A Figure of Speech
A Festschrift for John Laver

A Figure of Speech
A Festschrift for John Laver

Edited by

W. J. Hardcastle

and

J. Mackenzie Beck

2005

LAWRENCE ERLBAUM ASSOCIATES, PUBLISHERS

Mahwah, New Jersey   **London**

Lawrence Erlbaum Associates, Inc., Publishers
10 Industrial Avenue
Mahwah, New Jersey 07430

Cover design by Sean Trane Sciarrone

The cover design is based on a xeroradiographic photograph
of John Laver made by Frances MacCurtain, with additional
artwork by Elspeth Talbot and Janet Mackenzie Beck.

Library of Congress Cataloging-in-Publication Data
A figure of speech : a festschrift for John Laver / edited by William J. Hardcastle, J. Mackenzie Beck

    p. cm.

Publications by John Laver: p.
Includes bibliographical references and index.
ISBN 0-8058-4528-3 (alk. Paper)
    1. Phonetics.   I. Laver, John.   II. Hardcastle, William J.,
    1943–   III. Beck, J. Mackenzie (Janet Mackenzie)

P221.F48 2004
414'.8—dc22   2004050671
                                                      CIP

Books published by Lawrence Erlbaum Associates are printed
on acid-free paper, and their bindings are chosen for strength
and durability.

Printed in the United States of America
10 9 8 7 6 5 4 3 2 1

Contents

II.   Cognitive Aspects of Phonetic Processing

III.   Phonetics in Social Interaction

IV.   Voice Quality

Foreword

R. E. Asher

In all the three areas of endeavour that are traditionally in varying degrees the province of academics—teaching, research, and administration—John Laver has had an outstanding career. Generations of students know him as a brilliant and inspiring teacher, whether conducting a practical phonetics class, delivering a formal lecture, or directing research. Some of these talents were displayed when he delivered his inaugural lecture as Professor of Phonetics in the University of Edinburgh in 1986, at which both colleagues in the discipline and those in the audience with no knowledge of phonetics sat equally enthralled.

In the large number of administrative positions Professor Laver has held over a period of 40 years, a substantial majority have been concerned with research. Within a few years of his appointment in 1966 as lecturer in what was then the Department of Linguistics at the University of Edinburgh he was put in charge of the phonetics laboratory—a move that was predictable even apart from the fact that in the mid-60s he had the experience of running the phonetics laboratory in the Department of Linguistics and Nigerian Languages in the University of Ibadan (1963–1966), and that in 1971 he had spent 6 months in the Department of Linguistics at UCLA, where he worked in the phonetics laboratory directed by Peter Ladefoged, himself a former student in the Department of Phonetics in Edinburgh. This first administrative appointment in Edinburgh came at a time when the staff complement of the department included 10 phoneticians, the research of most of whom involved experimental work, with widespread use, for instance, of the techniques of kymography, palatography, and spectrography. Students in the postgraduate diploma course in phonetics received a thorough training in these areas, a training that most of those who went on to work for an MLitt or a PhD put to good use in their research. A well-organized and well-equipped laboratory was therefore a necessity, and this was fully achieved under John Laver's leadership—at a time when departments in the Faculty of Arts were not universally seen to have a legitimate claim on the university's equipment grant. It was under his guidance that new methods were developed for work in experimental phonetics and newer, more sophisticated techniques were introduced. Examples of these changes that he himself has provided follow: 'The classical kymograph was relegated to a museum, and airflow was instead measured by an electroaerometer coupled to a mingograph. The system of direct palatography gave way to electropalatography, using an artificial palate with embedded sensors for registering tongue-palate contact' (2002, p. 147). Credit for the latter development belongs to John Laver's first PhD student and the first editor of this volume.

With the passage of time and the growing awareness of the potential of computers in advancing the frontiers of phonetic research, the size of this claim for resources grew. John Laver's vision and persistence ensured that his subject and his department were not left behind. The foundations were thus laid for the realization of his wish to have an interdisciplinary research institute in Edinburgh to encourage the development of research on speech. With the enthusiastic support of the principal of the university, Dr. (later Sir) John Burnett, he succeeded in establishing the Centre for Speech Technology Research (CSTR) in 1984. The Centre got off to an unprecedented start by the award of a grant of 5 million pounds under the Alvey Programme on Information Technology which, by a happy coincidence, had been launched by the United Kingdom government in the same year. The grant was under a joint project with an industrial partner, first Plessey and later GEC Marconi. Apart from the fact of the size of the grant, which at the time was the largest that had been received by any university in Scotland, the project was important in illustrating a number of trends in academic research. There was collaboration not only with industry, but also with other universities (Loughborough and Dundee). Furthermore, the project was solidly interdisciplinary, with principal investigators being drawn from the departments of Artificial Intelligence, Electrical Engineering, and Linguistics.

Although continuing to direct the Alvey project through to its conclusion in 1991, John stepped down as director of CSTR in 1989 but maintained his central involvement with the Centre as chairman until 1994. During the decade since its establishment, the Centre had obtained more than 11 million pounds' worth of grants from a variety of industrial, research council, and other sources.

One important aspect of university administration is committee work. To this John Laver has made a very full contribution. It comes as no surprise when one observes that as often as not the committees of which he has been a member were in some way or another connected with research. At one time or another he acted as convener of the D.Litt. Committee, the Edinburgh University Press Committee, the Higher Degrees Committee, the Research Committee, and the Senatus Postgraduate Committee (twice), and was a member of the Personal Chairs Committee. He also chaired important working parties on postgraduate policy and on interdisciplinarity, producing reports which became the basis for university policy in these areas.

From John Laver's success in this multiplicity of roles, there seems a logical and almost inevitable progression to two posts that he filled in the late 1990s, one within and one outwith the University of Edinburgh. In the university, he was appointed to the post of Vice-Principal (1994–1997), with special responsibility for research, and most particularly for strategic aspects of the university's research policy. Just as he had earlier been responsible for putting some order into and codifying postgraduate policy in the university, so he now turned his attention to preparing a Code of Research Practice for the whole university in a form that gave it relevance to the widely differing research carried out in the University's four faculty groups. The comprehensiveness of the code was such that it had an impact in other universities both within the United Kingdom and internationally.

As the first Chairman of the Humanities Research Board (1994–1998), he did much to increase national awareness of research in the humanities and saw the board's budget in support of research rise to a sum in excess of 22 million pounds. His success in the post is to be measured not only by all that he achieved in that capacity but also, and no doubt more importantly in the long run, by the fact of government agreement in 2003 that an Arts and Humanities Research Council should be established under the auspices of the Office of Science and Technology.

John Laver has also played a multiplicity of administrative roles outside the institutions by which he has been formally employed. Since 1987, he has been chairman or member of, or consultant to, a large number of European Commission committees, in such areas as basic research, science and technology, speech communication, language technology, and multilingualism. In the British Academy, of which he was elected Fellow in 1990, he has acted as chairman of the Linguistics and Philology section (1998–2001). Elected Fellow of the Royal Society of Edinburgh in 1994, he has participated in the work of a number of its committees and has served as Vice-President (1996–1999) and Fellowship Secretary (1999–2001). His distinguished service to the Society was recognized by the award of its Bicentenary Medal in the summer of 2004.

For what will prove to be his last full-time university appointment, John Laver moved to another institution of higher education in the city of Edinburgh: Queen Margaret University College. The dilemma that faces competent all-rounders has once again been illustrated by the fact that his first designation was that of Research Professor of Speech Sciences, but that he was later invited to be Deputy Principal. For a period in the early part of 2003, he was also acting Principal.

To those who have had the opportunity to observe him closely, there are certain striking characteristics in the way that John Laver carries out any administrative duties that he has agreed to undertake. Among these are vision, an ability to think strategically, and a total commitment to the task in hand. Fortunately, this commitment to administrative duties undertaken has not prevented him from engaging in the third obligation of a member of the academic community and the one on which his wider and lasting reputation ultimately depends.

John Laver's many publications demonstrate a very broad view of his subject, a view that takes the domain of phonetics to be the study of all aspects of speech. This approach leads, as he himself has put it, to a conviction that 'phonetics and linguistics together make up the linguistic sciences, overlapping in the study of phonology, but each with legitimate interests outside the scope of the other' (2002, p. 139). It is, of course, possible to hold such a view of the subject and at the same time, quite reasonably, restrict one's research to a favorite corner of the field, but this has not been his way.

As is appropriate for anyone who has had the first professor of phonetics at the University of Edinburgh, David Abercrombie, as his guru, John Laver has shown an interest in the history of phonetics (1981). This, however, is not the normal point of departure for a young scholar, and his earliest publications, putting him in this respect in the Jonesian tradition, are concerned with the description of phonetic features of languages. Here he was taking advantage of his time in Nigeria in the mid-1960s to work on Etsako (1967, 1969) and Higi (1965). During the same period, Nigerian English, too, claimed his attention (1968).

Returning to Scotland in 1966 to take up a lectureship in phonetics, Laver embarked on research for a PhD on a topic in speech that had been remarkably underinvestigated and which was to remain a lifetime interest, namely voice quality. His thesis on *individual features in voice quality* was to form the basis of a major book (1980). Some of the original ideas in this work were later developed in collaboration with other colleagues that was made possible by two grants from the Medical Research Council. The first, in 1979 to 1982, was for the development of a technique for constructing vocal profiles of speech disorders. The key outcome of this project was the Vocal Profile Analysis Scheme, which aims to overcome the complex range of difficulties inherent in analyzing habitual voice quality by providing a standard and a system of objective measurement. The success of the scheme in making it possible to represent graphically the behaviour of all parts of the vocal apparatus during voice production was not only of great theoretical importance; it made possible clinical applications that have proved beneficial in the treatment of a range of speech and voice disorders. The second grant from the same source, following almost immediately (1982–1985), was to develop a technique for the acoustic analysis of voice features. The acoustic profiling system that resulted has been used in the clinical assessment of voice in hospitals in Edinburgh and Oxford. Applications of this research on voice quality have also proved to be of value in work by speech and language therapists, psychologists, sociolinguists, forensic phoneticians, and drama teachers. A summary of the range of applications is to be found in Laver, Wirz, Mackenzie, and Hiller (1991). John Laver's individual papers on this topic and related issues make up half of his 1991 book, *The Gift of Speech.*

Another interest that has continued through almost the same period is slips of the tongue, to which subject he was introduced by a request from Donald Boomer to apply his phonetic expertise to a body of examples that he had collected in recorded form. This led to a collaboration that produced important findings on neuro-linguistic strategies behind the production of utterances, findings whose publication (1968) was to prove a spur to further significant research by others. For John Laver himself it also led to an enduring interest in neurolinguistic aspects of speech. Five chapters of Laver, 1991, (originally published between 1968 and 1979) are devoted to an examination of the way in which the careful study of speech 'errors' can help our understanding of the way in which speech is generated by the brain.

A scholar's interests are shown not only by his books and articles and by the research projects he has directed, but also by collections of papers that he has edited. The diverse nature of John Laver's interest in speech is illustrated by collections concerned with socio-linguistics (Laver & Hutcheson, 1972), the importance of an understanding of phonetics in linguistic theory (Jones & Laver, 1973), the cognitive representation of speech (Myers, Laver, & Anderson, 1981), the use of computing techniques in the analysis of speech and the practical importance of research in this area (Jack & Laver, 1988; Laver & Jack, 1987), and the nature and scope of the phonetic sciences (Hardcastle & Laver, 1997).

Involvement in the preparation of such collections, taken along with the range of topics on which he has published articles and book chapters, gives some indication of the nature of John Laver's understanding of what it is that constitutes the speech sciences. The clearest indication of his views on the scope of phonetics, as a subject which of its nature is bound to be interdisciplinary, is shown by his principal ongoing piece of research and writing which is directed toward the production of the *Encyclopedic Dictionary of Speech,* which will cover the vocabulary with potential relevance to the discussion of speech in a wide range of disciplines. The book will show that the full understanding of the nature of human speech requires a familiarity with some part of the technical vocabulary of some 40 fields of study.

Breadth of vision does not, however, have to entail the lack of an ability to focus. John Laver's masterly textbook on phonetic theory (1994) manages to combine both these qualities. In presenting the author's approach to the domain of phonetics, it is the distillation of a lifetime of thought and experience. While making clear the ways in which phonetics relates to a mutiplicity of disciplines, it also demonstrates how phonetics, the one discipline that takes human speech as its central and principal concern, is an independent subject.

Apart from his election as Fellow of the British Academy and of the Royal Society of Edinburgh, already mentioned earlier, John Laver's scholarly reputation and his contribution to his subject have been recognized in a number of ways: by his own university, first by his appointment to a chair of phonetics in 1985 and later by the award of the degree of DLitt; by other universities—the University of Sheffield and De Montfort University, Leicester—through the award of an honorary DLitt (both in 1999); and nationally, by the award of CBE, also in 1999. It is fitting that friends and admirers among his former students and colleagues should add an expression of their regard by participating in this festschrift. The volume is an indication of the high esteem in which he is held as a major international figure in his chosen field. No less importantly, it is also an expression of the high value placed on his friendship by those fortunate enough to belong to the circle of his friends.

REFERENCES

Boomer, D. S., & Laver, J. (1968). Slips of the tongue. *British Journal of Disorders of Communication, 3,* 2–11.

Hardcastle, W., & Laver, J. (1997). *The handbook of phonetic sciences* (Blackwell Handbooks in Linguistics). Oxford, England: Blackwell.

Jack, M., & Laver, J. (1988). *Aspects of speech technology: A review* (EDIT Series). Edinburgh, Scotland: Edinburgh University Press.

Jones, W. E., & Laver, J. (1973). *Phonetics in linguistics.* London: Longman.

Laver, J. (1965). Some observations on alveolar and dental consonant articulations in Higi. *Journal of West African Languages, 2,* 59–61.

Laver, J. (1967). A preliminary phonology of the Aywele dialect of Etsako. *Journal of West African Languages, 4,* 53–56.

Laver, J. (1968). Assimilation in educated Nigerian English. *English Language Teaching, 22,* 156–160.

Laver, J. (1969). Etsako. In E. Dunstan (Ed.), *Twelve Nigerian languages* (pp. 47–56). London: Longmans Green.

Laver, J. (1980). *The phonetic description of voice quality.* Cambridge, England: Cambridge University Press.

Laver, J. (1981). The analysis of vocal quality: From the classical period to the twentieth century. In R. E. Asher, & E. J. A. Henderson (Eds.), *Towards a history of phonetics* (pp. 79–99). Edinburgh, Scotland: Edinburgh University Press.

Laver, J. (1991). *The gift of speech: Papers in the analysis of speech and voice.* Edinburgh, Scotland: Edinburgh University Press.

Laver, J. (1994). *Principles of phonetics* (Cambridge Textbooks in Linguistics Series). Cambridge, England: Cambridge University Press.

Laver, J. (2002). John Laver. In E. K. Brown, & V. Law (Eds.), *Linguistics in Britain: Personal histories* (Publications of the Philological Society of Great Britain, No. 36, pp. 139–154). Oxford, England: Blackwell.

Laver, J., & Asher, R. E. (in preparation). *The encyclopedic dictionary of speech.* Cambridge, MA: Blackwell.

Laver, J., & Hutcheson, S. (1972). *Communication in face to face interaction.* Harmondsworth, England: Penguin Books.

Laver, J., & Jack, M. (1987). *Proceedings of the European Conference on Speech Technology.* 2 vols. Edinburgh, Scotland: CEP Consultants Ltd.

Laver, J., Wirz, S., Mackenzie, J., & Hiller, S. M. (1991). A perceptual protocol for the analysis of vocal profiles. In J. Laver, *The gift of speech: Papers in the analysis of speech and voice* (pp. 265–280). Edinburgh, Scotland: Edinburgh University Press.

Myers, T., Laver, J., & Anderson, J. (1981). *The cognitive representation of speech.* Amsterdam: North-Holland.

Publications
by John Laver

General Phonetics

1965 Variability in vowel perception. *Language and Speech*, 8, 95–121.

1970 The production of speech. In J. Lyons (Ed.), *New Horizons in Linguistics* (pp. 53–75). Harmondsworth, England: Penguin.

1973 (2nd ed., with W. E Jones) *Phonetics in linguistics*. London: Longman.

1978 The concept of articulatory settings: An historical survey. *Historiographia Linguistica* 5, 1–14.

1992 The art and science of phonetics. In T. Balasubramanian & V. Prakasam (Eds.), *Sound patterns for the phonetician: Studies in phonetics and phonology in honour of J. C. Catford* (pp. 3–26). Madras, India: T. R. Publications.

1994 *Principles of phonetics* (Cambridge Textbooks in Linguistics Series). Cambridge, England: Cambridge University Press.

1994 Speech. In R. E. Asher & J. M. Y. Simpson (Eds.), *Encyclopedia of language and linguistics* (Vol. 8, pp. 4101–4109). Oxford, England: Pergamon.

1997 (2nd ed., with W. J. Hardcastle) *The handbook of phonetic sciences* (Blackwell Handbooks in Linguistics). Oxford, England: Blackwell.

2000 Linguistic phonetics. In M. Aronoff & J. Rees–Miller (Eds.), *Handbook of Linguistics* (pp. 150–178). Oxford, England: Blackwell.

2001 The nature of phonetics. *Journal of the International Phonetic Association, 30,* 31–38.

2001 Some future directions of phonetic research. *Journal of the Phonetic Society of Japan, 5,* 46–48.

Phonetics of West African Languages

1965 Some observations on alveolar and dental consonant articulations in Higi. *Journal of West African Languages, 2,* 59–61.

1967 A preliminary phonology of the Aywele dialect of Etsako. *Journal of West African Languages, 4,* 53–56.

1968 Assimilation in educated Nigerian English. *English Language Teaching, 22,* 156–160.

1969 Etsako. In E. Dunstan (Ed.), *Twelve Nigerian languages* (pp. 47–56). London: Longmans Green.

1971 Etsako in the Polyglotta Africana. *African Language Review, 9,* 257–262.

Voice Quality

1968 Voice quality and indexical information. *British Journal of Disorders of Communication, 3,* 43–54.

1970 Synthesis of components in voice quality. In B. Hála, M. Romportl, & P. Janota (Eds.), *Proceedings of the Sixth International Congress of Phonetic Sciences,* Prague, Czechoslovak Academy of Sciences, XX, 523–525.

1974 Labels for voices. *Journal of the International Phonetic Association, 4,* 62–75.

1979 *Voice quality: A classified research bibliography.* Amsterdam, Netherlands: Benjamins.

1979 Phonetic aspects of voice quality. *Northern Ireland Speech and Language Forum Journal, 5,* 6–20.

1980 *The phonetic description of voice quality.* Cambridge, England: Cambridge University Press.

1981   The analysis of vocal quality: From the classical period to the twentieth century. In R. E. Asher & E. J. A. Henderson (Eds.), *Towards a history of phonetics* (pp. 79–99). Edinburgh, Scotland: Edinburgh University Press.

1981   (1st author, with R. J. Hanson). Describing the normal voice. In J. Darby (Ed.), *Speech evaluation in psychiatry* (pp. 57–78). New York: Grune & Stratton.

1982   (1st author, with S. M. Hiller & R. J. Hanson). Comparative performance of pitch detection algorithms on dysphonic voices. *Proceedings of the IEEE International Conference on Acoustics, Speech, and Signal Processing, Paris,* 192–195.

1984   (1st author, with S. M. Hiller & J. Mackenzie). Acoustic analysis of vocal fold pathology. *Proceedings of the Institute of Acoustics,* London, England, 6, 425–430.

1985   (1st author, with S. Wirz, J. Mackenzie, & S. Hiller). Vocal profile analysis in the description of voice quality. In V. Lawrence (Ed.), *Transactions of the 14th Symposium on the Professional Care of the Voice* (pp. 184–192). New York: The Voice Foundation.

1986   (1st author, with S. M. Hiller, J. Mackenzie, & E. Rooney). An acoustic screening system for the detection of laryngeal pathology. *Journal of Phonetics,* 14, 517–524.

1991   (Guest ed.). Speaker characterization. [Special issue] *Speech Communication,* Vol. 10, Issues 5–6, pp. 431–562.

1991   *The gift of speech : Papers in the analysis of speech and voice.* Edinburgh, Scotland: Edinburgh University Press.

1991   Voice quality. In W. Bright (Ed.), *Oxford international encyclopedia of linguistics* (Vol. 4, pp. 231–232). London: Oxford University Press.

1991   The description of voice quality in general phonetic theory. In J. Laver (Ed.), *The gift of speech: Readings in the analysis of speech and voice* (pp. 184–208). Edinburgh, Scotland: Edinburgh University Press.

1991   (1st author, with S. Wirz, J. Mackenzie, & S. M. Hiller). A perceptual protocol for the analysis of vocal profiles. In J. Laver (Ed.), *The gift of speech: Readings in the analysis of speech and voice* (pp. 265–280). Edinburgh, Scotland: Edinburgh University Press.

1991   (2nd author, with J. Mackenzie & S. M. Hiller). Structural pathologies of the vocal folds. In J. Laver (Ed.), *The gift of speech: Readings in the analysis of speech and voice* (pp. 281–318). Edinburgh, Scotland: Edinburgh University Press.

1992   (1st author, with S. M. Hiller & J. Mackenzie Beck). Acoustic waveform perturbations and voice disorders. *Journal of Voice,* 6, 115–126.

1992   (3rd author, with A. A. Wrench, M. A. Jack, D. S. Soutar, A. G. Robertson, & J. Mackenzie). Objective speech quality assessment in patients with intra-oral cancers: Voiceless fricatives. *Proceedings of the International Conference on Spoken Language Processing*, Banff, Canada, 2, 1071–1074.

1994   (2nd author, with H. Eckert). *Menschen und ihre Stimmen: Aspekte der vokalen Kommunikation* (Humans and their voices: Aspects of vocal communication). Weinheim, Germany: Belz Verlag.

1995   Voice types in automated telecommunications applications. In J. Windsor Lewis (Ed.), *Studies in English and general phonetics: Essays in honour of professor J. D. O'Connor* (pp. 85–95). London: Routledge.

1997   (6th author, with J. M. Beck, A. Wrench, M. Jackson, D. Soutar, & A. G. Robertson). Surgical mapping and phonetic analysis in intra-oral cancer. In W. Zeigler & K. Deger (Eds.), *Clinical phonetics and linguistics* (pp. 485–496). London: Whurr.

2000   Phonetic evaluation of voice quality. In R. Kent & M. J. Ball (Eds.), *The handbook of voice quality measurement* (pp. 37–48). San Diego, CA: Singular Publications.

2001   (1st author, with Janet Mackenzie Beck). Unifying principles in the description of voice, posture and gesture. In C. Cavé, I. Guaïtella, & S. Santi (Eds.), *Oralité et Gestualité: Interactions et Comportements Multimodaux dans la Communication* (pp. 15–24). Paris: L'Harmattan. (Plenary lecture, Proceedings of ORAGE–2001, Aix–en–Provence, France, June 18–22, 2001).

Cognitive Aspects of Phonetic Processing and Neurolinguistics

1968   (2nd author, with D. S. Boomer). Slips of the tongue. *British Journal of Disorders of Communication*, 3, 2–11.

1973   (2nd author, with D. S. Boomer). Slips of the Tongue. In V. Fromkin (Ed.), *Speech errors as linguistic evidence* (pp. 120–131). The Hague, Netherlands: Mouton.

1973   The detection and correction of slips of the tongue. In V. Fromkin (Ed.), *Speech errors as linguistic evidence* (pp. 132–143). The Hague, Netherlands: Mouton.

1977   Neurolinguistic aspects of speech production. In C. Gutknecht (Ed.), *Grundbegriff und Hauptströmungen der Linguistik* (pp. 142–155). Hamburg, Germany: Forum Linguisticum.

1979   Monitoring systems in the neurolinguistic control of speech production. In V. Fromkin (Ed.), *Errors of linguistic performance* (pp. 287–305). New York: Academic.

1979   Slips of the tongue as neuromuscular evidence for a model of speech production. In H. W. Dechert & M. Raupach (Eds.), *Temporal variables in speech* (pp. 21–26). The Hague, Netherlands: Mouton.

1981   (2nd ed., with T. Myers & J. Anderson). *The cognitive representation of speech.* Amsterdam: North-Holland.

Communication in Social Interaction (Verbal and Nonverbal)

1972   (1st ed., with S. Hutcheson). *Communication in face to face interaction.* Harmondsworth, England: Penguin Books.

1975   Communicative functions of phatic communion. In A. Kendon, R .M. Harris, & M. R. Key (Eds.), *The organization of behavior in face to face interaction* (pp. 215–238). The Hague, Netherlands: Mouton.

1976   Language and nonverbal communication. In E. C. Carterette & M. P. Friedman (Eds.), *Handbook of perception* (Volume 7, pp. 345–363). New York: Academic.

1976   The semiotic nature of phonetic data. *York Papers in Linguistics*, 6, 55–62.

1979   (1st author, with P. Trudgill). Phonetic and linguistic markers in speech. In K. R. Scherer & H. Giles (Eds.), *Social markers in speech* (pp. 1–32). Cambridge, England: Cambridge University Press.

1981   Linguistic routines and politeness in greeting and parting. In F. Coulmas (Ed.), *Conversational routines* (pp. 289–304). The Hague, Netherlands: Mouton.

1999   Towards an integrated theory of nonverbal communication. In J. J. Ohala, Y. Hasegawa, M. Ohala, D. Granville, & A. Bailey (Eds.), *Proceedings of the XIVth International Congress of Phonetic Sciences* (Vol. 3, pp. 2433–2436). Berkeley: University of California.

2002   Nonverbal communication and tone of voice. In A. Braun & H. R. Mastoff (Eds.), *Phonetics and its applications: Festschrift for Jens–Peter Köster on the occasion of his 60th birthday* (pp. 280–288; in the series Zeitschrift für Dialektologie und Linguistik). Stuttgart, Germany: Steiner Verlag.

2003   Three semiotic layers of spoken communications. *Journal of Phonetics*, 31 (Special issue: Temporal integration in the perception of speech. Guest editors S. Hawkins & N. Nguyen), 413–415.

Speech Technology

1986   (3rd author with M. Terry, S. M. Hiller, & G. Duncan). AUDLAB: a speech signal processing system. *IEE Conference on Speech Input and Output*. (Institute of Electrical Engineers Publication number 258). 263–265.

1986   (2nd author with J. Harrington & D. Cutting). Word-structure reduction rules in automatic continuous speech recognition. *Proceedings of the Institute of Acoustics*, London, England, 8, 451–460.

1986   (2nd author with J. Dalby & S. M. Hiller). Mid-class phonetic analysis for a continuous speech recognition system. *Proceedings of the Institute of Acoustics*, London, England, 8, 347–354.

1987   (1st author, with M. Jack). *The prospect of future speech technology: An international survey to the year 2000*. (Report to the Scottish Development Agency, 3 volumes.)

1987   (1st ed., with M. Jack). *Proceedings of the European Conference on Speech Technology* (Vol. 1, 447 pp.; Vol. 2, 491 pp.). Edinburgh, Scotland: CEP Consultants Ltd.

1987   (Chief rapporteur, with three sous-rapporteurs). New horizons in European speech technology. *ESPRIT Workshop on Speech Technology*, Åarhus, Denmark, Jutland Telephone Company (published on behalf of the European Commission's Directorate XIII ESPRIT Programme).

1987   (2nd author, with H. S. Thompson). The Alvey speech demonstrator—architecture, methodology and progress to date. *Proceedings of SpeechTech–87*, New York: Media Dimensions, Inc.

1988   (2nd ed., with M. Jack). *Aspects of speech technology: A review* (EDIT Series). Edinburgh, Scotland: Edinburgh University Press.

1989   (2nd guest ed., with M. Jack & J. Blauert). Special section on speech technology. *Proceedings of the Institution of Electrical Engineers (Communications, Speech, and Vision)*, 109–168.

1989   Cognitive science and speech: A framework for research. In H. Schnelle & N.–O. Bernsen (Eds.), *Logic and linguistics* (Vol. 3, pp. 37–69), in N.–O. Bernsen (Ed.), *Research directions in cognitive science: European perspectives* (5 vols.; for the European Commission's DG XII, Forecast and Assessment in Science and Technology, and DG XIII, ESPRIT. Hillsdale, NJ: Lawrence Erlbaum Associates, Inc.

1990   European speech technology in perspective. *Terminologie et Traduction, 1*, 163–179.

1989   (1st author, with J. McAllister & M. McAllister). Pre-processing of anomalous text-strings in an automatic text-to-speech system. In S. Ramsaran (Ed.), *Studies in the pronunciation of English: A commemorative volume in memory of A. C. Gimson* (pp. 323–338). London: Croom Helm.

1990   (1st ed., with M. Jack & A. Gardiner). *Proceedings of the ESCA Tutorial and Research Workshop on Speaker Characterization in Speech Technology*, European Speech Communication Association, Amsterdam, Netherlands: North-Holland.

1990   (1st author, with J. McAllister, M. McAllister, & M. A. Jack). A Prolog-based automatic text-to-phoneme conversion system. In H. Fujisaki, (Ed.), *Second Symposium on Advanced Man-Machine Interface Through Spoken Language* (pp. 12.1–12.11). Tokyo, Japan: Ministry of Education, Science and Culture.

1991   (3rd author, with S. M. Hiller, E. Rooney, M.–G. Di Benedetto, & J.–P. Lefèvre). Macro and micro features for automated pronunciation improvement in the SPELL system. *ESPRIT '91: Proceedings of the Annual ESPRIT Conference*, November 25–29, 1991 (pp. 378–392). Brussels, Belgium: Commission of the European Communities.

1992   (4th author, with J.–P. Lefèvre, S. M. Hiller, E. Rooney, & M.–G. Di Benedetto). Macro and micro features for automated pronunciation improvement in the SPELL system. *Speech Communication, 11*, 31–44.

1992   (3rd author, with E. Rooney, S. M. Hiller, & M. A. Jack). Prosodic features for automated pronunciation improvement in the SPELL system. *Proceedings of the International Conference on Spoken Language Processing*, Banff, Canada, 413–416.

1992   (3rd author, with S. M. Hiller, E. Rooney, & M. A. Jack). An automated system for computer aided pronunciation teaching. *Proceedings of the Fourth Australian International Conference on Speech Science and Technology*, Brisbane, Australia, 658–663.

1992   (2nd author, with K. Edwards, M. A. Jack, & A. Simons). The design and performance of two accent-diagnostic 'Shibboleth' sentences. *Proceedings of the Institute of Acoustics Conference on Speech and Hearing*, Windermere, England, 14, Part 6, 199–206.

1993   Repetition and re-start strategies for prosody in text-to-speech conversion systems. In G. Fant, K. Hirose, & S. Kiritani (Eds.) [Special issue] *Speech Communication*, 13, 75–85 (Festschrift for Hiroya Fujisaki).

1993   (3rd author, with S. Hiller, E. Rooney, & M. Jack). SPELL: An automated system for computer-aided pronunciation teaching. *Speech Communication, 13*, 463–473.

1993   Subject Editor for articles on speech technology (185,000 words in total), in R. E. Asher & J. M. Y. Simpson (Eds.), *Encyclopedia of language and linguistics* (10 volumes). Oxford, England: Pergamon.

1994   (5th author, with S. Hiller, E. Rooney, R. Vaughan, M. Eckert, & M. Jack). An automated system for computer-aided pronunciation teaching. *Computer Assisted Language Learning, 7,* 51–63.

1994   Speech technology: An overview. In R. E. Asher & J. M. Y. Simpson (Eds.), *Encyclopedia of language and linguistics* (Vol. 8, pp. 4274–4289). Oxford, England: Pergamon.

1996   Repetition and re-start strategies for prosody in text-to-speech conversion systems. In G. Fant, K. Hirose, & S. Kiritani (Eds.), *Analysis, perception and processing: Festschrift for Hiroya Fujisaki* (pp. 75–85). Amsterdam: North–Holland (reprinted from special issue of Speech Communication, 1993, 13, 75–85.

1996   (1st author, with J. McAllister, M. McAllister, & M. A. Jack). A Prolog-based automatic text-to-phoneme conversion system for British English. In Fujisaki, H. (Ed.), *Recent research towards advanced man–machine interface through spoken language* (pp. 366–376), Amsterdam, Netherlands: Elsevier.

Research Strategy

1996   (1st author, with J. Roukens). The global information society and Europe's linguistic and cultural heritage. In C. Hoffmann (Ed.), *Language, culture and communication in contemporary Europe* (pp. 1–27). Clevedon, England: Multilingual Matters.

1997   *University research in Scotland: Developing a policy framework* (convener of editorial committee and of consortium; report of a project funded by the Scottish Higher Education Funding Council under its Regional Strategic Initiatives Programme, Phase 1). Edinburgh, Scotland: Scottish Universities Research Policies Consortium.

1997   *Interdisciplinary research: Process, structures and evaluation* (convener of editorial committee and of consortium; report of a project funded by the Scottish Higher Education Funding Council under its Regional Strategic Initiatives Programme, Phase 2). Edinburgh, Scotland: Scottish Universities Research Policy Consortium.

1997   The humanities: Afterthought or cynosure? In R. Crawford (Ed.), *The future of higher education in Scotland* (pp. 151–161). Glasgow, Scotland: Committee of Scottish Higher Education Principals (COSHEP).

1997   The need to invest in research in the humanities and arts. (Appendix 3 to *Higher Education in the Learning Society*, Report of the National Committee of Inquiry into Higher Education; Dearing Report, London: HMSO, pp. 9–24).

1997   Funding for research in the arts and humanities. *St Catherine's Conference Report*, 61, pp. 12–13, (King George VI and Queen Elizabeth Foundation of St Catherine's/Glaxo Wellcome Conference, 'What Are Universities For?').

1999   (5th ed. With V. Bruce, I. Carter, B. Ferrari, C. McKay, R. McGookin, G. McFadzean, J. Teppett, & T. Williams). *Collaboration in the use of research facilities* (Report of a project funded by the Scottish Higher Education Funding Council under its Regional Strategic Initiatives Programme, Phase 3). Edinburgh, Scotland: Scottish Universities Research Policies Consortium.

1999   The contribution of the humanities. In T. Kinoshita (Ed.), *Science and society: Research for the next generation* (Joint Symposium of the Japan Society for the Promotion of Science and the UK Research Councils, Churchill College, University of Cambridge, April 15–16, 1998, pp. 57–63). Yelvertoft Manor, Northants, England: Pilkington Press.

2002   (With V. Bruce, I. Carter, W. Hardcastle, G. McFadzean, L. Meagher, A. Murray, J. Penman). *Making the best decisions: A guide to strategic investment in research infrastructure* (Report of a project funded by the Scottish Higher Education Funding Council under the auspices of the Scottish Universities Research Policy Consortium). Edinburgh, Scotland: Scottish Higher Education Funding Council.

Other (Obituaries, Tributes, Autobiographical)

1992   A tribute to Peter Ladefoged. *Journal of the International Phonetic Association*, 21, 1–3.

1993   Obituary of Frank Fallside. *Speech Communication*, 12, 299.

2001   (2nd author, with A. Morpurgo Davies), Obituary of Katrina Hayward. *The Phonetician*, 84, 35–36.

2002   John Laver. In E. K. Brown & V. Law (Eds.), *Linguistics in Britain: Personal histories* (Publications of the Philological Society of Great Britain, number 36, pp. 139–154). Oxford, England: Blackwell.

Introduction

W. J. Hardcastle and J. Mackenzie Beck

Although the primary motivation for the publication of this book is as an expression of the great respect in which John Laver is held, the editors have aimed to produce a book which will be of interest to anyone who wishes to gain some understanding of the broad scope of phonetic sciences. It is no accident that the contributions are concerned with so many of the key themes in phonetics, since all of them have, in some way, been affected by John Laver's teaching, writing, and research. The range of topics included in this volume thus reflects not only the richness of phonetic theory and the range of applications of phonetics, but also the breadth of John Laver's own work and his keen interest in challenging and developing theoretical concepts and applying them to practical problems.

The content of this volume follows four general themes. The first of these focuses on some core theoretical issues within phonetics. The three chapters in the first section of the volume illustrate the ways in which instrumental data can enhance and challenge our understanding of theoretical concepts. These chapters mirror John Laver's own approach to research, in which data collection and theoretical modelling have always gone hand in hand. Peter Ladefoged speculates on the control of speech, which is still very poorly understood. The central problem addressed here is the fact that although we can observe that people produce certain gestures of the speech apparatus when they talk, it is not at all clear what the goals of these gestures are. This chapter presents data indicating that although sometimes speakers seem to be aiming at achieving certain movements, at other times they seem to aim at producing certain auditory effects. John Ohala's chapter explores the role of phonetic explanations for "natural" sound patterns. These have been successful within a purely phonetic study of speech but unsuccessful in purely phonological representations, that is, those supposed to be part of speakers' grammars. He concludes that phonetic naturalness has little or no role in speakers' grammars. The third chapter in this section, by Bill Hardcastle and Fiona Gibbon, shows how analysis of lingual dynamics, as revealed by electropalatography, can shed new light on aspects of normal and pathological speech, with both clinical and theoretical implications. The chapter focuses on a number of issues, including intersubject variability in assimilation of alveolars, abnormal articulatory patterns in cleft palate speech, in functional/phonological disorders, and temporal and serial ordering abnormalities in neurogenic disorders.

The second main theme concerns cognitive aspects of phonetic processing, encompassing speech production and perception. The ambition of increasing our understanding of the cognitive underpinning of spoken communication emerged early in John's career, and these chapters offer three very different approaches to fulfilment of this shared ambition. Although the first two chapters in this section have explicit implications for foreign language teaching, the third takes a more general view of the relationship between cognitive and physical aspects of speech production. Speech production is one side of the language user's competence; speech perception the other. Listening is a complex cognitive skill which usually seems effortless. Anne Cutler and Mirjam Broersma show how listening in the native language involves both phonetic precision, when needed, and imprecision, when appropriate; and how this delicate adjustment appears to be nearly unattainable in a second language learned in adulthood. Helen Fraser then presents an analysis of the concept of representation, using examples from pictorial representation, and points out that any representation requires both a creator and an interpreter, and must be essentially separate from the thing it represents. With phonetic representation, it is easy to lose sight of this sine qua non; bearing it more clearly in mind allows an interestingly different view of the relationships among the various phonetic and phonological representations. Implications for both theory and practice are explored, with a focus on the teaching of second language pronunciation. The chapter by Peter MacNeilage and Barbara Davis comes from an attempt to develop an embodiment perspective for speech, according to which the mental (cognitive) component of speech evolved and develops from the motor function. The argument is that a close–open cycle of mandibular oscillation is and was the main motor basis for the articulatory component of speech, and that a mental representation of this motor cycle evolves and develops as a frame for the programming of the segmental level of speech.

The natural environment for phonetic production and perception is, of course, within social interaction, and this gives us the third theme of the volume. The need for phonetic research to consider the social and interactional context of speech has been a significant recurring theme throughout John Laver's writings, and the chapters in this section provide a variety of perspectives on this. Ron Asher and Elinor Keane use detailed vowel data to highlight the importance of context and speech style on phonetic output. In the context of Tamil diglossia, the chapter examines the nature of Tamil diphthongs and the extent to which what is a diphthong in formal speech is realized as a monophthong in informal utterances. The investigation entailed a discussion of the difficulties inherent in eliciting authentic colloquial utterances in a laboratory environment. Gerry Docherty and Paul Foulkes focus more on the relationship between social background and speech output. This study investigates the phonetic properties of glottal and glottalised consonants in Tyneside English. They quantify the variable patterns of performance observed within a socially stratified sample of 32 speakers. As well as bringing to light interesting patterns of structured variation, the findings reveal that the phonetic properties of glottal variants may be more complex than is conventionally thought. Janet Fletcher acknowledges John Laver's championing of the importance of examining unscripted discourse in phonetic theory and her study is based on spontaneous narratives from three Northern Australian languages. She focuses on two aspects of their phonetic organisation: firstly examining vowel formant patterns with reference to prevailing theories of adaptive dispersion. Secondly, she examines the role of pitch range variation in signalling reported speech. Pitch reset serves as the primary cue to the latter, with often a total absence of grammatical framers such as "(s)he said", to signal reported speech fragments. In some cases, voice quality is also modified, suggesting it plays an important indexical role in this interactive context. The social context of the study by Jonathan Harrington, Sallyanne Palethorpe, and Catherine Watson could hardly be more different, but it is equally concerned with social context. This study shows that the diphthongs of Queen Elizabeth II have shifted since the early 1950s in the direction of a more mainstream and more widely spoken form of Received Pronunciation of the 1980s. The findings show that phonetic categories in adulthood are not immutable but continually change due to the forces exerted by sociolinguistic variables. In the final chapter in this section, John Local takes up the challenge of exploring the fine phonetic detail of everyday talk-in-interaction. He provides an analysis of a particular kind of interactional practice in which one participant completes a turn begun by another. Local seeks to develop an interactionally-grounded analysis of the phonetics of everyday talk and to provide a basis for grounding the description of the functioning of phonetic parameters in the observed behaviour of participants in naturally occurring spoken interaction.

Any book dedicated to John Laver would be incomplete without some comment on voice quality, and this forms the final theme in this book. John Laver is well known for his development of a theoretically rigorous framework for the phonetic description of voice quality, which culminated in the publication of *The Phonetic Description of Voice Quality* and the Vocal Profile Analysis Scheme. His work in this area has been characterised by a concern to explore the relationships among physiological aspects of voice production and their perceptual and acoustic correlates. All four chapters in this section draw very directly on this work, but this is perhaps especially true of the first. Janet Mackenzie Beck considers some general issues relating to perceptual analysis of voice quality, before focusing specifically on the role of Vocal Profile Analysis in voice research. She argues that perceptual analysis of voice quality offers insights into vocal performance that are not always available from instrumental measures, and illustrates the contribution of Vocal Profile Analysis to our understanding of voice by reference to a range of applications. The contribution by Ailbhe Ní Chasaide and Christer Gobl addresses a key question concerning the communicative role of voice quality. Although phonatory quality is known to be a major vehicle for the communication of emotions, moods, and attitudes, there is little empirical data on this important aspect of speech communication. The principal contribution of this chapter is that it provides an initial exploration, through perceptual experimentation, of the mapping of phonatory quality to affect. This function of voice quality variation is also placed within the broader context of within, and across, speaker voice source variation. Furthermore, the experiments demonstrate how different voice qualities might be synthesised, using a parametric voice source model.

John Esling and Jimmy G. Harris also acknowledge John Laver's influence, as a teacher and as an early pioneer in the study of voice qualities. The issues addressed in this chapter are in response to questions posed by John over the years: how laryngeal and supralaryngeal auditory categories are related, the nature of the difference between breathy and whispery modes of phonation, and the relationship of the actions of laryngeal and pharyngeal articulatory mechanisms to auditory sound quality designations. The final chapter, by Francis Nolan, discusses the role of Laver's phonetic framework for voice quality description as applied to forensic speaker identification. Surprisingly little use of the framework has been made considering how often 'voice quality' is referred to in this context, and the reasons for this are discussed, including the detrimental effect of the telephone on the percept of voice quality. Although the chapter concludes, in effect, that the auditory and acoustic properties of individual sounds must be the main focus of attention, it nonetheless suggests that the voice quality framework provides an invaluable conceptual infrastructure for thinking about how speakers differ.

We as editors are pleased that this book brings together the work of a number of authors in such a way as to exemplify the diversity of interests served by phonetics. We are enormously grateful for the authors' generosity in contributing to this book. Their willingness to do so is a clear indication of their regard for the Figure of Speech who has inspired this volume and done so much for phonetics. Most of all, we would like to express our personal gratitude to John Laver for his guidance, wisdom, and friendship over so many years.

Contributors

Professor R. E. Asher
Professor Emeritus of Linguistics
The University of Edinburgh
Scotland

Dr. Janet Mackenzie Beck
Senior Lecturer
Speech and Language Sciences
Queen Margaret University College
Edinburgh
Scotland

Mirjam Broersma, MA
Comprehension Group
Max Planck Institute for Psycholinguistics
Nijmegen
Netherlands

Dr. Ailbhe Ní Chasaide
Senior Lecturer
Phonetics and Speech Science Laboratory
Centre for Language and Communication Studies
Trinity College
University of Dublin
Eire

Professor Anne Cutler
Director
Max Planck Institute for Psycholinguistics
Nijmegen
Netherlands

Dr. Barbara Davis
Professor
College of Communication
The University of Texas at Austin
USA

Professor Gerry Docherty
Speech and Language Sciences Section
School of Education Communication and Language Sciences
University of Newcastle-upon-Tyne
England

Professor John H. Esling
Department of Linguistics
University of Victoria
Canada

Dr. Janet Fletcher
Department of Linguistics and Applied Linguistics
School of Languages
University of Melbourne
Australia

Dr. Paul Foulkes
Department of Language and Linguistics
University of York
England

Dr. Helen Fraser
Senior Lecturer
School of Languages Cultures and Linguistics
University of New England
Armidale
New South Wales
Australia

Professor Fiona Gibbon
Head of Speech and Language Sciences
Queen Margaret University College
Edinburgh
Scotland

Dr. Christer Gobl
Phonetics and Speech Science Laboratory
Centre for Language and Communication Studies
Trinity College
University of Dublin
Eire

Professor Bill Hardcastle
Director Scottish Centre for Speech
and Communication Science Research
Queen Margaret University College
Edinburgh
Scotland

Professor Jonathan Harrington
Director
Institute of Phonetics and Digital Speech Processing
University of Kiel
Germany

Professor Jimmy G. Harris
Department of Linguistics
University of Victoria
Canada

Dr. Elinor Keane
Junior Research Fellow
Christ Church College
Oxford
England

Professor Peter Ladefoged
Professor of Phonetics Emeritus
UCLA Department of Linguistics
Los Angeles
USA

Professor John Local
Department of Language and Linguistic Science
University of York
England

Professor John Ohala
Director of Phonology Laboratory
University of California at Berkeley
USA

Professor Peter MacNeilage
Department of Psychology
College of Liberal Arts
The University of Texas at Austin
USA

Dr. Francis Nolan
Reader in Phonetics
Department of Linguistics
University of Cambridge
England

Dr. Sallyanne Palethorpe
Macquarie Centre for Cognitive Science
Macquarie University
Australia

Dr. Catherine Watson
Lecturer in Linguistics
Macquarie University
Australia

Abbreviations

C	Consonant
CBE	Commander of the British Empire (in the UK Honours System)
DLitt	Doctor of Letters (University Degree)
EM(M)A	Electromagnetic (Midsaggital) Articulography
EPG	Electropalatography
F	(as in F1, F2, F3 etc) First, Second, Third etc Formant (in acoustic analysis)
Fo	Fundamental Frequency
Hz	Hertz (cycles per second)
IP	Intonational Phrase
IPA	International Phonetic Alphabet (or Association)
LF	(after liljencrants Fant) a four-parameter model of the rate of glottal flow
MLitt	Master of Letters (University Degree)
NMRU	Non-meaningful Recurrent Utterance
RP	Received Promotion (the so-called regionally neutral, prestige accent of British English)
SMA	Supplementary Motor Area (in the brain)
SPE	Chomsky's "Sound Patterns of English"
SSB	Standard Southern British accent
TESOL	Teaching English to Speakers of Other Languages
TIMIT	A large American English read-sentence database with time-aligned orthographic and phonetic transcripts.
UCLA	Univeristy of California at Los Angeles
V	Vowel
VPA	Vocal Profile Analysis
VPM	Ventral Premotor Cortex (in the brain)

PART I

Instrumental Evidence for Phonetic Theory

Chapter 1

Speculations on the Control of Speech

Peter Ladefoged
University of California, Los Angeles

Speech, like most skilled movements, is best described as goal directed activity, but it is not clear how the goals are defined. One possibility has been outlined by proponents of Articulatory Phonology (Browman & Goldstein, 1986, 1992; Saltzman & Kelso, 1987, int. al.), They suggest that the goals are a series of articulatory gestures, being careful to point out that we must distinguish between the higher level gestural goals and the lower level system that implements them. When you produce a word (e.g., *cat*) their notion is that the speech centers in the brain do not issue instructions for the use of particular muscles. Instead, they issue instructions equivalent to: "Make the following complex gestures: Voiceless aspirated velar stop, follow this by a low front vowel, finally make a voiceless glottaled alveolar stop," in which different parts specify goals for different parts of the speech mechanism. "Voiceless aspirated" is an instruction for a certain laryngeal gesture, "velar stop" a lingual gesture, and so on.

We can never be sure what are the goals of the speech centers in the brain. We cannot find out by asking speakers what they are trying to control. If you ask unsophisticated speakers of English what they are controlling when they say *cat* they will probably say that they don't know, or that they are trying to produce a 'c' followed by an 'a' and then by a 't'. Speakers of an African tone language do not know what they are doing when they say a word on a high tone. They do not know of their own knowledge, as the lawyers say (i.e., without being prompted or instructed) the goals of the gestures they are making. They are simply intending to say a particular word that happens, in the view of linguists, to have a high tone. Sophisticated speakers might say that they are trying to produce a high pitch. But it is still not clear what they mean by 'pitch' in these circumstances.

Determining the goals used by the speech centers of the brain is further complicated by the fact that we are apt to be biased by our linguistic analyses and think that the goals are the objects we use in our linguistic descriptions. It is an assumption that there are separate goals for vowels and consonants, just as one might assume that there are separate goals for the movements of the arms and legs when running to catch a ball. But running to catch a ball might be considered as a single action, just as producing a syllable or a word might be a coordinated whole.

A further problem is that speech may be goal directed, but we seldom achieve our goals. Observation of what happens when we talk will not provide direct evidence of the targets involved. We can only deduce what they might be, and try to formulate a set of statements—a formal model—that will account for our observations. The hypothesis advanced here is that there are at least three different kinds of goals involved in talking. Sometimes what matters most is achieving some articulatory gesture, sometimes there are auditory targets, and sometimes it seems that the aim is to achieve certain aerodynamic conditions. The notion of articulatory targets has been well described by articulatory phonologists, and is not illustrated further here. The next two sections illustrate the notion of auditory targets and aerodynamic targets.

AUDITORY TARGETS: TONE AND INTONATION

The first example of a goal oriented approach to phonetic universals that are considered in this chapter is the notion of pitch control. What are speakers of English doing when they say a sentence with a particular intonation? Of course, from one point of view, they are simply trying to produce a particular meaning. We must always remember that speakers are not consciously trying to produce a particular pitch pattern. If they have been given some instruction in phonetics, or if they are trained singers, then they may know how the vocal folds determine the pitch of a sound. Given some analytical knowledge, they may be able to make deliberate laryngeal adjustments. But this is not what happens in everyday life. The speech centers in the brain act to produce utterances in ways that are beyond our conscious thought processes. You can tell people to flex their biceps, and those of us who have watched tough guy movies will know what to do. But only the speech experts know how to increase the tension of the vocal folds.

Accordingly, we should reword the questions we were asking and say instead: What are the speech centers in the brain doing to implement the desire to produce an utterance with that particular meaning? Put this way, the answer almost certainly is that they are trying to produce a given pitch pattern. Extending the question, we can ask: How are they doing this? The primary control of the pitch of a speech sound is the tension of the vocal folds, and we might imagine that the speech centers achieve a pitch pattern by producing a particular sequence of vocal fold tensions. There is some evidence in favor of this notion, and some that goes against it.

The pitch of a sound is determined not only by the tension of the vocal folds, but also by aerodynamic factors such as the pressure drop across vocal folds and the rate of flow between them. It seems that the speech centers usually disregard the aerodynamic factors and control only the tension of the vocal folds when trying to produce a certain pitch. After a voiceless aspirated stop, the vocal folds often begin vibrating at a higher rate because of the greater flow of air. Conversely, there may be a drop in the rate of vibration during a voiced consonant when the flow is less, producing a lower pitch that may not be relevant.

These points are illustrated in Fig. 1.1. The speaker was asked to produce a series of similar sentences such as *Whatever pie you have in mind* ..., and *Whatever buy you have in mind* ... saying each of them with the same intonation pattern. As the parts of these sentences in Fig. 1.1 show, there is a considerable difference between the beginning of *buy* (which is virtually level) and the beginning of *pie* (which descends rapidly). The high pitch at the beginning of *pie* is due to the high rate of airflow for the [pʰ], which continues into the beginning of the vowel, producing a higher rate of vibration of the vocal folds. Even more noticeable is the drop in each phrase for the [v] in *whatever*. The speaker's intended pitch on *ever* was presumably fairly level. The drop in pitch was simply because the airflow dropped when the [v] was produced.

If the goal of the speech centers was to produce a given pitch pattern (and not just a particular vocal fold tension pattern), we might reasonably ask why there was no attempt to vary the tension of the vocal folds to compensate for aerodynamic factors. Experiments have shown that speakers are conscious of these small changes in pitch. When listening to someone else, they can use the pitch changes to help them decide whether a word begins with a voiced or a voiceless consonant (Ohde, 1984). However, the data in Fig.

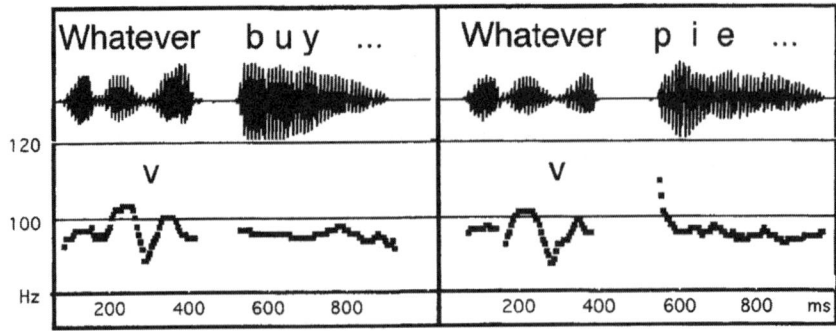

FIG.1.1. The waveform (upper panels) and fundamental frequency (lower panels) during parts of sentences beginning with *Whatever buy* ... and *Whatever pie*. Note the drop in pitch during the voiced consonant [v], and the high pitch at the beginning of the word *pie*.

1.1 show that the speech centers in the brain disregard aerodynamic factors, making no attempt to compensate for them. They arrange for a pattern of vocal fold tension that would produce the pitch pattern required for the sentence if there were no aerodynamic effects. So, it might seem that the goals are organized in terms of the vocal fold tension.

There are, however, two kinds of data suggesting that the speech centers are sometimes aiming directly for a pitch pattern, rather than a vocal fold tension pattern. The first comes from studies of pitch variation in vowels. When the tongue is pulled up to produce a high vowel such as [i], the hyoid bone is also pulled up. This, in turn, produces a pull on the thyroid cartilage, and when the thyroid moves upward, the vocal folds are further stretched and a higher pitch is produced. A speaker producing a set of words on the same tone will have a pitch that is 2 to 5 Hz higher on words that contain [i] in comparison with other words (Ladd & Silverman, 1984; Peterson & Barney, 1952). Whalen and Levitt (1995) discuss 58 studies involving 31 languages, in all of which the F0 of high vowels was higher than that of low vowels in similar phonetic contexts. Whalen, Gick, Kumada, and Honda (1998) point out that there is no fully agreed explanation of this finding, but they provide evidence that it is not a learned action but an automatic one. What is important from our point of view is that these variations are disregarded in the control of pitch.

It might be possible to retain the notion that the production of pitch is organized in terms of the tension of the vocal folds. We could say that, in gestural terms, the speech centers are trying to produce a particular sequence of vocal fold gestures in which the target is not the tension of the vocal folds themselves, but just that part of the tension that is achieved by particular muscles. This possibility, however, is excluded by other data, indicating that sometimes the goal may be the pitch and not the vocal fold tension, however defined.

Speakers do not all behave in the same way when it comes to making pitch variations. Ladefoged (1967) reported experiments in which 11 speakers produced a set of statements and questions such as *He's a pervert* and *He's a pervert?* An approximation to the subglottal pressure was obtained from a balloon in the esophagus attached to a pressure sensor. All 11 speakers had a rising intonation in the question form. Although actual values of the subglottal pressure could not be computed for these speakers, it was apparent that

4 of the 11 had a rise in subglottal pressure around the time in the sentence when the pitch increased. This rise in pressure alone may have been sufficient to cause the rise in pitch, and there may have been little or no increase in the tension of the vocal folds. Herman, Beckman, and Honda (1996) also report a "strong correspondence" between the subglottal pressure and the final part of the intonation contour in questions as opposed to statements.

Further evidence that speakers may produce pitch changes by varying the subglottal pressure comes from an unreported experiment by Lin Mao–can and myself (Ladefoged lab notebook, May 7, 1983). The speaker recorded 16 disyllablic words, each representing a possible sequence of the four tones of Putonghua. At the same time, his subglottal pressure was monitored by a balloon in the esophagus attached to a pressure sensor. There was a very high correlation between the pitch curves and the subglottal pressure curves. It was likely that, as in the case of the four subjects producing questions described earlier, the pitch variations in this speaker's Chinese words in citation form were produced by the variations in subglottal pressure.

These experiments show that meaningful pitch changes in speech can be produced in very different ways. Some speakers use primarily laryngeal muscles, others place greater emphasis on subglottal pressure, and some speakers use both systems in varying degrees. When there are different ways of achieving the same result, it is best to regard the result as the goal, and regard the way of achieving it as a lower level set of possibilities. It is likely that for all speakers in most circumstances the goal of the speech centers controlling an utterance is simply to achieve a particular pitch pattern.

Now let us consider the universal phonetic tendency for the pitch of vowels to be higher after aspirated stops. As we noted, this tendency may be said to be due to the aerodynamic situation. The greater rate of flow after aspirated stops produces a faster rate of vibration of the vocal folds. The speech centers may be aiming to produce a certain pitch, but do not (or cannot) adjust the vocal fold tension so as to allow for the greater flow rate during a small part of the vowel. This exemplifies a situation in which the speech centers aim at a certain pitch goal, but do not achieve it.

As we have noted, however, listeners are aware of these variations in the rate of vibration of the vocal folds. They disregard them, perhaps because they cannot do otherwise, when producing a given tone and intonation, but nevertheless they can hear them and use them when judging vowel quality, and assessing the differences between voiced and voiceless consonants (Ohde, 1984). Sometimes these pitch variations lead to changes in the goals for producing a sentence. In Korean, the increase in fundamental frequency after voiceless aspirated and fortis is higher than the increase due to the higher rate of flow through the glottis (Jun, 1996). Speakers have noticed the pitch difference between these consonants and other sounds and how the speech centers use laryngeal muscles and aim for a higher pitch, so as to make these sounds more distinctive. The variations in fundamental frequency that are usually disregarded have become phonologically relevant, so that these consonants are now marked by phonologically high tones.

AUDITORY TARGETS: VOWELS

Next, more speculatively, let us consider the possibility that consonantal gestures involve primarily articulatory goals, but that vowels have mainly auditory targets. Consonant gestures are things that you can feel, whereas vowel movements have to be heard to be appreciated. This is in accord with the finding that a statistically improbable number of languages tend to have five or seven vowels (Maddieson, 1984), with one so-called low central vowel and the same number of so-called back vowels as front vowels. As Liljencrantz and Lindblom (1972) and others have shown, these findings are readily explicable in auditory terms. The favored sets of vowels are those that have their formants well distributed in the acoustic vowel space. But, as we will see, they do not have their vocal tract shapes well distributed in terms of the possible set of tongue shapes.

There are always individual differences between speakers, and it is not advisable to attempt to make linguistic generalizations on the basis of data from only one speaker. However, there is a lack of data giving the mean formant frequencies and the corresponding tongue shapes for a set of speakers of a language with five or seven vowels. We can, however, make the point that vowels are best regarded as being organized in an auditory space rather than an articulatory one by first considering a set of English speakers producing different vowels. Fig. 1.2 shows the mean frequencies of the first two formants of the front vowels in *heed, hid, head, had, hod*, and the back vowels in *hod, hawed, hood*, and *who'd* for five speakers of American English (Harshman, Ladefoged, & Goldstein, 1977). In the case of the vowels in *hid, head, had, hod* and *hawed*, a steady state part of the second formant was selected. For the more diphthongal vowels in heed, *hayed, hoed, hood*, and *who'd*, a point shortly after the first consonant was selected. A cine x-ray film was made of the speakers as they were producing these vowels. The frame in the film corresponding to the time in

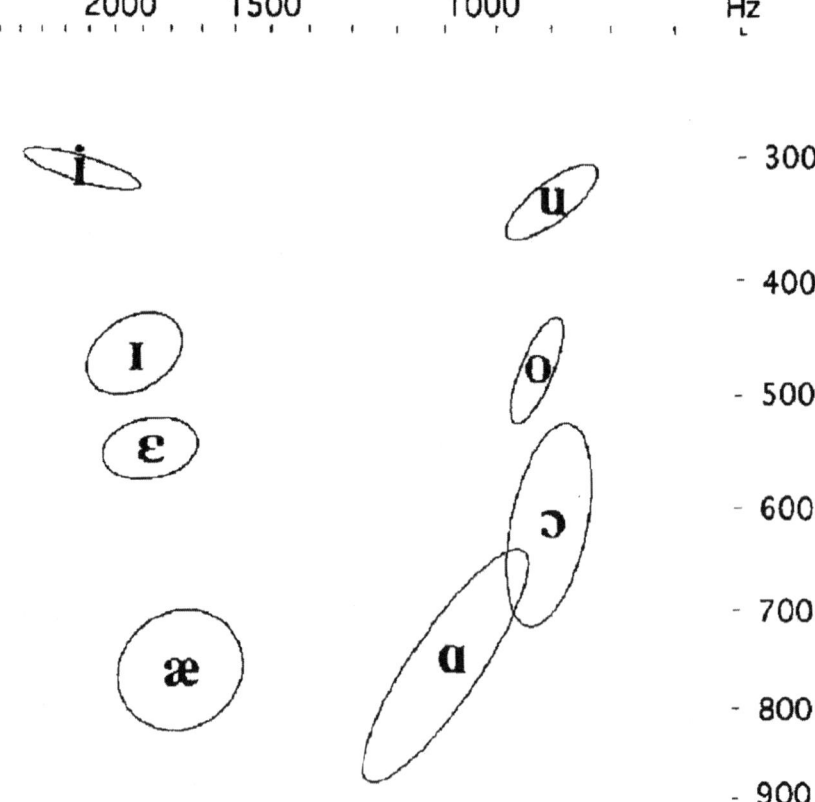

FIG. 1.2. A Bark scale formant plot of the vowels in *heed, hid, head, had, hod, hawed, hood*, and *who'd*, as spoken by five speakers of American English. The ellipses have their axes on the first two principal components and radii of one standard deviation around the mean of each vowel.

the acoustic record used for measuring the formants was located and the vocal tract shape traced.

The formant chart in Fig. 1.2 shows the mean formant values for the five speakers. The ellipses have their axes on the first two principal components of the dispersion of the points for each vowel, and radii of one standard deviation around the means. These eight vowels form an auditorily distinct set of vowels. If a low vowel [a] were substituted for the vowels [æ] and [ɑ], the pattern world be similar to that of a typical seven-vowel language.

Fig. 1.3 shows the mean tongue positions for these vowels. Calculating the mean tongue positions is more complex than calculating mean formant frequencies because the shape of the vocal tract differs from one individual to another. The procedure for obtaining a valid mean tongue shape has been described by Ladefoged (1976) and Ladefoged and Lindau (1989). The tongue positions for each of the five speakers were traced from the x-rays made at the same time as the audio recording. The variations in tongue shapes characteristic of different vowels can be described in terms of two factors: the differences between individuals being ascribed to different weightings of these factors (Harshman et al., 1977). The weightings correspond to personal characteristics. An average speaker will have a weighting of 1.0 on both factors.

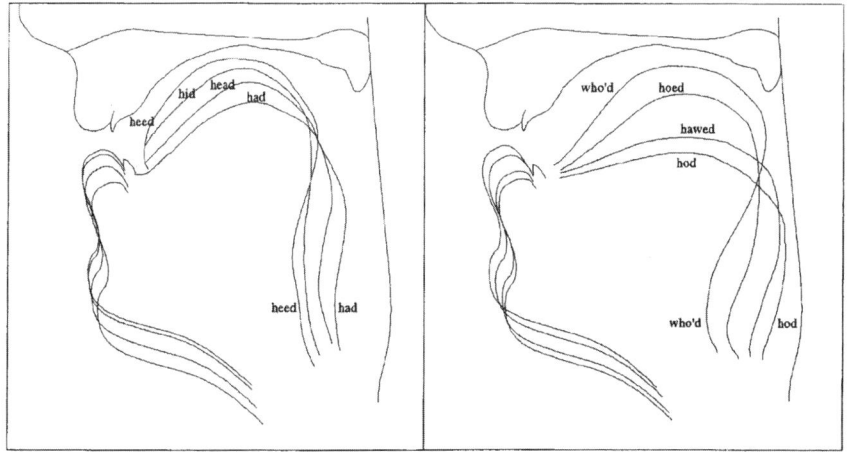

FIG. 1.3. The mean tongue positions of five speakers of American English in the vowels in *heed, hid, head, had, hod, hawed, hood.*

It is difficult to see how these vowels can be considered as being well organized in an articulatory space. The mean tongue positions in the first four vowels can be said to have similar changes in tongue height, but the other four vowels have very different tongue shapes, both from each other and from the first four vowels. The two sets of vowels also differ in that the first four vowels are close together, but the other four vowels differ considerably from one another.

The data linking the articulations of five speakers with the corresponding formant frequencies can be used in another way. An articulatory/acoustic model (Ladefoged & Lindau, 1989) can be used to reconstruct the tongue shapes appropriate for a language with five vowels. Fig. 1.4 shows the first two formants of five vowels that are dispersed within the vowel chart in a manner similar to the vowels of Spanish. Fig. 1.5 shows vocal tract shapes that will produce these sounds.

Figures 1.4 and 1.5 show that the vowels of languages with five vowels (the most common system in the languages of the world) are well distributed in the auditory space, but are less well organized in articulatory terms. The relations between articulations and the corresponding acoustic characteristics shown in these figures lend further credence to the notion that vowels are generally best considered to have auditory goals, and that accounts of universal

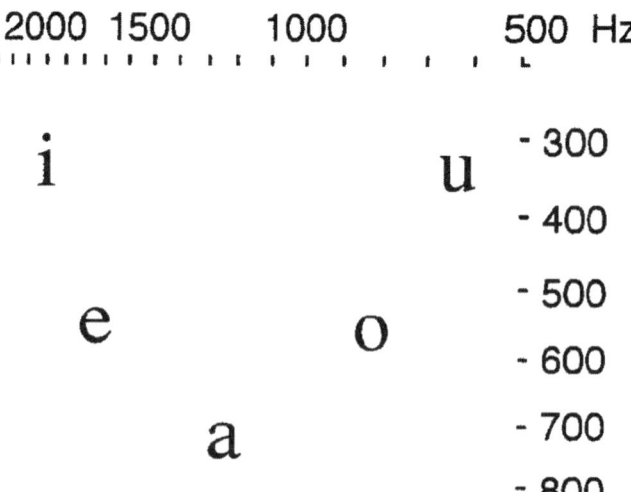

FIG. 1.4. A Bark scaled formant chart showing five vowels similar to those in Spanish.

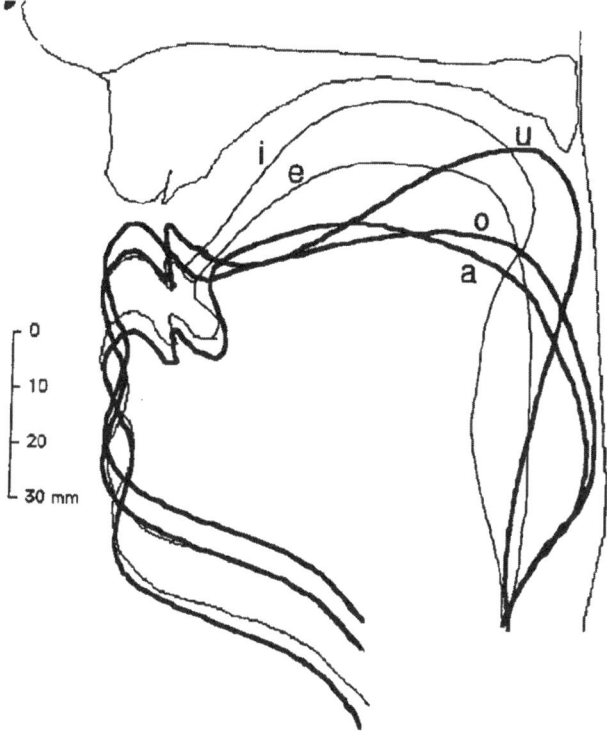

FIG. 1.5. Vocal tract shapes that produce the formant frequencies shown in Fig. 1.4. The shapes for the vowels [a, o, u] are shown with heavier lines.

tendencies among vowels are often more concerned with the sounds rather than the articulations. (There are exceptions to this notion, accounting for the 'often' in the previous sentence. Universal tendencies concerning lip rounding in vowels and in consonants may show that lip rounding is an articulatory goal, rather than an acoustic one, but this point is not pursued further here.)

Johnson, Ladefoged, and Lindau (1993) have also argued in favor of vowels having auditory targets. They point to the differences in the way in which individuals manipulate the tongue and jaw to produce the same vowel sounds, and propose an auditory theory of speech production. However, it must be admitted that their evidence still allows for a particular vocal tract shape to be the goal of the speech centers when producing a particular vowel. Individuals do not aim for one vocal tract shape at one moment and another shape at another, relying on the fact that different vocal tract shapes can produce the same formant frequencies. However, in the case of the next phonetic property that we consider, something like this occurs in that completely different movements are used to produce the same goal.

AERODYNAMIC TARGET: STRESS

In some cases, the goals of the speech centers cannot be considered to be auditory targets or articulatory gestures. Phrasal stress is a good example of a phonetic property that cannot be adequately described as an articulatory target or an acoustic one. Stress has been equated with a greater opening of the jaw (Fujimura, 2000), and a greater jaw opening certainly occurs on many stressed syllables. However, jaw opening is plainly not a defining characteristic. Some people hardly move the jaw at all, and anyone can produce properly stressed sentences while maintaining the jaw at a fixed height by holding an object between the teeth. These sentences sound completely natural, and are indistinguishable from those in which the jaw is free to move. Articulatory opening is equally not a defining characteristic. A sentence such as We *keep money* can be said with a strong emphasis on *keep* with an unusually close or a more open articulation than usual of the vowel [i]. Stressed syllables can also be produced with different actions of the respiratory system, depending on the amount of air in the lungs, as is illustrated later. These are all instances of motor equivalence, different systems being used to produce a goal that cannot be defined in articulatory terms.

Similarly, there do not appear to be any specific auditory goals for stressed syllables. Intensity is sometimes regarded as the major characteristic of stress, but this is also not correct. Consider three sentences that are the same except for a contrastive stress that has been placed on a different word in each of them:) (a) *I see three bees* (but I can't hear them), (b) *I see **three** bees* (not a swarm of them), and (c) *I see three **bees*** (but no wasps). In these circumstances, one might expect the stressed word to have a greater intensity than the other two words that have the same vowel. However, as the pitch and intensity records in Fig. 1.6 show, it is mostly the pitch and the duration that indicates which word received the contrastive stress. In

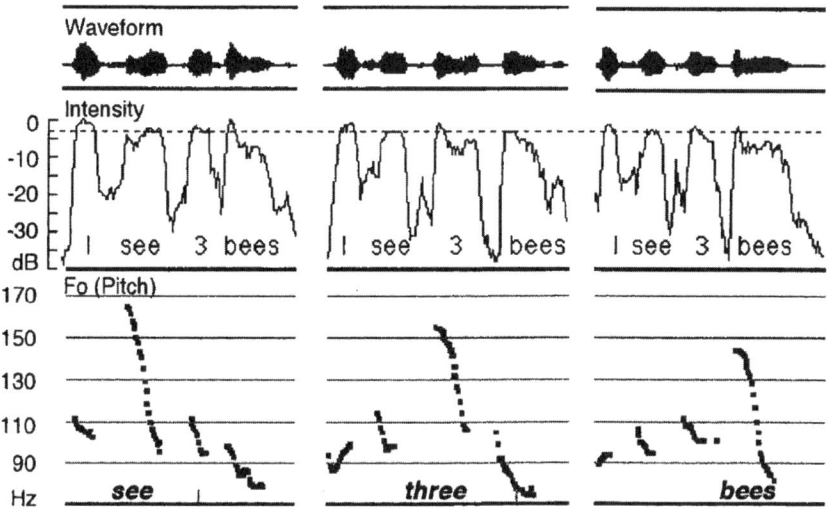

FIG. 1.6. Waveform, intensity, and pitch (fundamental frequency) records of *I see three bees* (but no wasps), *I see three bees* (not a swarm of them), and *I see three bees* (but I can't hear them). The dashed line shows the mean intensity of the word *see*.

every case, the stressed word has a high falling pitch and a greater length, but not a greater intensity. A dashed line has been drawn marking the intensity of the word *see*, showing that it is almost the same in all three phrases, irrespective of whether this word is stressed. In the first phrase, the word *bees* has the highest intensity although it is not stressed. In this particular set of phrases, the pitch is the more important indicator of stress.

We should not, however, presume that a high falling pitch is always the most important correlate of stress. Fig. 1.7 shows that it is possible to emphasize words without using an increase in pitch and a fall. This figure shows the waveform, pitch, and intensity in the phrase, *You saw what I meant*. The word *saw* has been emphasized as when replying to someone who had denied understanding an obvious statement. The pitch on *saw* is lower than that on *You* or *what I meant*. The intensity is higher and the vowel is longer than usual. These last two factors convey the information that this is the stressed syllable.

If the speech centers in the brain are not trying to produce a given articulation or a particular intensity or pitch pattern when producing a stressed syllable, what is the appropriate goal? The

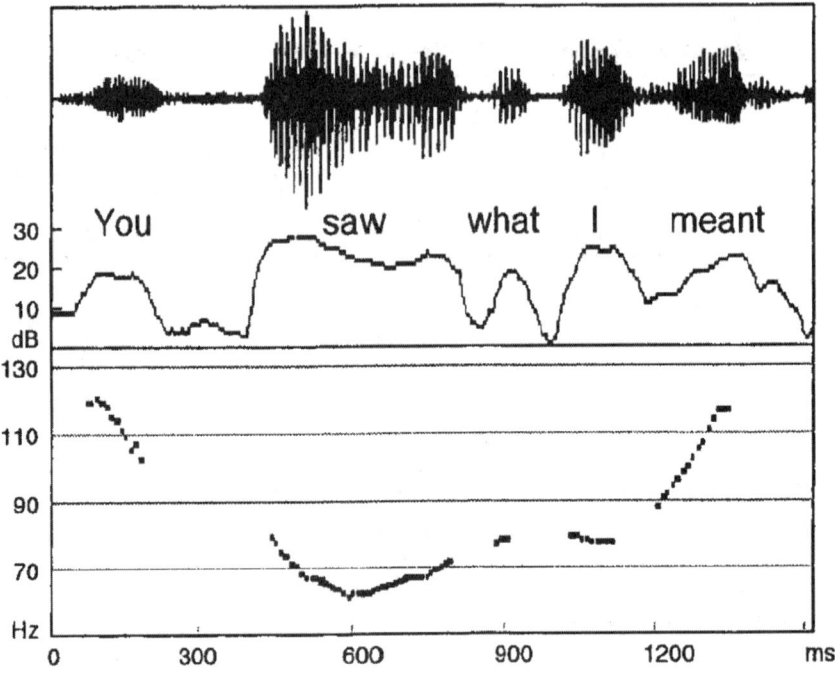

FIG. 1.7. The waveform, pitch, and intensity in the phrase *You **saw** what I meant*.

answer is that word stress always uses a greater amount of respiratory energy. The goal is probably an increased pressure below the vocal folds. There is evidence (Ladefoged, 1967, Ladefoged & Loeb, 2002) that stressed syllables use greater respiratory energy. However, this energy is not always produced in the same way. Fig. 1.8 (adapted from Ladefoged & Loeb, 2002) shows the most common way. The mean activity of the internal intercostals, the principal respiratory muscles for pushing air out of the lungs during speech, have been averaged over 17 repetitions of the phrase, *The old man doddered along the road*. The audio recording of one of the repetitions of the phrase is also shown. The speaker was slightly inconsistent in the way in which she said this phrase. There was always a stress on *man*, on the first syllable of *doddered* and on *road*, and on some occasions there was also a stress on *old*. The onsets of the stressed syllables are marked by open arrows.

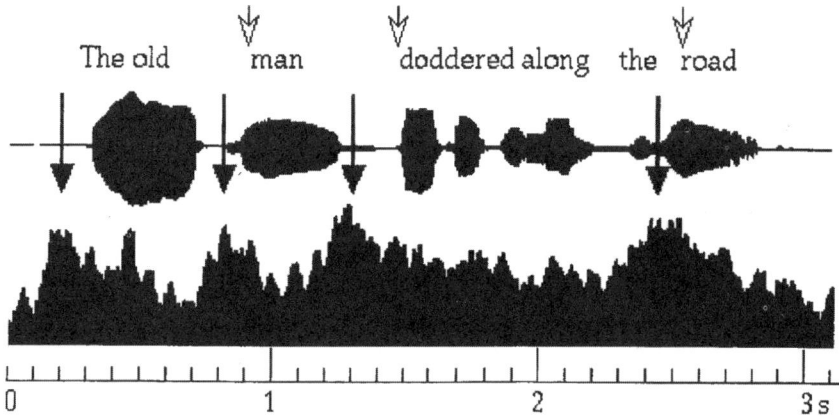

FIG. 1.8. A single audio record of *The old man doddered along the road* above the mean EMG activity of the internal intercostals during 17 repetitions of this phrase. The open arrows mark the onsets of the stressed syllables and the solid arrows mark four of the major peaks in the average activity. (For details of the procedure, see Ladefoged & Loeb, 2002.)

There are a number of peaks in the internal intercostal activity. Solid arrows mark four peaks with high amplitudes that are maintained for over 100 msec. The first peak occurs before the beginning of the utterance, and presumably reflects the generation of the respiratory power necessary to start vocal fold vibration. The second peak occurs before the word *man*. The third peak has the largest summed amplitude and occurs shortly before the first vowel of *doddered*, the syllable that carries the first primary stress in the utterance. At the end of the phrase, shortly before the stressed syllable *road*, there is another peak. There is also a sharp peak, not marked by an arrow in the figure, near the beginning of *old* in which the activity is confined within a 60-msec interval. This peak possibly reflects the occasional inconsistency in the stressing of the phrase. There are no peaks in the electromyographic (EMG) activity for the lengthy stretch of the utterance containing the unstressed syllables ... *ered along*.

The bursts of internal intercostal activity reduce the lung volume and produce a higher subglottal pressure. However, these controlled muscular actions cannot be regarded as gestures that produce stresses. The increase in pressure is the goal of the activity, and it is not always produced by respiratory muscles pushing air out of the lungs. Consider what happens after a speaker takes in a breath. After an inspiration the lungs are like inflated balloons containing air under pressure. In these circumstances, the problem is not how to push air out of the lungs, but how to stop it from going out at too high a pressure. Without muscular action to hold the rib cage up, the pressure beneath the vocal folds would be too great.

Fig. 1.9 shows what happens when a speaker takes two normal breaths and then starts talking after a third, slightly larger, inspiration. The external intercostals, the muscles that pull the rib cage up, are used to increase the volume of air in the lungs. They are active in all three inspirations shown in Fig. 1.9 at the times indicated by the

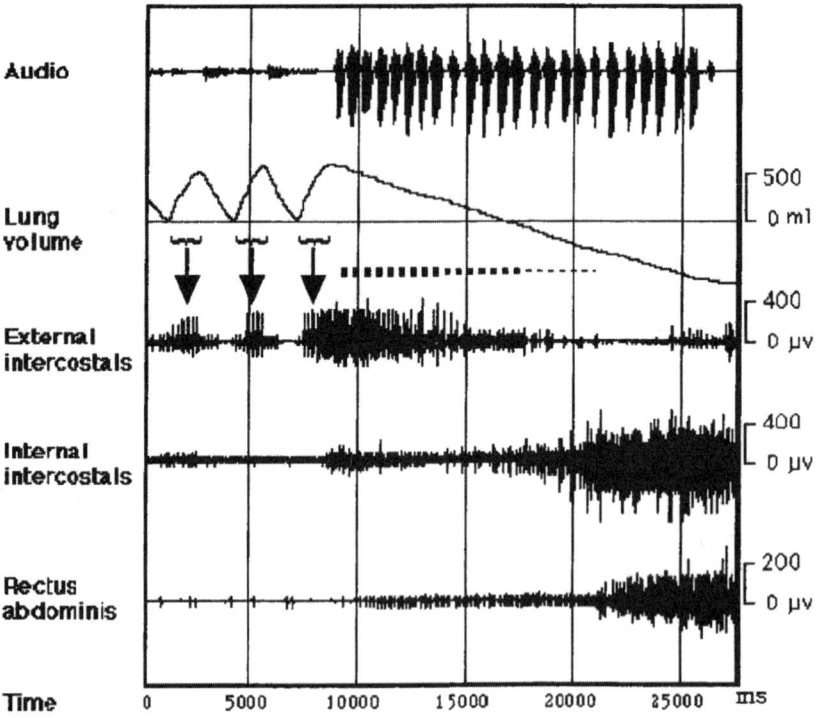

FIG. 1.9. Audio, lung volume, and EMG records from the external intercostals, internal intercostals, and rectus abdominis while producing two respiratory cycles followed by a lighter, deeper inspiration and 25 repetitions of the syllable [pa] at a quiet conversational level (adapted from Ladefoged & Loeb, 2002).

arrows. The external intercostals remain active for the first part of the utterance where there is a diminishing dotted line. The speech in this figure consists of repetitions of the single stressed syllable [ma]. For each of these syllables in the first part, the external intercostals relax slightly so as to allow the pressure of the air below the vocal folds to increase. As the utterance proceeds, the internal intercostals take over, producing contractions of the rib cage to increase the subglottal pressure. The relaxations of the external intercostals are difficult to see in Fig. 1.9, with its compressed time scale. Fig. 1.10 shows just the EMG and the audio for the central part of Fig. 1.9. The lessening of the external intercostal activity just before each stressed syllable is apparent.

There are other aspects of Figures 1.9 and 1.10 that are worth noting when considering the control of speech. As soon as speech starts, there is activity of both the internal intercostals and the rectus abdominis, a muscle that decreases the size of the abdominal cavity, thus pushing the diaphragm upwards so that the lung volume is reduced. These expiratory muscles are active while the external intercostals are still preventing the rib cage from descending. This pattern of activity may represent co-contraction to stabilize the musculoskeletal systems against stochastic fluctuations and external perturbations by taking advantage of the intrinsic mechanical properties of the active muscle (Hogan, 1984). It is evident that the respiratory muscles are operating as a complex system to control the pressure of the air in the lungs, and hence the respiratory power

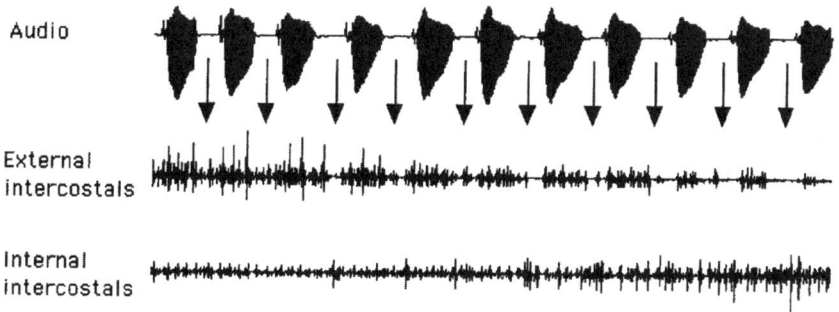

FIG. 1.10. An enlargement of the part of Fig. 1.5 from time 11,500 to 19,000 msec. The arrows mark onsets of stressed syllables and decreases of external intercostal activity.

used for speech. There is no way in which these actions can be considered as always being the same muscular gesture. Sometimes they involve pulling the rib cage down, and sometimes they simply allow it to collapse more rapidly.

Concluding this section, we note that stressed syllables may or may not have a greater jaw opening, they may or may not have a greater intensity or a higher pitch, and they may or may not have bursts of internal intercostals activity. However, they always use greater respiratory energy.

As a universal phonetic tendency, languages that use stress contrastively tend to avoid having two stresses close together. This is readily explicable in terms of the difficulty of consuming two bursts of respiratory energy close together.

CONCLUSION

This chapter has considered some of the ways in which the speech centers in the brain may be controlling speech acts. It is suggested that, generally speaking, tone and intonation are set as auditory goals consisting of pitch patterns. The targets for vowels are points in an auditory space. The target for a stressed syllable is an increased subglottal pressure, achieved through actions of the respiratory system. Note that these are all intended to be just general statements—in some circumstances, the speech centers may set other goals for these aspects of speech. However, it is my belief that we will not get much further in our investigation of the real nature of speech until we have discovered more about how speech is organized. We need to know what we are trying to do when we talk.

REFERENCES

Browman, C. P., & Goldstein, L. (1986). Towards an articulatory phonology. *Phonology Yearbook, 3,* 19–252.

Browman, C. P., & Goldstein, L. (1992). Articulatory phonology: An overview. *Phonetica, 49,* 155–180.

Fujimura, O. (2000). The C/D model and prosodic control of articulatory behavior. *Phonetica, 57,* 128–138.

Harshman, R. A., Ladefoged, P., & Goldstein, L. (1977). Factor analysis of tongue shapes. *Journal of the Acoustical Society of America, 62,* 693–707.

Herman, R., Beckman, M., & Honda, K. (1996). Subglottal pressure and final lowering in English. *International Conference on Spoken Language Processing, 1,* 145–148.

Hogan, N. (1984). Adaptive control of mechanical impedance by co-activation of antagonist muscles. *IEEE Transactions on Automatic Control, 29,* 681–690.

Johnson, K., Ladefoged, P., & Lindau, M. (1993). Individual differences in vowel production. *Journal of the Acoustical Society of America, 94,* 701–714.

Jun, S–A. 1996). Influence of microprosody on macroprosody: A case of phrase initial strengthening. *UCLA Working Papers in Phonetics, 92,* 97–116.

Ladd, D. R., & Silverman, K. E. A. (1984). Intrinsic pitch of vowels in connected speech. *Phonetica, 41,* 31–40.

Ladefoged, P. (1967). *Three areas of experimental phonetics.* London: Oxford University Press.

Ladefoged, P. (1976). How to put one person's tongue inside another person's mouth. *Journal of the Acoustical Society of America, 60,* S77.

Ladefoged, P., & Lindau, M. (1989). Modeling articulatory-acoustic relations. *Journal of Phonetics, 17,* 99–106.

Ladefoged, P., & Loeb, G. (2002). Preliminary experiments on respiratory activity in speech. http://www.jladefoged.com/respiratorystudies.pdf.

Liljencrantz, J., & Lindblom, B. (1972). Numerical simulation of vowel quality systems: The role of perceptual contrast. *Language, 48,* 839–862.

Maddieson, I. (1984). *Patterns of sounds.* Cambridge, England: Cambridge University Press.

Ohde, R. N. (1984). Fundamental frequency as an acoustic correlate of stop consonant voicing. *Journal of the Acoustical Society of America, 75,* 224–230.

Peterson, G. E., & Barney, H. L. (1952). Control methods used in a study of the vowels. *Journal of the Acoustical Society of America, 24,* 175–184.

Saltzman, E., & Kelso, J. A. S. (1987). Skilled actions: A task dynamic approach. *Psychological Review, 94,* 84–106.

Whalen, D. H., Gick, B., Kumada, M., & Honda, K. (1998). Cricothyroid activity in high and low vowels: Exploring the automaticity of intrinsic F0. *Journal of Phonetics, 27,* 125–142.

Whalen, D. H., & Levitt, A. G. (1995). The universality of intrinsic F0 of vowels. *Journal of Phonetics, 23,* 349–366.

CHAPTER 2

Phonetic Explanations for Sound Patterns

Implications for Grammars of Competence

John J. Ohala
University of California, Berkeley

Phonological grammars try to represent speakers' knowledge so that the 'natural' behaviour of speech sounds becomes self-evident. Phonetic models have the same goals but have no psychological pretensions. Phonetic models succeed in explaining the natural behaviour of speech, whereas phonological representations largely fail. The 'phonetic naturalness' requirement in phonological grammars should be reexamined and probably abandoned.

The quest to find a representation of speech sounds that makes their behaviour self-evident goes back at least three centuries (Amman, 1694; Jespersen, 1889; Key, 1855) but has been most intense in the past three decades. Two approaches to "natural" representation have been developed in parallel: one, the "mainstream" phonological one which employs discrete linguistic primitives and at the same time purports to represent the knowledge of the native speaker (Chomsky & Halle, 1968; Clements, 1985; Goldsmith, 1979; McCarthy, 1988) and another, phonetic models which are expressed with continuous physical primitives (Fant, 1960; Fujimura, 1962; Ohala, 1976; Scully, 1990; Stevens, 1971; Westbury & Keating, 1985) but which do not pretend to reflect psychological structure. In this chapter, I review certain well-known cases of sound patterns which are better explained by phonetic rather than mainstream phonological representations and then discuss the relevance of this for phonological (mental) grammars.

CONSTRAINTS ON VOICING

There is a well-known, aerodynamic constraint on voicing in obstruents. Some languages, like Korean and Mandarin, have only voiceless stop phonemes; in languages like English that possess both voiced and voiceless stops, the voiceless [p], [t], [k] tend to occur more often in connected speech than the voiced [b], [d], [g]. This constraint derives from the following: voicing (vocal cord vibration) requires sufficient air flow through the glottis; during an obstruent, air accumulates in the oral cavity such that oral air pressure rises; if the oral pressure nears or equals the subglottal pressure, air flow will fall below the threshold necessary to maintain vocal vibration and voicing will be extinguished. This constraint can be overcome (within limits) by expanding the oral cavity volume to absorb the accumulating air. Such expansion may be done passively, due to the natural compliance or "give" of the vocal tract walls to impinging pressure, or actively, by lowering the tongue and jaw, lowering the larynx, and so forth. However, there are fewer options for vocal tract enlargement the further back the obstruent is articulated. Thus, voiced velar stops are often missing in languages that use the voicing contrast in stops at other places of articulation; they may lose their voicing, their stop character, or both. This is the reason why /g/ is missing (in native vocabulary) in, for example, Dutch, Thai, and Czech. See Maddieson, 1984, and

Ohala, 1983 and 1994 for additional phonetic and phonological data reflecting this.

Additional considerations and variations on this constraint account for the greater bias against voicing in fricatives than stops, and in geminate (long) stops than in singletons (Ohala, 1983, 1994).

If back-articulated stops such as [g] and [G] are threatened in voiced stop series, it seems that it is the front-articulated stop [p] that is threatened in the voiceless series. This is not due as such to aerodynamic but rather to acoustic factors: an abrupt amplitude transient is one of the cues for a stop; the stop burst of a [p] is less intense and thus less noticeable than those for other, further back, places of articulation because a labially-released stop lacks any down-stream resonator. [p] seems thus frequently to become a labial fricative (which happened in the history of Japanese). (Although the burst form of the voiced [b] would be subject to the same factors, a rapid amplitude gradient on the voicing that follows it would still cue its stop character; with [p] and especially [pʰ], this additional stop cue would be weak.)

Thus, for aerodynamic reasons, place of articulation can influence what happens at the glottis and for acoustic reasons what happens at the glottis can influence the viability of place distinctions supraglottally.

How have these constraints been represented using conventional phonological notations? Although the phonetic reasons for the voicing constraint are clearly stated (in prose) by Chomsky and Halle (1968, pp. 330–331), and they explicitly recognize that the formal representation of phonological rules fails to reflect the 'intrinsic content' of the features, their response is the marking convention (p. 406):

$$[u \text{ voice}] \rightarrow [-\text{voice}] /$$

$$[\overline{-\text{son}}]$$

(read 'the unmarked value of voice is minus voice in combination with minus sonorant') which is to say that the voicing constraint on obstruents is just stipulated—it is not made self-evident; it is treated as a primitive. None of the newer formal notations in phonology have offered any improvement.

Feature geometry (Clements, 1985; McCarthy, 1988) proposed to capture dependency relations between features using a simple, transitive, asymmetric relation "dominates." 'Simple' in that it is the same relation everywhere it is used; 'transitive' in that if F_a dominates F_b and F_b dominates F_c, then F_a also dominates F_c; 'asymmetric' in that if F_a dominates F_b, then F_b cannot dominate F_a. The relation 'dominate' can be a one-to-many relation, such that a given feature may dominate more than one other feature but a given feature may itself be immediately dominated by only one other feature. It follows as a corollary of this that features at intermediate or terminal nodes in the resulting feature hierarchy may not dominate each other. A simplified version of this hierarchy is given in Fig. 2.1.

Such an arrangement makes it impossible to capture (other than by stipulation) the aerodynamic constraints between obstruency and voicing, between voicing and place of articulation, or the acoustic constraints between glottal state and supraglottal place of articulation. For the most part, Fig. 2.1 loosely embodies the configuration of the vocal tract by virtue of the particular dependency relations proposed, that is, separating the laryngeal mechanism from the supralaryngeal system which, in turn, is divided into nasal and oral

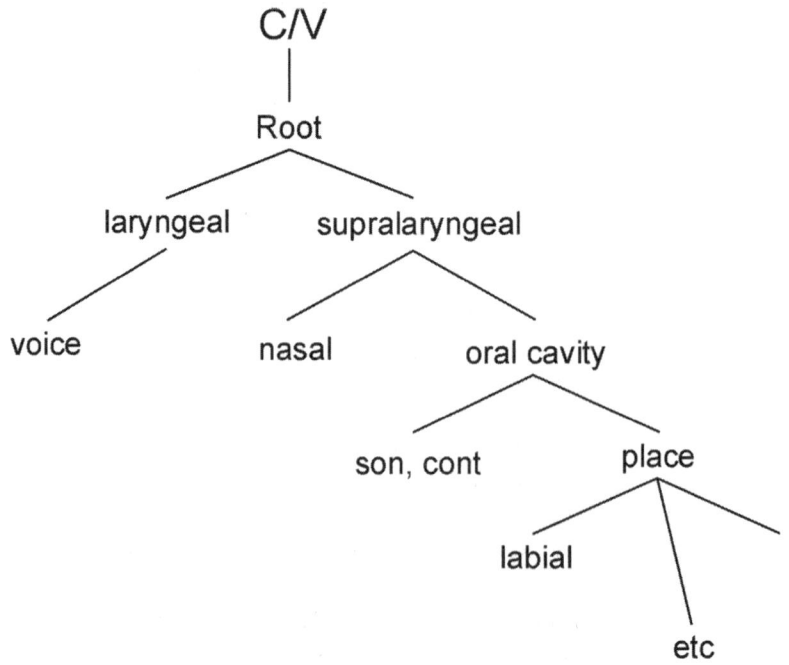

FIG. 2.1. Feature hierarchy proposed by Clements (1985).

cavities. The simple monolithic character of the relation 'dominates' prevents a separate encoding of dependency relations due to speech aerodynamics, acoustics, or perception. The asymmetric character of 'dominates' prevents simultaneous dominance of place by laryngeal features and vice versa and prevents dominance by features that are at terminal nodes or intermediate nodes of different branches of the feature hierarchy. In addition, there is nothing in the feature geometry mechanism to allow only *one* value of a feature, for example, [–voice], to dominate or be dominated by another feature without the other value of the feature ([+voice]) also sharing in the relation.

Within Optimality Theory, constraints are stated much as in SPE, for example,

OBS/VOI: 'If [–sonorant] then [–voice]; if [–sonorant] then not [+voice]' (Elzinga, 1999).

The difference is that such constraints are assumed to reflect elements of Universal Grammar, that is, they are part of the human genome. Unresolved (to everyone's satisfaction) is the question of why phonological constraints that arise from the way the physical world is structured need to be redundantly represented in human's genes (Menn, 2002).

Thus, as with the formalism used in SPE, the modern phonological representations can state (stipulate) things known to be true about the behaviour of speech sounds but they are inherently incapable of showing the "natural" or self-evident character of these relations. Phonetic models, however, which are also formal, succeed in deriving this behaviour from primitives, which are for the most part extra-linguistic, for example, entities and relations from the physical universe (Ohala, 1976; Scully, 1990; Westbury & Keating, 1985).

OBSTRUENTS FROM NONOBSTRUENTS.

There are morphophonemic alternations in Welsh and Kwakiutl (and other American languages in the vicinity of British Columbia and Washington State) where the voiced lateral approximant [l] alternates with the voiceless lateral fricative [ɬ] (Ball, 1990; Boas, 1947). Although perhaps not obvious, I think a related phonological phenomenon, an extremely common one, is the affrication of stops before high close glides or vowels; see examples in Table 2.1 (Guthrie, 1967–1970). Both are cases of what I call emergent obstruents (Ohala, 1997b).

Does the obstruent character of the [ɬ] or the affricated release of the stops have to be introduced explicitly by a special rule? Not at all; I claim they are directly derivable from preexisting elements. To see why, it is necessary to briefly review some of the aerodynamic factors giving rise to turbulence (Ohala, 1994, 1997a; Scully, 1990; Stevens, 1971).

Turbulence increases when the velocity, v, (so-called 'particle velocity') of the air increases. Particle velocity, in turn, varies as a function of volume velocity, U (how much air is moving past a given point per unit time), divided by the physical characteristics of the channel through which it moves, simplified as d (= diameter), in (1):

$$(1)\ v = U / d$$

Volume velocity, in turn, is determined by the area of the aperture, A, through which the air moves, and the pressure difference across that aperture (given as $P_{Oral}–P_{Atmospheric}$), as in (2; c is a constant and a varies between 1 and 0.5 depending on the nature of the flow).

$$(2)\ U = A\ (P_{Oral}–P_{Atmos})^a\ c$$

TABLE 2.1

Stops Become Affricated Before High, Close Vowels but not Before Lower Vowels

Proto–Bantu	Mvumbo	Translation
*–buma	bvumo	fruit
*–dib–	dʒiwo	shut
*–tiitʊ	tʃîr	animal
*–kiŋgo	tʃîuŋ	Neck, nape
*–kuba	pf̂uw	chicken
BUT		
*–bod	buo	Rot (v)
*–dl	di	eat

From these equations, we see that turbulence can be increased by decreasing the cross-dimensional area of the channel. This is the usual view of how fricatives differ from approximants. However, I don't think this is what is involved in the cases cited. Rather, another way to create turbulence is by increasing U, the volume velocity, and this, in turn, can be effected by increasing P_{Oral}. In the case of the [ɬ], the P_{Oral} is increased by virtue of its voicelessness: this reduces the resistance at the glottis to the expiratory air flow. The upstream pressure is then essentially the higher pulmonic pressure. Thus, the fricative character of the [ɬ] need not result from its having a narrower channel than the approximant [l] but simply from being [–voice]. In the case of the affrication developing on stops before high close vowels or glides, the higher P_{oral} occurs for different reasons: a stop generates a high upstream pressure; when the stop is released before a high close vowel or glide, some of the air must escape through the narrow channel present. It can take a few tens of msecs for the P_{Oral} to reach P_{Atmos} and during this time the air will be forced through the constriction at a higher rate. Hence, the initial portions of the vowel or glide can be fricated, especially after a voiceless stop but also after a voiced stop.

To my knowledge, there has been no attempt to use current phonological representations to capture the phonetic naturalness of such cases where [–son] elements emerge from [+son] segments simply by appearing simultaneously with [–voice] or sequentially after [–cont, –son]. But, again, the current models such as feature geometry would be inherently incapable of handling these cases because, first, they ignore the aerodynamic aspects of speech and, second, because of the prohibition on dependency relations between separate branches of the feature hierarchy (e.g., [voice] may not dominate [manner]).

EMERGENT STOPS

Occasionally, one finds a stop consonant emerging between a nasal consonant and an oral consonant:

Thompson (< *Thom* + *son*); *Alhambra* (< Arabic *al hamra*, "the red (edifice)"); *humble* (related to *humility*, < Latin hu "of the earth"); *empty* < Old English *amtig*; Sanskrit *viṣṇu* "Vishmu" > *Viṣṭṇu* > Bengali *biuṣṭu*

To understand how these stops arise, it is necessary to view speech production (in part) as a process controlling the flow of expiratory air using certain anatomical structures as valves. A nasal consonant is made by channeling air through the nasal cavity: there must be a valvular closure in the mouth and a valvular opening into the nasal cavity (by a lowering of the soft palate). The nasal consonant [m], for example, has the lips closed while the passage between the oral and nasal cavities is open (represented schematically in Fig. 2.2a). An oral consonant like [s], on the other hand, requires a closure of the nasal valve (by an elevation of the soft palate; see Fig. 2.2c). If the oral consonant's soft palate closure is made prematurely during the latter portion of the nasal, that is, undergoes anticipatory assimilation, then with both the oral and nasal valves closed (and there are no other outlet channels for the expiratory airflow), a complete stoppage of the air flow is produced (see Fig. 2.2b).

Fig. 2.2 also serves to show the basis for changes of the sort [ls] > [lts], except that in this case, the upper branch represents the lateral air

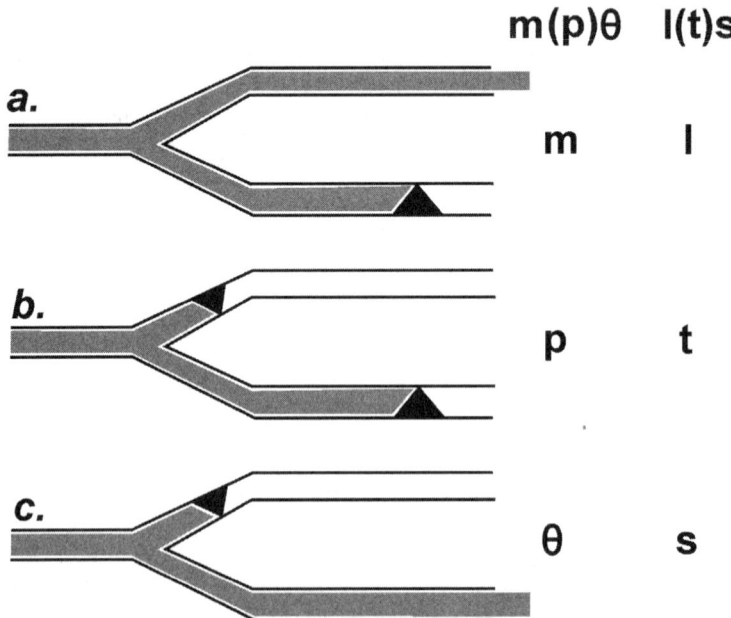

FIG. 2.2. Schematic representation of the vocal tract and the valves which regulate the flow of air; expiratory air symbolized by gray; valves by black triangles.

passage—which is open for the lateral [l] and closed for the fricative [s]—and the lower branch represents the midline passage—which is closed for [l] and open for [s]. In the transition between these two sounds, both air passages may be briefly closed, thus forming a stop. (See Ohala, 1995 and 1997b for more details, further data, and references, and discussion of how the same principles can account for some cases of emergent ejectives and clicks.)

Using autosegmental notation, Wetzels (1985) and Clements (1987) correctly characterized /mθ/ > [mpθ] as arising from the spreading of [–nasal] from the [θ] into the [m] (although they incorrectly assumed that such spreading could not occur from left-to-right as in Sanskrit *viṣṇu*, cited earlier). However, in the case of [ls] > [lts] or [sl] > [stl], they resort to a rule that simply inserts a consonant; it seems they are unable to generate a [–continuant] from the spreading of features from two [+continuants]. However, as detailed earlier, and illustrated in Fig. 2.2, the overlap of gestures from two continuants *can* create a noncontinuant or obstruent. The problem with the phonological representations here lies in taking [±continuant] or [±sonorant] as primitives, whereas they are in fact *derived* from the states of the valves which control airflow.

THE STORY OF [w]

The labial velars [w], [k͡p], [g͡b], and [ŋ͡m], are doubly-articulated consonants, having two simultaneous primary constrictions, labial and velar. In spite of their two constrictions, in certain cases, these sounds pattern with simple labials, such as [p], [b], and [m], and in other cases, with simple velars, [k], [g], and [ŋ]. However, their behaviour as labial or velar depends on the nature of the particular contextual effect involved.

When Generating Noise, Labial Velars are Labial

When generating noise (frication or stop bursts), labial velars tend to behave as labials. Some examples follow: British English [lɛftɛnənt] for *lieutenant*; in Tenango Otomi the /h/ before /w/ is realized as the voiceless labial fricative [ɸ]. The probable reason for this is that because noise is inherently a relatively high frequency sound, even if noise were generated equally at both the velar and labial places, the noise at the velar constriction would be attenuated by the low-pass filtering effect of the downstream resonator (see Fant, 1960; Stevens, 1971).

Nasals Assimilating to [w] Are Velar

A nasal assimilating to the labio-velar [w], insofar as it shows any assimilatory change and shows only one place of articulation, becomes the velar nasal [ŋ], not the labial nasal [m]. Tswana /–roma/ "send" + /wa/ (pass. sfx.) = /–roŋwa/; Melanesian dialects show the variant pronunciation /mwala/ ~ /ŋwala/ for the name of *Mala Island*.

Some principles adduced by Fujimura (1962) help to explain this pattern (see also Ohala & Ohala, 1993). Fig. 2.3 gives a schematic

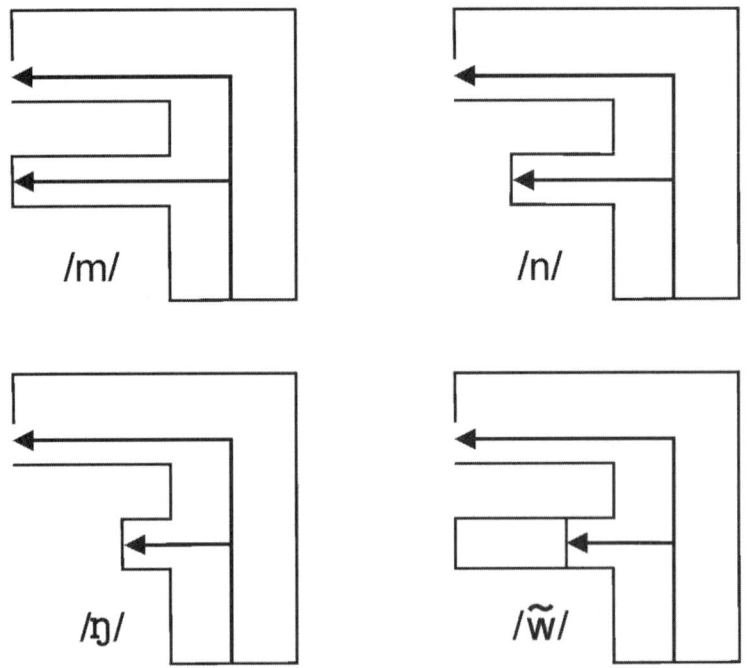

FIG. 2.3. Schematic representation of the air spaces creating the distinctive resonances for nasal consonants. The pharyngeal-nasal resonating air spaces are identical in all nasals; it is the oral air spaces, measured from the pharynx to the point of constriction in the oral cavity, that contribute resonances that differ between nasals.

representation of the air spaces that determine the resonances of nasal consonants. As shown in the figure, all nasal consonants have the pharyngeal-nasal air space in common. What differentiates one nasal from another is the length of the air cavity (marked by the lower arrow in the oral cavity), a cul-de-sac, which branches off of this pharyngeal-nasal air space. Measured from the point where the two air cavities diverge, this branch is quite long in the case of the labial nasal [m] but is quite short in the case of the velar nasal [ŋ]. In the case of the labio-velar nasal there are two constrictions, one labial and one velar, but only the rearmost constriction defines the extent of the branch (measured from the point where it diverges form the pharyngeal-nasal cavity); the forwardmost (labial) constriction will be largely irrelevant in determining the characteristic resonances. Thus, labio-velar nasals will tend to sound like simple velar nasals.

These labial velar sound patterns could not fall out from current phonological representations because they fail to incorporate aerodynamic and acoustic relations and do not allow for dependency relations between [nasal], [manner], and [place] features.

CONCLUSION: EXPLANATIONS FOR SOUND PATTERNS IN LANGUAGE

Mainstream phonological representations purport to simultaneously (a) reflect speakers' knowledge of the sound patterns in their language and (b) represent this knowledge in a way that makes the 'naturalness' of the sound patterns self-evident. I have tried to demonstrate in this chapter that the second goal is not achieved. Could this goal be met by some appropriate modification of the representations used, for example, by some new feature geometry having separate dependency relations for speech articulations, aerodynamics, acoustics, and so forth, including the interdomain dependencies (aerodynamics and acoustics together determine why the noise generated by labial velars is predominantly labial)? I submit that if such a revised representation were constructed, one that would then be capable of embodying the 'intrinsic content' of the elements of speech, it would be identical to the phonetic models referred to earlier. But this solution would be

unacceptable because such models use continuous physical parameters and physical relations between them such as Boyle–
Mariotte's Law—and with justification, no one believes that a
speaker's competence includes knowledge of physics.

I see no way out of this impasse except to abandon the requirement that phonological grammars reflect the phonetic naturalness
of the sound patterns in language. Can we justify this step and, if so,
what are its consequences?

A full justification would require more space than I am allotted
here but a few comments are possible. In searching for the origin of
the requirement that the rules in the speaker's mental grammar
reflect phonetic naturalness, it seems that it came about in two
steps. Chomsky's book, *Syntactic Structure* (1957; and earlier in
Chomsky, 1956), proposed that simplicity be a criterion for evaluation of competing grammars. By explicit projection, the criterion
used by the linguist to find a theory (grammar) of the language
should also be the criterion the language learner uses to evaluate
grammatical specifications of his language. Features, alpha variables, abstract underlying forms, ordered rules, the transformational cycle, and so forth, were subsequently shown to lead to
simplifications of grammar. At this, the 'quantitative' phase, simple
length was used to evaluate grammars and their parts. In *SPE*, Chapter 9, the authors declared that a simple quantitative evaluation of
rules was not sufficient and that further simplifications could be
achieved if a qualitative differentiation could be made between
common, widely-attested, sound patterns and those less common—a way that would reflect the 'intrinsic content' of features.
Thus, the burden was shifted to the representation of speech
sounds. The marking conventions, autosegmental notation, feature geometry, and so forth, were designed to incorporate more of
the inherent structure—presumably their phonetic structure—
which is responsible for the 'natural' behaviour of speech. But as
far as I have been able to tell, the proposals to make grammars
quantitatively and qualitatively optimal were made without any
serious consideration of psychological evidence or implications.
The whole notion of 'simplicity' is quite elusive and what sorts of
optimization speakers impose on their mental representation of
the phonological component of their language is largely unknown.

The amount of psychological evidence on speakers' awareness of what is phonetically natural is in inverse relation to the impact that the issue of 'naturalness' has had on mainstream phonological theory. Moreover, there is some evidence that nonphonetic factors, for example, morphology, and semantics, play a much more important role in speakers' conception and manipulation of sound patterns (Ohala & Ohala, 1987).

The existence of phonetically natural processes in the sound patterns of languages needs no special or extravagant explanation. Universal, physical, phonetic factors lead to a speech signal which obscures the speaker's intended pronunciation; listeners may misinterpret ambiguous phonetic elements in the signal and arrive at a pronunciation norm that differs from the speaker's. This is how sound change works (Ohala, 1993a, 1993b) and how natural sound patterns arise. Such changes will reflect phonetic constraints without speaker or listener having to "know" about them. Similarly, when we eat, walk, see, hear, and so forth, our behaviour is subject to a myriad of universal physical constraints without the necessity of our knowing them either consciously or unconsciously. Even a rock obeys the laws of physics without having to know them.

There is, in sum, more than ample justification to abandon the 'phonetic naturalness' requirement for the representation of speakers' competence.

What would the consequences of this move be for current phonological practice? Historical grammars or any account of phonological universals would, as now, still have to meet the requirement of representing speech sounds in a way that would accurately predict their behaviour. For this purpose, existing phonetic models suffice, as illustrated in this chapter. Of course, there is now and always will be a need to elaborate and revise existing models and to introduce new ones as we seek to explain more sound patterns in language. Adequate representations of native speakers' competence could—ironically—be much simpler, possibly formulated with no more than unanalyzed phonemes (Myers, 1994). There may be no need for features, underspecification, autosegmental notation, feature geometry, or similar speculative devices. However, whatever is attributed to the speaker's mental grammar should be subject to the same standards of empirical verification as are elements in phonetic models. Such evidence would probably come from psycholinguistic experiments.

No matter what sort of account or model is given of speech sounds and their behaviour, it would be beneficial if they were preceded by an explicit statement regarding what part of the universe the model represented, whether it be the speaker's vocal tract, the speaker's mind, or the speaker's DNA. That would determine the part of the universe where empirical verification of the model would be sought (Ohala, 1986; Ohala & Jaeger, 1986).

ACKNOWLEDGMENT

This a revision of a paper of the same title presented at the 13th International Congress of Phonetic Sciences, Stockholm, 1995.

REFERENCES

Amman, J. C. (1694). *The talking deaf man.* London: Tho. Hawkins.

Ball, M. J. (1990). The lateral fricative: Lateral or fricative? In M. J. Ball, J. Fife, E. Poppe, & J. Rowland, (Eds.), *Celtic linguistics/Ieithyddiaeth Geltaidd. Readings in the Brythonic Languages: Festschrift for T. Arwyn Watkins* (pp. 109–125). Amsterdam: Benjamins.

Boas, F. (1947). Kwakiutl grammar with glossary of the suffixes. [Monograph] *Transactions of the American Philosophical Society, 37,* (pt. 3).

Chomsky, N. (1956). The logical structure of linguistic theory. Cambridge, MA: Harvard University Press.

Chomsky, N. (1957). *Syntactic structure.* The Hague, Netherlands: Mouton.

Chomsky, N., & Halle, M. (1968). *Sound pattern of English.* New York: Harper & Row.

Clements, G. N. (1985). The geometry of phonological features. *Phonology Yearbook, 2,* 225–252.

Clements, N. S. (1987). Phonological feature representation and the description of *Chicago Linguistic Society Parasession, 23,* 29–50.

Elzinga, D. A. (1999). *The consonants of Gosiute.* Unpublished doctoral dissertation, University of Arizona, Tucson.

Fant, G. (1960). *Acoustic theory of speech production.* The Hague, Netherlands: Mouton.

Fujimura, O. (1962). Analysis of nasal consonants. *Journal of the Acoustical Society of America, 34,* 1865–1875.

Goldsmith, J. (1979). *Autosegmental phonology.* New York: Garland.

Guthrie, M. (1967–1970). *Comparative Bantu.* Farnborough, UK: Gregg.

Jespersen, O. (1889). *Articulation of speech sounds, represented by means of analphabetic symbols*. Marburg in Hesse, Germany: N. G. Elwert.

Key, T. H. (1855). On the vowel-assimilation, especially in relation to Professor Willis's experiment on vowel-sounds. *Transactions of the Philological Society [London], 5,* 191–204.

Maddieson, I. (1984). *Patterns of sounds*. Cambridge, England: Cambridge University Press.

McCarthy, J. J. (1988). Feature geometry and dependency: A review. *Phonetica, 45,* 84–108.

Menn, L. (2002). Retrieved from Phonetics and universal grammar: an open letter to Paul Smolens (sic) from Lise Menn. Https://mailman.rice.edu/pipermail/funknet/2002-March/002247.html

Myers, J. (1994). *Autosegmental notation and the phonetics-phonology interface*. Unpublished Manuscript, State University of New York, Buffalo, NY.

Ohala, J. (1976). A model of speech aerodynamics. *Report of the Phonology Laboratory, 1,* 93–107.

Ohala, J. (1983). The origin of sound patterns in vocal tract constraints. In P. F. MacNeilage (Ed.), *The production of speech* (pp. 189–216). New York: Springer–Verlag.

Ohala, J. (Ed.). (1986). The validation of phonological theories. *Phonology Yearbook, 3,* 3–252.

Ohala, J. (1993a). The phonetics of sound change. In C. Jones (Ed.), *Historical linguistics: Problems and perspectives* (pp. 237–238). London: Longman.

Ohala, J. (1993b). Sound change as nature's speech perception experiment. *Speech Communication, 13,* 155–161.

Ohala, J. (1994). Speech aerodynamics. In R. E. Asher & J. M. Y. Simpson (Eds.), *The Encyclopedia of Language and Linguistics,* (pp. 4144–4148). Oxford: Pergamon.

Ohala, J. J. (1995). A probable case of clicks influencing the sound patterns of some European languages. *Phonetica, 52,* 160–170.

Ohala, J. J. (1997a). Aerodynamics of phonology. *Proceedings of the Fourth Seoul International Conference on Linguistics [SICOL], Korea,* 92–97.

Ohala, J. J. (1997b). Emergent stops. *Proceedings of the Fourth Seoul International Conference on Linguistics [SICOL],* 84–91.

Ohala, J., & Jaeger, J. (Eds.). (1986). *Experimental phonology*. Orlando, FL: Academic.

Ohala, J., & Ohala, M. (1993). The phonetics of nasal phonology: Theorems and data. In M. Huffman & R. Krakow (Eds.), *Nasals, nasalization, and the velum* (pp. 225–249). San Diego, CA: Academic.

Ohala, M., and Ohala, J. (1987). Psycholinguistic probes of native speakers' phonological knowledge. In W. U. Dressler, H. C. Luschützky, O. E. Pfeiffer, & J. R. Rennison (Eds.), *Phonologica* 1984 (pp. 227–233). Cambridge, UK: Cambridge University Press.

Scully, C. (1990). Articulatory synthesis. In W. J. Hardcastle & A. Marchal (Eds.), *Speech production and speech modelling* (pp. 151–186). Dordrecht, The Netherlands: Kluwer.

Stevens, K. N. (1971). Airflow and turbulence noise for fricative and stop consonants. *Journal of the Acoustical Society of America, 50,* 1180–1192.

Westbury, J., & Keating, P. (1985). On the naturalness of stop consonant voicing. *Working Papers in Phonetics, 60,* 1–19.

Wetzels, W. L. (1985). The historical phonology of intrusive stops. A nonlinear description. *Canadian Journal of Linguistics, 30,* 285–233.

Chapter 3

Electropalatography as a Research and Clinical Tool

30 Years on

W. J. Hardcastle and F. Gibbon
Queen Margaret University College
Edinburgh, Scotland

Electropalatography (EPG) has its origin in older forms of palatography and other methods of recording details of tongue contact with the palate during speech. Earlier versions of palatography such as "direct palatography" described by Abercrombie (1957) involved spraying the roof of the mouth with a black powder (e.g., a mixture of charcoal and chocolate) and photographing the area of "wipe-off" on the palate and teeth following tongue contact for the targeted sounds. The problem with this technique was that it recorded a single snapshot only and was therefore unsuitable for examining details of tongue dynamics, for example, the changing patterns of tongue contacts as they occurred during normal contin-uous speech. During the late 1960s and early 1970s, the first author was working on a new form of dynamic palatography in the Phonet-ics Laboratory at Edinburgh University.[1] The technique involved the subject wearing an artificial palate made of acrylic incorporat-ing an array of silver electrodes which could respond to contacts made by the tongue. The changing patterns of contacts were dis-played on a panel of light-emitting diodes and a permanent record of the patterns was obtained by a high speed cine-camera (Hardcastle, 1972).

This early EPG system was used to record the details of tongue contact under controlled conditions of altered auditory and tactile feedback (Hardcastle, 1975). With the development of the PC, the technique evolved into a convenient laboratory tool for phonetic research and has been used in a wide range of studies since (see online EPG bibliography at http://sls.qmuc.ac.uk). The technique has also now found an important place in the speech therapy clinic where the provision of a visual display of tongue-palate contacts on the computer screen makes the technique very useful as an aid in the diagnosis, assessment, and treatment of a wide range of speech dis-orders manifesting problems with lingual articulation (see review in Hardcastle & Gibbon, 1997). In this chapter, we illustrate the appli-cation of the technique in phonetic and clinical research with the results of some recent studies. As these results illustrate, the tech-nique continues to reveal details of lingual dynamics undetected by other more conventional methods and, in many cases, is encourag-ing us to reconsider some of our preconceived notions about how speech works.

THE EPG TECHNIQUE

As mentioned earlier, EPG involves the subject wearing an acrylic palate incorporating miniature silver electrodes arranged on the surface. In the EPG system in widespread use, the Reading EPG3 system, 62 elec-trodes are arranged according to anatomical landmarks (Hardcastle, Gibbon, & Jones, 1991, and Fig. 3.1) and characteristic contact patterns can be registered for all English lingual obstruents /t, d, k, g, s, z, ʃ, ʒ, ʧ, ʤ/, the palatal approximant /j/, nasals /ŋ, n/ lateral /l/, relatively close

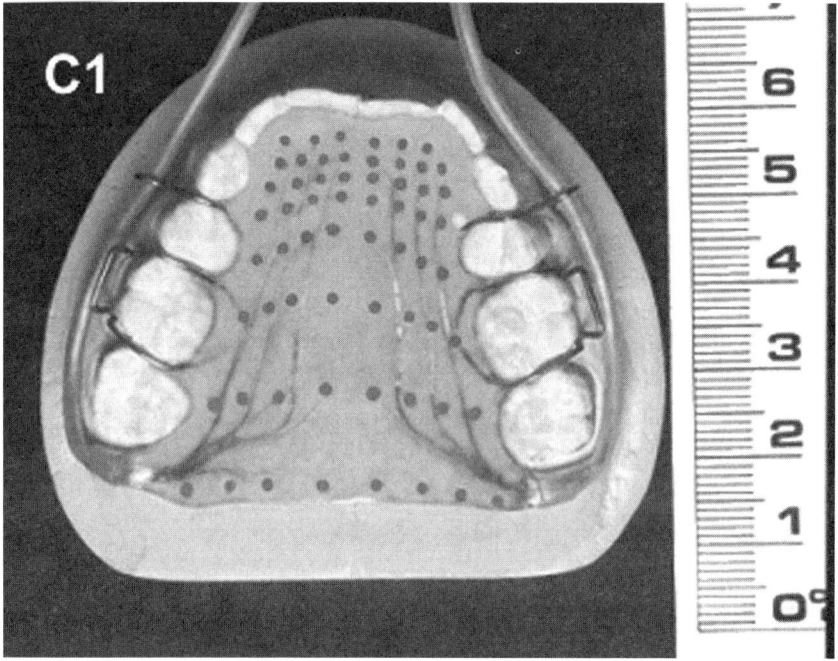

FIG. 3.1. Artificial palate for Electropalatography moulded to fit plaster cast of the subject's upper palate and teeth (from Gibbon & Crampin, 2001).

vowels such as /i, e/, and diphthongs with a close vowel component such as /ei, ai, oi/. Analysis of lingual-palatal patterns is available from computer processing and the sequence of contact patterns can be displayed in terms of a printout such as that in Fig. 3.2.

The range of spatial and temporal detail can be readily seen in such a printout. Major articulatory landmarks and their spatial-temporal patterns identifiable from the printout include alveolar closure for /t/ (released at frame 60), approach and closure for the first /k/ (79–96 with a period of simultaneous velar–alveolar closure due to the influence of the upcoming /t/ 94–96), followed by release of the /t/ (frame 109), closure for the second /k/ (132–143), and alveolar grooved constriction for the /s/ (145–167). Simultaneous recording of the acoustic signal allows the EPG patterns to be displayed on the computer screen along with either the wave-form or a spectrogram (Fig. 3.3 shows a computer display from a new Microsoft Windows version of EPG developed at Queen Margaret University College, Edinburgh, Scotland).

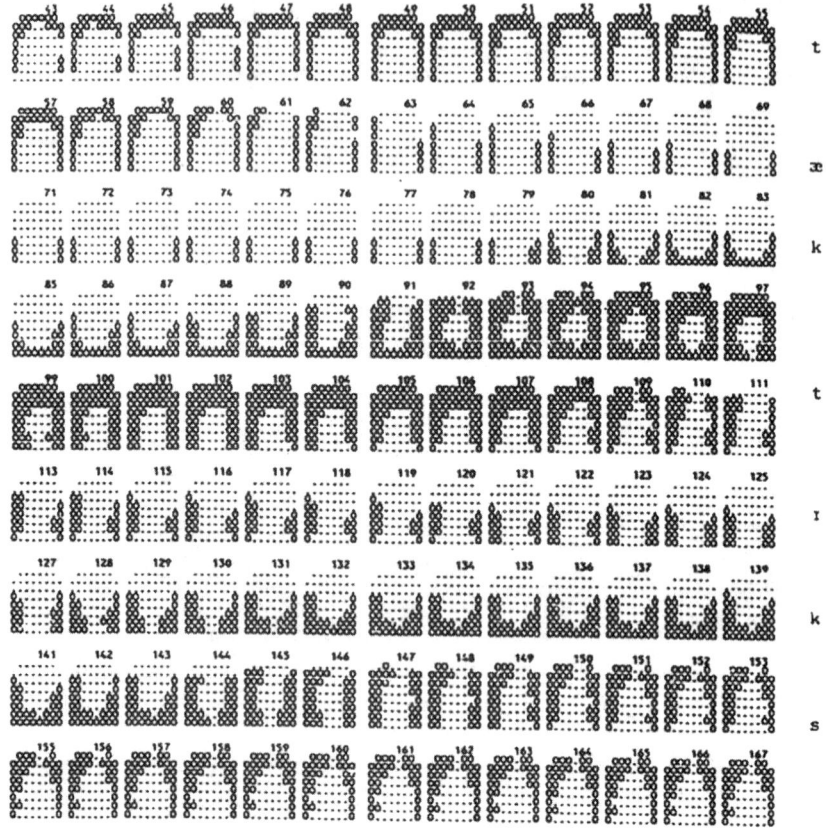

FIG. 3.2. Computer printout of the word 'tactics.' Individual palate displays are at 10-msec intervals and are read from left to right with the alveolar region at the top of each diagram and the velar at the bottom.

EPG IN PHONETIC RESEARCH

A wide range of different data reduction procedures have been developed for analysing EPG patterns. These have been described at length elsewhere (e.g., Byrd, Fleming, Mueller, & Tan, 1995; Hardcastle, Gibbon & Nicolaidis, 1991) and include such indexes as the centre of gravity, asymmetry, coarticulation, and variability indexes. These and other analytical procedures have made EPG extremely useful for investigating many different phenomena in phonetic research such as coarticulation (see, e.g., the surveys in

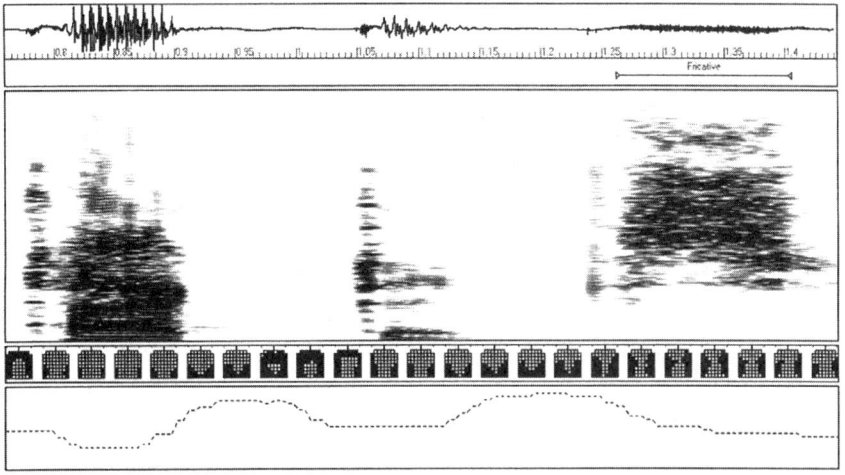

FIG. 3.3. Computer display from the new Microsoft Windows EPG showing waveform, spectrogram, and Electropalatography (EPG) patterns for the word 'tactics.' The EPG display is synchronised to the acoustic pattern and one in every three palate displays are shown here. The bottom trace represents total number of EPG contacts in the velar region (bottom three rows of the palate). Annotation marks can be inserted such as, for example, the period of friction for the /s/.

Hardcastle & Hewlett, 1999), fricative production (e.g., Hoole, Nguyen–Trong, & Hardcastle, 1993), palatalization (e.g., Recasens, 1984), 'vocalised' /l/ (e.g., Hardcastle & Barry, 1989), lingual dynamics (e.g., Recasens, 1989), timing of /kl/ gestures (e.g., Hardcastle, 1985), and rate variation (e.g., Byrd & Tan, 1996).

An illustration of the insights EPG analysis can provide into the dynamics of tongue articulation is a recent study carried out by Lucy Ellis (Ellis & Hardcastle, 2002). The phenomenon under investigation in this study is the so-called "instability of alveolars," the tendency for alveolar stops to be assimilated into the following bilabials or velars (see, e.g., Gimson, 1989). Thus, in a sequence such as "red banner," the final /d/ of "red" often assimilates into the initial /b/ of "banner" and so, according to some analyses, "disappears." This is a common phenomenon in most varieties of English but does occur in other languages as well, such as German (Kohler, 1976). It is common in fast colloquial rates of speech. According to the Articulatory Phonology Framework (Browman & Goldstein, 1992), this type of phenomenon is accounted for by postulating a coalescence of gestures for the alveolar and bilabial stops. The theory is that the separate gestures associated with the alveolar and bilabial stops get closer and closer together in fast rates until they are superimposed, and this results perceptually in a /b/. The phenomena has been observed with nasals in a sequence such as /n # g/ manifested either as [ŋg] or as [ng]. Previous EPG studies had suggested that these alveolar place assimilations are the result of a gradual process rather than a categorical process with evidence of "residual" or "partial" alveolar gestures present in the assimilated forms (Hardcastle, 1995; Wright and Kerswill, 1989). Investigators such as Barbara Kühnert (1993) saw the prevalence of partial assimilations as evidence that higher-order phoneme substitution rules have no part to play in assimilation. Instead they argue that the mechanism is likely to be located at a speaker's phonetic representation, a level which permits noncategorical variation such as stop-closure weakening. This process, it is argued, would presumably be constrained by the inherent biomechanical properties of the articulatory organs themselves.

In the Ellis and Hardcastle (2002) study, EPG was combined with the technique of Electromagnetic Articulography (EMA) to investigate assimilatory patterns in nasal alveolar and velar stop sequences with a view to testing whether the assimilations were gradual or categorical. EMA tracks the movement in two dimensions of miniature coils attached to the surface of the tongue (Hoole & Nguyen, 1999) and so provides information on tongue proximity to the palate which complements the EPG contact data.

Ten speakers produced, at two different rates of speech, 10 repetitions of sentences containing the experimental sequences /n # k/ and /ŋ # k/ (the latter a lexical velar–velar sequence with which apparent cases of complete assimilation could be compared). Fig. 3.4 shows an EPG and EMA printout of the sequence "ban cuts" spoken at fast speed. The EMA traces show vertical displacement of the tongue tip and tongue dorsum as well as velocity of tip and dorsum, together with EPG contact patterns for the sequence. The cursor marks the position of minimum velocity of the tongue tip gesture coinciding with the EPG closure and maximum vertical displacement of the tip. Analysis of the results showed that for fast speech, four distinct assimilatory strategies were employed by the subjects. Two subjects never assimilated, four always assimilated

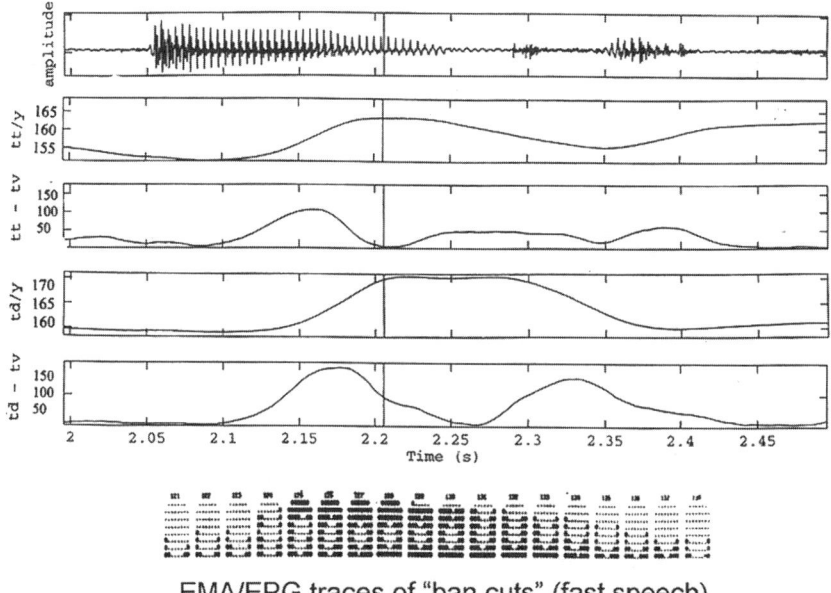

EMA/EPG traces of "ban cuts" (fast speech)

FIG. 3.4. Electropalatography (EPG) and Electromagnetic Articulography (EMA) traces for the sequence "ban cuts" (fast speech). The traces show (from the top) waveform, vertical tongue tip displacement, tongue tip velocity, vertical displacement of the tongue dorsum, tongue dorsum velocity, and EPG printout.

in what appeared to be a complete fashion (i.e., without any evidence of "residual" alveolar contact), and the remaining four showed considerable intraspeaker variability. Two of these latter four produced the expected continuum of assimilatory forms including partials (see, e.g., repetitions 4 and 5 in Fig. 3.5). Unexpectedly, the other two produced either full alveolars or complete assimilations in the manner of a binary opposition. This did not appear to be related to timing so a biomechanical explanation would probably be inappropriate.

One obvious question is whether there was some residual alveolar gesture present in the assimilated forms that was not evident in EPG records (which show contact only, not proximity of the tongue to the palate). The question was resolved by a simultaneous EMA recording of two of the speakers showing that when they assimilated, they did

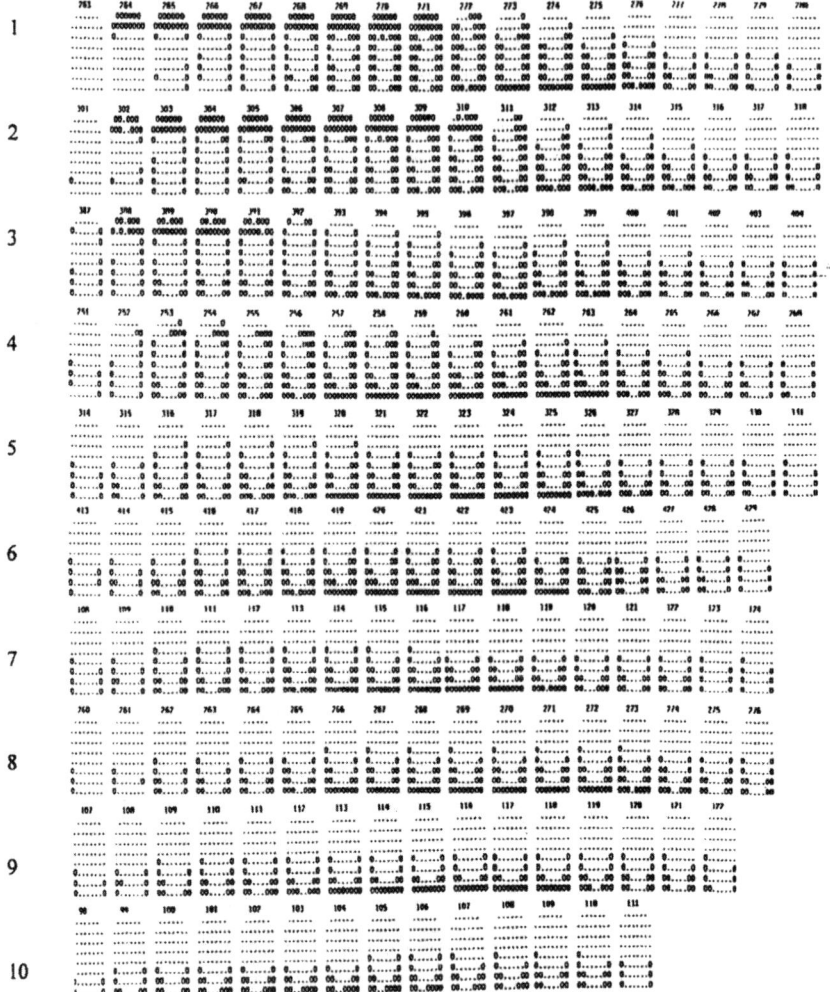

FIG. 3.5. Electropalatography (EPG) traces of the alveolar-velar sequence in one subject's 10 repetitions of "ban cuts" (fast speech; from Ellis & Hardcastle, 2002).

so in a complete fashion. The experiment seemed to suggest that some speakers do make a binary choice at a cognitive level, that is, whether or not to assimilate, and that the assimilatory process for these speakers at least is not an automatic consequence of lower-level biomechanical constraints.

EPG AS A CLINICAL ASSESSMENT AND DIAGNOSTIC TOOL

The value of EPG as a diagnostic and assessment tool in speech therapy lies in the fact that it reveals atypical lingual patterns that are not detected by an auditory-based analysis. Experiments have shown that assessments of speech disorders based solely on auditory-based analysis are often unreliable and miss potentially valuable clinical data (see, e.g., Gibbon & Crampin, 2001). The limitations of auditory-based analysis are well known (see Hardcastle, Morgan Barry, & Nunn, 1989; Kent, 1996; Santelmann, Sussman, & Chapman, 1999) and EPG in many cases has provided an additional objective insight into speech articulatory patterns that have prompted us to reexamine traditional notions about the nature of some disorders. These insights have come from the analysis of a number of atypical patterns which we have grouped under two main headings: (a) distorted spatial patterns, and (b) temporal and serial ordering abnormalities.

Distorted Spatial Patterns

The following types of distorted spatial patterns have been identified by EPG analysis and their presence has been found to have important clinical implications:

- Middorsum palatal stop patterns in cleft palate speech.
- "Undifferentiated lingual gestures" in children with functional/ phonological speech problems.
- Double labial-lingual articulatory patterns in cleft palate speakers.

Middorsum Palatal Stops

Trost (1981) describes the middorsum palatal stop as a particular type of abnormal articulation in cleft palate speakers frequently used as a substitution for both target alveolar and velar stops. The articulation is said to involve raising of the tongue dorsum with accompanying lowering of the tongue tip and often the perceptual boundary between /t/ and /k/, and /d/ and /g/, is lost (Trost, 1981, p. 196). An EPG investigation of a cleft palate speaker is reported in Gibbon and Crampin (2001), where a middorsum articulatory pattern was produced for both target /t/ and /k/. Perceptually-based analysis showed that /t/, /d/, /k/, and /g/ targets were all produced as palatal plosives [c, ɟ]. However, a detailed study of the EPG patterns produced for target /t/ and /k/ showed subtle differences undetected by the perceptual analysis.

Fig. 3.6 shows the cleft palate speaker's composite EPG patterns for target /t/ and /k/ compared to the control subjects' productions. Analysis using the centre of gravity index during the maximum constriction phase revealed that D had a significantly more anterior place of articulation for /t/ targets than for /k/ targets, although both targets were heard by listeners as identical palatal stops. This instrumentally measurable difference between target phonemes that is neutralised in listeners' perceptions has been called covert contrast by Hewlett (1988) and has been investigated further in children with functional phonological disorders by a number of researchers (e.g., Edwards, Gibbon, & Fourakis, 1997; Gibbon & Scobbie, 1997, and, see, Gibbon, 2002, for a recent review). There are important implications of such contrasts for speech therapy in that they reveal a pho-

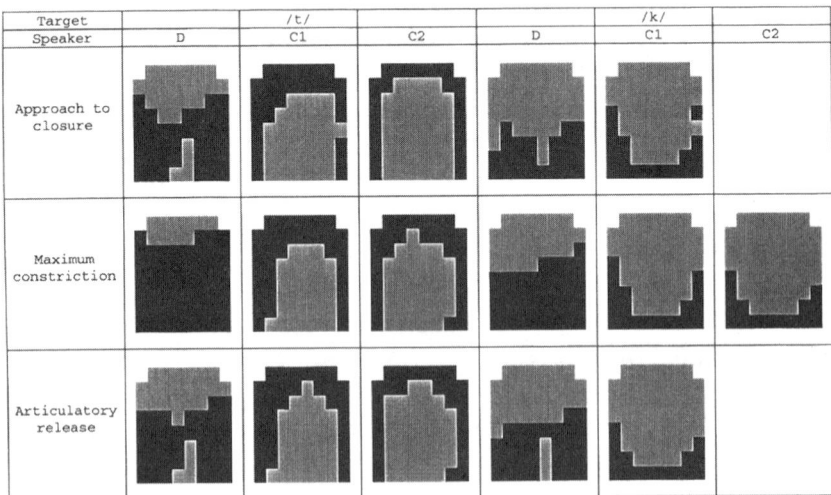

FIG. 3.6. Electropalatography (EPG) patterns of the production of /t/ and /k/ target phonemes at the point of approach to closure, maximum constriction, and just before articulatory release for an adult cleft palate speaker, D, and two control subjects, C1 and C2. Patterns are averaged over a total of 12 productions of the targets (from Gibbon & Crampin, 2001, p. 101).

netic problem rather than a phonological one, thus warranting a motor-orientated approach to treatment (Sell, Harding, & Grunwell, 1994).

Undifferentiated Lingual Gestures

Gibbon (1999) has identified a particular error pattern in the speech of school-age children with articulation and phonological disorders. These patterns are characterised by a relatively higher amount of lingual-palatal contact than "normal-speaking" children. She refers to the underlying articulation in these patterns as involving "undifferentiated lingual gestures" (see, e.g., Fig. 3.7). The inference is that these gestures are symptomatic of a lack of coordinated control between the tip and blade system of the tongue, the tongue body, and the lateral margins of the tongue (see Hardcastle, 1976, for a description of these separately controllable functional parts of the tongue). Standard, perceptually-based, analysis does not typically identify such abnormal gestures which may be transcribed variably as distortions, substitutions, or even as correct targets (such as in Fig. 3.7). In an analysis of EPG literature from 17 children, 12 showed evidence of producing undifferentiated gestures (Gibbon, 1999). Gibbon (1999) interprets the undifferentiated gestures as reflecting a speech motor constraint involving either delayed or deviant control of functionally independent regions of the tongue. The undifferentiated pattern may be more widespread than was previously thought and may explain much of the variability noted by previous investigators whose observations were based on perceptually-based judgments. For example, a recent study by Gibbon and Wood (2002) measured the change in place of articulation during stop closures that can occur during undifferentiated gestures. Their results showed that changes in placement were greater during undifferentiated gestures than for normal articulations. It was hypothesised by Gibbon and Wood that abnormal placement change during stop closure generates conflicting acoustic cues for place that listeners find difficult to interpret.

Double Labial-Lingual Articulatory Patterns

Double articulations have frequently been noted in the speech of children with cleft palate. However, this phenomenon was thought to be most commonly confined to simultaneous glottal and pharyn-

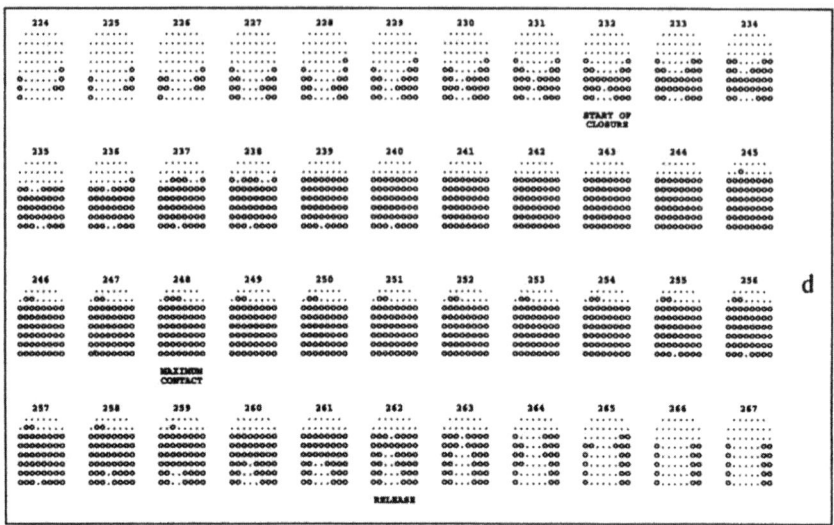

FIG. 3.7. Undifferentiated gesture for word-final /d/ in 'shed' produced by a child with articulatory/phonological disorder, judged by listeners as a correct /d/ (from Gibbon, 1999).

geal articulations (e.g., Trost–Cardamone, 1990). EPG studies have revealed another type of double articulation involving simultaneous bilabial and lingual gestures (Dent, Gibbon, & Hardcastle, 1992; Gibbon & Crampin, 2002; Gibbon & Hardcastle, 1989). Fig. 3.8 shows an EPG printout of a child with cleft palate producing the /p/ target in the phrase "a pig." The EPG printout clearly indicates an abnormal velar closure simultaneous with the bilabial stop. This velar closure was not detected by the listener.

Gibbon and Crampin (2002) speculated on how labial-velar double articulations might become established in children's speech. They noted that a strong backing pattern involving velar substitutions for bilabial targets occurred at an early age in many of the children who were found at a later age to produce these double articulations (Gibbon & Hardcastle, 1989). The velar substitution stage was followed by a period of perceptually variable productions where bilabials were heard by listeners as correct some of the time, but as incorrect velar substitutions at other times. It is possible that following a period of substituting velars for bilabials, some children "superimpose" labial closures onto existing lingual closures for

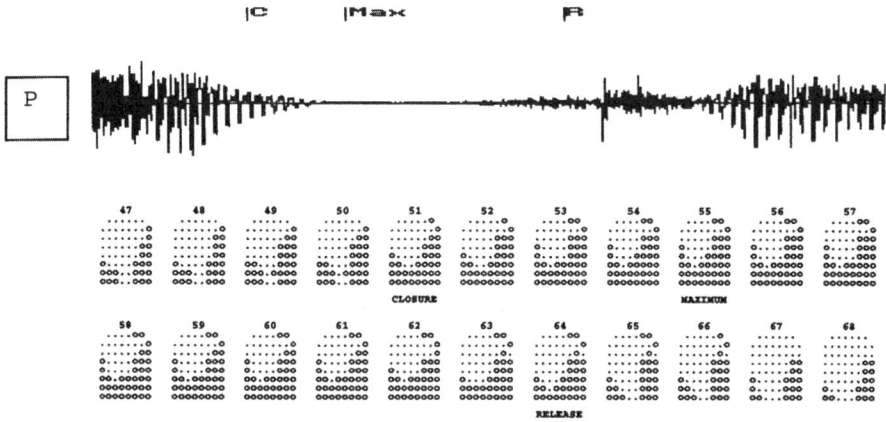

FIG. 3.8. Electropalatography (EPG) printout and waveform for the phrase "a pig" as spoken by a child age 9.07 years with a unilateral cleft lip and palate (from Gibbon & Crampin, 2002).

bilabial targets, thus creating simultaneous labial and lingual closures. The addition of bilabial closure onto an existing closure could occur spontaneously, or following a period of speech therapy. Golding–Kushner (1995) noted that double articulations, such as [p͡ʔ], can develop in the speech of individuals who originally had glottal replacement (e.g., /p/ targets produced as a substituted glottal stop [ʔ]), and were instructed in speech therapy to produce lip closure but were inadvertently not given sufficient guidance about correct airstream management.

Labial-velar double articulations are relatively minor speech errors in the sense that they tend to be judged by listeners as correct bilabial realizations and so do not have an obvious detrimental impact on intelligibility. Nevertheless, previous studies (e.g., Gibbon & Hardcastle, 1989) highlighted the importance of eliminating them as part of a therapy programme. These double articulations do not occur as isolated errors, but observation of the EPG data shows that other high-pressure consonants, such as lingual obstruents /s/, /z/, /t/, /d/, are similarly affected by this strong backing pattern. The perceptual consequences of the backing pattern is often readily identifiable for other targets such as lingual consonants. Therapy goals for these children are to eliminate the underlying articulatory abnormality in all affected consonant targets. A few studies report therapy to eliminate abnormal tongue involvement in these double articulations, and the evidence suggests that these abnormal articulations may respond positively to therapeutic intervention. In particular, the visual feedback facility available with EPG has been used successfully in therapy (Gibbon & Hardcastle, 1989). The real-time visual feedback provided by EPG reduced abnormal posterior tongue movement for a range of targets in this case.

Temporal and Serial Ordering Abnormalities

Many disorders such as neurogenic disorders in adults manifest temporal and serial ordering abnormalities affecting speech production. A number of EPG studies (e.g., Hardcastle & Edwards, 1992; Hardcastle, Morgan Barry, & Clark, 1985; Howard & Varley, 1995; Wood & Hardcastle, 1999) have identified temporal and serial ordering problems, which were undetected in an auditory-based analysis, such as the following: increased duration of lingual-palatal contact, increased variability of target gestures, distortions in target configurations, increase in area of lingual-palatal contact, and misdirected articulatory gestures. Misdirected articulatory gestures occurring in the speech of adult apraxic speakers as identified in such studies as Wood (1997) and Wood and Hardcastle (1999) are particularly interesting as they provide possible insights into the nature of the errors themselves and have potential implications for models of speech production. Previous work (e.g., Hardcastle & Edwards, 1992) identified a velar misdirected gesture in an apraxic speaker during production of the word "deer" (transcribed as a correct [d]). Fig. 3.9 shows the EPG printouts of a normal speaker's production of the word and the apraxic speaker's production. In the apraxic speaker's production the clearly defined velar gesture at the onset of the word is followed by a normal [d] pattern. The listener does not hear the "intrusive" velar gesture because the velar closure is "masked" by the alveolar and it is the alveolar release that provides the perceptual cues to its identity.

In Wood's study (Wood & Hardcastle, 1999), which examined errors in aphasic speakers following stroke, alveolar as well as velar misdirected gestures were observed in the EPG records (e.g., Fig.

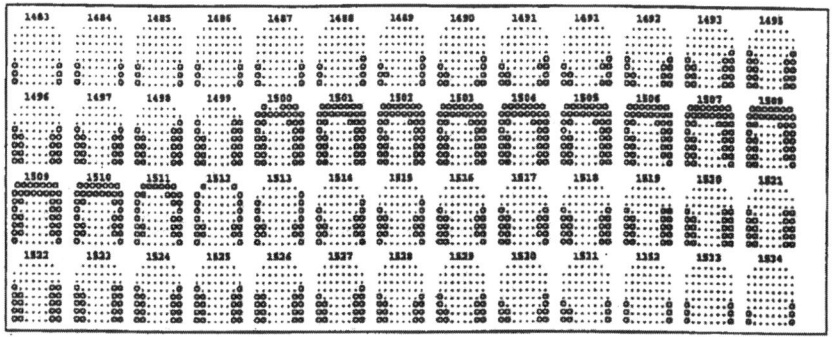

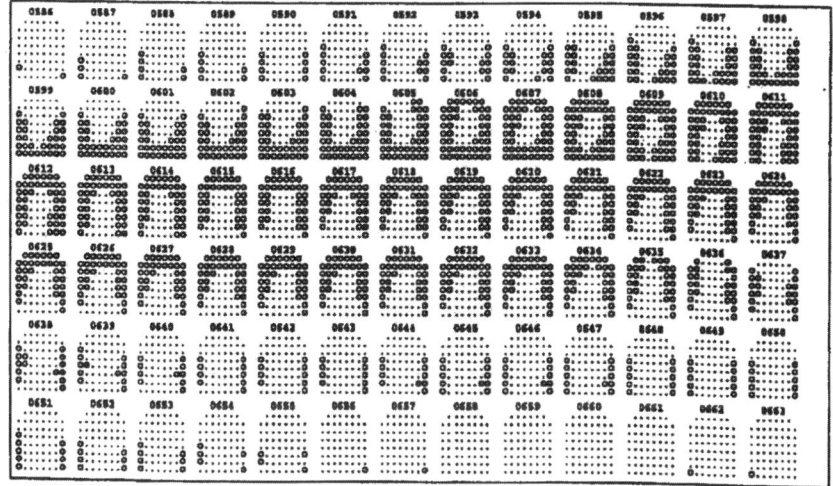

FIG. 3.9. Electropalatography (EPG) printouts of the word "deer" spoken by a normal speaker (above) and a speaker with apraxia of speech (below). Note the velar gesture at the onset of the apraxic speaker's production which is followed by a (correct) alveolar gesture (from Hardcastle et al, 1985).

3.10 which shows the EPG record of a speaker with conduction aphasia producing the word "key" heard as "tea"). In this case (illustrated in Fig. 3.10), the speaker begins with a clearly defined velar stop pattern (at frame 51) which continues until frame 56. During the latter part of the closure phase of the velar stop, an intrusive alveolar stop pattern occurs, which results in a brief period of simultaneous velar-alveolar closure from frames 53 to 56. The alveolar stop is finally released at frame 67. These alveolar and velar misdirected

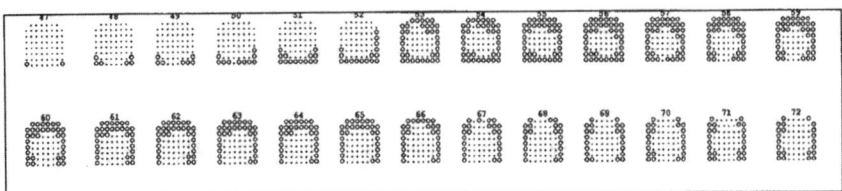

FIG. 3.10. Electropalatography (EPG) printout for the word "key" heard as "tea" spoken by an adult with conduction aphasia.

gestures illustrated in Figures 3.9 and 3.10 were spatially normal in their EPG configurations and were typical of target alveolar and velar stops for the speaker (that is, they occurred elsewhere in other words spoken by this speaker) but here they occurred in the wrong place, that is, they were "misdirected."

It is clear that in an example as in Fig. 3.10, where the word "key" is heard as "tea," there is more happening than a straightforward substitution of one target phoneme for another, that is, the /t/ for the /k/. This may have been the conclusion if it were based on an auditory judgment only and in fact the results of this study call into question the theoretical basis for differential diagnosis of these disorders based on such subjective judgments alone. One of the characteristics of aphasic speech is reported to be substitutions of phonemes but, according to these EPG results, the nature of such perceptual substitutions needs to be scrutinised.

Errors such as the misdirected gestures may reveal some important aspects about the process of speech production. It seems as if competing places of articulation (alveolar and velar and probably also bilabial) interact with each other during a neurolinguistic planning stage in the generation of an utterance and the wrong choice for the target may not always be inhibited as in the case of certain types of neurogenic disorders.

EPG AS A THERAPY TOOL

The EPG system offers a direct visual display in real time of lingual contacts as they occur and so can be used as a visual biofeedback aid for correcting abnormal articulatory patterns. The technique has been particularly successful in treating the intractable problems which have resisted conventional therapy for many years (see Fig. 3.11 which shows a therapist treating a child with an articulation disorder).

Functional articulation disorders and cleft palate speech have responded particularly well to EPG therapy. Typical is a child, Robbie, described in Gibbon, Stewart, Hardcastle, and Crampin, (1999) who, prior to EPG therapy, manifested a "backing" articulatory pattern where /t/ was heard as /k/ and /d/ as /g/. Fig. 3.12 shows EPG patterns before and after therapy.

This improvement in articulatory patterns was reflected in better intelligibility and is typical of the often quite dramatic changes in abnormal motor patterns that can result from therapists using the technique as a complement to conventional procedures.

CONCLUSION

Since its early development over 30 years ago, EPG has proven to be a key technique for the investigation of lingual activity in both nor-

FIG. 3.11. Photograph of a clinician undertaking Electropalatography (EPG) therapy with a child with cleft palate.

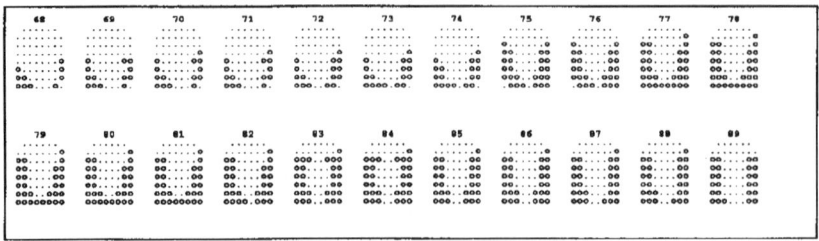

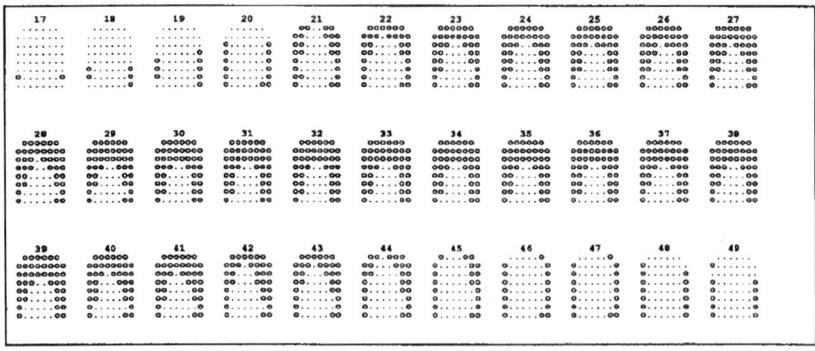

FIG. 3.12. Electropalatography (EPG) patterns for two productions of target /t/ in "a tip" spoken by an 8-year-old child with a functional speech disorder, before (above) and after (below) therapy with EPG (from Gibbon et al, 1999).

mal and atypical speakers. Its dual role in both assessment and treatment of a wide range of speech disorders has established it as a useful clinical tool for speech and language therapists and we can look forward to the day when EPG therapy will be offered routinely as part of a rehabilitation programme for children with intractable speech problems. A number of new developments currently underway, such as the design of a cheaper artificial palate, will make the technique even more attractive to the therapist and will encourage its widespread use in clinics throughout the world. By revealing details of lingual activity often undetected by an auditory-based analysis, the technique has certainly encouraged a fresh look at some of our accepted theories about the nature of speech disorders. Many of these additional insights have had implications for diagnosis and treatment. For example, for some children with speech disorders, the identification of subtle differences in lingual contact for target phonemes heard as identical demonstrates that these children are able to make some distinction between the phonemes, and this knowledge influences the approach to treatment of such children. Similarly, perceived phonemic substitutions in some adults with neurogenic disorders have been associated with undetected abnormal lingual contacts and this has had implications for differential diagnosis of disorders such as apraxia and dysarthria.

Our understanding of processes involved in normal speech production has also been enhanced by EPG research. In particular, theories of coarticulation and speech timing in many different languages have benefited from EPG studies over a period of years. Especially when combined with tracking and imaging techniques such as Electromagnetic Articulography and Ultrasound, EPG can be a very powerful tool in helping to unravel many of the remaining mysteries surrounding the control of the dynamic processes involved in producing continuous speech.

NOTE

[1] This work was part of a PhD programme supervised by John Laver. The first author remains indebted to John not only for his excellent supervision at that time in the Phonetics Laboratory at Edinburgh but for his encouragement and support of Electropalatography research ever since.

REFERENCES

Abercrombie, D. (1957b). Direct palatography. *Zeitschrift für Phonetik, 10,* 21–25.

Browman, C. P., & Goldstein, L. (1992). Articulatory phonology: An overview. *Phonetica, 49,* 155–180.

Byrd, D., Fleming, E., Mueller, C. A., & Tan, C. C. (1995). Using regions and indices in EPG data reduction. *Journal of Speech and Hearing Research, 38,* 821–827.

Byrd, D. & Tan, C. C. (1996). Saying consonant sequences quickly. *Journal of Phonetics, 24,* 263–282.

Dent, H., Gibbon, F., & Hardcastle, W. (1992). Inhibiting an abnormal lingual pattern in a cleft palate child using Electropalatography. In M. M. Leahy & J. L. Kallen (Eds.), *Interdisciplinary perspectives in speech and language pathology* (pp. 211–221). Dublin, Ireland: Trinity College School of Clinical Speech and Language Studies.

Edwards, J., Gibbon, F. E., & Fourakis, M. (1997). On discrete changes in the acquisition of the alveolar/velar stop consonant contrast. *Language and Speech, 40,* 203–210.

Ellis, L., & Hardcastle, W. J. (2002). Categorical and gradient properties of assimilation in alveolar to velar sequences: Evidence from EPG and EMA data. *Journal of Phonetics, 30,* 373–396.

Gibbon, F. (2002). Features of impaired motor control in children with articulation/phonological disorders. In F. Windsor, L. Kelly, and N. Hewlett (Eds.), *Investigations in clinical linguistics and phonetics* (pp. 299–309). London: Lawrence Erlbaum Associates, Inc.

Gibbon, F., & Hardcastle, W. (1989). Deviant articulation in a cleft palate child following late repair of the hard palate: A description and remediation procedure using electropalatography. *Clinical Linguistics and Phonetics, 3,* 93–110.

Gibbon, F. E. (1999). Undifferentiated lingual gestures in children with articulation/phonological disorders. *Journal of Speech, Language, and Hearing Research, 42,* 382–397.

Gibbon, F. E., & Crampin, L. (2001). An electropalatographic investigation of middorsum palatal stops in an adult with repaired cleft palate. *Cleft Palate Craniofacial Journal, 38,* 96–105.

Gibbon, F. E., & Crampin, L. (2002). Labial-lingual double articulation in speakers with cleft palate. *Cleft Palate Craniofacial Journal, 39,* 40–49.

Gibbon, F. E., & Scobbie, J. M. (1997, Autumn). Covert contrasts in children with phonological disorder. *Australian Communication Quarterly,* 13–16.

Gibbon, F. E., Stewart, F., Hardcastle, W. J., & Crampin, L. (1999). Widening access to electropalatography for children with persistent sound system disorders. *American Journal of Speech-Language Pathology, 42,* 382–397.

Gibbon, F. E., & Wood, S. E. (2002). Articulatory drift in the speech of children with articulation/phonological disorders. *Perceptual and Motor Skills, 95,* 295–307.

Gimson, A. C. (1989). An introduction to the pronunciation of english (4th ed.). London: Edward Arnold.

Golding–Kushner, K. J. (1995). Treatment of articulation and resonance disorder associated with cleft palate and VPI. In R. J. Shprintzen & J. Bardach (Eds.), *Cleft palate speech management: A multidisciplinary approach* (pp. 327–351). St Louis, MO: Mosby.

Hardcastle, W. J. (1972). The use of electropalatography in phonetic research. *Phonetica, 25,* 197–215.

Hardcastle, W. J. (1975). Some aspects of speech production under controlled conditions of oral anaesthesia and auditory masking. *Journal of Phonetics, 3,* 197–214

Hardcastle, W. J. (1976). Physiology of speech production: An introduction for speech scientists. London: Academic.

Hardcastle, W. J. (1985). Some phonetic and syntactic constraints on lingual co-articulation during /kl/ sequences. *Speech Communication, 4,* 247–263.

Hardcastle, W. J. (1995). Assimilation of alveolar stops and nasals in connected speech. In J. Windsor–Lewis (Ed.), *Studies in general and english phonetics* (pp. 49–67). London: Routledge Kegan Paul.

Hardcastle, W. J. & Barry, W. (1989). Articulatory and perceptual factors in /l/ vocalisation in English. *Journal of International Phonetics Association, 15,* 3–17.

Hardcastle, W. J. & Edwards, S. (1992). EPG–based descriptions of aphasic speech errors. In R. Kent (Ed.), *Intelligibility in speech disorders: Theory measurement and management* (pp. 287–328). Philadelphia: John Benjamins.

Hardcastle, W. J., Gibbon, F. E., & Jones, W. (1991). Visual display of tongue-palate contact: Electropalatography in the assessment and remediation of speech disorders. *British Journal of Disorder of Communication, 26,* 41–74.

Hardcastle, W. J. & Gibbon, F. E. (1997). Electropalatography and its clinical applications. In M. J. Ball & C. Code (Eds.), *Instrumental clinical phonetics* (pp. 149–193). London: Whurr.

Hardcastle, W. J., Gibbon, F. E., & Nicolaidis, K. (1991). EPG data reduction methods and their implications for studies of lingual coarticulation. *Journal of Phonetics, 19,* 251–266.

Hardcastle, W. J. & Hewlett, N. (Eds.) (1999). *Coarticulation: Theory, data and techniques.* Cambridge, UK: Cambridge University Press.

Hardcastle, W. J., Morgan Barry, R. A., & Clark, C. (1985). Articulatory and voicing characteristics of adult dysarthric and verbal dyspraxic speakers: An instrumental study. *British Journal of Disorders of Communication, 20,* 249–270.

Hardcastle, W. J., Morgan Barry, R. A., & Nunn, M. (1989). Instrumental articulatory phonetics in assessment and remediation: Case studies with the electropalatograph. In J. Stengelhofen (Ed.), *Cleft palate: The nature and remediation of communicative problems* (pp. 136–164). Edinburgh, Scotland: Churchill Livingstone.

Hewlett, N. (1988). Acoustic properties of /k/ and /t/ in normal and phonologically disordered speech. *Clinical Linguistics and Phonetics, 2,* 29–45.

Hoole, P., & Nguyen, N. (1999). Electromagnetic articulography. In W. Hardcastle & N. Hewlett (Eds.), *Coarticulation: Theory, data and techniques* (pp. 260–269). Cambridge, UK: Cambridge University Process.

Hoole, P., Nguyen–Trong, N., & Hardcastle, W. J. (1993). A comparative investigation of coarticulation in fricatives: Electropalatographic, electromagnetic and acoustic data. *Language and Speech, 36,* 235–260.

Howard, S., & Varley, R. (1995). Using electropalatography to treat severe acquired apraxia of speech. *European Journal of Disorders of Communication, 30,* 246–255.

Kent, R. D. (1996). Hearing and believing: Some limits to the auditory-perceptual assessment of speech and voice disorders. *American Journal of Speech-Language Pathology, 5,* 7–23.

Kohler, K. (1976). Die Instabilität wortfinaler Alveolarplosive im Deutschen-eine elektropalatographische Untersuchung. [The instability of word-final alveolar plosives in German: An electropalatographic investigation.] *Phonetica, 33,* 1–30.

Kühnert, B. (1993). Some kinematic aspects of alveolar to velar assimilations. *Forshungsberichte des Institut für Phonetik und Sprachliche Kommunikation der Universität München (FIPKM), 31,* 263–272.

Recasens, D. (1984). Timing constraints and coarticulation: Alveolar-palatals and sequences of alveolar +[j] in Catalan. *Phonetica, 41,* 125–139.

Recasens, D. (1989). Long range co-articulation effects for tongue dorsum contact in VCVCV sequences. *Speech Communication, 8,* 293–307.

Santelmann, L., Sussman, J., & Chapman, K. (1999). Perception of mid-dorsum palatal stops from the speech of three children with repaired cleft palate. *Cleft Palate Craniofacial Journal, 36,* 232–242.

Sell, D., Harding, A., & Grunwell, P. (1994). A screening assessment of cleft palate speech (Great Ormond Street Speech Assessment). *Journal of Disorders of Communication, 29,* 1–15.

Trost, J. E. (1981). Articulatory additions to the classical description of the speech of persons with cleft palate. *Cleft Palate Journal, 18,* 193–203.

Trost–Cardamone, J. E. (1990). The development of speech: Assessing cleft palate misarticulation. In D. A. Kernahan & S. W. Rosenstein (Eds.), *Cleft lip and palate: A system of management* (pp. 227–235). Baltimore: Williams & Wilkins.

Wood, S. (1997). *Electropaltographic study of speech sound errors in adults with acquired aphasia.* Unpublished doctoral dissertation, Department of Speech and Language Sciences, Queen Margaret University College, Edinburgh, Scotland.

Wood, S., & Hardcastle, W. J. (1999). Instrumentation in the assessment and therapy of motor speech disorders: A summary of techniques and case studies with EPG. In I. Papathanasiou (Ed.), *Acquired neurogenic communication disorders* (pp. 203–248). London: Whurr.

Wright, S., & Kerswill, P. (1989). Electropalatography in the study of connected speech processes. *Clinical Linguistic and Phonetics, 3,* 49–57.

PART II

Cognitive Aspects of Phonetic Processing

Chapter 4

Phonetic Precision
in Listening

Anne Cutler and Mirjam Broersma
Max Planck Institute for Psycholinguistics
Nijmegen, The Netherlands

————

Not many people know very much about ... how speech actually works
.... It is the privilege and the pleasure of phoneticians, with their colleagues from related disciplines professionally concerned with speech,
to engage themselves in the analysis of this most intricate of our communicative skills. (Laver, 1994, p.592)

————

Among the skills which great phoneticians possess is the ability to
perceive many subtle articulatory distinctions. However, it is indeed

true that not many people share this ability. How precise is the phonetic perception of the ordinary listener?

Paradoxically, listeners' phonetic processing is both precise and imprecise. It is imprecise in that what matters ultimately for the listener is not phonetic detail but categorisation. Discrimination of speech sounds is hugely better across phoneme category boundaries than within categories. Imprecision of listening effectively does not matter within categories; the ordinary listener would just be distracted by analysing precise details of each speaker's pronunciation of each speech sound. This is because, after all, the point of phonetic perception is to understand spoken messages. What matters is to make distinctions between words, and phonemic categories make (by definition) distinctions between words.

However, listeners are also capable of extremely precise distinctions in the service of interword decisions, in cases where subphonemic information is available and can be of assistance. In this sense, phonetic perception can be highly precise. The next section discusses some relevant evidence. Furthermore, listeners' phonemic category boundaries are highly sensitive and can be adjusted to deal with distributional variation in the input; section 3 discusses some relevant recent evidence on this issue. Given these listening abilities, it is all the more striking how difficult it is for most people to acquire fully the perceptual phonemic categories of a second language in adulthood; the remaining sections discuss the implications of this for the ordinary listener.

HOW WORD RECOGNITION WORKS

—◆◈▸—

> Phonological units (including, but not only, consonant and vowel phonemes) have the sole linguistic function of being combinable and permutable, within narrowly defined structural constraints of sequence, to give distinctive shape to the very large number of grammatical units (words) whose identity and sequence in their turn make up the lexical and syntactic patterns of the language. (Laver, 1989, p. 40)

—◆◈▸—

Precise phonetic category decisions are not a necessary component of word recognition—in fact, word recognition does not necessarily involve phonetic category decisions at all. The point of word recognition is to convert the incoming speech signal into known meaningful units, and phonetic units do not in themselves carry meaning; morphemes, whether stand-alone or combinable, are the smallest units that can do that. Of course, phonetic decisions are indirectly involved in word recognition in that any acceptance of a word (*phone*) involves rejection of other words differing from it by minimally one phoneme (*fine*, *shown*, *foal*). But whether spoken-word recognition involves a stage of explicit conversion of the input into a representation in terms of phonemes is one of the most disputed questions in psycholinguistics, which has received more than three decades of attention without being resolved. The discussion continues unabated (see, e.g., Pallier, Colomé, & Sebastián–Gallés, 2001; Pierrehumbert, 2002), but the present authors do not intend to contribute further to it here.

Instead, we highlight some characteristics of the word recognition process which play a significant role in the research issues involved which underlie the new findings we discuss in later sections. The most important factors are multiple activation and competition. As the first of these terms suggests, the word to be recognised may not be the only lexical form actively participating in the recognition process. The arrival of incoming speech information calls up an array of potential word candidates which form at least temporarily a partial match to the speech input. Although the temporal nature of speech processing prompted early proposals that lexical forms could be recognised in sequential order of arrival, this is in practice hardly possible for the listener given the extent to which words in any vocabulary are similar and overlapping. Vocabularies contain tens or hundreds of thousands of words, but these are constructed using only a handful of phonetic categories (on average around 30; Maddieson, 1984). Moreover, languages (and presumably language users) prefer short words to long ones. The inevitable result is large numbers of minimal pairs of shorter words, and longer words with shorter words embedded within them. In fact, only about 2% of English words do not contain some other word form (Cutler, McQueen, Jansonius, & Bayerl, 2002). And, because more of these embeddings occur at the beginning than in the middle or at the end of the matrix word, the first full word a listener hears may not be the intended word, but only a spuriously embedded form occurring within it. Thus *star* may not be *star* but may turn into *start* or *stark* or *starve* or *starling* as more speech input arrives; *start* may become *starch* or *startle; starch* may turn out to have been *star chart* after all.

Under these circumstances, efficiency appears to be served by making available all the potential options in parallel: *star* and *start* and *stark* and *starve* and *starling* and *starch* and *startle* may all be simultaneously activated given the input *star-*. There is abundant experimental evidence for this phenomenon by now (see McQueen, 2004, for a review). The superfluity of simultaneously available candidates is resolved by a process of competition between them. That is, the more one candidate is favoured, the more it can disadvantage its rivals. Thus, incoming information which matches one candidate but not others (a /k/, for instance, after *star-*) does not simply result in the preferred candidate (*stark*) accruing more points in its favour and increasing in activation, but it also leads to a decrease in activation of the alternative candidates (*starling, starve,* etc.). Again, evidence from laboratory experiments attests to this inhibitory effect. Thus, lexical decision responses to a visual presentation of TRAFICO are significantly faster after an immediately preceding spoken fragment *trafi-* than after a control prime, but after the fragment *tragi-*, (matching *tragico, tragic,* rather than *trafico, traffic*) responses are significantly slower than the responses in the control condition (Soto–Faraco, Sebastián–Gallés, & Cutler, 2001). Words embedded within other words may be similarly inhibited (such as *mess* in *domestic;* McQueen, Norris, & Cutler, 1994). Obviously, the competition process is primarily constrained by incoming information from the speech signal, but because speech is continuous, word boundaries may not be apparent to the listener, so that multiple candidates may temporarily enjoy full support. Direct competition between all words supported (fully or partially) by the input offers an efficient means of evaluating such candidates without processing delays (see McQueen, Cutler, Briscoe, & Norris, 1995, for discussion of this issue). However, the more competition arises, the slower words may be recognised (Norris, McQueen, & Cutler, 1995).

The modulation of competition by incoming speech information is rapid; here the precision of the listener's processing is remarkable. Matching or mismatching, such information is put to use immediately, and this includes early arriving coarticulatory cues which can resolve a competition process. For instance, suppose a listener hears the fragment *jo-* from the word *jog*. Velar cues in the vowel are already sufficient to boost the activation of *jog* and inhibit competitor words such as *job*. This can be seen from the fact that if by cross-splicing a version of *job* is created in which the *jo-* actually comes from *jog*, positive lexical decision responses to that form are significantly slower than to a cross-spliced *job* in which the *jo-* comes from *jod*, a nonword. Further, if the nonword *smob* is presented, and its *smo-* comes from the real word *smog*, negative lexical decision responses are slower than if the *smo-* were taken from *smod*, another nonword (Dahan, Magnuson, Tanenhaus, & Hogan, 2001; Marslen–Wilson & Warren, 1994; McQueen, Norris, & Cutler, 1999). In both cases, the coarticulatory information in the vowel about the place of articulation of the upcoming consonant was passed on to influence lexical activation, favouring *jog* and *smog*, respectively.

These data, and many further demonstrations of effects of subphonemic mismatch on lexical activation (e.g., Streeter & Nigro, 1979; Utman, Blumstein, & Burton, 2000; Van Alphen & McQueen, 2003; Whalen, 1984) and of listeners' efficient use of coarticulatory information in distinguishing both vowels and consonants (e.g., Martin & Bunnell, 1981, 1982; Strange, 1989), clearly show that spoken-word recognition involves precise processing of contextually induced phonetic variability. Note that although attempts have been made to argue, on the basis of such findings, that a phonemic level of representation has no place in models of speech understanding, the data are actually neutral with respect to this issue. In activation/competition models, information may be probabilistically weighted to reflect degree of match or mismatch to more than one alternative during prelexical processing, just as more than one candidate may be simultaneously active at the lexical level. The data could certainly be held to rule out discontinuous models in which correct phonemic category decisions would form a prerequisite for lexical access, but in fact no such models enjoy current support in the psycholinguistic literature.

WORD RECOGNITION AND ADJUSTMENT
OF PHONETIC PRECISION

Two speakers may share the same vowel and consonant systems, have the same structural possibilities, choose the same lexical selection of phonemes, and yet have slightly different accents. The fine detail of how a given speaker pronounces his sounds can act as a marker of group membership, but it can also function as an individuating marker. (Laver & Trudgill, 1979, p. 19).

Precision would be served by constancy in the definition of phoneme categories; the more exact the better, if the decision about a particular category of the native language were subject to the same constraints in each and every instance. But this is not the case. There is considerable variation in the realisation of tokens of any other phonemic category, and the amount of variation changes as a function of context, of rate of speech, and across speakers and dialects. That in itself is not problematic; the category definitions can be loosely set. But categories are also not constant across speakers of a given language or dialect, and they are not immutable across time. The realisation of categories, and by extension the range of the associated variation, changes over time for the language community as a whole (Labov, 1994) and for individual speakers (Bauer, 1985; Harrington, Palethorpe, & Watson, 2000; Yaeger–Dror, 1994).

How can listeners adapt the definitions of phoneme categories? The only reasonable assumption is that such adaptation occurs as a by-product of word recognition. Even if an individual token is somewhat different from other tokens of the same phoneme that we have previously heard, the word best matched by the input as a whole will still win the competition process, and the ensuing lexical recognition will motivate a record of the altered input for future use. Of course, in practice, a shift within a language community will occur gradually, as a shift of the clustering within an existing range of variation. But the adaptation needed to shift is arguably the same adjustment that occurs when we accommodate to a new, unfamiliar speaker with a variant pronunciation (foreign accent, speech impediment, etc.). It is a familiar experience that such adjustment can occur quite rapidly; a new speaker can sound quite strange and hard to understand at the beginning of a lecture, but within quite a short space of time the strangeness has disappeared and the accent is no longer hard to process.

If these processes are the same, then it should not be necessary for native categories to undergo a gradual process of shift of centre of gravity in a variation space; it should be possible to induce adjustment of phonemic categories in the laboratory very quickly by supplying lexical support for the adjustment. We tested this hypothesis in our laboratory in a series of experiments involving the fricative sounds [s] and [f] in Dutch (Norris, McQueen, & Cutler, 2003). The lexical support was provided by placing the sounds in question at the end of real words which would normally end in [s] or [f]. Some examples are the Dutch words for *carcase* (*karkas,* with final stress) and *carafe* (*karaf*). These words have no minimally paired companions ending with the other fricative, just as English *carcafe* and *carase* are not words.

The series of experiments began with a standard phonetic categorisation study. Dutch listeners made forced-choice [s]-[f] decisions about stimuli along a continuum from a good [s] to a good [f] through 12 intermediate tokens created by sampling the two natural endpoints in different proportions. The results of this study produced a maximally ambiguous token between [s] and [f]. This token was then grafted onto the end of spoken tokens of Dutch words of the *carcase-carafe* type, in place of the originally produced fricative.

New groups of Dutch listeners then took part in the crucial experiment. They carried out a lexical decision task: they heard spoken items and had to decide for each one whether it was a real Dutch word. There were 200 items in the experiment, and nothing in the instructions called attention to phonetic processing; only the lexical decision was emphasised. Nearly all the items contained no occurrences of [s] or [f] at all; the exceptions were 20 real words of the *carcase* type and 20 of the *carafe* type.

There were two experimental groups of listeners, and they differed in how they heard these words. One group heard the 20 [s] words in natural form, and the 20 [f] words with the final [f] replaced by the selected ambiguous fricative. The other group heard the 20 [s] words with the final [s] replaced by the ambiguous sound, and the 20 [f] words in natural form. The objective was to shift the boundary of the [s]-[f] distinction for these two groups, but to shift it in opposite directions. Would exposure to only 20 words be enough to bring this about?

In the lexical decision task, the listeners certainly treated the items ending with the ambiguous sounds as words, that is, they signalled a YES decision (although their response times to do so were slower than responses to unmanipulated word tokens). But the real test came afterward. Once the lexical decision task had been completed, the listeners were given a phonetic categorisation task, using a subset of the same continuum used in the pretest study. And, indeed, their decisions had been affected by the experience in the lexical decision experiment, as Fig. 4.1 shows. The listeners who had heard the *carcase*-type words with the ambiguous sound made more [s] decisions in the categorisation task, and the listeners who had heard the *carafe*-type words with the ambiguous sound made more [f] decisions. The responses of control groups of listeners fell in between.

The control groups were crucial to the demonstration that the adaptation depended on lexical information. There were control lis-

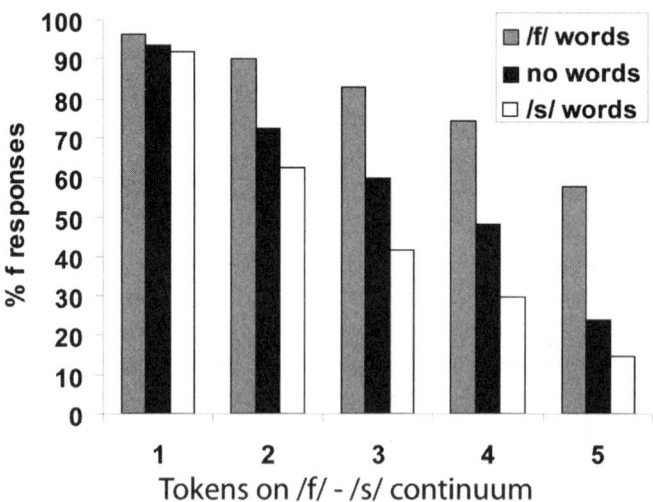

FIG. 4.1. Mean percentage of /f/ responses to ambiguous tokens lying on a continuum from Dutch /f/ to /s/, by listeners who had heard words containing token 3 in place of /f/ (mean of two groups), listeners who had heard no words containing the ambiguous tokens (mean of five different control groups), and listeners who had heard words containing token 3 in place of /s/ (mean of two groups; averaged data from Norris, McQueen, & Cutler, 2003).

teners who heard the ambiguous sound at the end of nonwords, but heard no words ending in [s] or [f]; or who heard the ambiguous sound at the end of nonwords and heard words ending with one or the other of the natural fricatives; or who heard words ending with one or other of the natural fricatives but no ambiguous sound at all. None of these groups showed the significant response shift that was observed with the experimental groups. Only the experimental groups had heard the ambiguous sound with lexical support signalling its interpretation, and only those groups showed an effect of this experience in their subsequent categorisation responses. The listeners who had received lexical support for interpreting the ambiguous sound as [s] shifted their category decisions toward [s], those who had received support for interpreting it as [f] shifted toward [f]. Moreover, this shift was not specific to the actual ambiguous sound that they had been exposed to, but embraced the other intermediate sounds which they received in the categorisation test. The whole continuum shifted for these listeners; just a short exposure, involving only 20 words, had been sufficient to adapt their phonemic category decisions. Thus, the precision of ordinary listeners' phonetic processing is sufficient to support considerable flexibility in phonetic category assignment.

WHEN PRECISION IS UNATTAINABLE

Learning a language other than one's own native language is always a process in which the patterns of the first language interfere with the learning of the foreign language (Laver, 1994, pp. 78–79).

Given that the native phonetic processing is so precise when needed, imprecise when sufficient, and even flexible when appropriate, it is disturbing that mastering the categories of a second language acquired after childhood can be so extraordinarily difficult. Foreign accent is the most conspicuous symptom, and far more research attention has been given to phonetic imprecision in second-language production than perception. But of perception it is nevertheless well attested that responding to non-native category distinctions is already hard by the end of the first year of life (Werker & Lalonde, 1988; Werker & Tees, 1983), and adult listeners find it very difficult indeed to improve their performance (see Strange, 1995, for a review), although huge amounts of training can bring about some improvement (Lively, Pisoni, Yamada, Tohkura, & Yamada, 1994; Logan, Lively, & Pisoni, 1991). Perception of native contrasts remains more categorical than perception of non-native contrasts (Burnham, Earnshaw, & Clark, 1991).

Adult listeners appear to be imprisoned within the categories of the native language. It is not the case that they cannot perceive non-native contrasts for some auditory reason (e.g., a loss of sensitivity due to lack of exposure). Rather, native phonology captures speech input and categorises it although this may mean forgoing much of the precision which the listener's auditory system could have delivered. Only when experimenters can contrive somehow to switch off phonological processing does the sensitivity of auditory processing have a chance of being revealed. Werker and Tees (1984) found that adult English speakers were able to perceive non-English phonemic distinctions (between Hindi retroflex versus dental alveolar voiceless stops, and Thompson—an Amerindian language— ejective uvular versus velar stops) if the distinctions were apparently nonlinguistic; that is, they could successfully discriminate vowel-less stops (which don't sound very much like speech), but failed to discriminate the same stops in syllable-initial position. Similarly, Japanese-speaking adults who cannot discriminate between [r] and [l] can make the (very similar) distinction between [r] and [w], sounds which are not contrasted in Japanese but are also not conflated (Best, MacKain, & Strange, 1982).

When non-native contrasts are similar to native contrasts it can be argued that auditory experience with the non-native sounds does occur in the native language—for instance, the sounds may occur as allophonic variations (e.g., unaspirated voiceless stops occur in English in postfricative position). Thus, the listener in effect has experience with assigning the sounds to native categories rather than to the categories which may be required for precise perception of a newly encountered language. Best, McRoberts, and Sithole (1988; see also Best, 1995) distinguished four principal possibilities for the mapping of a non-native phonemic contrast to a particular listener's native system:

1. The contrasting sounds are both assimilated to the same category in the listener's native language. This is the case with [r] and [l] for Japanese speakers, for instance. Such Single-Category Assimilations constitute the most difficult non-native contrast to perceive.

2. The contrasting sounds may be assimilated to the native language, but to different categories. This is the case with French unaspirated stops for English speakers. These Two-Category Assimilations are easy to perceive, because the sounds are assimilated to categories which also contrast in the native language.

3. One of the contrasting sounds assimilates well to a native category but the other does not. This is the case with Hindi dental versus retroflex stops for English speakers. These contrasts should appear as differences in relative "goodness of fit" to the native category. Best et al. (1988) predicted that such Category Goodness differences should be difficult but perceptible, especially if the goodness difference was extensive.

4. Finally, it might be the case that neither contrasting sound can be assimilated to the native phonemic space. Then the sounds may not even be heard as speech. Because the world's languages have selected their phonetic stock from a relatively limited range, such cases are rare; however, an example is found in the click contrasts characteristic of many African languages, which for speakers of nonclick languages are unlike any of their native sounds.

Best et al. (1988) argued that only the Nonassimilable case (as in number 4) would truly show whether adult listeners retain perceptual capabilities in the absence of any relevant auditory experience. Accordingly, they presented English-speaking listeners with Zulu click contrasts. Discrimination performance was excellent—as good, in fact, as that of adult Zulu speakers. Infants, needless to say, could also perform the same discrimination. Best et al. concluded that the perceptual narrowing for phonetic contrasts which is shown by adult listeners is not simply due to lack of relevant auditory experience, leading to sensori-neural atrophy or simply to loss of phonetic capabilities. These remain intact; what happens in the transition from prelinguistic infant to fully capable language user is a phonological reorganisation of speech sound percepts. Efficient recognition of speech requires rapid identification of (native) phonetic categories; it is therefore expedient for categorisation according to the native system to override super-fluous phonetic precision.

Adult language users, therefore, have perceptual capacity which they do not always exploit. But although unused, the perceptual abilities are intact, and the discriminatory skills of highly expert phoneticians show that it is possible (at least for some speakers) to learn to ignore native phonological categorisations on occasion. Extended linguistic exposure can help even untrained speakers to improve their discrimination; Flege and Eefting (1987) found that Dutch native speakers with good English shifted the boundary of their categories [t] and [d] as a function of whether they thought they were listening to Dutch or English. However, some types of contrast are more difficult to acquire than others. Flege and Hillenbrand (1986) examined [s]-[z] discrimination in syllable-final position by speakers of English and French (in which this contrast occurs), and Swedish and Finnish (in which it does not occur). They separately manipulated vowel duration and fricative duration, and found that only English listeners fully exploited both cues; French listeners relied mainly on fricative duration (as per the French native cues), whereas the speakers of the languages without this contrast used vowel duration cues only. In this case, degree of exposure to English had no effect on the non-English-speakers' performance. Flege and Hillenbrand concluded that contrasts requiring integration of more than one cue are particularly difficult for adults to acquire.

Interestingly, cues which are indeed present in productions of a native contrast may not be exploited if they are not phonologically significant in the language. Gottfried and Beddor (1988) also found that French listeners did not make use of variations in vowel duration, this time as a cue to vowel identity. Their productions of the same vowel showed systematic variation in vowel duration as well as spectral information, but in perceptual identification they used the spectral information alone. English listeners presented with the same French stimuli, however, were able to make use of both temporal and spectral variation. Gottfried and Beddor explain these results by pointing to differences in the French and English vowel systems: in English, temporal and spectral information trades off to distinguish vowels (and indeed, the English listeners reported that they were assimilating the French stimuli to English categories); in French, however, duration is an unreliable cue to vowel identity, so French speakers have learned to ignore it.

To date, the model proposed by Best et al. (1988) makes the most explicit predictions concerning the effects of native phonetic categories on the perceptibility of second-language categories. Best (1995) refined and extended the original typology, allowing for the possibility of uncategorizable cases (second-language phonemes which map to a point in phonetic space distant from any native category). The model has been supported by data from Japanese perception of English (Best & Strange, 1992) and English perception of Zulu (Best, McRoberts, & Goodell, 2001; Best et al., 1988); it also accounts well for English perception of German vowels (Polka, 1995) and Japanese ratings of English consonants for "goodness of fit" to Japanese categories (Guion, Flege, Akahane–Yamada, & Pruitt, 2000).

It is true, however, that the model provides a better fit to data involving perception of a more complex system by listeners with a simpler native system—that is, where potentially larger native categories capture smaller second-language categories. The model effectively predicts the reverse case to be, in comparison, less problematic for the listener. For instance, perception of vowels in a language with a five-vowel system by listeners with a more densely populated native vowel space would be predicted by Best's (1995) model to involve assimilation to the nearest native peripheral vowel categories, all of them distinct, and hence misidentifications should be avoidable. As Escudero and Boersma (2002) point out, however, the existence of multiple native categories in the space occupied by tokens of a single second-language category may also cause problems. They presented Dutch listeners with tokens of Spanish /i/ and /e/ in labelling tasks; in one case, the listeners thought they were labelling Dutch tokens. Dutch has three vowels in the relevant area of vowel space occupied by the two Spanish vowels, and those listeners who more often used the three Dutch categories in labelling the vowel set also performed worse when identifying the same stimulus set in terms of the two Spanish categories.

As the next section describes, there are also other aspects in which the modelling of second language phonemic perception is in need of further elaboration. We consider the whole issue from the point of view which is also the most burning question for the average listener: what effect does insoluble imprecision have on success in understanding? That is, what are the consequences of inaccurate phonetic processing for the recognition of spoken second-language words?

THE WORST BEST CASE

Variability in vowel perception ... a vowel located in one position on one occasion may well be located in a distinctly separate position one week, one day, or even ten minutes later (Laver, 1965, p. 95).

When two distinct categories of a second language map onto one native-language category, which corresponds better to neither of them, the perceptual situation is notoriously difficult. If the native category corresponds fairly well to one of the second-language categories, then discrimination may be assisted by a difference in category goodness between the two second-language sounds. But if both are possible approximations to the native category, the native category can potentially capture all tokens of either category in the second-language speech.

That is the case, for instance, with English /r/-/l/ for Japanese listeners or /æ/-/ɛ/ for Dutch listeners. In the former case, English distinguishes two kinds of voiced alveolar approximant, and Japanese has neither, but instead a voiced alveolar flap, which offers the only available category for capturing the English sounds—equally badly, but neither worse than the other. In the latter case, a similar situation arises, but with vowels: standard southern British English distinguishes two open midfront unrounded vowels, whereas Dutch has only one vowel in this part of the vowel space. The Dutch vowel is written with IPA's epsilon so that the transcription of English *neck* and Dutch *nek* is identical. However, in fact, the vowel in a *nek* is just that bit lower or more open than the vowel in a *neck*, bringing it closer to English /æ/ (as in *knack*), with the effect that, again, neither of the two southern British vowels maps well to the Dutch category but both are possible approximations. Dutch rhyme dictionaries list English loan words with both vowels as rhymes for Dutch words with /ɛ/ (e.g., besides *check* also *crack, snack* and *Jack* as rhymes for *nek*; Bakker, 1986, p. 163).

What happens to word recognition then? First, the listener is notoriously incapable of distinguishing between word pairs based on this distinction: *knack* and *neck* for the Dutch, *right* and *light* for the Japanese.

Second, phantom words could be recognised. There is no need for a minimal pair to satisfy the conditions for this, given the extent of spurious within-word embedding described earlier. Thus, hearing the word *phantom* may activate the pseudoembedding *fan* for any listener; and similarly, hearing *chastise* might activate *chess* for a Dutch listener and hearing *regular* might activate *leg* for a Japanese listener. There are no real English words *chass* or *reg*, so this is a case where no comparable competition arises for the native listener.

Does this happen? Is *chass* perceived as a token of *chess* by a listener with Dutch as first language?

One way to find out is simply to ask non-native speakers if *chass* is a word. Unfair, perhaps, but psycholinguists actually spend a lot of their time presenting lists of nonwords and words and asking people to decide which is which. This procedure is called the lexical decision task, and was described earlier. It is probably the most widely used laboratory method in experimental psycholinguistics. Accordingly, we approached the present question via a lexical decision experiment (Broersma, 2002) in which Dutch and English listeners were presented with real English words (*share, wish*), clear cases of English nonwords (*plog, strisp*), and what we called "near words:" spoken forms such as *chass*. Twenty-four native speakers of Dutch and 24 native speakers of British English (from the University of Birmingham) took part. The Dutch participants had a high level of proficiency in their second language English, whereas the English participants did not know any Dutch.

Altogether there were 32 monosyllabic English words involved in the /æ/-/ɛ/ comparison, 16 with /ɛ/ (*chess, desk*) and 16 with /æ/ (*fact, gang*). Further criteria for selection were that the word did not sound like an existing Dutch word, and that replacement of the target phoneme with its confusable counterpart did not result in an existing English or Dutch word. Near words were formed by replacing the target phoneme with its confusable counterpart (e.g., *chess* became *chass* and *gang* became *geng*). The target words were divided into two lists, balanced for frequency of occurrence, and contained equal numbers of each of the two base vowels. For both the Dutch and the English groups, half the listeners heard the words from one list in their real-word form and those from the other list in near-word form, whereas the other half heard the reverse mapping. Thus, if *chass* was indeed accepted as a real word, we could compare how often this happened in comparison with the acceptance of the correct pronunciation *chess.*

With real English words and clear nonwords as filler items, the experiment contained 200 items in all. Participants read instructions about the task, then heard the items binaurally over headphones; after each item was heard, they pressed one response button if they thought the presented item was an English word and another if they thought it was not. Presentation of the next item started 500 msec after the response was given.

The results were very clear, as can be seen from Fig. 4.2. First, the Dutch were very good at performing lexical decisions on English input. Their rate of positive responses to real words and of negative responses to clear nonwords did not differ from that of native Eng-

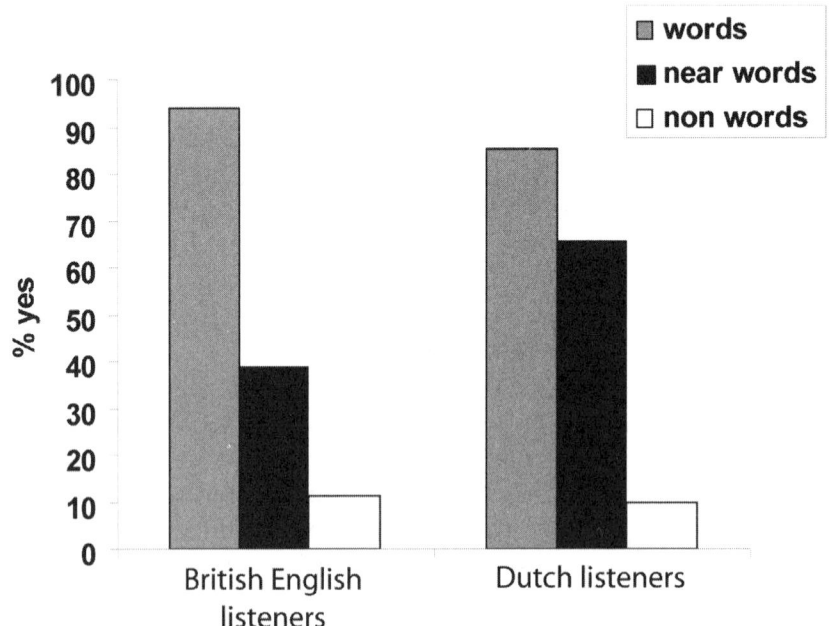

FIG. 4.2. Mean percentage of YES responses to real English words containing /æ/ or /ɛ/ (e.g., *chess, gang*), near words formed from them (e.g., *chass, geng*), and clear nonwords (e.g., *plog, strisp*) for native British English listeners and Dutch-native listeners (from Broersma, 2002).

lish speakers. Second, the near words were indeed rather confusing even for the native speakers, who were more likely to make a false positive response to a near word than to a clear nonword. Third, however, the Dutch listeners were significantly more likely to fall into this sneaky experimenter-set trap. In 66% of the cases, they simply responded yes to near words like *chass* and *geng* (significantly more often than did native listeners). That is, for these Dutch listeners, most of the tokens of *chass, geng,* and the like, were as good as canonical English words.

An extension of the same type of test to a competition situation was carried out in a second experiment within the same study (Broersma, 2002). This experiment involved minimal pairs based on the same vowel contrasts: *flash-flesh, mansion-mention,* and the like. Here a cross-modal priming paradigm was used: the task was again lexical decision, but this time with visually presented targets, and these were preceded by spoken primes. With visually presented targets, we assume that the Dutch listeners and the native listeners will not differ substantially in how they process the form of the targets, so that the dependent variable is, in this case, time to make a response rather than proportion of positive versus negative responses. Crucially, we compare the effects of a previously presented prime which is the same word as the target (e.g., FLESH preceded by spoken *flesh*) versus a prime which is the target's minimal pair (e.g., FLESH preceded by spoken *flash*), plus a control condition in which the prime is phonologically and semantically unrelated to the target (e.g., FLESH preceded by spoken *spite*). As described earlier, this kind of experiment usually shows that targets preceded by a minimally mismatching prime are responded to least rapidly, due to inhibitory effects (Soto–Faraco et al., 2001); note that vowel and consonant mismatches exercise equivalent inhibition (thus, Soto–Faraco et al.'s 2001 study included pairs like *sardina-sardana* as well as pairs like *tragico-trafico*).

Seventy-two native speakers of Dutch and 72 native speakers of British English, from the same populations used in the preceding experiment, took part. There were more participants because there were more conditions to counterbalance in this case: each target word could be preceded by an identical prime, a minimal-pair prime, or a control prime, and for each minimal pair of words either one could be the target word, but any one participant should only be presented with one member of the pair. This made for six presentation conditions in the experiment. Again, the potential target words were divided across conditions in such a way that the frequency of occurrence of the target words was balanced as closely as possible.

As in the auditory lexical decision experiment, none of the items were phonetically similar to any Dutch words, and in addition, none of the words that were used as visual targets in this set of materials were orthographically similar to Dutch words. The experiment contained in all 168 trials, including many filler trials with word and nonword targets. The listeners heard the prime words over headphones, then saw a target word on a computer screen; as before, they were asked to decide if the target word was an existing English word, and to indicate their response through button press.

The mean response times for each group in each condition can be seen in Fig. 4.3. As expected, the English native speakers showed

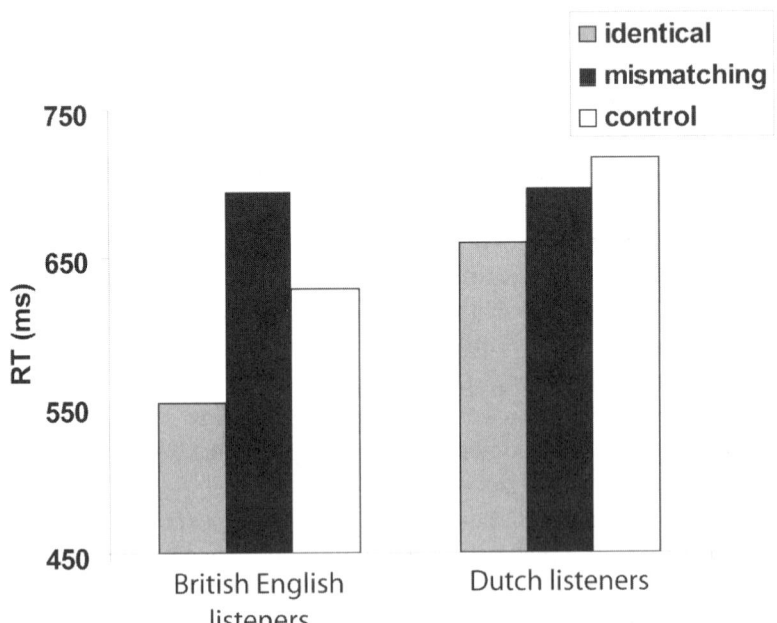

FIG. 4.3. Mean response time (msec) to visually presented English words containing /æ/ or /ɛ/ (e.g., *flesh*) preceded by an identical spoken prime (e.g., *flesh*), a minimally mismatching prime (e.g., *flash*), or a control prime (e.g., *spite*), respectively, for native British English listeners and Dutch-native listeners (from Broersma, 2002).

the well-known dual pattern of facilitation and inhibition: compared with the control condition, responses to targets were significantly faster after matching primes but significantly slower after minimally mismatching primes. This is exactly the pattern that was found in the experiments of Soto–Faraco et al. (2001) and others. The Dutch listeners, however, showed a different pattern of results. They did show significant facilitation in the matching condition in comparison with the control condition, but there was no trace of inhibition (and there was no facilitation) in the minimally mismatching condition. Their responses were, naturally, slower than those of the native speakers (this can be most easily seen in a comparison of the two control condition means); but the important aspect of the results is how each group's matching-prime and mismatching-prime conditions compare to the control condition, and in this the two groups clearly differ.

The Dutch listeners' pattern can be explained by assuming that competition between prime and target words remained unresolved. Neither one of the lexical competitors obtained sufficient activation to inhibit the other. However, it is not just the case that Dutch listeners treat English /æ/ and /ɛ/ as equally valid exemplars of a single category (and, accordingly, *flash* and *flesh* as homophones). In the auditory lexical decision experiment, as we saw, over one third of near words were correctly rejected by these listeners. In this experiment, too, responses in the minimally mismatching condition were longer than those in the matching condition, which implies that the primes must have activated identical targets more strongly than minimal-pair targets. This, in turn, must mean that the non-native listeners succeeded in differentiating to some extent between the English vowels, albeit not as clearly as did the native listeners. We suggest that the non-native listeners may maintain separate vowel categories for /æ/ and /ɛ/, but these will not be as distinct as those of the native listeners; indeed, they may even overlap, which would allow for (weaker) support to be given to the minimally mismatching words. Thus, *flesh* would activate *flesh* more than *flash* for native and non-native listeners alike; however, whereas for native listeners *flesh* would decisively mismatch *flash*, for non-native listeners *flash* would be partially matched by *flesh*. The mismatch of *flash* would then not be large enough to lead to inhibition. Phonetic imprecision would thus extend the competition process in non-native word recognition.

However, although this kind of explanation can be easily applied to the worst case in Best's (1995) classification, in which two second-language categories cover space containing only one native language category, there are other situations in which it seems less obviously applicable. The following section describes such a case.

ANOTHER NON-BEST CASE

The brain obviously transmits different neural commands for a phoneme occurring in initial as opposed to final syllable position (Laver, 1970, p. 71).

In fact Best's classification, as Escudero and Boersma (2002) also observed, does not fully cover the range of possibilities. Consider a distinction which is made in the same way in the first and the second language, but is restricted in its distribution in the native language such that listeners of that language have experience with making the distinction only in certain positions or under certain conditions. An example here is the voicing distinction for obstruents. This is independent of syllable position in English: *dough, toe, ode,* and *oat* are all words and no two of them are homophonous. In German and Dutch, however, a syllable-final devoicing rule bars voicing contrast in final position: German *Rat* and *Rad* are homophones, as are Dutch *raat* and *raad*.[1] In syllable-initial position, on the other hand, the contrast is as effective as in English: German *Deich* and *Teich* and Dutch *dij* and *tij* are nonhomophonous minimal pairs.

This situation is clearly not a cut-and-dried mapping of one set of categories exactly or inexactly against another. German or Dutch users of English will be able to map English obstruents contrasting in voicing against their native categories for [t] versus [d], [p] versus [b], [f] versus [v], and so forth. They will have had plenty of native experience in making these distinctions. Yet this experience will have been limited to syllable-initial contrasts, and in their native language at least they will never have needed to attend to a voicing distinction in syllable-final position. As a result, although they will be familiar with the English distinction, they may simply overlook it in positions in which it never occurs in their native language. This may be because they cannot attend to the distinction in those positions, or because awareness at a phonological level is insufficient, and to be useful must be accompanied by relevant phonetic processing experience; English correlates of the voicing distinction differ in syllable-initial versus syllable-final position, and listeners unfamiliar with the cues used in final position, such as preceding vowel duration, may be unable to exploit them. (Of course, both inattention and insufficient experience may exercise simultaneous effect!)

Indirect evidence from loan words in rhyme dictionaries can be again adduced in support of the complete irrelevance of the voicing distinction in final position: not only *snack* but also *shag* is listed as a possible rhyme for *nek*, both *sweet* and *tweed* as rhymes for Dutch *friet* ('chips'), and both *cop* and *job* as rhymes for Dutch *drop* ('licorice;' Bakker, 1986, pp. 163, 238, 330).

Thus, voicing contrasts in syllable-final position may present our Dutch listeners with exactly the same problems as the English vowel contrasts discussed earlier; they may consider *glope, sice,* and *quode* to be words in the same way as they misclassified *chass* and *geng*. We tested this in the auditory lexical decision experiment reported earlier, which contained 32 near words differing vocalically from real English words, and 32 near words differing from real words in the voicing of a final obstruent.

Fig. 4.4 shows the results (with clear nonwords again included to facilitate comparison). In this case, the native listeners had no problem making the relevant distinctions and hardly ever produced a false positive response to a near word like *glope*. However, the Dutch listeners did. Again, a majority of these items received a false positive response, that is, were treated as words.

The cross-modal priming experiment which we reported in the preceding section also examined English syllable-final voicing distinctions. Minimal pairs such as *bride* versus *bright, phase* versus *face,* and *robe* versus *rope* formed part of the stimulus set, and again, either member of a pair could appear as a visual target, preceded by a matching, minimally mismatching, or control spoken prime (thus BRIDE could be preceded by spoken *bride, bright,* or *shave*). The results for this group of items are shown in Fig. 4.5. It can be seen that obstruent voicing contrasts produced the same pattern of results as vowel contrasts: for the native listeners, facilitation and inhibition appeared in tandem, again both significantly differing

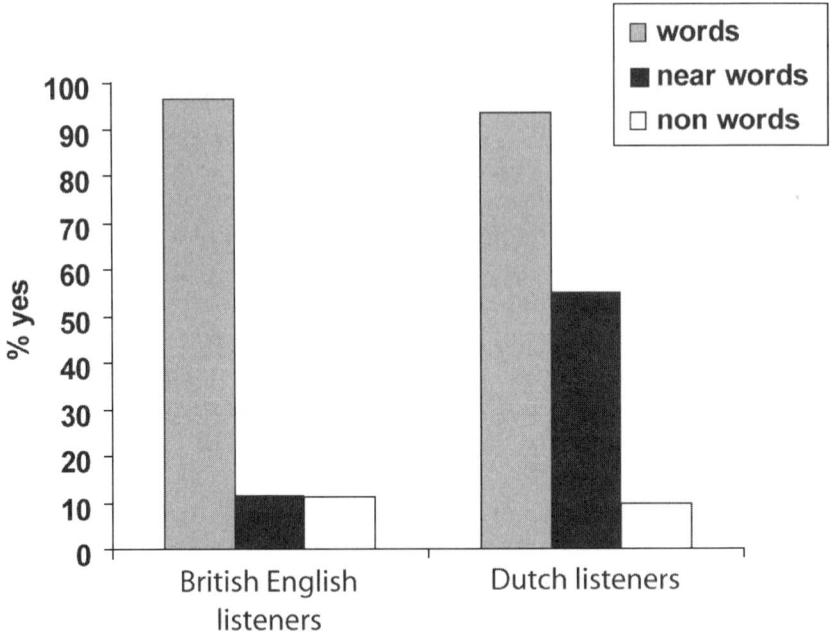

FIG. 4.4. Mean percentage of YES responses to real English words containing final obstruents (e.g., *globe, quote*), near words formed from them (e.g., *glope, quode*), and clear nonwords (e.g., *plog, strisp*) for native British English listeners and Dutch-native listeners (from Broersma, 2002).

from the control condition; but for the Dutch listeners, there was facilitation by matching primes but no inhibition from minimally mismatching primes.

Thus, the position-specific mismatch between the repertoires of English and Dutch voicing contrasts seems to cause the same problems for spoken-word recognition as the complete absence of a second-language contrast from the native repertoire: near words can treacherously pass for real words, and competition between minimal pairs can be unnecessarily extended. Our results suggest that comparisons across the phonemic repertoires of languages cannot be made on the basis of the category repertoire alone; Best's (1995) classification must be separately applied for syllable-initial versus syllable-final position (and possibly according to further relevant differences affecting contrast occurrence). The category repertoire may match in one area of

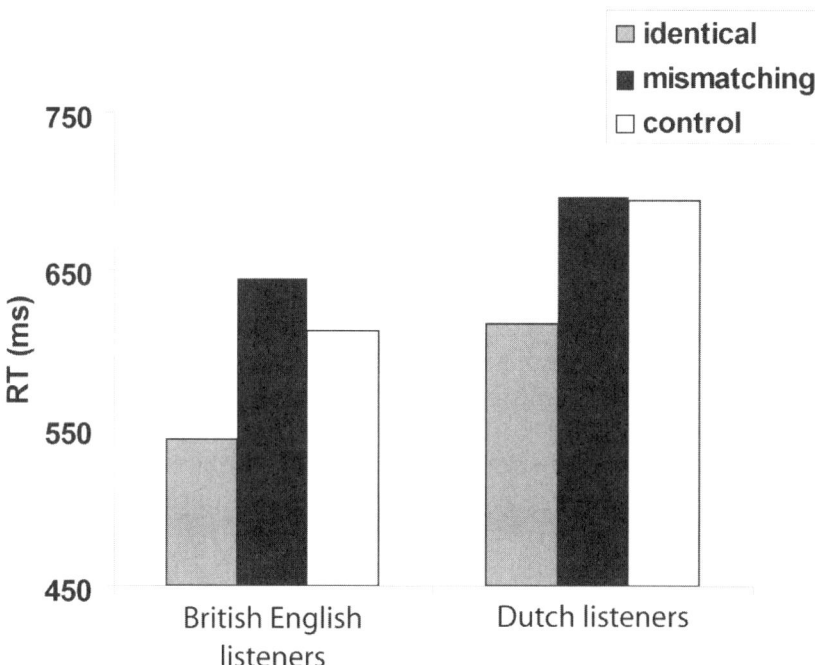

FIG. 4.5. Mean response time (msec) to visually presented English words containing final obstruents (e.g., BRIDE) preceded by an identical spoken prime (e.g., *bride*), a minimally mismatching prime (e.g., *bright*), or a control prime (e.g., *shave*), respectively, for native British English listeners and Dutch-native listeners (from Broersma, 2002).

application but mismatch in another, leading to overlapping representations in the latter situation only.

CONCLUSION

The perceptual skills that allow us to participate successfully in face-to-face conversation are very complex (Laver, 1976, p. 345).

Phonetic processing in listening to speech is a balancing act in which the aim is to achieve the highest precision where it does good, and abandon precision where it is not necessary. This general conclusion holds good as well for listening to a second language as for listening to speech in the native tongue. Yet the degree to which listeners achieve the necessary balance in a second language falls far short of their success with the native language.

Where the second language makes distinctions which are not made in the native language, the native language can override the distinction; and where the native language makes distinctions which are not made in the second language, these distinctions can intrude despite their irrelevance. Over decades of research, speech perception investigators have amassed a formidable body of evidence of this listening imprecision. However, for the second language user, the consequences are conspicuous not so much in the phonetic realm as in the effects on communication. Imprecise phonetic processing delays communication.

Comprehension of speech involves rapid selection of the correct sequence of words from a panoply of potential word candidates which are fully or in part supported by the spoken input. The more candidates are active, the more competition arises, and the more competition there is (and the longer it lasts), the more difficult successful word recognition becomes. Imprecise phonetic decisions can result, as we have seen, in phonetic sequences which are in fact not words at all being recognised as words: a Dutch listener who hears *chass* or *glope* is likely to activate the English words *chess* and *globe*.

Of course, we hope that native speakers do not in general go around uttering nonwords to hapless non-native listeners. We (two authors who grapple daily with our imprecise perception of our respective second languages) would beg readers of this book never to take up such a tormenting pastime. But the continuity of speech and the construction of vocabularies make it highly likely that non-native listeners will hear relevant near words anyway. Thus, *chass* is embedded within *chastise,* as we pointed out; likewise, *eace* occurs in *easterly* and *sice* in *precise.* The native speaker should experience little unwarranted competition from *chess, ease,* and *size* in these contexts, but our results suggest that many non-native listeners will. Not only within but across words such sequences can be found: where /æ/ and /ɛ/ cannot be distinguished, *stamp* may be activated in *the last emperor,* and where voiceless final obstruents are not distinct from voiced, then *cheese* may be heard in *each Easter.* Combine the two cases and *friend* is activated in *frantic* and *sand* in *this entrance.*

On top of the near-word recognition problem there is also the failure to distinguish minimal pairs incorporating the distinctions in question. For Japanese listeners, as we pointed out earlier, English pairs requiring the /r/-/l/ distinction, such as *right* and *light* or *brew* and *blue,* may collapse to a single phonetic form. Likewise the Dutch listeners to English in our experiments can experience the same problem with *flash* and *flesh,* or with *hard* and *heart,* or *beck* and *beg.* Speakers of languages which do not maintain intervocalic voicing distinctions will confuse English pairs such as *waver* and *wafer,* or perhaps hear *Laver* in *souffle for dinner.* All of these consequences of phonetic imprecision in listening combine to exacerbate the problem of interword competition for the non-native listener. Speech, the "most intricate of our communicative skills," requires from its users quite formidable precision in determining when and when not to be precise.

NOTE

[1] Extensive research has in fact shown that in both languages there is evidence of incomplete neutralisation: Port and O'Dell, 1985, for German; Warner, Jongman, Sereno, and Kemps, 2004, for Dutch. However, in each case the incomplete neutralisation effects seem to be in part a reflection of orthographic awareness, and native speakers of each language certainly consider the relevant minimal pairs to be homophones, for example, for use as rhymes. For ease of exposition of the experiments reported here, which concerned the perceptibility of English syllable-final voicing contrasts only, we also pass over all other aspects of the obstruent phonology of German and Dutch, for example, restrictions on certain fricative voicing contrasts in syllable-initial position as well, availability of voicing assimilation in certain contexts, and absence of some English obstruent categories from the German and Dutch repertoires.

REFERENCES

Alphen, P. M. van, & McQueen, J. M. (2003). *The effect of voice onset time differences on lexical access.* Manuscript submitted for publication.
Bakker, J. (Ed.). (1986). *Nederlands rijmwoordenboek* [Dutch rhyming dictionary]. Amsterdam: Ooievaar Pockethouse.
Bauer, L. (1985). Tracking phonetic change in the received pronunciation of British English. *Journal of Phonetics, 13,* 61–81.

Best, C. T. (1995). A direct realist view of cross-language speech perception: Standing at the crossroads. In W. Strange (Ed.), *Speech perception and linguistic experience: Issues in cross-language research* (pp. 171–204). Baltimore: York Press.

Best, C. T., MacKain, K. S., & Strange, W. (1982). A cross-language study of categorical perception for semi-vowel and liquid glide contrasts. *Journal of the Acoustical Society of America, 71* (Suppl. 1), S76.

Best, C. T., McRoberts, G. W., & Goodell, E. (2001). Discrimination of non-native consonant contrasts varying in perceptual assimilation to the listener's native phonological system. *Journal of the Acoustical Society of America, 109,* 775–794.

Best, C. T., McRoberts, G. W., & Sithole, N. M. (1988). Examination of perceptual reorganization for non-native speech contrasts: Zulu click discrimination by English-speaking adults and infants. *Journal of Experimental Psychology: Human Perception & Performance, 14,* 345–360.

Best, C. T., & Strange, W. (1992). Effects of phonological and phonetic factors on cross-language perception of approximants. *Journal of Phonetics, 20,* 305–330.

Broersma, M. (2002). Comprehension of non-native speech: Inaccurate phoneme processing and activation of lexical competitors. *Proceedings of the 7th International Conference on Spoken Language Processing,* (pp. 261–264). Denver, Colorado: Center for Spoken Language Research.

Burnham, D. K., Earnshaw, L. J., & Clark, J. (1991). Development of categorical identification of native and non-native bilabial stops: Infants, children and adults. *Journal of Child Language, 18,* 231–260.

Cutler, A., McQueen, J. M., Jansonius, M., & Bayerl, S. (2002). The lexical statistics of competitor activation in spoken-word recognition. *Proceedings of the 9th Australian International Conference on Speech Science and Technology, Melbourne,* 40–45.

Dahan, D., Magnuson, J. S., Tanenhaus, M. K., & Hogan, E. M. (2001). Subcategorical mismatches and the time course of lexical access: Evidence for lexical competition. *Language and Cognitive Processes, 16,* 507–534.

Escudero, P., & Boersma, P. (2002). *The subset problem in L2 perceptual development: Multiple-category assimilation by Dutch learners of Spanish.* Paper presented at the 26th annual Boston University Conference on Language Development.

Flege, J. E., & Eefting, W. (1987). Cross-language switching in stop consonant perception and production by Dutch speakers of English. *Speech Communication, 6,* 185–202.

Flege, J. E., & Hillenbrand, J. (1986). Differential use of temporal cues to the /s/–/z/ contrast by native and non-native speakers of English. *Journal of the Acoustical Society of America, 79,* 508–517.

Gottfried, T. L., & Beddor, P. S. (1988). Perception of temporal and spectral information in French vowels. *Language & Speech, 31,* 57–75.

Guion, S. G., Flege, J. E., Akahane–Yamada, R., & Pruitt, J. C. (2000). An investigation of current models of second language speech perception: The case of Japanese adults' perception of English consonants. *Journal of the Acoustical Society of America, 107,* 2711–2724.

Harrington, J., Palethorpe, S., & Watson, C. I. (2000). Does the Queen speak the Queen's English? *Nature, 408,* 927–928.

Labov, W. (1994). *Principles of linguistic change.* Cambridge, MA: Blackwell.

Laver, J. (1965). Variability in vowel perception. *Language and Speech, 8,* 95–121.

Laver, J. (1970). The production of speech. In J. Lyons (Ed.), *New horizons in linguistics* (pp. 53–75). Harmondsworth, Middlesex, England: Penguin.

Laver, J. (1976). Language and non-verbal communication. In E. C. Carterette & M. P. Friedman (Eds.), *Handbook of perception, Vol. 7, Language and Speech* (pp. 345–363). New York: Academic.

Laver, J. (1989). Cognitive science and speech: A framework for research. In H. Schnelle & N.–O. Bernsen (Eds.), *Logic and linguistics, vol. 2* (pp. 37–69). Hillsdale, NJ: Lawrence Erlbaum Associates, Inc.

Laver, J. (1994). *Principles of phonetics.* Cambridge, England: Cambridge University Press.

Laver, J., & Trudgill, P. (1979). Phonetic and linguistic markers in speech. In K. R. Scherer & H. Giles (Eds.), *European studies in social psychology: Social markers in speech* (pp. 1–32). Cambridge, England: Cambridge University Press.

Lively, S. E., Pisoni, D. B., Yamada, R. A., Tohkura, Y., & Yamada, T. (1994). Training Japanese listeners to identify English /r/ and /l/ III: Long-term retention of new phonetic categories. *Journal of the Acoustical Society of America, 96,* 2076–2087.

Logan, J. S., Lively, S. E., & Pisoni, D. B (1991). Training Japanese listeners to identify English /r/ and /l/: A first report. *Journal of the Acoustical Society of America, 89,* 874–886.

Maddieson, I. (1984). *Patterns of sounds.* Cambridge, England: Cambridge University Press.

Marslen–Wilson, W., & Warren, P. (1994). Levels of perceptual representation and process in lexical access: Words, phonemes, and features. *Psychological Review, 101,* 653–675.

Martin, J. G., & Bunnell, H. T. (1981). Perception of anticipatory coarticulation effects. *Journal of the Acoustical Society of America, 69,* 559–567.

Martin, J. G., & Bunnell, H. T. (1982). Perception of anticipatory coarticulation effects in vowel-stop consonant–vowel sequences. *Journal of Experimental Psychology: Human Perception and Performance, 8,* 473–488.

McQueen, J. M. (2004). Speech perception. In K. Lamberts & R. Goldstone (Eds.), *The handbook of cognition* (pp. 255–275). London: Sage.

McQueen, J. M., Cutler, A., Briscoe, T., & Norris, D. (1995). Models of continuous speech recognition and the contents of the vocabulary. *Language and Cognitive Processes, 10,* 309–331.

McQueen, J. M., Norris, D., & Cutler, A. (1994). Competition in spoken word recognition: Spotting words in other words. *Journal of Experimental Psychology: Learning, Memory and Cognition, 20,* 621–638.

McQueen, J. M., Norris, D., & Cutler, A. (1999). Lexical influence in phonetic decision-making: Evidence from subcategorical mismatches. *Journal of Experimental Psychology: Human Perception and Performance, 25,* 1363–1389.

Norris, D., McQueen, J. M., & Cutler, A. (1995). Competition and segmentation in spoken word recognition. *Journal of Experimental Psychology: Learning, Memory and Cognition, 21,* 1209–1228.

Norris, D., McQueen, J. M., & Cutler, A. (2003). Perceptual learning in speech. *Cognitive Psychology, 47,* 204–238.

Pallier, C., Colomé, A., & Sebastián–Gallés, N. (2001). The influence of native-language phonology on lexical access: Exemplar-based versus abstract lexical entries. *Psychological Science, 12,* 445–449.

Pierrehumbert, J. B. (2002). Word-specific phonetics. In C. Gussenhoven & N. Warner (Eds.), *Laboratory Phonology 7* (pp. 101–139). Berlin, Germany: Mouton de Gruyter.

Polka, L. (1995). Linguistic influences in adult perception of non-native vowel contrasts. *Journal of the Acoustical Society of America, 97,* 1286–1296.

Port, R., & O'Dell, M. (1985). Neutralization of syllable-final voicing in German. *Journal of Phonetics, 13,* 455–471.

Soto–Faraco, S., Sebastián–Gallés, N., & Cutler, A. (2001). Segmental and suprasegmental mismatch in lexical access. *Journal of Memory and Language, 45,* 412–432.

Strange, W. (1989). Dynamic specification of coarticulated vowels spoken in sentence context. *Journal of the Acoustical Society of America, 85,* 2135–2153.

Strange, W. (Ed.), (1995). *Speech perception and linguistic experience: Issues in cross-language research.* Baltimore: York Press.

Streeter, L. A., & Nigro, G. N. (1979). The role of medial consonant transitions in word perception. *Journal of the Acoustical Society of America, 65,* 1533–1541.

Utman, J. A., Blumstein, S. E., & Burton, M. W. (2000). Effects of subphonetic and syllable structure variation on word recognition. *Perception & Psychophysics, 62,* 1297–1311.

Warner, N., Jongman, A., Sereno, J., & Kemps, R. (2004). Incomplete neutralization and other sub-phonemic durational differences in production and perception: evidence from Dutch. *Journal of Phonetics, 32,* 251–276.

Werker, J. F., & Lalonde, C. E. (1988). Cross-language speech perception: Initial capabilities and developmental change. *Developmental Psychology, 24*, 672–683.

Werker, J. F., & Tees, R. C. (1983). Developmental changes across childhood in the perception of non-native speech sounds. *Canadian Journal of Psychology, 37*, 278–286.

Werker, J. F., & Tees, R. C. (1984). Phonemic and phonetic factors in adult cross-language speech perception. *Journal of the Acoustical Society of America, 75*, 1866–1878.

Whalen, D. H. (1984). Subcategorical mismatches slow phonetic judgments. *Perception & Psychophysics, 35*, 49–64.

Whalen, D. H. (1991). Subcategorical phonetic mismatches and lexical access. *Perception & Psychophysics, 50*, 351–360.

Yaeger–Dror, M. (1994). Phonetic evidence for sound change in Quebec French. In P. A. Keating (Ed.), *Phonological structure and phonetic form: Papers in Laboratory Phonology III* (pp. 267–292). Cambridge, England: Cambridge University Press.

Chapter 5

Representing Speech in Practice and Theory

Helen Fraser
University of New England

Speech is a fleeting phenomenon. In order to study it, we must capture it—keep it 'present' to us, re-present it to ourselves—by letting something more permanent stand in for it, or represent it.

Representation is thus a necessary precursor to any analysis of speech, whether practical or theoretical. However, representation faces us with several kinds of problems. First, we have to choose appropriately among many ways of representing speech—any of several kinds of writing systems, any of several kinds of transcription systems, output from any of several kinds of phonetic analysis equipment (spectrograms, electropalatograms, etc.), abstract diagrams in any of several specialist theories. Second, whatever choice we make inevitably brings with it the danger that we might confuse character-istics of our representation with characteristics of the speech itself.

For these reasons, issues to do with phonetic representation have long been a focus of debate, both in relation to practical tasks such as transcription, speech technology, and pronunciation teach-ing, and in relation to a wide range of theoretical issues (e.g., Anderson, 1999; Carello, Turvey, Kugler, & Shaw, 1984; Fowler, 1986; Keating, 1983; Nolan, 1990; Perkell & Klatt, 1986; Pierrehumbert, 1990; Rischel, 1990; Rumelhart & McClelland, 1986). Changes in the ways we represent speech have driven many of the practical developments within our discipline, while con-versely, discovery of inadequacies of particular representations for achieving practical goals (e.g., Cooper, 1950) has spurred much of its theoretical development.

However, questions about phonetic representation in general, as opposed to questions about which specific representations to use in particular contexts, are rarely tackled in their own right. John Laver's work is one exception, and many appreciate his careful analysis (1994), using the philosophies of Peirce and Vaihinger, of the subtle interplay of considerations of speech as a physical sub-stance, and speech as a vehicle of linguistic communication, which is needed to define representations suitable for use in a General Phonetic Theory.

In this chapter, I offer some observations on the nature of repre-sentation in general, and explore their implications for several practical and theoretical goals of phonetics. I argue that represent-ing speech is a much more complex process than is usually recog-nised, and one that by its nature is particularly prone to errors of judgment which are easy to leave undiagnosed. These need to be guarded against through ongoing attention to matters of meta-theory as well as theory. I use as examples several types of 'external' representations of speech, such as transcriptions and dictionary pronunciation guides, and various views of 'internal,' or mental, representation, as used in theories of speech processing. However, the special focus throughout is on an application which perhaps more than any other requires detailed attention to the inter-rela-tionship of practice and theory—the teaching of second language pronunciation.

WHY DO WE NEED AN ANALYSIS OF PHONETIC REPRESENTATION?

For Practical Tasks

One reason to undertake an analysis of the concept of representation in phonetics is to improve our ability to undertake practical tasks. Every phonetician has felt the frustration of seeing an important practical task carried out by someone with an inadequate understanding of the nature of speech and its representations.

Consider, for example, the marketing of computer-based language-teaching materials which use speech waves as a representation of pronunciation: the screen displays a model speech wave and users are asked to modify their pronunciation until their own speech wave matches the model. An elementary understanding of acoustic phonetics is enough to know that this will never work: a speech wave is just not the right kind of representation. Waves of different words can look very similar, whereas the same word said twice by the same speaker can yield two quite different waves.

Or consider the painstaking but thoroughly wrong-headed systems for representing pronunciation often found in dictionaries and phrasebooks of English or another language (e.g., Jegtheesh, 1981). Representations like this may make sense to the author, but they are of little help to the intended user.

These two examples allow us to make several preliminary points about the representation of speech. First, accuracy is not the only issue, although it is of course important. There is nothing 'inaccurate' about the speech waves used in multimedia pronunciation tutors. This kind of representation is perfect for some purposes, just not for this purpose. And although many bad dictionary pronunciation guides certainly are inaccurate, some perfectly accurate ones can be very hard for users to interpret, as we see later. Phonetic representation is not a question with a single, accurate 'right answer'. The key issue is appropriacy to context, not accuracy alone.

Second, demonstrating that one representation is *not* appropriate is far from sufficient to demonstrate which representation *is* appropriate. How *should* we represent English for learners in multimedia teaching materials? What *is* the best representation of pronunciation to use in a dictionary? More importantly, what principles should we use in deciding on an appropriate representation in any given context? These questions require an understanding of the nature of representation in general, to which we return shortly. But first let us open some discussion of the use of phonetic representation in various kinds of theories.

For Phonological and Psycholinguistic Theory

Rather than simply looking at speech and its representations, what is usually considered theoretically interesting is to look at the relationships among representations. This is done by two distinct but closely related disciplines: phonology and psycholinguistics.

A great deal of phonological and psycholinguistic theorising involves a phonetic transcription, which the theory aims to relate to a phonological representation. The nature of that phonetic transcription obviously then has a profound effect on the ensuing theories. In many phonological theories, for example, it defines the architecture needed for theoretically principled representations (Kenstowicz, 1994). In psycholinguistic theories, it determines the processing needed to account for speech acquisition, production, and comprehension.

As has been pointed out before, however, because phonetics as such is generally not the main focus of phonological and psycholinguistic theory, the phonetic transcription used in such theories is often quite rough (Anderson, 1999). Often, too, this fairly rough transcription becomes the main reference for the phonetic nature of speech on which the theory rests, with little further recourse to the actual speech on which the transcription is based (Ohala, 1990).

As with the practical applications discussed earlier, however, accuracy alone is not the key issue. A maximally accurate phonetic representation treats speech as mere sound with insufficient attention to its linguistic aspects—not to mention creating overly huge quantities of detail (Laver, 1994). The more important issue is the appropriacy of the representation to the context.

Also similarly to the practical applications, identifying what is wrong is not the same as knowing what is right. The history of phonology can be seen as an interplay of the effects of changing representations on processes, and changing processes on representations (Anderson, 1985).

Again, then, in theory as well as practice, we have a wide range of possible types of phonetic representations, and yet rather little general consideration of criteria for choosing amongst them. Development of such criteria is greatly helped, I think, by more attention to questions of representation in general, to which we now turn.

WHAT IS A REPRESENTATION?

Representation in General

A representation is, precisely, a 're-presentation,' a way of capturing some aspect of experience, pinning it down, enabling it to seem 'present' even when it is not literally there, by letting something else stand for it, or do duty for it, or refer to it. Since representation of speech is particularly complex, it is useful to consider a more straightforward type of representation first. A classic example of a representation is a picture, in which marks on a surface cause something to appear present, in a certain sense, to the viewer. A picture, then, is more than just marks on a surface; it somehow points beyond itself and represents something other than itself, or as is often said, it has a *content* distinct from its *form*. This is part of the fundamental nature of all representations. They require and presuppose the existence of something other than themselves.

This ability of a representation to point beyond itself is not simply a 'property' of the representation. Rather it is the result of actions by those who use it. The existence of a representation presupposes not just the existence of something represented (as we will see, this 'something' need not be a real thing), but also the activity of two parties: someone who has made the representation, and someone who is interpreting the representation. These may in fact be the same person in different roles, but the roles of creator and interpreter must both be filled for the representation to function as a representation.

It is worth pursuing this thought for a moment. Although when stated like this its truth seems so simple and obvious as to be hardly worth mentioning, it is surprising how easy it is to lose sight of it, as we will see. I want to insist that every representation does indeed represent something separate to itself (not, of course, necessarily something that really exists—consider a representation of a unicorn, or of a voiced labio-uvular stop), and also that any representation presupposes the actions of someone who has made the representation, and of someone who interprets the representation. Each of these three (represented, representer, and interpreter) is necessary to making a representation a representation, and the characteristics of each contribute to the representation in particular ways.

It is relatively easy to keep these roles of representation, represented, representer, and interpreter clear and distinct when discussing pictorial representation. As we will see, this can be much more difficult with representations of speech. A picture of my dog can evoke feelings in me similar to those evoked by my dog itself, but I generally don't really confuse the picture of my dog and the dog itself—even though our language makes it easy for me to say 'That's my dog' when I really mean 'That's a picture of my dog' (and actually makes the more accurate statement awkward to say: 'That's a picture of the artist's concept of my dog').

Similarly, even if I don't know who painted the picture of my dog, or what their intention was in the context in which they did so, I am quite clear that *someone* painted it. Pictures of dogs don't 'just happen'.

The role of interpreter can be more difficult to keep sight of. It is easier for me to forget my own role in interpreting the picture as a representation of my dog than to forget the role of the 'someone' who made it. It seems such a realistic picture that it would be impossible *not* to interpret it as what it simply *is*—a picture of my dog. However, a little reflection makes clear that there is indeed something about *me* that goes into making the marks on a surface into a representation of my dog: after all, *my dog* doesn't interpret the picture as a representation of itself. Even considering other humans, someone who has never met my dog, or any dog, or is unfamiliar with the style of pictorial representation used, might interpret the marks on the surface very differently.

Preliminary Implications

This brief outline of representation allows us to make several important points. First, the word *representation* can refer either to the process of representing (the drawing of the picture), or the product of that process (the picture itself). The product, a representation, presupposes the process, representing. This is a fundamental ambiguity which, as we will see, can cause confusion in discussion of representations of speech.

Second, the process of representing always, even when we do not explicitly acknowledge it, presupposes the playing of several roles by various people (or other entities): a 'something' to be represented, a 'someone' to do the representing, and a 'someone' to interpret the representation.

Third, there is often a many-to-one relationship between a representation and the 'something' it represents. I can use one drawing to represent many dogs, or dogs in general. I can make many drawings of one dog. Each of them can be a quite different kind of representation. For example, I might make one very realist drawing, another naïve, childlike drawing, and a third highly abstract drawing. It is interesting to note that although the realist drawing might seem in a sense to be the one which represents my dog most straightforwardly, it is actually, in both cultural and personal terms, a highly sophisticated achievement.

Finally, we can raise the question of the relationship among representations themselves. Bearing in mind the analysis of representation just given, it is clear that this relationship can only be understood with reference to the external roles played in the process of their creation and interpretation. For example, my realist and abstract drawings are related because they are both drawings of my dog, or because they are both drawings by me. They are not related purely through their own characteristics. Without reference to the creator and the thing represented, there is nothing in the drawings themselves to indicate a relationship between them.

Representation and Language

Let us look now at the roles and contributions of the various parties in creating another seminal type of representation—a much more complex one—our representation of experience through language.

Representation of experience in words and sentences is very significantly different from pictorial representation (Stewart, 1996). It uses and refers to a system which is more abstract, more conventionalised, and syntactically and semantically very much more sophisticated than that of art.

It does, however, share with pictorial representations the key qualities already discussed: representation in language involves the existence, beyond the words and sentences themselves, of a 'something' that the words represent, and also the action of both a creator and an interpreter of the representation.

In fact, linguistics has contributed greatly to our general interdisciplinary understanding of representation (Harris & Taylor, 1989; Seuren, 1998). It is linguistics that has made clear that words do not represent concrete things, and comprehensively discredited a referential theory of meaning (de Saussure, 1916/1983).

Representation of anything is now well agreed to be representation of a concept (or some other mediating device) rather than a thing (Palmer, 1976). Only in this way can we account for the fact that different languages, and different individuals, represent experience in different ways. These ideas have been crucial in the development through the 20th century of ideas to do with conceptualisation and categorisation, not just in linguistics but in many other disciplines.

THE STUDY OF REPRESENTATION

Representation is a key concept, along with closely related concepts such as *sign* and *symbol,* in a number of academic disciplines, including philosophy of mind, cultural studies, mathematics, and computer science, as well as linguistics, semiotics, and cognitive science. Similar definitions of representation to the one we have been discussing are commonly used (although obviously with differences of terminology and emphasis) in all of these disciplines: a representation is seen as part of a relationship involving *someone who represents*, the *representation* itself, and *something which is represented*.

In the vast majority of cases, however, in these disciplines as in phonetics, once this definition has been made, the discussion moves on quickly to classify types of representation (e.g., sign vs. symbol), define the relationships among them (e.g., their relative levels of abstractness), or argue for one kind of representation over another, with little opportunity made for a return to the definition to check that it has been correctly applied, or to analyse it further in light of observations made.

This means that there are relatively few wide-ranging and open-ended analyses and explorations of the concept of representation itself for us to turn to in considering questions about phonetic representation.

Two of which I am aware are Judge (1985) and Shanon (1993). It is interesting that both of these make extensive use of the concepts of phenomenological philosophy, although neither of them started off as apologists for phenomenology. In fact, it is hard to imagine a careful analysis of issues of representation which would not end up accepting the main principles of phenomenology, and although there are many texts which dismiss phenomenology, I have never seen one which both understands it and also clearly refutes it.

Phenomenology is a philosophical tradition which focuses on the analysis of human experience and the ways we interpret the world we live in and our position in it. It has had a huge influence on 20th century thought, but is itself poorly understood. It often receives bad press—due in some part to its own unconventional use of language, but in large part to the unjustified linking of some of the most extreme brands of postmodernism to it.

The main principles of phenomenology are not particularly difficult to understand, however. In fact, the most important ones are by now quite familiar—for example, that 'point of view' plays a crucial role in any interpretation, so there is no such thing as a 'neutral' interpretation. What is difficult is to follow the implications of these principles. This is why it is said that phenomenology is a method, rather than a system of ideas. In fact, it is a method for maintaining rigour in complex analyses by constant reference back to the provenance of concepts and representations used in the analysis. The rest of this chapter uses many ideas from phenomenology, without acknowledging each one explicitly. For background and justification see Fraser (1992). For a brief introduction to phenomenology itself I recommend Magee (1987) or Passmore (1968).

The Natural Attitude

One of the most useful concepts from phenomenology is that of the 'Natural Attitude.' We discussed earlier the well-accepted idea that words and sentences represent concepts rather than reality. It is interesting that despite this idea being almost universally accepted when stated explicitly, it is not always applied rigorously in discussions of representation. This is because, when we represent our experience with language, we have a strong tendency (much stronger than in the case of pictorial representation discussed earlier) to *negate* the distinction between reality and our representation of it, and to *forget* our own role in creating and interpreting the representation.

Thus, I feel strongly that I call a dog a dog because, "Dammit, it *is* a dog!" Perhaps on reflection I will admit that I do so also because I speak English, and because I have built up a prior concept of 'dog' through a complex and lengthy process of guided experience and socialisation—but that is certainly not at the front of my mind when I use the word 'dog'. Indeed, our language *encourages* us to ignore the creators and interpreters of our linguistic representations, just as agentless passives encourage us to ignore the perpetrators of deeds ("Dad, the window got broken").

This tendency is called by the phenomenologists the Natural Attitude. It is indeed quite natural, and serves us well in ordinary life. It would probably be impossible to function without it. Unfortunately it has a downside when it comes to scientific analysis—it is extremely difficult to escape from the Natural Attitude, especially when we are actually engaged in a project, rather than reflecting philosophically.

NO NEUTRAL REPRESENTATION

The upshot of our discussion of representation so far is the assertion that there is no such thing as a 'neutral' representation—hardly a radical proposition at the beginning of the 21st century. Any representation is a product of some action by some person on some aspect of experienced reality; any representation requires interpretation by some person in some context if it is to function as a representation. This statement in itself is simple and straightforward. What is difficult is to follow its implications. To some, this idea that there can be no neutral representation has implied the 'postmodern' view that there can be no *reliable* representation, that all representations are suspect, and that we should therefore try to theorise a world without representations, even without any foundational facts or values (Sarup, 1988). Of course, this extreme position is impossible to maintain in theory or practice, and analysis of attempts to do so usually find it not difficult to pinpoint representations, facts, and values on which the attempt itself is resting.

Perhaps in opposition to this untenable position (sometimes unfortunately but erroneously ascribed to phenomenology), others have reacted by clinging more tightly to the representations that work for them, acknowledging that in principle they may not be neutral, but arguing that because they 'work' they must be OK, at least until something better comes along.

The position I am advocating here, and which I believe is much closer to the spirit of real phenomenology, is that the fact that we cannot have a neutral representation means only that we cannot have a neutral representation—not that we should somehow try to have no representations at all. Representation and its related activities of categorisation and conceptualisation are absolutely central to our cognition and our theorising—we certainly cannot pretend that we are not using representations. We do have to be aware, however, especially when theorising representation itself, of what each representation entails, of our own role in creating and interpreting it, and of the distracting tendencies of the Natural Attitude. We must be prepared to use representations flexibly in accord with the different demands of different contexts, and to justify our use of each particular representation in relation to the particular context in which it is being used.

Such justification of a representation clearly cannot involve a claim that it is 'neutral' in any sense. Rather, representations should be justified with reference to the process of their creation and interpretation, by looking beyond or behind the end product, the representation, to the reality it represents. Otherwise we risk the danger, mentioned right at the beginning, of confusing characteristics of the representation with characteristics of the 'something' being represented.

This justification requires, in the face of the Natural Attitude, a constant return to first principles regarding representation. We can achieve this by taking time to identify all the representations we use within a theory or application, including all the technical terms we use, and simply asking of them a series of what we can call 'Framework Questions':

Framework Questions

- What does this representation represent? In what context is it created and used?
- Who made this representation? What prior knowledge or experience did they need to make it?
- Who will interpret this representation? What prior knowledge and experience will they need to use it properly?

REPRESENTING SPEECH

In studying representation, it is usual, as we have seen, to emphasise the role of language (and also culture) in shaping our representation of the world. Language is often seen as a system or tool with which we can represent our experience, and which shapes and influences that representation, mediating our access to reality. It is less usual to focus on the metalinguistic representation of language itself, and the influence our language and culture have on the ways that we can do this.

However, a little reflection makes it clear that this influence must be there. There is no such thing as a 'neutral' representation of speech, any more than there is of anything else. A metalinguistic representation of language is no more neutral than any other kind of representation. Individual speech sounds are often considered to be components of words. However, the terms we use for speech sounds (such as *syllable*, *question intonation*, *consonant*, *the letter 'y,' the phoneme* /s/, and so on) are themselves words, and fall under the same semantics as other words: the word for a sound is a representation of a concept of a sound, not a direct label for the sound.

When we represent speech with transcriptions or diagrams or output of phonetic analysis equipment, even when we simply talk about the sounds of speech, we are making representations of speech in just the way we make pictures of dogs—with just the same implications and presuppositions of roles and processes, and, more importantly, with the same risk of the Natural Attitude blurring crucial distinctions. We need the Framework Questions to avoid this risk.

What does a phonetic representation represent? Behind any representation of speech is a 'something' that we might call 'raw speech,' because it is by definition not yet represented. Obviously this is difficult to talk about, because to describe it is to represent it, thus rendering it no longer 'raw.' Nevertheless, we can learn a great deal about it by working with it and representing it in a wide range of ways, and most phoneticians have considerable experiential knowledge about 'raw speech.'

Who can make a phonetic representation of speech? Only, I claim, someone who has a prior understanding of the same speech represented as phrases, words, and syllables. This is shown by two kinds of evidence, among many others. First, the kind of phonetic representation we can make with a computer operating only with 'bottom-up' acoustic information is nothing like the representation made by a human, who can't help but have 'top-down' knowledge of words and phrases (Perkell & Klatt, 1986). Second, if we try to present human listeners with speech in a segment-by-segment fashion (e.g., through 'gating' experiments), they cannot understand the segments until they have heard enough of the speech to make an interpretation at the word and phrase level (Shockey, 2003).

This well known evidence shows that a phonetic representation of speech is more sophisticated than a representation of speech as words and phrases. And yet, almost every theory treats phonetic representation as more basic, closer to the reality of 'raw speech' than words and phrases. This shows an interesting analogy to the common Natural Attitude view, discussed earlier, that a highly sophisticated 'realist' drawing must be more basic or closer to reality than a naïve childlike drawing.

It is interesting, also, that the view that the phonetic representation is more basic than a lexical representation, while useful for many purposes, also causes a number of theoretical problems for phonetics and phonology. For example, it is necessary to explain the 'conversion' of a string of discrete segments into a continuous flow of speech, and vice versa. The usual account is in terms of coarticulation, the influence of each segment upon its neighbours. However, as has been pointed out before (Ohala, 1986b; Ohala, 1990), this account can only go so far, since segments cannot influence each other directly, but only through a speaker's behaviour.

Later, I will argue the value of developing theory, for use in appropriate contexts, based on the unconventional but well-justified idea that representation of speech as words and phrases is more basic than phonetic representation. Now, let us look at the implications of the argument so far for practice and theory.

IMPLICATIONS FOR PRACTICE

Let us return now to the examples with which we started, dictionary pronunciation guides and pronunciation teaching, to see the implications of our discussion so far for practical applications. When we use representations of speech for practical applications, we are either creating a representation for someone, whether ourselves or another person, to interpret, or interpreting a representation made by someone, whether ourselves or another person. Understanding the nature of the creator and the interpreter, and the context in which they work, is critical, especially if the creator and interpreter are different kinds of people, or working in different kinds of context. This situation, of course, arises frequently in practical applications where someone with linguistic training is creating a representation to be interpreted by someone without such training.

Consider, first, dictionary pronunciation guides. Who makes such representations? Hopefully, it is someone who understands enough about phonetics not to be misled by simplistic ideas about pronunciation and its relationship to orthography. But beyond this, it should also be someone who understands the type of person who will be using the dictionary, and how they are likely to interpret different kinds of representation. Who interprets dictionary pronunciation guides? Asking the question makes it obvious that there are many different kinds of people who use these representations, and many different contexts in which they use them. For example, some users are not interested in pronunciation as such, but simply want a quick-and-easy indication of how to pronounce a difficult word. Others are professional linguists and want considerable detail as to how words are generally pronounced in different dialects, or at different historical times. The guide needs to be tailored to these different uses and users.

Although this is obvious as soon as the 'who' question is posed, surprisingly it has not often been explicitly considered in creating dictionary pronunciation guides, and there are virtually no published experiments looking at how different groups of users interpret different types of guides (see Fraser, 1997a). Rather, the usual practice has been to make assumptions (inaccurate, as we will see) about which representations will be easier for users to interpret, based on considerations of which representation is simplest from a linguist's point of view.

The most obvious type of guide from a linguist's perspective is a phonemic transcription of the words using special symbols such as those of the International Phonetic Alphabet (IPA). This is good for people with training in IPA transcription, but, of course, it is recognised that for some users the symbols are unfamiliar and quite difficult to interpret. Several solutions have been proposed.

Consider, first, 'Oxford diacritics', in which ordinary letters of English spelling are used, rather than strange phonetic symbols. To overcome the ambiguities of English orthography, the ordinary letters must be augmented with diacritics. This makes sense on the assumption that we need to keep the systematic nature of IPA transcription without using the special symbols. However, it is generally agreed to be very hard to use, and various alternatives have been proposed.

Unfortunately, this has generally been done without full analysis of the reason for the failure of Oxford diacritics, with the result that many of the alternatives do not really overcome the problems. One of these new systems is 'phonemic respelling', in which each phoneme is represented systematically, not by a letter with diacritics, but by a single letter or digraph from the English alphabet. Thus, in one system, /u/ is 'ooh', /ai/ is 'uy', and the 'schwa' vowel is 'uh' (Blair 1987). However, although the system of letters and digraphs looks fine when set out as a table of phoneme correspondences, it makes for very bizarre sequences when the phonemes are strung together to show the pronunciation of words. Consider the following examples:

pyooh-uh	pure
jooh-uhl	jewel
duh-**lish**-uhs	delicious
muys	mice
thuh-**mom**-uh-tuh	thermometer

Not only are these difficult to interpret, they are also highly confusable with ordinary orthography (Fraser, 1997a). In many cases, the user is better off relying on the word's spelling as a guide to pronunciation.

Let us pause now to consider *why* these representations are unsuccessful as a representation for dictionary pronunciation guides, by asking the Framework Questions. Phonemic respelling seems like a good idea on the analysis that it is the strange-looking diacritics that cause the problems with Oxford diacritics—but is this the real crux of the problem?

Who can create and interpret Oxford diacritics? Surely only someone who can first do phonemic transcription, and then translate this into Oxford diacritics can do this. There is no way Oxford diacritics is 'simpler' than IPA transcription (Nisbet, 1994). Both the systems we have considered so far (diacritics and phonemic respelling) have aimed to keep the systematic one-symbol-one-phoneme style of IPA phonemic transcription without the difficult symbols. What is lacking is consideration of the nature of average dictionary users, who not only do not know IPA, but may not even have a clear systematic phonemic representation of speech in their minds (as discussed further later).

The most familiar and most effective method of representing speech for these people is via the orthographic rules of English (see Fraser, 1997a, for empirical justification and further discussion of this claim, as well as a system for representing pronunciation with orthography in nonphonemic respelling; see also Fraser, 1999, for application of the same reasoning to creation of a pronunciation-to-spelling guide). In particular, ordinary users find any representation of 'schwa'—whether with a diacritic, a digraph, or an IPA symbol—very confusing, because this is not represented in English orthography. Drawing attention to it makes them emphasise it, which is the exact opposite of what is required. Rather than representing 'schwa' directly, a better solution is to allow it to emerge from a clear representation of the stressed syllables—in combination with the users' native speaker knowledge of the stress patterns of English.

Turn now to learners of second language pronunciation. We have seen that speech waves are not a useful representation for them—but what would be better? We are still left with the question of exactly *which* type of representation is most useful to the learner.

This is not a question that can be answered purely with reference to linguists' representations of speech—we need to observe and analyse learners' creation and use of representations. This requires closer attention to the process of representation rather than representations as products and takes us into the realm of phonological and psycholinguistic theory.

IMPLICATIONS FOR THEORY

Phonological Theory

We saw earlier that much phonological theorising requires a phonetic representation, and that, because it is not the main focus of the theory, this phonetic representation is often quite rough. Much more attention in phonological theorising has been paid to the 'higher level' or 'more abstract' phonological representations. However, the key interest has been in neither the phonetic nor the phonological representations, but in the relationships among them.

It has been common to think about these relationships in terms of processes by which one sound is changed into another, such as palatalization, lenition, or devoicing. Of course, recent developments have questioned the idea that these processes are literally ones of transformation, and a range of alternatives is available (Anderson, 1985; Kenstowicz, 1994). However, most theories of phonology still aim, explicitly or implicitly, to specify a direct relationship between two representations, one phonetic and the other phonological.

As with the practical applications discussed earlier, these new theories have generally been developed without a deep analysis of what it was that was wrong with the transformational theories in the first place. Again, analysis of the representations according to the Framework Questions is helpful in understanding their relationship. This emphasises that the relationship between representations at different levels must be mediated through the mind of someone who understands both representations, and also the 'raw speech' being represented. This makes their relationship much more like translation than transformation. Consider that the translation of a sentence from one language to another must be mediated through the mind of someone who understands both languages and also the meaning being represented—at least if we are to avoid rendering "The spirit is willing, but the flesh is weak" as "The whisky is strong, but the meat is rotten." That is why general definitions of phonological processes (as opposed to definitions within particular contexts) are often very difficult to give (e.g., Bauer, 1988).

Of course, all this does not imply that we should abandon the traditional view of the relationships between representations of speech. These are obviously useful for typological description, generalisation, and prediction. It does mean we should respect the boundaries of appropriacy of this traditional view.

Taking the notion seriously, believing that there really is some kind of 'process' relationship between the representations of speech, raises more problems than it solves.

Nevertheless, there has been a tradition, since the publication of *The Sound Pattern of English* (Chomsky & Halle, 1968), of deliberately blurring the distinction between the grammar created by a linguist and the grammar 'in people's heads.' This has the unfortunate effect of encouraging just such a 'really is' view of phonetic and phonological representation.

Psycholinguistic Theory

So far we have been talking about 'external' representations, such as paintings and transcriptions. One of the most significant uses of the concept of representation in 20th century thought, however, is that of 'mental representation,' or what we might call by contrast 'internal representation.' The idea that thought depends on the manipulation of subconscious mental representations is very widely accepted in our era despite ongoing criticisms, such as those of Shanon and Judge, discussed earlier, and is the basis of the many computational models of mind. The discipline of cognitive science, of which psycholinguistics is a subbranch, remains based firmly on this insight, although there have been major changes in the exact workings of the models proposed (Lepore & Pylyshyn, 1999) as our insights into computation have increased.

Consider speech perception, for example. It is common to assume that word recognition depends on the processing of acoustic cues into a phonetic representation, through some stages of sublexical representation, to a lexical representation, which allows access to the mental lexicon, for association with the word's meaning. The close analogy to phonological theorising is hard to miss.

Also similarly to the case in phonological theory, although strict transformational models have been outmoded for some time, most new psycholinguistic theories retain the interest in defining the processes which relate these representations—when, according to the argument so far, the key question to be addressed in psycholinguistics is not 'How do people manipulate representations?' but 'How do people create representations of speech in the first place?'

To understand this point, let us look at each of the representations involved in theories of speech perception in terms of our Framework Questions and the process view of representation. As we saw earlier, existence of sublexical representations *presupposes* understanding of words. Isn't it a little odd to consider that they are intermediate representations involved in *creating* representations of words?

An analogy with pictorial representation might make the point clearer. Consider a series of representations of my dog: a highly realistic, figurative drawing, an abstract image emphasising the forms and colours of my dog, a 'naïve' style drawing showing my dog with all its legs the same length and two eyes on the same side of its face, and an expressionist depiction of the essential joy and silliness that is my dog, chasing sticks on the beach. How are these related to one another? Surely any understanding of their relationship must refer to the dog they all represent, to the artist who creates them all, and to me, the interpreter who sees them all as representations of my dog. The suggestion that you could create a 'processor' that would take one of these drawings as input, and generate another by computation which passes through intermediate representations like the remaining drawings is decidedly unlikely, if not actually impossible. The idea that drawings *really are* created by this type of computational process is ludicrous: of course, each drawing must be made by an artist with reference to (a concept of) the dog.

Where is the difference, we must ask, then, from the situation in speech perception? The only difference is that the Natural Attitude allows us to blur the distinctions between 'raw speech' and its representation, and to ignore the contribution of the creator and interpreter of representations even more easily than we can with pictures.

This 'oddity' we have uncovered is an instance of what is known in philosophy as the homunculus problem. For a theory like this to work it requires within it a 'little man' (homunculus) who understands the words being spoken enough to create the sublexical representations at each level. But, of course, there is no little man. His work is done, unnoticed, and unacknowledged within the theory, by the scientist, stuck in the Natural Attitude, forgetting his or her own contribution to the representations used in the theory, and thus neglecting to account for it.

The Natural Attitude means that few theorists notice this oddity. Those who do, and yet wish to retain the computational view of mind, are forced into convoluted arguments that mental representations are somehow different from other representations, in requiring no interpretation (e.g. Pylyshyn, 1983).

It is worth asking now why speech perception might be theorised in terms of computation of mental representations in the first place. Again, the Natural Attitude is behind this. Once we have identified levels of representation 'below' the word, we feel that these more physical, more orderly representations are somehow more 'real' than lexical representations, that they represent what speech is 'really like' as it 'enters our ears.' Yet we also have the strong percept of words—somehow one 'must be' transformed into the other. We are unaware of this transformation taking place so it 'must be' happening subconsciously. Someone suggesting that there is no need for intermediate representations seems to misunderstand the issue, to have some crazy notion that meaning alone 'enters the ear' and is transformed into phonetic representations.

Basically what we have here is a failure to recognise that the representations being related within these theories are representations made by two different kinds of people—the lexical and phonological representations can be created by 'ordinary people,' whereas phonetic representations can only be made by people with significant scientific training. We can theorise the relationships between these representations in all kinds of computational ways, but we will never fully understand their relationship unless we recognise that the relationship is mediated through their creators and interpreters, that it is a translation, not a transformation. This is why no simple computational relationship has been found after 50 years of searching. It is not just because we happen not to have found it, but because it is impossible in principle—the relationship must refer to the creator and interpreter, which are necessarily noncomputational.

I hasten to add that this argument does not mean we should throw out computational models of either phonology or psycholinguistics.

Clearly they have been and continue to be helpful to linguists in gaining knowledge about the patterns of speech in languages of the world, and predictive powers about sound change, and as a source of abstract knowledge and prediction about human linguistic behaviour. They are also valuable in applications which actually involve computation, such as speech technology.

They are far less useful in understanding and theorising applications involving real humans. For that we need a theory based on the processes of representation that are relevant to language users, as opposed to scientists or computers.

THEORISING CONCEPTUALIZATION AND REPRESENTATION

We have seen that representations are representations not of things, but of concepts. What are ordinary people's concepts of speech like? Because of the focus of research on linguists' representations and their relationships, there has been little direct study of this question. However, most linguists who work with speech have a good deal of informal knowledge about how ordinary people conceptualise speech and what they can and can't do with different kinds of representation.

There is also a growing body of serious research which takes an explicit interest in the categorisation and conceptualisation of speech by ordinary people, and which fits well with the views on representation presented here (e.g., Jaeger, 1986; Nathan, 1996; Ohala, 1986a; Schachter, 1993; Taylor, 1989, pp. 222–238). This approach seems to me to make the basis for a good alternative to computational models (not a replacement, as it does a quite different job), for use in cases where the focus is on how ordinary people conceptualise and represent the sounds of speech, and on how they use concepts and representations of speech.

Such an account would be useful, in combination with the considerable body of knowledge in other disciplines about concepts and how they drive behaviour, and how they are formed, and modified (e.g., Neisser, 1987). For example, a well-agreed aspect of concept formation is that it is much less likely to happen through application of information and facts, and much more likely through experience and activity.

What we need, then, is a systematic framework for understanding the concepts that drive our speech behaviour, of the many ways we can represent speech, and the relationships among them. Work is in progress to develop such a framework and the next section summarizes some results. For further detail and justification see Fraser (2004).

RELATIONSHIPS AMONG REPRESENTATIONS OF SPEECH

We have seen that 'raw speech' can be conceptualised and represented in many different ways, and that the relationships among these representations can also be theorised in many different ways, depending on the context (e.g., whether the theory is intended for use in speech technology, psycholinguistics, or language typology). The framework proposed in this section is intended for use in contexts involving applications with real humans, such as creating pronunciation guides, or teaching pronunciation. It is important to recall that all of these representations are representations of (concepts of) 'raw speech,' which is always distinct from all the representations. It is also important to be clear that all of these representations are focusing on the raw sound of speech in its linguistic interpretation, as opposed to an interpretation as 'mere sound' or as sound that is meaningful in nonlinguistic ways (e.g., indicating the presence of a particular person, or for diagnosing some problem with the vocal folds).

The aim is to rank the representations in terms of how basic or sophisticated they are as representations of speech, from the point of view of language users. This is quite a different ranking from that generally understood in linguistics, but follows from all that has been said so far (and is further justified and explored elsewhere).

The claim is that, for units at later levels in the hierarchy below to be fully understood, the language user must have a good understanding of earlier levels. This does not mean that terms from later levels cannot be learned at all, but that they cannot be understood fully and used effectively unless prior levels are also understood.

There is no claim that language users have no concept of standard linguistic units, or that linguistic theory should avoid reference to phonemes, features, and so forth. However, accepting the hierarchy of concepts proposed here makes it unjustifiable to impute such concepts to speakers at 'low levels' of language processing—because they depend on prior understanding of larger units, particularly words.

Word

A representation of raw speech in terms of meaningful words is the most basic of all, from the language user's point of view, and understanding words requires no prior mental processing. This is the first way young children learn to represent speech, and throughout life it remains the most basic—as is seen when we consider how difficult it is to listen to speech without hearing words. This view is clearly quite different from the standard idea that a meaningless unit such as the phoneme, or Distinctive Feature, is the fundamental building block of language. It is worth considering, then, that the definition of a phoneme depends on knowledge of 'word' (in terms of minimal pairs).

Sound Versus Meaning

The first analysis of words involves a distinction between their sound and their meaning. This distinction presupposes an understanding of words, and children develop it—not without difficulty—after they have learned to talk (Gombert, 1992; Vihman, 1996). Again, this is different from the standard view, which sees words as formed from the arbitrary union of a sound with a meaning.

Sublexical Units

Once we have distinguished the sound of words from their meaning, we can break the sound up into various types of sublexical units—such as rhythmic patterns, syllables, onsets, and rhymes—which at this level are informal and unsystematised. Detailed study of this type of representation has tended to be outlawed in scientific linguistics but it is observable and theorisable (e.g., Ohala & Jaeger, 1986). It certainly has its own rationality, despite its differences from the neat systematic representations of formal linguistics, to which it would appear to relate in much the same way as ordinary reasoning is related to formal logic (e.g., Margolis, 1987).

Orthography

It is well established that it is only through acquisition of alphabetic literacy that an analysis of speech into segments becomes available to language users—that is, that literacy fundamentally changes a person's way of representing speech (Linell, 1988; Olson, 1996). It is also well established that the acquisition of literacy *requires* such an analysis of speech into sounds (Byrne, 1998). 'Whole language' methods, which aim to teach literacy without inflicting the burden of such analysis on the learners, simply do not work (Gough, Ehri, & Treiman, 1992). The analysis of speech into sounds at this level, however, is very informal and unsystematic. Writing systems (as opposed to transcription systems) are primarily intended to represent language rather than speech (Olson, 1994)—even in regular, shallow, so-called 'phonetic' writing systems (DeFrancis, 1989). They always—with only the most marginal of exceptions (Byrne, 1998)—work at an emic level, regardless of the size of the unit with which they operate.

However, once a language user has become literate, the symbols of the writing system (whether alphabetic, syllabic or other) provide a handy means for users to refer to the sounds of speech, as distinct from the meanings of words, for example, in giving a 'phonetic spelling' of an irregular word. Indeed, the Natural Attitude ensures that literate people come to believe that the symbols of their writing system actually are accurate representations of speech sounds, even where, as in English, the writing system provides a representation quite different from the actual pronunciation. This belief can be hard to shake, as anyone who has taught first-year linguistics will attest, and is of course the basis of so-called 'spelling effects' in psycholinguistics (e.g., Derwing, 1992).

Phonemic Representation: Systematised Orthography

Many well-educated literate people never get beyond the level of orthography in terms of the sophistication of their representations of speech. Special training, available to a much smaller group of people, is needed to replace orthographic representation with a more systematic representation such as phonemic transcription, or some other 'emic' representation.

Interestingly, just as, when people learn to read, they come to believe that the orthography of their writing system provides an accurate representation of speech, so too, when people learn phonemic representation, they come to believe that phonemic transcription represents speech accurately. They also generally believe that phonemes are constitutive of words, and that when they speak they 'speak in phonemes.' Of course, this shows the operation of the Natural Attitude, in two important ways: first, because phonemic representation is in fact a highly abstract representation of speech, which bears little resemblance to the 'raw speech' from which it is derived; and second, because people's ability to represent speech phonemically—beyond the basics of 'cat' is 'c-a-t'—is very much more limited than their own self-assessment suggests (Scarborough, Ehri, Olson, & Fowler, 1998). The reason is that although people use an elementary phonemic analysis to 'bootstrap' literacy, they become fluent readers long before a full phonemic system is developed.

Allophonic Representation

Some people who learn phonemic transcription go on to notice that it is inadequate as a representation of what speech is 'really like.' These people become aware of some subphonemic differences, and develop the concept of allophone. Allophonic representation is a rough phonetic representation of the kind discussed earlier. It is intuitively important as a way of referring to subphonemic differences but very hard to define phonetically, because it depends on phonemic awareness. Nevertheless, this type of representation remains highly influential on linguists' thinking, and it is natural for most linguists to do their pretheoretical thinking about speech in terms of phonemes and allophones.

Phonetic Representation

Only with yet further training and experience do people gain some understanding of the continuous and multifaceted phonetic nature of speech, as seen through laboratory-based observation of the perception, production, and acoustics of speech.

Problematizing Phonetic Representation

By this stage, it becomes possible to engage in effective analysis of the relationships among the various levels of representation, to consider general questions about the nature of phonetic representation, and to propose and evaluate new technical and specialised theoretical representations (e.g., disyllables, autosegmental 'tiers,' feature geometry, optimality 'tableaux') intended to overcome the theoretical difficulties of segmental transcription. More relevant to present concerns, it is at this level that it is possible to gain a good understanding of the theoretical problems involved in explaining speech processing. Without traversing all the levels, it is difficult to gain full understanding of the advantages, disadvantages, and presuppositions of representation at different levels.

To see an example of this, consider the case of 'schwa.' As we have seen, ordinary English speakers are quite unaware of 'schwa,' because it is not represented in orthography. In many cases, however, 'schwa' is taught early in linguistic training as part of phonemic transcription, the 'systematised orthography' level discussed earlier. Unless students go on to later stages of analysis, the Natural Attitude affects their understanding, so that schwa comes to be used as another letter in such a systematised orthography. It is only with understanding of later levels of representation that they can see it as a symbol of transcription, whose interpretation varies depending on the level of the transcription. Much uncertainty and many misunderstandings about schwa ensue (see, for example, the extended discussion on the Linguist List, http://www.linguistlist.org, Issue 11.499 and following).

APPLICATION IN SECOND LANGUAGE PRONUNCIATION TEACHING

We mentioned at the beginning the close link that has existed between theory and application in phonetics generally—seen, for example, in the way that observations from practical applications in speech technology have fed back into theory development.

One area in which this close link has *not* existed is pronunciation teaching. There has been little communication between academic phonetics and phonology on the one hand, and pronunciation teaching on the other, and in what communication there has been, the flow of information is generally one way—from theory to application rather than vice versa. Note that I am talking here about the actual practice of teaching and teacher education, as opposed to the use of data from second language speakers as input to theory development, which is discussed further later.

To the extent that knowledge from academic phonetics and phonology has been made available to language teachers and teacher educators (Pennington, 1996; Roach, 1991; Yallop, 1995), it has been in highly simplified form—mainly restricted to providing very basic information about English phonetics and phonology, usually taking readers only to the level of systematised orthography in the hierarchy outlined earlier, and discussing only English. This is understandable on the grounds, well-evidenced, that teachers are impatient with more detailed and complex information for which they have trouble seeing the direct relevance to their classroom work.

The issue is in the last clause. Existing theories, as we have seen, are based on computational models which, by their nature (I have argued), have little application in contexts involving work with humans. Their inadequacies in this area have left the field wide open to exploitation by multimedia programmers or professional development providers with grossly inadequate understanding of phonetics and psycholinguistics.

The result has been that, until recently, and always with honourable exceptions (see Fraser, 2000), pronunciation has often not been taught at all, or been taught very badly (Celce–Murcia, Brinton, & Goodwin, 1996) in English language courses. Many students finish their course with good knowledge of English grammar and vocabulary but very poor ability to make themselves understood. This, coupled with prejudice or lack of familiarity with foreign accents (Lippi–Green, 1997), is very bad for intercultural communication.

The situation is often blamed on the Critical Age Hypothesis. However, the fact that language learning begins after puberty means only that the learner is likely to need explicit tuition in pronunciation, and is likely to retain a foreign accent—not that they cannot learn to speak intelligibly (Derwing, Munro, & Wiebe, 1998). Perhaps a better explanation is that many existing theories of second language pronunciation really are not relevant to the classroom, as teachers suspect.

Theorising Second Language Pronunciation (SLP)

We argued earlier that theories of phonetics, phonology, and psycholinguistics need to distinguish carefully the representations of speech made by linguists and those available to ordinary people. In language teaching contexts, the theoretical situation is even more complex, with not two but three quite different points of view involved in creating and interpreting representations of speech—those of the linguist, the teacher, and the learner (Mohanan, 1992).

Many theories of second language pronunciation are really contributions to general phonology using data from second language pronunciation (Archibald, 2000). This is valuable in itself but has little to say about the process of acquiring second language pronunciation. For example, many seek to specify processes that relate the phonology of the target language to the learner's speech. This obviously cannot be how the learning really works—for the same reason as showing a derivational relationship between adult phonology and child phonology cannot really explain children's acquisition: to do so presupposes the child has some underlying knowledge of the adult phonology.

A common way of theorising processes of acquisition is through the concept of 'transfer,' in which aspects of the learner's first language phonology are 'transferred' to their pronunciation of the target language. This is useful for basic prediction of characteristics of learners' pronunciation, but cannot be the actual process of learning a language. After all, acquisition of pronunciation is not a direct relationship between two phonologies, but a change in a person's behaviour, driven by a change in their conceptualisation of speech.

The idea of transfer is more useful if it is recalled that what is transferred is not phonemes, or phonological processes, but habits of conceptualisation of 'raw speech' (Gass & Selinker, 1993). What people need to do when they learn pronunciation is form new phonological concepts, and learn to apply them habitually, skilfully, and subconsciously in interpreting the 'raw speech' of the new language. Their activity in doing this is seen in some well-known but counterintuitive observations. Consider, for example, the observation that the sounds of the target language that are most difficult for learners are not generally those which are most different from those of their first language, but rather those which are quite similar— enough so as to be confusable (Flege, 1987). However, this notion of similarity is difficult to define purely phonetically (Major, 1998), and requires reference to the viewpoint of the learner rather than that of the linguist (Markham, 1996).

This view of pronunciation learning as a cognitive process of concept formation and skill development has a range of advantages in relation to the practicalities of teaching pronunciation.

Teaching Pronunciation

I have claimed that adults can learn pronunciation if it is taught effectively (see also Derwing et al., 1998). Let us consider now what this involves. It is useful to start by looking at some methods that don't work well, to analyse the reasons for their failure in light of the discussion so far. I should say at the outset that I am not denying that elements of these methods can be usefully incorporated into tuition, or that they can be effective for particular kinds of students. Rather, I am suggesting that it is not optimal for most teaching to let them form the main focus of work on pronunciation.

We know that giving information about English phonology or the physical articulation of sounds (even if this information is accurate) does not work well. First, this kind of information requires a certain level of proficiency in English for its comprehension (so it can be useful to advanced learners). More importantly, it does not affect the subconscious concepts which drive pronunciation, as evidenced by the many learners of English who can cite facts about English phonetics and phonology—in pronunciation that is very hard to understand.

We also know that simply providing auditory input, for example, through tapes and videos, or exposure to native speakers, does not work. It is too passive and does not engage the concept-formation parts of consciousness.

So what does work? Recall that speech behaviour, like all behaviour, is driven by subconscious concepts. To change behaviour we must influence those subconscious concepts. This involves getting 'behind' all the various representations of speech. The learner must create new concepts, not manipulate representations of old concepts, and the teacher's role is to facilitate this.

Pronunciation, on this view, is a cognitive skill. It requires a lot of practice. It also requires information. For most adult learners, this information is difficult to pick up spontaneously by listening alone (although some can learn in this way) but requires explicit instruction. What form should this instruction take? A full answer to this question is still a long way off, but a few points can be made briefly here (see Fraser, 2001a, 2001b, for further detail and justification). First, it is essential to pay considerable attention to the meta-linguistic communication between teacher and learner, to make sure that the information being imparted by the teacher is accessible and usable to the learner. Thus, it is no good telling a learner that they have stressed the wrong syllable in a word if they do not yet fully understand the concept of stress.

An important element of this communication is visual representation of the speech, enabling a 'multimedia' (not necessarily computer-based) approach to the concepts the learner needs to acquire. In general, continuous representations of speech (such as raw pitch traces) seem not to be as useful as discrete ones for this purpose. Work in progress is exploring the value of using English orthography as the basis of this type of visual representation.

Second, it is essential to spend considerable time training learners' listening. This is not the usual 'listening for meaning' but 'critical listening' to the details of pronunciation, in an extension of the successful programme of 'focus on form' (Doughty & Williams, 1998) into the area of pronunciation. Several studies (Strange, 1995) have shown a benefit to production from training perception. I suggest—and work in progress seeks to demonstrate this empirically—that what is called perception here is really conception, and that more attention to the needs of concept formation allows us to develop more effective listening-based training—valuable in itself and also because it is something that learners can do alone with computer-based materials.

Teacher Education

Let us consider now, finally, the training that language teachers need to teach pronunciation effectively according to the principles just outlined. Currently, pronunciation is being brought back into TESOL courses after a long absence (Celce–Murcia et al., 1996), and there are many innovative programs. In general, however, pronunciation is covered by giving trainee teachers a very basic account of the

English phoneme system, and an even more basic account of its word and sentence prosody.

Is this the best way to ask trainee teachers to spend the limited time they have for pronunciation? Its effect is to move them through to the 'systematised orthography' level of understanding in terms of the hierarchy proposed earlier. At this level, they retain the natural nonlinguists' understanding of speech and speech processing. They still have a strong sense of the 'reality' of their own representation of English phonology; in fact, it will be reinforced by their tuition (which often enough encourages them to call phonemic representation 'phonetics').

As a consequence, they are likely to retain Natural Attitude ideas about how to teach pronunciation (i.e., by giving learners information about English sounds and their production). They are likely to prefer a curriculum that moves through the main categories of English phonology in an orderly progression, giving information about its long and short vowels, its stops, fricatives, and other consonants, its sentence prosody. As they implement this type of curriculum and find it doesn't work well, they come to believe that pronunciation can't be taught and leave it out of their classes (Macdonald, 2002). The errors learners make will confuse them ('my students don't seem to be able to hear the phonemes properly').

Surely it is better in the limited time available to try to move teachers quickly through the levels of representation encouraging them to critique, not reinforce, their natural attitude beliefs, and providing them with a good general understanding of the task their students face in learning pronunciation, and a strong sense of what they need to do to facilitate this learning.

This will encourage them to choose a curriculum which teaches first what the learners most need to be able to say, and to work most on aspects of pronunciation which most affect the average native listener's comprehension. More importantly, it will encourage them to observe and learn from their learners' speech behaviour, rather than finding it baffling, and to adapt exercises in textbooks to what their own students are capable of. For example, many textbooks, in teaching word stress, take the apparently logical progression of asking learners to count syllables before identifying stressed syllables. Teachers need the skill and confidence to recognise that, in fact, for many learners, it is much harder to do the former than the latter, and to reverse this strategy in appropriate circumstances.

CONCLUSION

There is no doubt that much remains to be done in developing both the theory and the practice of using representations of speech in ways appropriate to the context and the users. It is an interesting reversal of the relationship that has existed between linguistics and applied linguistics for several decades, offering an opportunity to 'theorise what works in practice' rather than 'applying what works in theory' (c.f. Davies, 1999).

I like to think it is also an extension of the theoretical principles that John Laver used in developing his theoretical foundation for General Phonetic Theory, and his long-standing interest in theoretical and practical issues of phonetic representation—in light of his strongly held view that phonetics should always remain an interdisciplinary science.

REFERENCES

Anderson, S. (1985). *Phonology in the twentieth century: Theories of rules and theories of representation.* Chicago: University of Chicago Press.

Anderson, S. (1999). *The nature of phonetic representation.* Talk given at Keio University March 4, 1999. Retrieved from http://bloch.ling.yale.edu/recentPapers.html.

Archibald, J. (Ed). (2000). *Second language acquisition and linguistic theory.* Oxford, England: Benjamins.

Bauer, L. (1988). What is lenition? *Journal of Linguistics, 24,* 381–392.

Blair, D. (Ed). (1987). *My First Macquarie dictionary.* Brisbane, Australia: Jacaranda.

Byrne, B. (1998). *The foundation of literacy: The child's acquisition of the alphabetic principle.* Hove, England: Psychology Press.

Carello, C., Turvey, M. T., Kugler, P. N., & Shaw, R. E. (1984). Inadequacies of the computer metaphor. In M. S. Gazzaniga (Ed.), *Handbook of Cognitive Neuroscience* (pp. 229–248). New York: Plenum.

Celce–Murcia, M., Brinton, D., & Goodwin, J. (1996). *Teaching pronunciation: A reference for teachers of English to speakers of other languages.* Cambridge, England: Cambridge University Press.

Chomsky, N., & Halle, M. (1968). *The sound pattern of English.* New York: Harper & Row.

Cooper, F. S. (1950). Research on reading machines for the blind. In P. A. Zahl (Ed.), *Blindness: Modern approaches to the unseen environment* (pp. 512–543). Princeton, NJ: Princeton University Press.

Davies, A. (1999). *An introduction to applied linguistics: From practice to theory.* Edinburgh, Scotland: Edinburgh University Press.

DeFrancis, J. (1989). *Visible speech: The diverse oneness of writing systems.* Honolulu: University of Hawaii Press.

Derwing, B. (1992). Orthographic aspects of linguistic competence. In P. Downing, S. Lima, and M. Noonan (Eds.), *The linguistics of literacy* (pp. 193–210). Amsterdam: Benjamins.

Derwing, T., Munro, M., & Wiebe, G. (1998). Evidence in favour of a broad framework for pronunciation instruction. *Language Learning, 48,* 393–410.

de Saussure, F. (1983). *Course in general linguistics* (R. Harris, Trans.). London: Duckworth (Original work published 1916).

Doughty, C., & Williams, J. (1998). *Focus on form in classroom second language acquisition.* Cambridge, England: Cambridge University Press.

Flege, J. (1987). The production of "new" and "similar" phones in a foreign language: Evidence for the effect of equivalence classification. *Journal of Phonetics, 15,* 47–65.

Fowler, C. A. (1986). An event approach to the study of speech perception from a direct-realist perspective. *Journal of Phonetics, 14,* 3-28.

Fraser, H. (1992). *The subject of speech perception: An analysis of the philosophical foundations of the information-processing model of cognition.* London: Macmillan.

Fraser, H. (1997a). Dictionary pronunciation guides for English. *International Journal of Lexicography, 10,* 181–208.

Fraser, H. (1999). Pronunciation spellings. In J. Lambert, S. Butler, & A. Moore (Eds.), *Macquarie bad speller's friend: A guide to correct spelling.* Sydney, Australia: The Macquarie Library.

Fraser, H. (2000). *Coordinating improvements in pronunciation teaching for adult learners of English as a second language.* Canberra, Australia: Department of Education, Training, and Youth Affairs.

Fraser, H. (2001a). Teaching Pronunciation: A Guide for Teachers of English as a Second Language [Computer software]. Canberra, Australia: Department of Education, Training, and Youth Affairs.

Fraser, H. (2001b). *Teaching pronunciation: A handbook for teachers and trainers.* Canberra, Australia: Department of Education, Training, and Youth Affairs.

Fraser, H. (2004). Constraining abstractness: Phonological representation in the light of color terms. *Cognitive Linguistics, 15*(3), 293–288.

Gass, S. M., & Selinker, L. (Eds.). (1993). *Language transfer in language learning.* Amsterdam: Benjamins.

Gombert, J.-E. (1992). *Metalinguistic development.* Hemel Hempstead, London: Harvester.

Gough, P., Ehri, L., & Treiman, R. (Eds.). (1992). *Reading acquisition.* Hillsdale, NJ: Lawrence Erlbaum Associates, Inc.

Harris, R., & Taylor, T. J. (1989). *Landmarks in linguistic thought: The Western tradition from Socrates to Saussure.* London: Routledge.

Jaeger, J. (1986). Concept formation as a tool of linguistic research. In J. Ohala & J. Jaeger (Eds.), *Experimental phonology* (pp. 211–237). Orlando: Academic.

Jegtheesh, N. (1981). *Learn Tamil in 30 days.* Madras, Tamil Nadu, India: Balaji Publications.

Judge, B. (1985). *Thinking about things: A philosophical study of representation.* Edinburgh, Scotland: Scottish Academic Press.

Keating, P. A. (1983). Phonetic and phonological representation of stop consonant voicing. *University of California at Los Angeles, Working Papers in Phonetics, 57,* 26–60.

Kenstowicz, M. (1994). *Phonology in generative grammar.* Cambridge, England: Blackwell.

Laver, J. (1994). *Principles of phonetics.* Cambridge, England: Cambridge University Press.

Lepore, E., & Pylyshyn, Z. (Eds.). (1999). *What is cognitive science?* Malden, MA: Blackwell.

Linell, P. (1988). The impact of literacy on the conception of language: The case of linguistics. In R. Saljo (Ed.), *The written world: Studies in literate thought and action* (pp. 41–58). Berlin, Germany: Springer–Verlag.

Lippi–Green, R. (1997). *English with an accent: Language, ideology and discrimination in the United States.* London: Routledge.

Macdonald, S. (2002). Pronunciation: Views and practices of reluctant teachers. *Prospect, 17,* 3–15.

Magee, B. (1987). *The great philosophers.* London: BBC Books.

Major, R. (1998). Interlanguage phonetics and phonology: An introduction. *Studies in Second Language Acquisition, 20,* 131–137.

Margolis, H. (1987). *Patterns, thinking and cognition: A theory of judgment.* Chicago: University of Chicago Press.

Markham, D. (1996). Similarity and newness—Workable concepts in describing phonetic categorisation? In P. E. McCormack & A. Russell (Eds.), *Sixth Australian International Conference on Speech Science and Technology* (pp. 497–502). Canberra, Australia: Australian Speech Science and Technology Association.

Mohanan, K. P. (1992). Describing the phonology of non-native varieties of a language. *World Englishes, 11,* 111–128.

Nathan, G. (1996). Steps towards a cognitive phonology. In B. Hurch & R. Rhodes (Eds.), *Natural phonology: The state of the art* (pp. 107–120). Berlin, Germany: Mouton.

Neisser, U. (Ed.). (1987). *Concepts and conceptual development: Ecological and intellectual factors in categorisation.* New York: Cambridge University Press.

Nisbet, B. (1994). *The representation of pronunciation in English native-speaker dictionaries.* Unpublished Master of Arts in Applied Linguistics thesis, Macquarie University, Sydney, Australia.

Nolan, F. (1990). Who do phoneticians represent? *Journal of Phonetics, 18,* 453–464.

Ohala, J. (1986a). Consumer's guide to evidence in phonology. *Phonology Yearbook, 3,* 3–26.

Ohala, J. (1986b). Phonological evidence for top-down processing in speech perception. In J. Perkell & D. Klatt (Eds.), *Invariance and variability in speech processes* (pp. 386–401). Hillsdale, NJ: Lawrence Erlbaum Associates, Inc.

Ohala, J. & Jaeger, J. (Eds.). (1986). *Experimental phonology.* New York: Academic.

Ohala, J. J. (1990). The phonetics and phonology of aspects of assimilation. In J. Kingston and M. E. Beckman (Eds.), *Papers in laboratory phonology I: Between the grammar and physics of speech* (pp. 258–275). Cambridge, England: Cambridge University Press.

Olson, D. (1994). *The world on paper: The conceptual and cognitive implications of writing and reading.* Cambridge, England: Cambridge University Press.

Olson, D. (1996). Language and literacy: What writing does to language and mind. *Annual Review of Applied Linguistics, 16,* 3–13.

Palmer, F. R. (1976). *Semantics: a new outline.* Cambridge, England: Cambridge University Press.

Passmore, J. (1968). *A hundred years of philosophy.* Harmondsworth: Pelican.

Pennington, M. (1996). *Phonology in English language teaching.* Essex: Addison-Wesley Longman.

Perkell, J., & Klatt, D. (Eds.). (1986). *Invariance and variability in speech processes.* Hillsdale, NJ: Lawrence Erlbaum Associates, Inc.

Pierrehumbert, J. (1990). Phonological and phonetic representation. *Journal of Phonetics, 18,* 375–394.

Pylyshyn, Z. (1983). Representation, computation and cognition. In F. Machlup and V. Mansfield (Eds.), *The study of information: Interdisciplinary messages* (pp. 115–118). New York: Wiley–Interscience.

Rischel, J. (1990). What is phonetic representation? *Journal of Phonetics, 18,* 395–410.

Roach, P. (1991). *English phonetics and phonology: A practical course* 2nd, ed. Cambridge, England: Cambridge University Press.

Rumelhart, D. E., & McClelland, J. L. (Eds.). (1986). *Parallel distributed processing: Explorations in the microstructures of cognition.* Cambridge, MA: MIT Press.

Sarup, M. (1988). *An introductory guide to post-structuralism and postmodernism.* New York: Harvester.

Scarborough, H. S., Ehri, L. C., Olson, R. K., & Fowler, A. E. (1998). The fate of phonemic awareness beyond the elementary school years. *Scientific Studies of Reading, 2,* 115–142.

Schachter, J. (1993). A new account of language transfer. In S. M. Gass & L. Selinker (Eds.), *Language transfer in language learning* (pp. 32–46). Amsterdam: Benjamins.

Seuren, P. A. (1998). *Western linguistics: An historical introduction.* Oxford, England: Blackwell.

Shanon, B. (1993). *The representational and the presentational: An essay on cognition and the study of mind.* New York: Harvester.

Shockey, L. (2003). *Sound patterns of spoken English.* Oxford, England: Blackwell.

Stewart, J. (Ed.). (1996). *Beyond the symbol model: Reflections on the representational nature of language.* Albany: State University of New York Press.

Strange, W. (Ed.). (1995). *Speech perception and linguistic experience: Issues in cross-language research.* Baltimore, MD: York Press.

Taylor, J. R. (1989). *Linguistic categorisation: Prototypes in linguistic theory.* Oxford, England: Clarendon.

Vihman, M. (1996). *Phonological development.* Oxford, England: Basil Blackwell.

Yallop, C. (1995). *English phonology.* Sydney, Australia: National Centre for English Language Teaching and Research.

Chapter 6

A Cognitive-Motor Syllable Frame for Speech Production

Evidence From Neuropathology

Peter F. MacNeilage and Barbara L. Davis
University of Texas at Austin

Phonetics is the study of the nature of speech. In the past few years, there has been increasing interest in the most fundamental question regarding the nature of speech: the question of how it evolved. Recent work in this area can be found in a series of three volumes based on biennial international conferences on the evolution of language (Hurford, Studdert–Kennedy, & Knight, 1998; Knight & Hurford, 2000; Wray, 2002). The most comprehensive present view of the evolution of speech *production* is contained in the Frame and Content theory (e.g., MacNeilage, 1998; MacNeilage & Davis, 1990; MacNeilage & Davis, 2000; MacNeilage, Studdert–Kennedy, & Lindblom, 1985). This theory involves an attempt to integrate evidence from speech phylogeny, speech ontogeny, and the neuro-biology of speech. In this chapter we summarize phylogenetic and ontogenetic aspects of this theory and focus on evidence from neuropathology that is crucial to a central tenet of the theory, namely that a cognitive–motor syllable frame has evolved as part of the inter-face between cognitive and motor levels of speech production.

THE FRAME AND CONTENT THEORY
OF THE EVOLUTION OF SPEECH PRODUCTION

The focus of the Frame and Content theory is on the evolution of the syllable and its internal organization, as the syllable lies at the core of speech production. The theory takes as its point of departure one of the main conclusions of modern psycholinguistic research: "Probably the most fundamental insight from modern speech error research is that the word's skeleton or frame and its segmental content are inde-pendently generated" (Levelt, 1992, p. 10). This conclusion is based on the presence of a syllable structure (frame) constraint on the mis-placement of segments (content) in otherwise correct utterances. The most general of these constraints is that consonants can never be put in a position in a syllable which was intended for a vowel (the syl-lable nucleus) and vowels can never be put into a position intended for consonants (syllable margins). For example, "no" is never pro-nounced as "own," or "abstract" as "bastract." This conclusion is the basis for our view that the main target for a theory of evolution of speech should be the phenomenon of *programmable syllable frames* in modern adult speech production.

What is the phylogenetic basis for this most central property of modern speech organization? The primary basis for the distinction between consonants and vowels at the level of *action* is amount of mouth opening. In the context of speech utterances, the mouth usually makes a closing movement for consonants and an opening movement for vowels. Our view is that because these *movements*—primarily movements of the mandible—are in opposite directions, and always have been, there has never been an opportunity for their neural accompaniments to get interchanged in the time domain. In other words, the movement pattern for the conso-nant–vowel alternation has been responsible for the mutual exclusiveness in the placement of consonants and vowels into a syllable frame structure in the premovement programming stage.

We suggest that the close–open cycle of the mandible provided an initial *Motor* Frame for speech; that is, the original form was just a movement cycle. As to the origin of the capacity for repeated close–open mouth alternations, and its basis in mandibular oscillation, we suggest that it may have initially evolved in the context of mammalian ingestive processes—chewing, sucking, and licking (MacNeilage, 1998). Then there may have been an intermediate visuofacial communicative stage, in the form of lipsmacks, tongue-smacks, and teeth chatters, before this close–open cycle was paired with phonation to form the basis for syllable production.

Why would the ontogeny of speech be relevant to its phylogeny? One highly relevant property of babbling and early speech is that both stages are dominated by the consonant vowel (CV) syllabic form, whether occurring monosyllabically or in multisyllabic strings. In addition, this CV syllable form is the only universal syllable form (Bell & Hooper, 1978) as well as probably being the dominant syllabic form in most languages (Maddieson, 1999). The fact that speech-like behaviour of infants *begins* with the CV form as the predominant form, whether or not this form is the main form in the language to which the infant is exposed, suggested to us that infant babbling and early speech may provide a window into the structure of the first words of hominids.

Our work on speech acquisition (e.g., Davis & MacNeilage, 1995; Davis, MacNeilage, & Matyear, 2002) has shown that babbling and early speech are subject to Frame Dominance, in that most of the variance in these early utterances is a result of mandibular oscillation, and the utterances are otherwise highly subject to biomechanical constraints. For example, within syllables, there are three co-occurrence constraints on consonants and following vowels: Coronal consonants tend to co-occur with front vowels, dorsal consonants with back vowels, and labial consonants with central vowels (MacNeilage & Davis, 2000). In all three cases, there is a relative lack of tongue movement between consonant and vowel. In addition, in multisyllabic utterances, particular CV forms tend strongly to be reduplicated (repeated), indicating a lack of change in articulators other than the mandible from one syllable to the next, as well as from one segment to the next.

We have also found that these three CV co-occurrence patterns are typical in a study of 10 languages (MacNeilage, Davis, Kinney, &

Matyear, 2000). This suggests that not only the CV syllable of bab-bling and early speech, but also aspects of its internal structure, are fundamental to speech, and may therefore have been basic to the evolution of the first words (MacNeilage & Davis, 2000).

The CV alternation is the dominant vocalization form from the beginning of babbling. It is also the dominant form in early word pro-duction, and this often remains so for years. It is well known, for example, that infants often have persistent problems in producing word-final consonants or consonant clusters. In addition, we have recently found that the first two-segment consonant clusters pro-duced by infants in an English-speaking environment have a much stronger tendency to be homorganic than do two-element clusters in the language in general, suggesting that they are produced by modu-lations of a single closing phase rather than involving two successive closures by different articulators (heterorganic; Jakielski, Davis, & MacNeilage, 2004).

Perhaps word-initial vowels and word-final consonants are better regarded as additions to the basic close–open cycle rather than devel-opments beyond it. Initial vowels involve adding an initial open phase, and final consonants involve adding a final closing phase to the basic CV form. In other words, the basic cycle is elaborated to include beginning and ending with a different phase than was favoured ini-tially. The fact that when final consonants develop in CVC forms they usually have the same place of articulation as the initial consonant suggests this possibility. Similarly, homorganic consonant clusters can be regarded as minor internal modifications of a single closing phase and heterorganic clusters can be regarded as a more major modifica-tion of a single closing phase.

In this view, the close–open alternation remains the canonical syl-lable-related form throughout life, even in speakers of languages like English in which phonological organization goes well beyond the usual predominance of the CV syllable. If so, it would stand to reason that this close–open cyclicity would become represented in some way in the planning stage of production. In our opinion, this repre-sentation plays an important role in the syllable structure or frame constraint that infants eventually develop as they become adults, capable of segmental serial ordering errors. There is, in fact, a good deal of evidence for the existence of a CV cyclicity at the representa-tional level in human neuropathology and it is to that evidence that we now turn.

BRAIN ORGANIZATION FOR THE FRAME AND CONTENT MODE

In higher primates, two subsystems cooperate in the control of movement in general (e.g., Goldberg, 1995). One is an "intrinsic" system, primarily involved in self-generated behaviour. The main substrate for this system is the medial cortex of the Supplementary Motor Area (SMA). It receives extensive input from the prefrontal cortex and forms a control loop with the basal ganglia. As Gazzaniga, Ivry, and Mangun (2000) put it, "Due to their anatomical connections, these areas are in a position of allowing limbic structures to convey information related to the animal's current motivational state and internal goals" (p. 397). The other system is an "extrinsic" system. It involves Ventral Premotor Cortex (VPM), which consists, in humans, of Brodmann's area 6, and area 44, the latter being part of Broca's Area. VPM receives input from posterior cortical centres concerned with vision and audition, and also from the cerebellum, which is thought to be important in timing of movements. This system plays a role in the imitation of speech.

The different roles of the two systems are illustrated by results of experiments on monkeys (Gazzaniga et al., 2000). Damage to the SMA disrupts monkeys' ability to perform learned sequences of movement, in the absence of an external cue to the required sequence, (i.e., when the sequence is internally generated) but not when such cues are present. Contrarily, VPM lesions affect the ability to perform such tasks in the presence of external cues, but not in their absence.

Evidence for the importance of the SMA in spontaneous movement generation in humans comes from the lack of movement in general (akinesia), including an initial mutism, that follows SMA damage. A clinical observation reported by Jasper (1995) nicely shows that a normal role of the SMA is the internal generation of movements:

> Following excision of the SMA ... with Dr Bertrand, we observed a very curious effect. There was no obvious defect in testing motor function following the removal but the patient found that in the morning when he got up and read the newspaper while drinking his coffee for breakfast, he could no longer automatically drink his coffee and read the paper. He had to change and watch his hand moving from the coffee to his mouth and take his eyes off the paper, otherwise he would spill the coffee. So somehow or other, sequences of motor functions which are performed automatically were disrupted by this supplementary motor excision. (p. 270)

We have argued that in modern humans the intrinsic system is primarily responsible for the generation of frames whereas the extrinsic system is primarily concerned with segmental content (MacNeilage, 1998; MacNeilage & Davis, 2001). The role of the VPM in the control of segmental content is indicated by the phenomenon of Apraxia of Speech (Ziegler, 2002). Damage to the VPM, also including the insula, results in an impairment of the programming of individual speech sounds. From the standpoint of the Frame and Content theory, the involvement of this region in speech is to be expected, as the VPM is the main cortical region for the control of ingestive processes in mammals (Woolsey, 1951). However, although the initial involvement of the motor frame in speech might have occurred via VPM, as an adaptation from ingestive cyclicities, there is evidence that in modern humans, the frame for speech is primarily controlled by the SMA.

One of the most surprising findings of the era of brain imaging has been the important role of the SMA in movement control. It is considered to play a higher order role in the generation of movement. It has been shown, for example, that merely thinking about movements leads to activation of the SMA, typically without activation of the VPM (Roland, 1993). It has also been implicated in the initiation of movement. For example, the SMA is an important component of a medially located Bereitschaftpotential, a negative potential which is initiated several hundred millisec before the beginning of a movement (Roland, 1993). In addition, as mentioned earlier, in many studies of damage to the SMA, patients display an initial mutism and akinesia (Ziegler, Kilian, and Deger, 1997). In a meta-analysis of 45 imaging studies of word production, Indefrey and Levelt (2000) conclude that "the SMA is in some complex way related to motor planning and imagination of articulation" (p. 8).

But what is the role of the SMA in motor planning for spontaneous speech in particular? Evidence that the SMA is involved in frame generation for speech comes from a number of sources which we now consider. Brickner (1940) was the first to report evoking rhythmic repetitive vocalization from electrical stimulation of the SMA, before the area was even formally named. This property of the area "was discovered accidentally during routine exploration. The patient suddenly uttered syllables resembling 'err, err, err', in what seemed a stereotyped manner" (Brickner, 1940, p. 128). Since his study, there have been numerous other reports of this phenomenon. Some of these reports are summarized in Table 6.1.

Although specific findings varied, the theme of repetition of a nonmeaningful speech form in a rhythmic manner continually recurs. The most common phonetic description is of a series of consonant–vowel syllables, typically repetitions of the same syllable. This particular phenomenon has not been observed in studies of stimulation in any other part of the brain. In contrast, stimulation of Broca's area results in interference with or suppression of ongoing speech, but not in evocation of phonetically well-formed utterances, either meaningful or nonmeaningful (Ojemann, 1983).

TABLE 6.1

Electrical Stimulation Effects on the Supplementary Motor Area

Summary of case material

	Patient	Utterance/s
Brickner, 1940	(only)	"Err, err, err"[1]
Erikson and Woolsey, 1951	G. W.	"Rapid repetitive vocalization … with "T" sound as a component"
Penfield and Welch, 1951	K. H.	"Da da da da;" "repeated a vocal sound"
	H. R.	Rhythmic vocalization (four instances)
	L. R.	"Vocalize(d) in a rhythmic manner"[2]
Penfield and Jasper, 1954	(Summary)	"Vocalization … rhythmic or interrupted (and) at times resembles … kata, kata, or wata, wata"
Lim et al., 1994	4	"Vocalization … usually associated with rhythmic movements involving both sides of the jaw and mouth"

[1]Brickner's patient also perseverated on whatever letter of the alphabet was being spoken when electrical stimulation was turned on.

[2]Penfield and Welch (1951) noted that overall, "Vocalization was produced 15 times in seven patients … The most characteristic response was a rhythmic or intermittent sound, but instantaneous exclamation, continuous prolongation of a vowel sound, and the repetition of a word or of a meaningless syllable or combination of syllables, have been observed as well."

A similar phenomenon has repeatedly been observed in patients with irritative lesions affecting the SMA. An example would be an adjacent tumour exerting pressure on SMA tissue. A clinical description by Jonas (1981) gives the flavour of the phenomenon:

> A 37 year-old lady ... suddenly found herself saying "la, la, la, la", at 6:05 P.M. on 2/19/79. This preceded a seizure in which she became unconscious. On 2/24/79 she had a spell during which she said "da, da, da, da"; she neither could stop making this sound nor could she speak. There were some other motor signs of a seizure. The phenomena subsided in 7 or 8 minutes. (Jonas, Case 3, p. 355)

This patient proved to have a meningioma lying against the SMA. Jonas (1981) described 12 patients in this category: 11 in five other studies, and the one he studied (see Table 6.2.).

The similarity between these irritative lesion effects and the electrical stimulation effects is quite striking, as was noted by some of the other researchers (see footnotes to Table 6.2). The highly specific and speech-like nature of these phenomena suggests that they are not examples of artificially evoked disorganization of function, but examples of release of a function normally used in speech but not normally revealed independently of meaningful speech acts in adults. We believe that Penfield and Welch (1951) exhibited considerable prescience in remarking, with regard to the electrical stimulation findings, that "these mechanisms, which we have activated by gross artificial stimuli, may, however, under different conditions, be important in the production of the varied sounds which men often use to communicate ideas" (p. 303).

Ziegler et al. (1997) have made the most comprehensive study of the speech of a patient with problems involving the SMA. They showed, in a word repetition task, that onset latencies increased as the number of syllables in the word increased, but the patient showed no effect of the complexity of the syllables involved. Their conclusion that the SMA is involved in "downloading temporarily stored multisyllabic strings" is consistent with our claim that the SMA is involved in frame generation.

When the thesis that the SMA was responsible for frame generation was first presented (MacNeilage, 1998), three reviewers responded with the contention that both frames and content are mediated primarily by ventral premotor cortex (Abbs & de Paul, 1998; Jürgens, 1998; Lund, 1998). None of these reviewers dealt

TABLE 6.2

Irritative Lesion Effects on the Supplementary Motor Area: Summary of Case Material on 12 Patients Reviewed by Jonas, 1981

Study	Patient	Utterance/s
1. Jonas, 1981	No. 3	"la, la, la, la" "da, da, da, da, …"
2. Erikson and Woolsey, 1951	D. K.	(see notes below)[a]
3. Patient described in discussion of E & W paper by Sweet		"I, I, I, I, I, I, I"
4. Arseni and Botez, 1959	No. 2	"verbal repetition"[b]
5.	No. 8	"verbal repetition"[b]
6.	No. 11	"verbal repetition"[b]
7.	No. 12	"verbal repetition"[b]
8. Alajouanine, Castaigne, Sabourauch, and Contamin, 1959	No. 2 F. F.	"tati, tati, tati, tati … "[c]
9.	No. 3	"ah-ah-ah-ah-ah-ah-ah-ah"
10.	No. 4	"oh-oh-oh"
11. Botez and Wertheim, 1959	D. M.	uncontrolled repetitive vocalizations
12. Petit–Dutaillis, Guiot, Messimy, and Bourdillon, 1954	M. L.	"seizures of verbal repetition"

[a]Patient No. 2.—Intermittent vocalization reminiscent of that produced in other patients by stimulation of the Supplementary Motor Area.
[b]Arseni and Botez (1961) defined "verbal repetition" as "the exact counterpart of what is induced by electric stimulation of the supplementary motor area" (p. 233).
[c]Note also that Alajouanine et al.'s (1959) patient No. 1 was classified by Jonas as producing "paroxysmal rhythmic repetition of a brief phrase"—"oui, oui, oui, oui, oui, oui" repeated about 20 or 30 times.

with the evidence from electrical stimulation studies and irritative lesion studies of the SMA summarized earlier. They also did not provide any evidence for their alternative conception. However, another group of reviewers did produce evidence that patients can generate frames even when Broca's area has been destroyed. Abry and coauthors (Abry, Boe, Laboissière, & Schwartz, 1998; Abry, Stefanuto, Villain, & Laboissière, 2002) called attention to a subclass of global aphasics who produce speech automatisms called 'non-meaningful recurrent utterances' (NMRUs; Blanken, Wallesch, & Papagano, 1990). Like babbled utterances and the involuntary utterances of patients subject to electrical stimulation or irritative lesions of the SMA, NMRUs characteristically consist of a sequence of the same CV syllable (Blanken et al., 1990; Brunner, Kornhuber, Seemuller, Suger, & Wallesch, 1982; Code, 1982, 1994, 2002; De Bleser & Poeck, 1985; Poeck, De Bleser, & Graf von Keyserlingk, 1984; Wallesch, 1990). As global aphasia typically results from destruction of the entire perisylvian language cortex, Broca's area cannot be involved in these utterances. It is of interest to note that Broca's first patient, Leborgne, suffered from this syndrome. He was nicknamed "Tan" because the only speech he could produce was repetitions of this syllable (Abry et al., 2002). (It is actually a CV syllable because "..an" stands for a nasal vowel in French.)

A relatively large number of specific utterances of these patients have been reported. This data allows a detailed comparison of the structure of these utterances with the structure of infant babbling. Code (1982) has presented 30 examples of utterances produced by 17 English patients. All but two produced only a single form. Blanken et al. (1990) presented utterances from 27 German patients. Table 6.3 shows a comparison of aspects of the structure of these utterances described in these two studies with that of the babbling of six infants (Davis & MacNeilage, 1995). The babbling indexes were derived from databases of over 1,000 syllables per infant.

The babbling and aphasic corpora are remarkably similar. At least three quarters of all syllables were CV syllables in all groups. In addition, when pairs of successive syllables were compared, the two syllables were the same approximately half of the time.

TABLE 6.3

Comparison of the Structure of Babbling (Davis & MacNeilage, 1995) With Multisyllabic Nonmeaningful Recurrent Utterances (NMRUs) of English and German Global Aphasics

	Percentage of Syllables Which Were CV*	Percentage of Second Syllables Which Were Reduplicative
Babbling	86	50%
English Global Aphasics	79	51
German Global Aphasics	75	62

*consonant–vowel

Why do some global aphasics produce NMRUs whereas others do not? Brunner et al. (1982) found that although both subgroups were similar in terms of perisylvian involvement, the group who produced NMRUs also had damage to the basal ganglia. They hypothesized that the basal ganglia damage resulted in a disinhibitory effect on speech, but as perisylvian cortex was unable to supply detailed segmental content, the outcome was these simple stereotyped forms. The implication is that these forms are in some sense present in the normal brain, but do not manifest themselves under ordinary circumstances. The similarity between NMRUs and babbling makes unlikely the alternative suggestion that patients producing NMRUs may have had atypical organization of language in the brain before they incurred the damage (De Bleser & Poeck, 1985). We prefer our conclusion that some fundamental organizational property of speech developing in the context of early speech-like behaviour of infants continues to be present in adults.

The most important recipient of the basal ganglia's contribution to movement is the SMA. Therefore, any disinhibitory effect of basal ganglia damage on movement must have its primary effect on the SMA. In patients with perisylvian and basal ganglia damage, the only remaining region of the brain characteristically involved in the organization of speech production is the SMA. Therefore, the SMA must be primarily responsible for the production of NMRUs. This contention is supported by the similarity of NMRUs to the automatisms produced by electrical stimulation and irritative lesions of the SMA. The NMRUs and the SMA automatisms seem to be instances of the same phenomenon, elicited in the first case by disinhibition, and in the second by tissue perturbations.

CONCLUSION: A COGNITIVE–MOTOR FRAME FOR SPEECH

How can the existence of these speech automatisms be explained? Our conclusion is that the speech automatisms reveal the existence of a component of the mental–motor interface for speech production, and that it evolved and develops from the motor frame in the course of establishing a mental representation for speech. We first reconsider the ontogenetic situation.

In an infant, the motor frame first appears at the onset of canonical babbling, before the infant can produce any meaningful speech. A short time after the infant begins to acquire words (in production, at about 1 year), a general-purpose superstructure for his or her mental representation perhaps begins to crystallize out by means of self-organization. Adult speech errors show us that this mental representation eventually includes independent segmental and syllable structure components. As we said earlier, the close–open alternation is a constant part of the developmental process. Consequently, this movement alternation eventually acquires a separate abstract representational status, somewhat independent of the actual close–open movements for individual words as well as the detailed syllable structure of words. In short, the motor frame spawns a premotor frame. The derivation of this premotor or cognitive frame structure from speech behaviours early in ontogeny allows us to understand why adult patients produce such a childlike form, so superficially unrelated to their premorbid speech behaviour. As befits its intermediate status between detailed movements and abstract mental structures for words, this frame is best described as a cognitive–motor entity. It is cognitive enough to allow elaborate modifications for particular syllables. In English, for example, detailed modifications might involve not one but several consonants (e.g., "*spr*ing"). The ordering of these sounds in syllables is premotor in that it must be laid down before the movements needed to proceed from one segment to the next are computed. However, it is still sufficiently closely related to actual movements to have its own basic rhythmic figure, resulting in a characteristic average cycle time or period, which, when varying as it does across individuals, results in their different basic speaking rates. (See Smith, 2002, on the range of speaking rates in adults.)

We see the phylogenetic derivation of this cognitive–motor frame as being similar to its ontogenetic derivation. We believe the first words were produced with *motor* frames with a predominant CV form (MacNeilage & Davis, 2000). However, as words continued to accumulate, a general-purpose CV superstructure for the mental representation of this action constant must have begun to crystalize out, and the cognitive–motor frame played a role in this as part of the mental–motor interface necessary for producing individual speech events required by various lexical representations. Thus, in both phylogeny and ontogeny, mental structure is considered to derive from regularities in movement patterns, rather than being somehow specified in advance, as typically postulated in generative phonology (Davis et al., 2002).

ACKNOWLEDGMENT

This chapter was prepared with support from research grant No. HD–27733–9 from the Public Health Service.

REFERENCES

Abbs, J. H., & de Paul, R. (1998). Motor cortex fields and speech movements: Simple dual control is implausible. *Behavioral and Brain Sciences 21*, 511–512.

Abry, C., Boe, L.–J., Laboissière, R., & Schwartz, J.–L. (1998). A new puzzle for the evolution of speech. *Behavioral and Brain Sciences, 21*, 512–513.

Abry, C., Stefanuto, M., Villain, A., & Laboissière, R. (2002). What can the utterance "tan, tan" of Broca's patient Leborgne tell us about the hypothesis of an emergent "babble-syllable" downloaded by SMA? In J. Durand & B. Laks (Eds.), *From Phonetics to Cognition* (pp. 432–468). Oxford: Oxford University Press.

Alajouanine, T., Castaigne, P., Sabouraud, O., & Contamin, F. (1959). Palilalie paroxystiqe et vocalizations iteratives au cours de crises epileptiques par lesion interssant l'aire motrice supplementaire. *La Revue Neurologique [The Neurology Review], 101*, 186–202.

Arseni, C., & Botez, M. I. (1959). Speech disturbances caused by tumors of the supplementary motor area. *Acta Psychiatrica Neuroliogica Scandinavia, 36*, 279–298.

Bell, A., & Hooper, J. B. (1978). Issues and evidence in syllabic phonology. In A. Bell & J. B. Hooper (Eds.), *Syllables and segments* (pp. 3–22). Amsterdam: North-Holland.

Blanken, G., Wallesch, C.–W., & Papagno, C. (1990). Dissociations of language functions in aphasics with speech automatisms (recurring utterances). *Cortex, 26*, 41–63.

Botez, M. I., & Wertheim, N. (1959). Expressive aphasia and amusia. *Brain, 82*, 186–202.

Brickner, R. M. (1940). A human cortical area producing repetitive phenomena when stimulated. *Journal of Neurophysiology, 3*, 128–130.

Brunner, R. J., Kornhuber, H. H., Seemuller, E., Suger, G., & Wallesch, C.–W. (1982). Basal ganglia participation in language pathology. *Brain and Language, 16*, 281–299.

Code, C. (1982). Neurolinguistic analysis of recurrent utterance in aphasia. *Cortex, 18*, 141–152.

Code, C. (1994). Speech automatism production in aphasia. *Journal of Neurolinguistics, 8*, 149–156.

Code, C. (2002). Are syllables hard wired? Evidence from brain damage. In R. J. Hartsuiker, R. Bastiaanse, A. Postma, & F. N. K. Wijnen (Eds.), *Phono-

logical encoding and monitoring in normal and pathological speech (pp. 312–331). Hove, Sussex, England: Psychology Press.

Davis, B. L., & MacNeilage, P. F. (1995). The articulatory basis of babbling. *Journal of Speech and Hearing Research, 38,* 1199–1211.

Davis, B. L., MacNeilage, P. F., & Matyear, C. L. (2002). Acquisition of serial complexity in speech production: A comparison of phonological and phonetic approaches to first word production. *Phonetica, 59,* 75–107.

De Bleser, R., & Poeck, K. (1985). Analysis of prosody in the spontaneous speech of patients with CV-recurring utterances. *Cortex, 21,* 405–416.

Erikson, T. C., & Woolsey, C. N. (1951). Observations on the supplementary motor area of man. *Transactions of the American Neurological Association, 76,* 50–52.

Gazzaniga, M. S., Ivry, R. B., & Mangun, G. R. (2000). *Cognitive neuroscience: The biology of mind.* New York: Norton.

Goldberg, G. (1995) Supplementary motor area structure and function: Review and hypothesis. *Behavioral and Brain Sciences, 8,* 567–616.

Hurford, J. R., Studdert–Kennedy, M. G., & Knight, C. (Eds.). (1998). *Approaches to the evolution of language: Social and cognitive bases.* Cambridge, England: Cambridge University Press.

Indefrey, P., & Levelt, W. J. M. (2000). The neural correlates of language production. In M. S. Gazzaniga (Ed.), *The new cognitive neurosciences* (2nd Ed.) (pp. 845–866). Cambridge, MA: Bradford.

Jakielski, K. J., Davis, B. L., & MacNeilage, P. F. (2004). *Place change restrictions in early consonant cluster acquisition.* Manuscript submitted for publication.

Jasper, H. H. (1995). Discussion in H. H. Jasper, S. Riggio, & P. S. Goldman–Rakic (Eds.), *Advances in neurology, volume 66. Epilepsy and the functional anatomy of the frontal lobe* (p. 270). New York: Raven.

Jonas, S. (1981). The supplementary motor area and speech omission. *Journal of Communication Disorders, 14,* 349–373.

Jürgens, U. (1998). Speech evolved from vocalization, not mastication. *Behavioral and Brain Sciences, 21,* 519–520.

Knight, C., & Hurford, J. R. (2000). *The evolutionary emergence of language.* Cambridge, England: Cambridge University Press.

Levelt, W. J. M. (1992). Accessing words in speech production: Stages, processes and representations. *Cognition, 42,* 1–22.

Lim, S. H., Dinner, D. S., Pillay, P. K., Luders, H., Morris, H. H., Klem, G., et al. (1994). Functional anatomy of the human supplementary sensorimotor area: Results of extraoperative electrical stimulation. *Electroencephalograpy and Clinical Neurophysiology, 91,* 179–193.

Lund J. P. (1998). Is speech just chewing the fat? *Behavioral and Brain Sciences, 21,* 522.

MacNeilage, P. F. (1998). The frame/content theory of evolution of speech production. *Behavioral and Brain Sciences, 21,* 499–546.

MacNeilage, P. F., & Davis, B. L. (1990). Acquisition of speech production: Frames, then content. In M. Jeannerod (Ed.), *Attention and performance XIII: Motor representation and control* (pp. 452–468). Hillsdale, NJ: Lawrence Erlbaum Associates, Inc.

MacNeilage, P. F., & Davis, B. L. (2000). On the origin of internal structure of word forms. *Science, 288,* 527–531.

MacNeilage, P. F., & Davis, B. L. (2001). Motor mechanisms in speech ontogeny: Phylogenetic, neurobiological and linguistic implications. *Current Opinion in Neurobiology, 11,* 696–700.

MacNeilage, P. F., Davis, B. L., Kinney, A., & Matyear, C. (2000). The motor core of speech: A comparison of serial organization patterns in infants and languages. *Child Development, 71,* 153–163.

MacNeilage, P. F., Studdert–Kennedy, M. G., & Lindblom, B. (1985). The planning and production of speech. *ASHA Reports, 15,* 15–21.

Maddieson, I. (1999). In search of universals. *Proceedings of the 14th International Congress of Phonetic Sciences, San Francisco, 4,* 2521–2528.

Ojemann, G. (1983). Brain organization for language from the perspective of electrical stimulation mapping. *Behavioral and Brain Sciences, 6,* 189–230.

Penfield, W., & Jasper, H. H. (1954). *Epilepsy and the functional anatomy of the human brain.* New York: Little, Brown.

Penfield, W., & Welch, K. (1951). The supplementary motor area of the cerebral cortex: A clinical and experimental study. *Archives of Neurology and Psychiatry, 66,* 289–317.

Petit–Dutaillis, D., Guiot, G., Messimy, R., & Bourdillon, C. (1954). Apropos d'une aphemie par atteinte de la zone motrice supplementaire de Penfield, au cours de l'evolution d'un anevrisme arterio-veineux. Guerison de l'aphemie par ablation de la lesion [An aphemia following an arteriovenous aneurysm in Penfield's supplementary motor area is alleviated by ablating the lesion.] *La Revue Neurologique [The Neurological Review], 90,* 95–106.

Roland, P. E. (1993). *Brai*Poeck, K., De Bleser, R., & Graf von Keyserlingk, D. (1984). The neurolinguistic status and localization of lesion in aphasic patients with exclusively consonant–vowel (CV) recurrent utterances. *Brain, 107,* 200–217.*n activation.* New York: Wiley–Liss.

Smith, B. (2002). Effects of speaking rate on temporal patterns of English. *Phonetica, 59,* 232–244.

Wallesch, C.–W. (1990). Repetitive verbal behaviour: Functional and neurological considerations. *Aphasiology, 4,* 133–154.

Woolsey, C. N. (1951). Organization of somatic sensory and motor areas of the cerebral cortex. In H. F. Harlow & C. N. Woolsey (Eds.), *Biological and biochemical bases of behavior* (pp. 28–46). Madison: University of Wisconsin Press.

Wray, A. (Ed.). (2002). *The transition to language.* Cambridge, England: Cambridge University Press.

Ziegler, W. (2002). Psycholinguistic and motor theories of apraxia of speech. *Seminars in Speech and Language, 4,* 231–244.

Ziegler, W., Kilian, B., & Deger, K. (1997). The role of left mesial frontal cortex in fluent speech: Evidence from a case of left supplementary motor area hemorrhage. *Neuropsychiatry, 35,* 1197–1208.

PART III

Phonetics
in Social Interaction

Chapter 7

Diphthongs in Colloquial Tamil

R. E. Asher
University of Edinburgh

E. L. Keane
University of Oxford

'Wise men now agree, or ought to agree, in this, that there is but one way to the knowledge of nature's works; the way of observation and experiment.'

—*Thomas Reid (1764, p. 3)*

This chapter analyses one aspect of the difference between formal and informal Tamil. Since the appearance of Ferguson's article on diglossia (1959), Tamil has been seen as one of the clearest representations of the phenomenon (see Britto, 1986). As is common in such situations, the formal, or 'higher,' variety is not only the language of writing but is also used in such contexts as the reading of news bulletins on the radio or television or the delivering of a lecture or a political speech. It is true that in the middle decades of the 20th century, two senior political figures, C. Rajagopalachari (Rajaji) and E. V. Ramaswami Naicker (E.V.R.) normally spoke from the platform in the informal, or 'lower,' variety, but this was very exceptional. For the most part, the nature of the social context determines the choice made by the speaker.

The two varieties are clearly distinct at all levels: phonetic and phonemic, morphological, syntactic, and lexical, and it is possible to tell from even a small fragment of an utterance with which variety one is concerned. That is not to say that features of one variety never intrude into the other (see Asher & Annamalai, 2002, p. 73), but that the intrusive elements will be very limited. Our concern here is principally the phonetic and phonemic, in that we focus on the colloquial equivalent of what in the formal style is a diphthong.

Analyses of the phonology of the formal variety of Tamil have tended to be strongly influenced by the Tamil writing system (see Annamalai & Steever, 1998, p. 101). The justification for this is that, as far as native Tamil elements are concerned, the script is both economical and systematic and, indeed, very close to what a phonemic transcription would be.

The Tamil script recognizes two diphthongs and the two orthographic symbols that represent these are usually transcribed as *ai* and *au*. However, there are other vocalic sequences within a single syllable that are phonetically diphthongs. Firth (1934, p. xxi) speaks of these as 'special diphthongs'—special in the sense that rather than being written with a single vowel symbol, they are made up of an orthographic sequence of vowel + <y>. They fall into two groups, namely orthographic *ey* [ɛi] and *oy* [ɔi], and orthographic *aay* [aːi], *eey* [eːi], and *ooy* [ɔːi]; that is to say, two in which the first vocalic element is short, and three in which it is long. Certain generalizations emerge from these facts. Diphthongs in formal Tamil are all, in Daniel Jones terms, falling diphthongs and all are closing diphthongs. With regard to the latter feature, *au* is exceptional in closing toward a back vowel. It is also of relatively infrequent occurrence. Moreover, unlike any of the others, it does not occur as the vocalic component of a monosyllabic word. Among monosyllables involving the other six are *kai*, 'hand;' *cey*, 'do;', *poy*, 'untruth;' *vaay*, 'mouth;' *peey*, 'demon;' *pooy*, 'past participle of *poo* "go."' These raise the issue of how such vocalic sequences should be treated at the phonological level. That is to say, in the simplest terms, are there underlying diphthongs in Tamil? Or are such sequences all better treated as V + y (or, in the case of the second set of Firth's 'special diphthongs,' $\bar{V}$ + y)?[1] This would mean that the three items *kai, cey,* and *poy* would all have the structure CVC. This, to revive a term from orthodox phonemic theory, would satisfy the demands of pattern congruity and would allow all to be accommodated by the same phonological rules. Thus, in the case of root morphemes having the structure C_1VC_2, C_2 is doubled before a vowel-initial suffix, giving the following (with *kai* taken to be *kay*): *kayyil* (locative), *ceyya* (infinitive), and *poyyil* (locative). These are then all of the same pattern as one finds with other consonants in the C_2 position; for example, *pallil,* 'tooth.loc;' *kaḷḷil,* 'toddy.loc;' and *maṇṇil,* 'earth.loc.' Root morphemes having the structure $C_1\bar{V}C_2$ do not have doubling of C_2: *vaayil,* 'mouth;' *paalil,* 'milk.loc;' and *vaaḷil,* 'sword.loc.' The rules that generate these suffixed forms in formal Tamil also provide a formula to express the relation between the uninflected forms in the formal and informal varieties, in that the latter commonly have an 'enunciative vowel' (see Bright, 1990, pp. 86–117): *kayyi, ceyyi, pallu, vaayi, pooyi,* and *paalu*—where, as is apparent, the nature of this vowel is determined by the nature of the preceding consonant.

There are other generalizations to be made about diphthongs in formal Tamil. First, only *ai* occurs in noninitial syllables of monomorphemic word forms. Second, only *ai* and *aay* occur as suffixes, the former as the marker of accusative case and the latter as an adverbalizing suffix when added to a noun stem. It is the particularly wide privilege of occurrence of *ai* that makes it of particular interest in a comparison of formal and informal spoken Tamil.

It is possible to give an account of the differences between the vowel systems of the two varieties by taking the formal variety as basic and the informal as derived from it. In these terms, vowels in formal Tamil may undergo either modification or deletion in the informal variety. Such modification or deletion can reasonably be seen as related to the stress patterns of the language. The greater the degree of salience of a syllable in relation to other syllables in a word, the less likely is the vowel nucleus to undergo change or to be lost. It has been shown that unstressed *i, u,* and *a* are subject to these forces (see Keane, 2001, p. 125).

A number of analyses have concluded with regard to *ai* that it is subject to reduction to a short vowel in all environments except that of a word-initial syllable (or alternatively, of course, that the *y* of *ay* is subject to deletion in the same environments; see, for example, Asher, 1982, pp. 220 and 259; Balasubramanian, 1972, p. 224; and Schiffman, 1999, p. 3). While there is no explicit discussion of the issue, the roman transcription in Kumaraswami Raja and Dora-swamy, 1966, and Shanmugam Pillai, 1965 and 1968, implicitly supports the same analysis. The resulting vowel has been transcribed as *e* and *a*, depending on the dialect being described, and so assuming a range of realizations from [ɛ] to [ə]. Examples of corresponding forms in the two varieties follow:

Formal	Informal	
pai	payyi[2]	'bag'
aiyoo	ayyoo	'alas'
manaivi	manevi	'wife'
talai	tale	'head'
veelai-y-ai	veeleye	'work.acc'

Descriptions that equate written *ai* with colloquial *e* are quite clear that the latter is a short monophthong. However, a careful experimental analysis of examples of colloquial utterances has shown diphthongs occurring in comparable environments. An explanation has been sought for the discrepancy. In this quest, one must take account of the fact that most of the accounts are based on an impressionistic analysis; that is to say that phonetically trained analysts have concluded that what they hear is a monophthong. The possibility must be allowed for that this conclusion is the result of the reduced duration of the syllable as compared with the formal style, even though the formants diverge.

An alternative hypothesis is that the effect of the presence of recording equipment has had the result that informants providing examples of utterances have modified their pronunciation in the direction of the formal style. Support for this is to be found in the fact that speakers who are ready to agree that, for instance, *talai* has a different realization in informal speech from its pronunciation in formal speech, will commonly, in making a written version in the Tamil script as an aid to memory in making a recording, use the written symbol for *ai* in word-final position, regardless of how they believe they pronounce it. This, it is argued, then leads them to produce a reading pronunciation rather than a totally natural colloquial utterance. There is support for this argument in the fact that there is no universally agreed system for writing informal Tamil in the Tamil script and in the fact that there are strict conventions taught in schools for reading from a written text.

With such thoughts in mind, other recordings, differently organized, were subjected to the same experiments. In view of its wider distribution as compared with other diphthongs in the language, these experiments focussed on *ai*.

METHOD

Materials were designed to elicit formal and informal utterances of a range of sentences, so that the production of the *ai* in each could be compared. In the formal condition, subjects were required to read sentences presented in Tamil orthography, following the standard conventions for written texts. The informal data were elicited by asking subjects to respond to prerecorded questions on the basis of pictorial stimuli, a method that had been found to produce genuinely colloquial utterances in previous work. It has the advantage of avoiding any orthographic representation, which is highly problematic given the lack of standards for writing informal Tamil, and the limitations of the script. For example, nasalized vowels, which are common in informal speech, cannot be represented as such in the orthography. The colloquial nature of the questions, which were prerecorded by a native speaker, also encouraged an informal response.

An example of a formal and informal pair is provided in the following numbered list, the first transliterated, the second an indication of the expected pronunciation. As mentioned earlier, the formal and informal varieties are distinct at all levels, and this is reflected by differences not only in the realization of what in the formal register at least is a diphthong but also in the form of the noun and the verbal inflection:

1. *kumaar* *taṇṇiir* *kotikka* *vaikkiraaṉ*
2. *kumaar* *taṇṇi* *kodikka*[3] *vekrāā*
   Kumar water boil.infin cause.pres.3sm
   'Kumar is boiling the water.'

For both conditions, the stimuli were presented on a computer screen, a sentence or a picture at a time, and the subject controlled the rate of presentation by pressing the return key to move between stimuli. In the informal condition, this prompted not only presentation of the picture but also automatic playing of the relevant question. There were in all 28 target words containing *ai* diphthongs, equally divided between seven different categories, as illustrated in Table 7.1.

The different categories were chosen to investigate a possible effect of the position of the syllable containing *ai*—initial, medial, or final. Word length, in terms of number of syllables, was also varied for word-final *ai*, from monosyllabic to quadrisyllabic words. Finally, the trisyllabic word-final *ai* category contained instances where the diphthong was part of a single lexical morpheme and also cases

TABLE 7.1

Target Words

Set	Number of Syllables	Syllable Position	Lexical or Inflectional	Target Words			
A	1	final	lexical	*kai*	*pai*	*tai*	*vai*
				hand	bag	sew!	put!
B	2	final	lexical	*yaanai*	*talai*	*puunai*	*cilai*
				elephant	head	cat	statue
C	3	final	lexical	*cakkarai*	*kutirai*	*maattirai*	*kaɻutai*
				sugar	horse	tablet	donkey
D	3	final	inflectional	*marattai*	*paʈattai*	*siŋkattai*	*paɳattai*
				tree.acc	picture.acc	monkey.acc	money.acc
E	4	final	inflectional	*cakkarattai*	*veŋkaayattai*	*pustakattai*	*kaʈitattai*
				wheel.acc	onion.acc	book.acc	letter.acc
F	2/3	initial	lexical	*taikkiraan*	*taippaan*	*vaikkiraan*	*vaittaan*
				(he) is sewing	(he) will sew	(he) is causing	(he) caused
G	3/4	medial	lexical	*Cennaikku*	*Maturaikku*	*puunaikku*	*manaivi*
				Chennai.dat	Madurai.dat	cat.dat	wife

where it formed the accusative marker, to see whether its status as providing lexical or inflectional information had any effect. A number of fillers were also included to disguise the purpose of the investigation from the subjects, giving 50 different stimuli for each condition, and three tokens of each were recorded.

In the informal condition, the stimuli were presented in four blocks of decreasing length (57, 39, 36, and 18 sentences) and increasing difficulty, and were preceded in each case by a training session with the experimenter. This involved modeling the required response, and also checking that the pictures were correctly identified. In the first block, subjects were asked to respond according to the following pattern:

niiŋga	enna	paakriiŋga?		naan	oru ____	paakrēē.
you	what	see.pres.2pl		I	a ____	see.pres.1s
'What do you see?'				'I see a ____.'		

In the second block, the format changed slightly so as to ensure that accusative endings would be included on the nouns:[4]

niiŋga	enda ____	paakriiŋga?		naan	anda ____	paakrēē.
you	which ____	see.pres.2pl		I	that ____	see.pres.1s
'Which ____ do you see?'				'I see that ____.'		

In all these examples, the objects were easily identifiable common nouns, many of them animals. As far as possible, the diphthongs were enclosed between stops, to aid segmentation. The target words were chosen so that consonants with the same place of articulation (dental/alveolar) preceded the diphthong, to control for coarticulatory effects. In the last two carrier phrases shown earlier, the diphthongs were all followed by labial stops, since these do not involve any lingual articulation and hence might be expected to induce less coarticulatory influence on preceding vowels. There were, however, a number of target words for which these frames were inappropriate—verb forms or dative case-marked names—and for these various different questions had to be devised; for example, 'What must I do?' to elicit commands. The pictorial stimuli also needed to be more elaborate in these cases; for example, the question 'Where did Kumar go?' was accompanied by a map of India with the relevant place marked by a dot and the initial of the place name in Tamil script. In all cases, the question and answer pairs were designed so that the target word represented new information, and so might be expected to bear the sentence accent.

Within each block the first two stimuli and the last one were fillers, and the other fillers were interspersed amongst the target stimuli in a pseudorandom order. Three tokens of each stimulus were included in the blocks. This differed from the order used in the practice session, but was kept constant across subjects. A pilot study did not use the block design, having a single randomized order for all the stimuli, but this was found to be too taxing for the subject and resulted in inconsistent use of the accusative marker, with confusion between the response patterns (shown earlier). The reading task, however, was much more straightforward and so the complete set of stimuli was presented in a single sequence in the formal condition, but with breaks between the three repetitions. Four fillers were included at the beginning and two at the end in each case, but the order of the rest of the stimuli was randomized and different orders were used for the three repetitions and for each subject. The informal condition was run first for all subjects, to avoid a recent formal utterance affecting the informality of the colloquial sentences. Since the conventions for reading texts are strict, it was thought unlikely that there would be any influence of the informal on the formal condition.

Three speakers were recorded, two female (CS and NK) and one male (SS), with ages ranging between 38 and 68 years. They were born in Tamil Nadu: the male speaker near Thanjavur and the female speakers near Coimbatore and Madras, although all are now resident in the U.K. In each case, at least part of their formal education had been in Tamil. The recordings were made in three different locations: a sound-treated room at Oxford University Phonetics Laboratory, the anechoic chamber in the Phonetics Department of University College London, and a quiet room in the speaker's own home.

The questions used in the informal condition were recorded by a female speaker who also served as the pilot subject. She was explicitly instructed to make the questions as colloquial as possible, and read from an orthographic representation in which the Tamil symbol corresponding to <e> was used for the *ai* diphthong.

ANALYSIS

The recorded data were digitized at a rate of 16kHz and 16-bit resolution, and segmented into files corresponding to each sentence using the software package ESPS/*xwaves*™. For each token of *ai,* cursors were set manually at particular points, and various measurements were taken automatically. For the frequency parameters, linear predictive coding analysis was used, applying auto-correlation within a pitch period to identify broad spectral peaks corresponding to the vocal tract resonances. Twelve coefficients were used in the linear predictive equation, and the window duration was 49 millisec, with 5-millisec steps between analysis frames. The accuracy of the formant tracking was checked by inspection during the measuring process, and in the few instances where the tracking had gone astray, manual measurements were substituted for those recorded automatically.

Studies of *ai* diphthongs in different languages have revealed cross-linguistic variation in their internal structure, and also variation conditioned by speech rate. There appear to be maximally five stages or components that can be differentiated: a transition from the preceding consonant, an onset steady state, an interior transition, an offset steady state, and a transition into the following consonant. Languages differ in the relative proportions occupied by the successive stages. Informal inspection of the Tamil data revealed considerable variation in the internal structure of the diphthongs, but relatively little evidence of an onset steady state. The predominant pattern in the formal condition involves F2 rising from the onset of voicing, and then leveling out, whilst the frequency of the first formant changes relatively little over the course of the diphthong, falling only very gradually. No marked transitions from the preceding consonant could be identified in the majority of cases, but there was a steep fall in F2 before the closure of a labial plosive and a rise in the few instances where it was followed by a velar consonant. A schematic representation is given in Fig. 7.1, which also illustrates the points at which measurements of duration and frequency (for F1 and F2) were taken. 'A' marks the point at which voicing starts, taken to be the onset of the diphthong; 'B' marks the point at which there is a clear change in the gradient of F2; 'C' marks the start of the transition into the following conso-

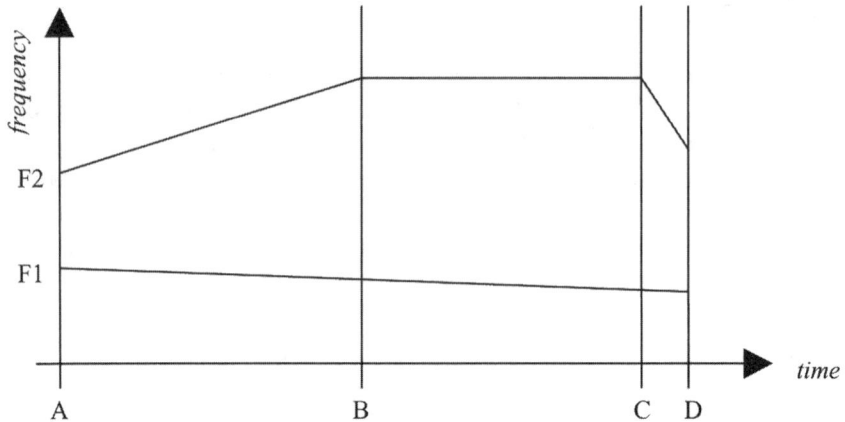

FIG. 7.1. Schematic display of measurements.

nant; and 'D' marks the cessation of voicing, that is, the offset of the diphthong. In tokens where no turning point in F2 could be identified, no measurements corresponding to point 'B' were taken, and in cases where the target word was utterance final and there were no final consonant transitions, no measurements were taken corresponding to point 'C.' The spectrogram of the third repetition of *pai* by speaker CS is provided in Fig. 7.2 as an example of how the measurements were applied in practice.

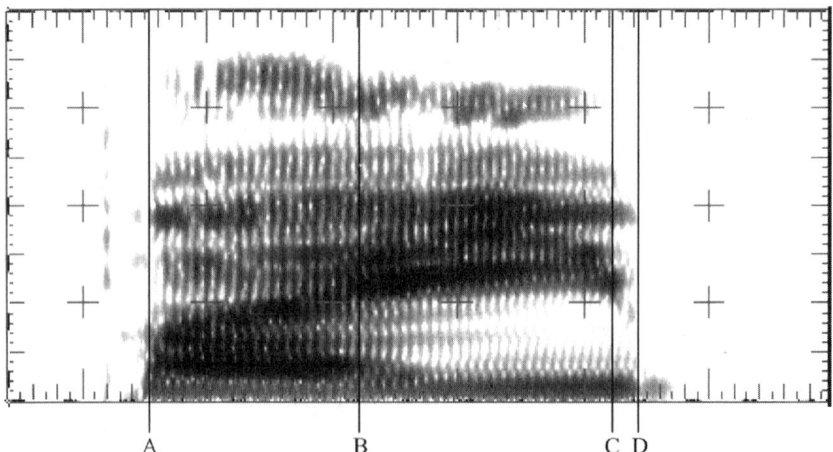

FIG. 7.2. Measurement parameters applied to the wide-band spectrogram of *pai* by speaker CS.

RESULTS

Evidence for Monophthongization

Comparison of matching sentences in the formal and informal conditions revealed some differences, although their nature and extent varied considerably between speakers. Cases where no turning point in F2 (i.e., no point corresponding to 'B' in Fig. 7.1) could be identified formed a relatively small proportion of the total data set, accounting for just 57 of the 494 tokens. Of these, nine examples belonged to speaker SS but all the rest were informal tokens produced by speaker CS. Moreover, the different realizations of *ai* in her speech, with and without a turning point in the formant structure, fell into clearly differentiated groups coinciding with different sets from Table 7.1. The monophthongs were found in tokens from sets 'B,' 'C,' 'D,' and 'E,' that is, instances of word-final *ai* in nonmonosyllabic words, and the diphthongs were found in sets 'A,' 'F,' and 'G,' that is, instances of *ai* in medial or initial syllables (including monophthongs). The differences between the two realizations are clearly seen in Fig. 7.3, which dis-

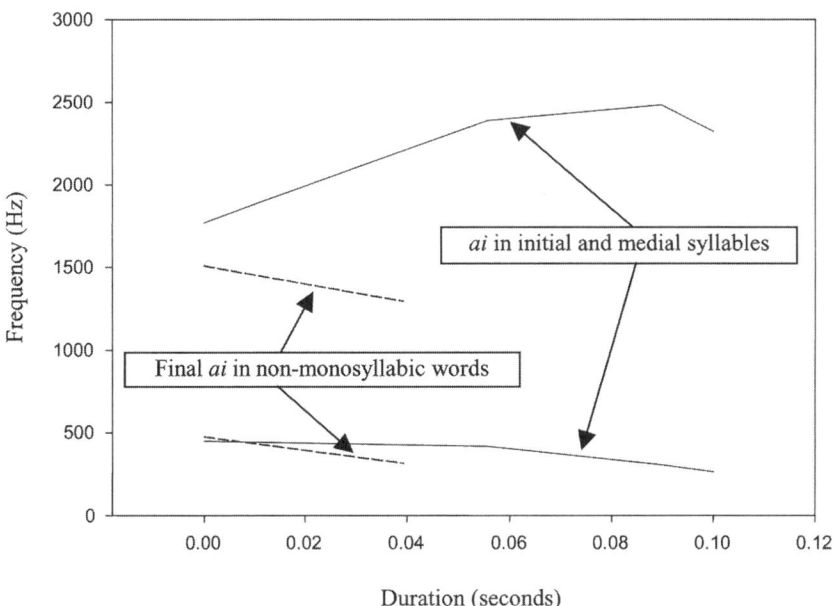

FIG. 7.3. Mean formant frequency values for speaker CS in the informal condition, comparing final *ai* in nonmonosyllabic words with *ai* in initial and medial syllables.

plays the changing formant frequency values for the two groups by plotting the mean measurements for points 'A,' 'B,' 'C,' and 'D.'

In addition to the distinction between complex and simple structure, there is a striking contrast in duration, the monophthongs being on average less than half the length of the diphthongs. The direction of formant movement is also markedly different, especially for F2. The downward movement of both F1 and F2 in the monophthongs can probably be attributed to the influence of the following consonant, which was p in every case. Because the monophthongs were of such short duration, it was not possible to distinguish between a steady state and a final transition phase, so there were no measurements corresponding to point 'C.' The onset formant frequencies also differ between the two groups, with F1 starting slightly higher in the monophthongs and F2 somewhat lower, and these differences are statistically highly significant ($p < .006$ and $p < .0005$, respectively, according to the nonparametric Mann–Whitney test).

Analysis of the informal speech of speaker CS thus provides confirmation of the monophthongization reported in the literature for colloquial Tamil. It also suggests that the correct generalization is that monophthongization applies to word-final *ai* in nonmonosyllabic words. This supports the description of Balasubramanian (1972, p. 224) over that of Britto (1986, p. 198), Steever (1998, p. 14), and Schiffman (1999, p. 23), who state that monophthongization also applies to *ai* in word-medial syllables. In the speech of speaker CS, at least, tokens from set 'G' clearly pattern with the diphthongal realizations.

Comparison of Formal and Informal Conditions

The monophthong–diphthong distinction found in the informal speech of speaker CS was not replicated in the formal condition, as Fig. 7.4 illustrates. The formant structures for tokens of *ai* in initial and medial syllables are of very similar shape in both conditions, although the durations are significantly longer in the formal condition ($p < .0005$ on the Wilcoxon signed ranks test). However, the formal tokens of final *ai* in nonmonosyllabic words differ markedly from their informal counterparts: a turning point in the second formant can be identified in all cases, putting them firmly in the class of diphthongal realizations. There is again a clear contrast in duration within the formal condition between

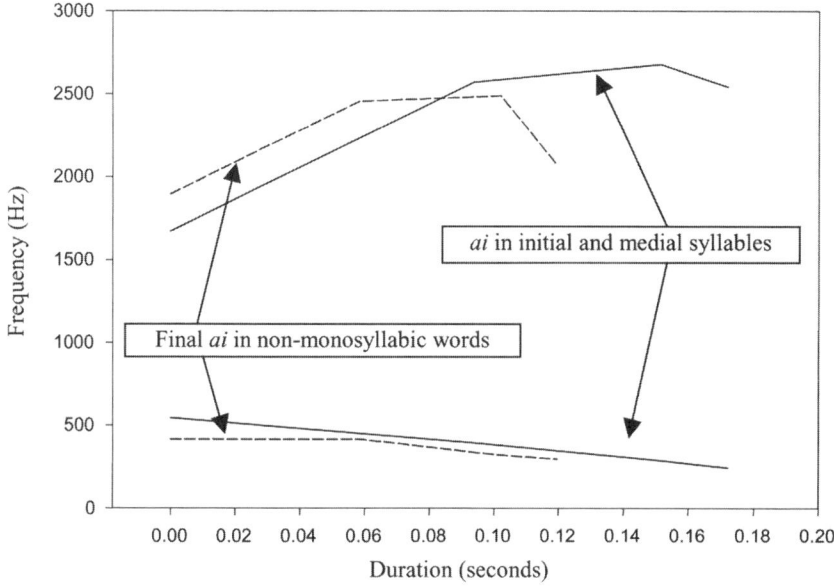

FIG. 7.4. Mean formant frequency values for speaker CS in the formal condition, comparing final *ai* in nonmonosyllabic words with *ai* in initial and medial syllables.

the two sets of tokens ($p < .0005$), but the difference is less extreme than in the informal condition.

There is no clear distinction between monophthongs and diphthongs of the kind seen in the informal speech of speaker CS in either of the other speakers. Instead, both conditions roughly follow the pattern seen in the formal speech of speaker CS, that is, tokens of word-final *ai* in nonmonosyllabic words are generally shorter than the rest but still diphthongal in structure, as illustrated in Fig. 7.5. In order to investigate how the two conditions differ, the Wilcoxon signed ranks test, which is suitable for a repeated measures design, was applied to various measurements for matched formal–informal pairs. For speakers SS and NK, there were no significant differences between the onset formant frequencies in the formal and informal conditions, or in the gradient of the glide, that is, the rate of change of F2 between points 'A' and 'B' of Fig. 7.1. Two overall measures, the total duration and total difference in F2 (calculated between points 'A' and 'C' to discount the effect of the final transition) did, however, differ significantly for both speakers, informal tokens being shorter and involving a smaller F2 difference ($p < .0005$ in

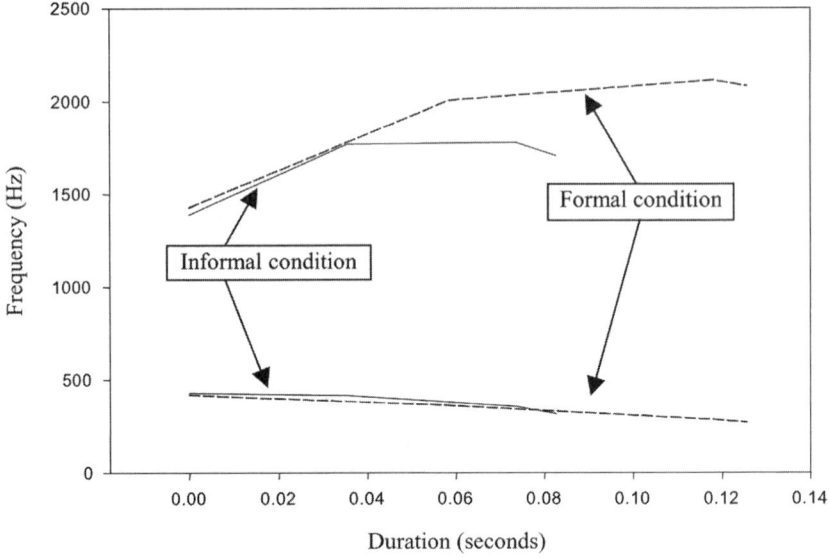

FIG. 7.5. Mean formant frequency values of *ai* for speaker SS, comparing formal and informal conditions.

each case). The turning point in F2 was lower in the informal condition by a considerable margin, as the results of *t*-tests on the difference demonstrate: $t = 42.595$ for speaker SS and $t = 73.685$ for speaker NK. There was also a highly significant difference in the pretransition level of F2 at point 'C' ($p < .0005$ for both speakers), although the t values were less extreme ($t = 8.077$ for speaker SS and $t = 7.408$ for speaker NK). Finally, the proportion of the total duration occupied by the glide differed significantly ($p < .023$ for speaker SS and $p < .032$ for speaker NK), with the glide forming a greater percentage of the whole in the informal condition.

There were, therefore, some consistent and significant differences between formal and informal realizations of *ai* even in the speech of the two speakers who did not produce the monophthong–diphthong contrast. Although these do include reduced duration, and hence a smaller overall difference in F2 values, the stability of the rate of change of F2 makes it difficult to regard the informal tokens as an intermediate stage between monophthong and diphthong. Instead, the distinction between monophthong and diphthong in these data seems to be categorical rather than gradient, and found only in the one speaker. The contrasts in the speech of speakers SS and NK may therefore arise from differences in the nature of the task in the two conditions (answering questions on the basis of visual stimuli, as opposed to reading), rather than a genuine contrast between colloquial and formal Tamil.

These results demonstrate very clearly the difficulty of eliciting genuinely colloquial Tamil, even when possible interference from the orthography has been precluded. All three speakers understood that their responses in the informal condition were intended to be colloquial, and yet in the artificial situation of being recorded, only one seems to have produced authentically informal speech. It is, perhaps, no accident that she was also the only one of the three to have participated in recordings of colloquial Tamil on a previous occasion (for the audio materials accompanying Asher & Annamalai, 2002). This outcome strongly suggests that when diphthongs have unexpectedly been reported for colloquial utterances, they may be due to speakers modifying their pronunciation in the direction of the formal variety.

Effects of Word Length and Syllable Position

The effect of the length of the word on the realization of a final *ai* was explored by comparing tokens from sets 'A,' 'B,' 'C,' and 'E' of Table 7.1, which range from one to four syllables in length. Fig. 7.6 illustrates the general pattern: it displays data from speaker SS only, but, as the statistical results reported below show, the same trends were found in all three speakers. The spread of the data is shown by boxplots: the boxed areas are bounded by the first and third quartiles, with the line marking the median value, and the whiskers extend to the furthest points not classed as outliers (i.e., lying a distance of more than 1.5 times the interquartile range beyond the end of the box). Outliers are marked individually by empty circles. The duration of *ai* in monosyllables is clearly greater than in polysyllabic words and the difference between the two was found to be statistically significant for all speakers and in both formal and informal conditions ($p < .008$ on the nonparametric Mann–Whitney test). It was thought possible, however, that this result might have been skewed by effects of sentence-final lengthening (Cooper & Paccia–Cooper, 1980): two of the four monosyllabic words (*tai* and *vai*) were verbs and thus limited to sentence-final position (unmarked sentences being verb-final in

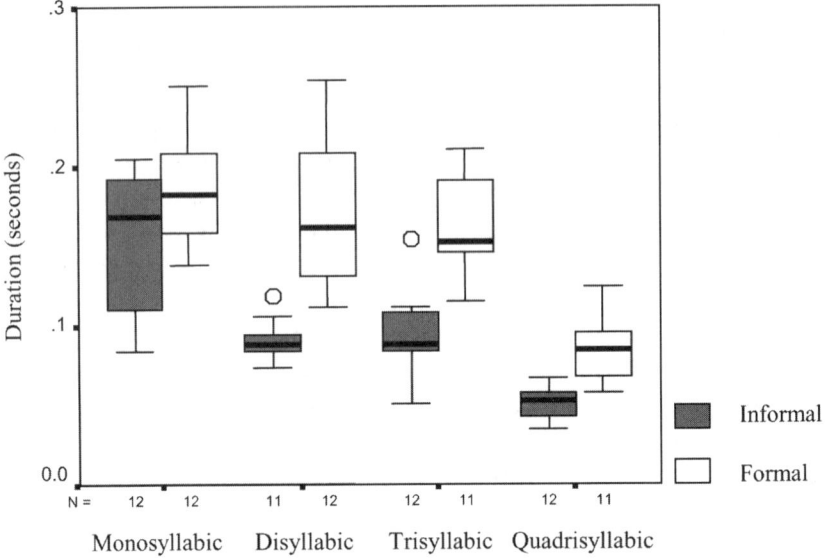

FIG. 7.6. Boxplots of the total duration of word-final *ai* against word length for speaker SS, clustered by condition.

Tamil). The statistical tests were therefore repeated after excluding tokens of *ai* from the relevant words, but the significance of the differences was unaffected.

Inspection of Fig.7.6 suggests that there may be a gradient effect, with duration diminishing in proportion to word length. The nonparametric Mann–Whitney test was used to conduct two-way comparisons between monosyllabic and disyllabic words, disyllabic and trisyllabic words, and trisyllabic and quadrisyllabic words. Highly significant differences were found in the first case, as expected, for each speaker and each condition (with the sole exception of the formal condition for speaker SS, where there was no significant durational difference). The other comparisons, however, yielded no significant results, for any speaker or either condition (excepting the informal condition for speaker NK). This suggests that the primary effect on duration is between initial and noninitial syllables, at least for examples of word-final *ai*.

To test whether syllable position within the word has any effect, tokens of *ai* in word-medial syllables (set 'G' from Table 7.1) were contrasted with cases of *ai* in the initial syllables of polysyllabic words (set 'F'). For all three speakers in the formal condition, instances of *ai* in word-initial syllables proved to be significantly longer ($p < .011$ for speaker SS, $p < .045$ for speaker CS, and $p < .003$ for speaker NK on the nonparametric Mann–Whitney test), although there were no significant results for the informal condition. Tokens of *ai* in word-medial syllables were also significantly shorter than final *ai* in disyllabic words (set 'B' from Table 7.1) for speakers SS and NK, which probably reflects the occurrence of word-final lengthening in Tamil. Overall, therefore, these results provide some confirmation of a durational distinction between initial and noninitial syllables and hence support for the hypothesis that initial syllables receive word-level prominence in Tamil (Keane, 2003).

Interaction Between Duration and Internal Structure

Several factors have already been identified that affect the total duration of *ai* tokens: word length, syllable position, and the formality of the recording conditions. With the exception of the monophthongs in the speech of speaker CS, the internal structure of *ai* conforms loosely to the scheme shown in Fig. 7.1. No attention has yet been paid, however, to the details of how this structure is affected by changes in duration. A priori various possibilities can be envisaged: the onset and offset frequencies might be fixed, which could result in the gradient of the glide changing in proportion to the length of the diphthong. Alternatively, the end of the diphthong might be truncated, reducing the steady state portion but maintaining constant onset and offset frequencies. If the start of the diphthong were truncated, the onset frequency might be raised so that the same offset was reached, or perhaps the onset frequency would be fixed, resulting in the offset level of F2 decreasing. In either case, the relative proportions of the total duration taken up by the glide and offset steady state would change. Fig. 7.7 illustrates what happens in Tamil: it displays the mean measurements of word-final *ai* in the formal condition, comparing monosyllabic words with quadrisyllabic words (sets 'A' and 'E'), for all three speakers combined.

The rate of change of F2 remains constant across durational changes: there is no significant difference in the gradients of either the F2 glide or the steady state portion. The proportion of the total

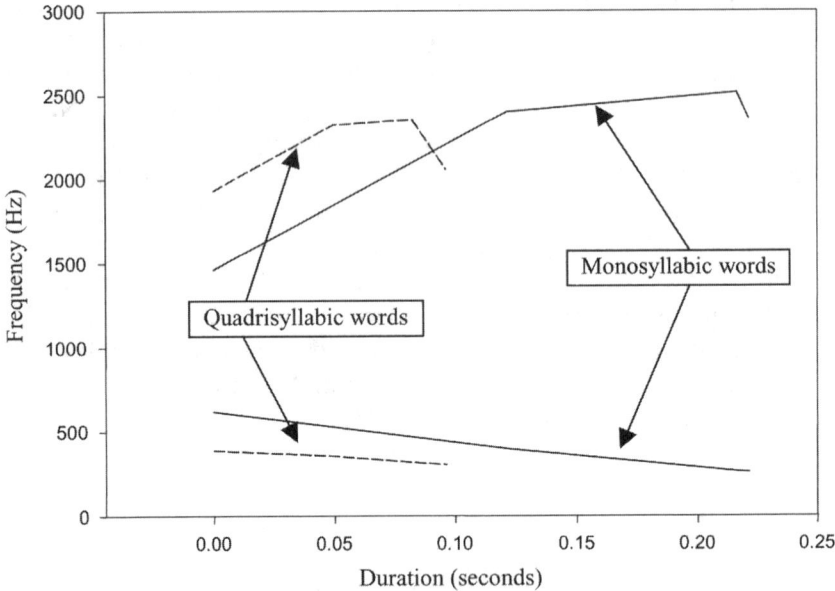

FIG. 7.7. Mean formant frequency values of *ai* for all speakers in the formal condition, comparing monosyllabic with quadrisyllabic words.

duration occupied by the glide is also unaffected by the change in duration, as is the frequency level of the turning point in F2. The effect of reducing the duration thus seems to be truncation of both ends of the diphthong, whilst the F2 turning point is stable, both in terms of its frequency and its timing relative to the diphthong as a whole. As Fig. 7.7 illustrates, the F2 trace for the shorter duration is simply a section from the middle of the longer trace that has been transposed across horizontally. The first formant behaves in a similar fashion, although the turning point for the shorter duration is slightly lower. Both onset and offset[5] frequencies are therefore affected: the F1 onset is significantly lowered ($p < .005$ on the nonparametric Mann–Whitney test) and its offset raised ($p < .0005$) in shorter tokens, whereas the F2 onset is raised ($p < .0005$) and the F2 offset lowered ($p < .005$).

The pattern described here seems to be fairly robust. It is clearly replicated in the data for each individual speaker. It does not, however, coincide exactly with the differences between the formal and informal conditions reported earlier, although these, too, are associated with a reduction in the overall duration of the diphthong, and indeed a generally faster speech rate. As described earlier, and illustrated in Fig. 7.5, the gradient of the glide again seems to be constant, but the onset frequencies are also fixed. Although the glide occupies a slightly greater proportion of the shorter tokens, it is not lengthened sufficiently to allow the same F2 turning point to be reached, resulting in a pattern of 'undershoot' in the shorter tokens. Durational differences associated with different factors—word length versus the formality of the condition—thus seem to affect the internal structure of the diphthong in slightly different ways. The data sample here is clearly not large enough to propose definite connections between particular patterns and particular factors. It does, however, demonstrate that differences in formant trajectories are multidimensional.

Comparison of Lexical and Inflectional *ai*

A further factor that might influence the realization of *ai* is whether it conveys lexical or grammatical information. According to Schiffman and Arokianathan (1986, p. 376), orthographic representations of colloquial Tamil treat grammatical and lexical morphemes in an asymmetric fashion, representing the former as phonetically as possible, whilst using the formal equivalent for lexical morphemes. It was hypothesized, therefore, that lexical *ai* might also have a more careful pronunciation than its grammatical counterpart. To test this, a repeated measures general linear model analysis was conducted on durational data for tokens of final *ai* from trisyllabic words, half being lexical and half grammatical (sets 'C' and 'D' from Table 7.1). Examples from both formal and informal conditions were included, for speakers SS and NK (the results from speaker CS were excluded because of the monophthongization affecting these words in her informal speech). The data were arranged by word, with speaker (two levels) and repetition (three levels) as within-word factors, and condition and lexical~inflectional as between-word factors. No significant results were found for repetition, suggesting that the data were unaffected by ordering effects. Speaker did, however, prove to be a significant factor ($p < .037$), and both condition and the lexical~inflectional distinction were highly significant ($p < .0005$), although not their interaction. For both speakers inflectional *ai* was shorter than lexical *ai,* which is consistent with a slightly more careful production of the lexical morpheme.

Interestingly, comparison of the internal structures of the two sets of diphthongs revealed different strategies on the part of the two speakers: Speaker SS adopted the 'undershoot' strategy also seen in his contrast between formal and informal speech (see Fig. 7.5), keeping onset frequencies fixed and terminating the glide at a lower frequency level for inflectional *ai.* Speaker NK, by contrast, followed the pattern outlined in the last section, raising the F2 onset of her inflectional *ai* tokens but keeping the frequency of the turning point constant. The fact that the two different patterns are here associated with the same factor (the lexical or inflectional status of *ai*) suggests that there may be some flexibility, and certainly interspeaker variability, in the way that durational differences are realized.

Cross-Linguistic Comparisons

In this final section, the results for Tamil are placed in the wider context of research on diphthongs, and particularly *ai* diphthongs, in other languages. One respect in which Tamil immediately stands out is the general absence of a steady state onset in tokens of *ai.* The numerous descriptions of American English *ai* agree that at a normal speech rate, it comprises an onset steady state, a glide, and an offset steady state (e.g., Gay, 1968, p. 1571; Hertz, 1991, p. 99; Lehiste & Peterson, 1961, p. 276; Thomas, 2000, p. 10). Furthermore, it is the onset steady state that is held to be crucial for *ai:* Lehiste and Peterson (1961, p. 276) describe it as longer than the offset and Gay (1968, p. 1571) reported that it is maintained in fast speech, although the offset may be lost.

Perception experiments conducted by Peeters (1991) comparing diphthongs in Southern British English, Dutch, and German revealed language-specific preferences for different internal temporal structures, which were also reflected to some degree in production data. Synthetic stimuli of constant overall duration were used, but the relative proportions occupied by onset steady state, glide, and offset steady state were systematically varied. Dutch and German speakers preferred stimuli in which the glide formed the single greatest component. A pattern of relatively longer onsets and shorter offsets was preferred by Dutch subjects, whereas the German speakers favored onsets and offsets of equal duration or else longer offsets. By contrast, the preferred pattern for the British English speakers involved no off-set steady state at all, with the onset and glide either of equal duration, or the onset slightly longer. According to Jha (1985), Maithili *əi* contains a consistent sequence of onset steady state, glide, and offset steady state, although he reported that the offset is always longer than the onset steady state. Clearly, therefore, languages differ over the relative prominence of onset and offset, to the point that British English may dispense with the offset entirely. Tamil, however, is alone among the languages mentioned in not having a consistently identifiable onset steady state, even in isolated productions of monosyllables containing the diphthong. A possible explanation for Tamil's apparent peculiarity in this respect is the need to keep *ai* distinct from the 'special diphthong' *aay*.

Some further data on how languages vary in the internal structure of their *ai* diphthongs is reported by Lindau, Norlin, and Svantesson (1990). They give figures for the percentage of the whole diphthong occupied by the internal glide or transition in several languages: 16% to 20% in Arabic and Hausa, 40% to 50% in Chinese, and 60% in American English. The same calculation was performed on the Tamil data, giving an overall figure of 50.74%, which is roughly comparable with Chinese. Moreover, individual results for the three speakers proved to be surprisingly consistent: 49.52% for speaker SS, 50.83% for speaker CS, and 51.82% for speaker NK. Lindau et al. also calculated the correlation between the duration of the glide and the acoustic distance it travels, measured as the Euclidean distance in the F1–F2 space measured in mel. They note that the correlation coefficient for *ai* is fairly high (.87 for 18 speakers of three languages), certainly in comparison with other diphthongs. The figure for Tamil *ai* is considerably lower: the Pearson correlation coefficient is .657 for all three speakers, for the Euclidean distance in the F1–F2 space measured in hertz against duration (the final transition phase was ignored for the purposes of the calculation). However, the correlations for individual speakers are slightly more in line with Lindau et al.'s results, (.741 for speaker SS, .77 for speaker CS, and .752 for speaker NK), and thus lend some support to their principle: 'the further to go, the longer it takes' (Lindau et al., 1990, p. 12).

As the preceding sections have shown, there is some variability in the way that durational differences are realized in Tamil, depending on whether the frequencies of the onset or the offset are fixed. A common characteristic, however, is stability in the rate of change of F2, a finding that has also been reported for other languages. Gay (1968) is the classic paper on this subject. He found little consistent difference in the F2 rate of change across three different speech rates in American English. Onset frequencies for F2 were also fairly fixed, whereas offset frequencies changed significantly, with the F1 offset being higher and F2 offset lower in shorter tokens of *ai*. This pattern of undershoot is also reported for Maithili by Jha (1985, p. 113), and has been found in the Tamil data for differences between formal and informal speech, the latter involving a faster overall speech rate. A possible parallel for the other Tamil pattern, in which the diphthong is truncated from both ends, is a contrary finding by Gottfried, Miller, and Meyer, 1993, p. 226, that an increase in tempo causes centralization of both onset and offset frequencies of *ai* in American English. Their study did, however, support Gay's proposal that different diphthongs display distinctive F2 rates of change, which would provide some explanation for the stability of this particular parameter. Since the Tamil data also point in this direction, it would be interesting to compare the gradient of the glide in *ai* with that of the other complex vocalic nuclei found in Tamil.

CONCLUSION

This investigation has shown, first, that speakers have a tendency to resist producing colloquial Tamil utterances in a situation, such as a recording session, which has even a small element of formality. One can speculate that this may relate to the very high prestige accorded to formal Tamil. Nevertheless, it is clear that, when colloquial forms are produced, there are differences between formal *ai* and the equivalent vocalic segments in informal speech. Of the three speakers who participated in the investigation, only CS appears to have fully overcome the impact of the recording situation. The analysis of the recordings she provided shows that, in her speech at least, the colloquial equivalent of *ai* is a monophthong in certain environments. That is to say that word-final *ai* is realized as a monophthong, both when it is part of the root of a word and when it is the accusative suffix. There is, however, a difference between the two, in that the latter is consistently of a shorter duration than the former. In other positions in the word, that is to say in initial or medial syllables in nonmonosyllabic words, CS realizes what is written as *ai* as a diphthong. With regard to monosyllabic words of the form C*ai,* it is clear that the realization is dynamic. There does not in CS's speech seem to be a difference between such monosyllabic words in formal and informal conditions that would justify the representation of *pai* as *payyi.* This may indicate that this feature of colloquial Tamil is not universal.

This study, deliberately limited to the treatment of formal *ai* in colloquial Tamil, suggests that there would be value in conducting a more wide-ranging enquiry into the whole set of Tamil diphthongs.

NOTES

[1] This has been proposed for Proto-Dravidian, the phonology of which can be seen as remarkably similar to that of classical, and, indeed, modern formal, Tamil (see Krishnamurti, 2003, p. 48). Interestingly, some of the Tamil–Brahmi inscriptions of some two millennia ago have the spelling *ay* to represent the diphthong *ai* (see Mahadevan, 2003, p. 253).

[2] This transcription to represent the colloquial form of written *pai* assumes (as does the earlier discussion of the question) both that the colloquial realization of such CVC words is longer in duration than in a formal utterance and that it is disyllabic at the allophonic level. It is to be noted, however, that these assumptions are not based on a careful acoustic analysis, and there remains the question of whether the relatively longer duration commonly observed in informal utterances is such as to justify regarding the colloquial equivalents of *pai, kai, cey,* and so on, as disyllabic.

[3] In this sort of context, the letter *t* in the representation of a formal utterance and the letter *d* in the representation of an informal utterance do not represent different phonetic segments; both indicate a voiced dental fricative. The apparent discrepancy is the result of different established conventions of transcription. For a transcription of a written form, a simple transliteration of the Tamil writing system is used (with the exception here of the use of a sequence of two vowel letters to represent a long vowel), and this system does not differentiate between voiced and voiceless plosives, which, in native Tamil words, are in complementary distribution. However, because of the number of loanwords in colloquial Tamil with voiced plosives occurring in environments where only a voiceless plosive is possible in the indigenous vocabulary (for example, in word-initial position), it has been found useful to differentiate in the transcription between members of such homorganic pairs.

[4] Use of the accusative marker in Tamil is generally limited to definite contexts in the case of [–animate] nouns. It is always used with [+human]

nouns and commonly with nouns that are [+animate] but [–human]. Definite contexts include noun phrases in which one of the constituents is a demonstrative adjective (*inda* 'this,' or *anda* 'that').

[5] Note that 'offset' here refers to the formant frequency values at point 'C' of Fig. 7.1, that is, the level before the final transition phase.

REFERENCES

Annamalai, E., & Steever, S. B. (1998). Modern Tamil. In S. B. Steever (Ed.), *The Dravidian languages* (pp. 100–128). London: Routledge.

Asher, R. E. (1982). *Tamil* (Lingua Descriptive Studies No. 7). Amsterdam: North-Holland.

Asher, R. E., & Annamalai, E. (2002). *Colloquial Tamil.* London: Routledge.

Balasubramanian, T. (1972). *The phonetics of colloquial Tamil.* Unpublished doctoral dissertation, University of Edinburgh, Scotland.

Bright, W. (1990). *Language variation in South Asia.* New York: Oxford University Press.

Britto, F. (1986). *Diglossia: A study of the theory with application to Tamil.* Washington, DC: Georgetown University Press.

Cooper, W. E. & Paccia–Cooper, J. (1980). *Syntax and speech.* Cambridge, MA: Harvard University Press.

Ferguson, C. A. (1959). Diglossia. *Word, 15,* 325–340.

Firth, J. R. (1934). A short outline of Tamil pronunciation. Appendix to A. H Arden, *A progressive grammar of common Tamil.* 4th ed., revised by A. C. Clayton (pp. i–xxxiv). Madras, India: Christian Literature Society for India.

Gay, T. (1968). Effect of speaking rate on diphthong formant movements. *Journal of the Acoustic Society of America, 44,* 1570–1573.

Gottfried, M., Miller, J. D., & Meyer, D. J. (1993). Three approaches to the classification of American English diphthongs. *Journal of Phonetics, 21,* 205–229.

Hertz, S. R. (1991). Streams, phones and transitions: toward a new phonological and phonetic model of formant timing. *Journal of Phonetics, 19,* 91–109.

Jha, S. K. (1985). Acoustic analysis of the Maithili diphthongs. *Journal of Phonetics, 13,* 107–115.

Keane, E. L. (2001). *Echo words in Tamil.* Unpublished doctoral dissertation, University of Oxford, England.

Keane, E. L. (2003). Word-level prominence in Tamil. In M. Solé, D. Recasens, & J. Romero (Eds.), *Proceedings of the 15th International Congress of Phonetic Sciences,* 2, 1257–1260. Adelaide, Australia: Causal Productions Pty Ltd.

Krishnamurti, Bh. (2003). *The Dravidian languages.* Cambridge, England: Cambridge University Press.

Kumaraswami Raja, N., & Doraswamy, K. (1966). *Conversational Tamil* (Dept. of Linguistics, Publication No. 9). Annamalainagar, India: Annamalai University.

Lehiste, I., & Peterson, G. E. (1961). Transitions, glides and diphthongs. *Journal of the Acoustic Society of America, 33,* 268–277.

Lindau, M., Norlin, K., & Svantesson, J.–O. (1990). Some cross-linguistic differences in diphthongs. *Journal of the International Phonetic Association, 20,* 10–14.

Mahadevan, I. (2003). *Early Tamil epigraphy. From the earliest times to the sixth century A.D.* Chennai, India: Cre–A & Cambridge, MA: The Department of Sanskrit and Indian Studies & Harvard University.

Peeters, W. J. M. (1991). *Diphthong dynamics.* Unpublished doctoral dissertation, Rijksuniversiteit te Utrecht, Netherlands.

Reid, T. (1764). *An inquiry into the human mind, on the principles of common sense.* Edinburgh: A. Millar, A. Kincaid & J. Bell.

Schiffman, H. F. (1999). *A reference grammar of Spoken Tamil.* Cambridge, England: Cambridge University Press.

Schiffman, H. F., & Arokianathan, S. (1986). Diglossic variation in Tamil film and fiction. In Bh. Krishnamurti (Ed.), *South Asian languages: Structure, convergence and diglossia* (pp. 371–381). Delhi, India: Motilal Banarsidass.

Shanmugam Pillai, M. (1965). *Spoken Tamil* (Part I, Publications in Linguistics No. 4). Annamalainagar, India: Annamalai University.

Shanmugam Pillai, M. (1968). *Spoken Tamil* (Part II, Publications in Linguistics No. 12). Annamalainagar, India: Annamalai University.

Steever, S. B. (Ed.). (1998). *The Dravidian languages.* London: Routledge.

Thomas, E. R. (2000). Spectral differences in /ai/ offsets conditioned by voicing of the following consonant. *Journal of Phonetics, 28,* 1–25.

Chapter 8

Glottal Variants of /t/ in the Tyneside Variety of English

G. J. Docherty
University of Newcastle

P. Foulkes
University of York

A fundamental goal of phonetic investigation is to build up an account of the systematic properties of speech performance. This, in turn, informs the development of rigorous phonetic taxonomies and the formulation of models of the learning, representation, and processing which underpin speech communication. The past 50 to 60 years of research (since the development of the spectrograph) has provided theoretical clarity in respect of many of these areas. However, there is a strong sense in which phonetic research has really only scratched the surface of what on closer inspection appear to be ever more complex areas of human behaviour. So, for example, it is clear that the range of languages covered by quantitative phonetic research is heavily skewed to the relatively few languages spoken by the investigators themselves. Even within those languages which have received the bulk of the attention from phonetic research, there has tended to be relatively little quantitative research on the differences between varieties. Laboratory studies have typically been designed to focus on relatively small numbers of speakers producing material which is highly controlled. Furthermore, in order to test experimental hypotheses, they have tended to emphasise the statistically typical patterns of performance across groups of speakers, giving much less attention to the variability found *within* corpora of data. Finally, despite all the instrumental work that has been carried out over the years, there are still large tracts of our phonetic knowledge of languages which are cast exclusively within the terms of the auditory-segmental symbolic representations offered by the IPA (see Docherty & Foulkes, 2000, for further discussion).

In this chapter[1], we draw on the findings of the *"Phonological Variation and Change"* project, a large-scale investigation of phonological variation and change within the Tyneside variety of English (Docherty & Foulkes, 1995; Docherty, Foulkes, Milroy, Milroy, & Walshaw, 1997; Milroy, Milroy, & Docherty, 1997; Milroy, Milroy, Docherty, Foulkes, & Walshaw, 1999; Milroy, Milroy, Hartley, & Walshaw, 1995).[2] We present a study which addresses our knowledge of one aspect of the systematic phonetic properties of a nonstandard variety of English. In the process, we shed light on a category of sounds (glottal and glottalised consonants), the properties of which are currently a matter of some debate. In pursuing this, we set out to quantify the variable patterns of performance observed within a socially stratified sample of 32 speakers. We are assisted in this by making use of an acoustic profiling methodology. This, on the one hand, reveals that the phonetic properties of glottal variants may be somewhat more complex than is conventionally thought, and, on the other hand, brings to light interesting patterns of structured variation.

THE PHONETIC PROPERTIES OF GLOTTAL AND GLOTTALISED CONSONANTS

A number of studies published in recent years have challenged conventional views of glottal articulation. Based on their programme of laryngographic studies of glottal and pharyngeal articulations across a number of languages, Esling, Fraser, and Harris (in press) advise that 'terms like glottalized, preglottalized, postglottalized, laryngealized, prelarygealized and postlaryngealized should never be used without precise phonetic specification.' Their work sheds some much needed light on the complexity of articulations in this region of the vocal apparatus. For example, Esling (1996) demonstrates the importance of a laryngeal sphincter mechanism in the production of these sounds (involving the true and false vocal folds and, in many cases, the aryepiglottic folds) as opposed to a narrowing in only one of the components of the sphincter (e.g., occlusion of the true vocal folds). Other writers also recognise that the properties of glottal articulations may be complex. Nolan (1995, p. 366) suggests that '[t]he term 'glottal stop' probably covers a range of realizations all of which may be associated with perturbed phonation, from brief creaky voice alone, through actual full-glottal closure, to glottal closure reinforced by closure of other structures above the true vocal folds,' highlighting that strong candidates for these 'other structures' are the ventricular folds and the aryepiglottic folds (see Catford 1977, p. 163; Lindqvist, 1969; Trigo, 1991, p. 131). Ladefoged and Maddieson (1996) point out that different types of glottal stops can be observed across languages. They suggest that 'true stops' only occur reliably in cases of gemination, and that more typically, glottal 'stops' do not have complete glottal occlusion, especially in intervocalic position. Instead, they are likely to be realised as an interval of creaky voice or 'stiff phonation.' Ladefoged and Maddieson further point out that glottal stop and creaky or laryngealised voice quality[3] share the property of having a high degree of constriction in the glottis, and they place them as close neighbours on a continuum of laryngeal articulation, which ranges from glottal abduction to glottal stop, 'in which the vocal folds are even more tightly together than in creaky voice' (p. 49).

The stance taken by these investigators contrasts sharply with what we might refer to as the 'conventional' view that the term 'glottal' fits into phonetic taxonomy as simply another label for place of articulation on a par with 'bilabial,' 'alveolar,' and so forth, that is, denoting a locus for producing varying degrees of approximation. Thus, the 'conventional' view implies that (place of articulation apart) glottal stops are similar in most respects to other stops. This is a view with a long history (traced in some detail by Esling, Fraser, & Harris, in press), which resonates through to more recent standard texts. For example, Gimson (3rd ed., 1980) provides one of the clearest statements, pointing out that in [ʔ]

> the obstruction to the airstream is formed by the closure of the vocal folds, thereby interrupting the passage of air into the supra-glottal organs. The air pressure below the glottis is released by the sudden separation of the vocal folds. The compression stage of the articulation consists of silence, its presence being perceived auditorily by the sudden cessation of the preceding sound or by the sudden onset (often with an accompanying strong breath effort) of the following sound. (p. 167)

This view of the glottal stop is in accord with that put forward by Catford (1977, p. 109), who states that a 'glottal stop requires total tight closure of the glottis maintained for an appreciable time.' The notion that a glottal stop involves a sustained articulatory occlusion as found with other stops is also reinforced in some instrumental studies. Byrd (1993) reports a study of the 4,834 glottal stops contained in the TIMIT database in which she found that [ʔ] had a mean duration of 65 msec (with a standard deviation of 32 msec),[4] the implication being that there is a sustained configuration (presumably an occlusion) of the articulators during this period. This mean figure corresponds to the claim by Henton, Ladefoged, and Maddieson (1992) that glottal stops have a closure duration at least as long as that of other stops (although the authors do not explore the basis for this assertion).

It is noteworthy that nearly all of the accounts which diverge from the view that glottal stops are simply the same as other stops but produced at a different place of articulation are based on instrumental evidence of some sort, suggesting that this is an area where there may be a complex relation between auditory impression and articulatory and acoustic characteristics. Of course, it is undeniable that speakers are indeed capable of producing a glottal stop which has all of the characteristics of the conventional description, but it seems evident that this is only one of a number of articulatory patterns associated with percepts of glottal articulation. In light of this situation, it is striking that there have been very few instrumental studies which provide anything more than a cursory account of the phonetic characteristics of any substantial sample of this category of sounds. This is in spite of the fact that they are found to be extremely common in the phonetic inventories of unrelated languages from around the world—146 out of 317 languages surveyed by Maddieson (1984) are classified as having a 'glottal plosive' as part of their consonant inventory. Most of what we find in the literature on this topic is based either on auditory judgement, the instrumental representation of a small number of tokens from individual speakers, or is simply a view expressed without any supporting evidence. This study aims to contribute to filling this gap by looking at the acoustic characteristics of a relatively large sample of glottal variants of voiceless plosives in Tyneside English.

GLOTTAL VARIANTS IN BRITISH ENGLISH

British English (BrE) is a fruitful focus of investigation for furthering our understanding of the phonetic properties of glottal consonants. There is abundant evidence that glottal variants have been spreading into varieties of BrE, particularly in recent decades. Andrésen (1968) offers an exhaustive review of the early literature on glottals. He suggests that the 'increasing space given by phoneticians from about 1920 onwards to the treatment of the glottal stop in the speech of non-dialectal speakers may indicate that the use of the reinforcing and/or replacing glottal stop is actually on the increase among educated people' (p. 34). More recently, Collins and Mees (1996) review the evidence for glottals in RP, and argue that glottals have been present for much longer than is usually acknowledged. Fabricius (2000, 2002) also traces the history of t-glottaling in RP, focusing in particular on its gradual change in sociolinguistic status such that it is no longer a feature which is stigmatised among younger speakers.

Previous work has also shown that there is considerable social and geographical variation with regard to the frequency with which glottal variants occur, the environments in which they occur and the extent to which stops other than /t/ are affected (e.g., Andrésen, 1968; Chirrey, 1999; Christophersen, 1952; Docherty & Foulkes, 1999b; Docherty et al., 1997; Higginbottom, 1964; Jones, 1967; Kingsmore, 1995; Macaulay, 1977, 1991; Mees, 1987; Mees & Collins, 1999; Newbrook, 1986; O'Connor, 1947; Przedlacka, 2002; Reid, 1978; Roach, 1973; Stoddart, Upton, & Widdowson, 1999; Stuart–Smith, 1999; Tollfree, 1999; Trudgill, 1974; Wells, 1982).[5]

Most writers identify two types of glottal variant in BrE: glottal replacement (sometimes referred to as glottaling), where a glottal stop is produced in contexts where an oral stop (typically [t]) would often occur; and glottal reinforcement (sometimes referred to as glottalisation), where a glottal stop is produced in a double-articulation with an oral occlusion. To be more precise, the latter, in most accents, is actually preglottalisation, with the reinforcing glottal gesture being established just prior to the supralaryngeal gesture and being removed before the latter's release (Roach, 1973). The main focus of this previous work has been on describing the environments in which glottal variants can be found.[6] In general, the conventional view of glottal stop articulations, as described earlier, seems to prevail (see, for example, Clark & Yallop, 1995; Gimson, 1980; Henton et al., 1992; Jones, 1967; and O'Connor 1973), but, as is the case more generally, there has been relatively little direct instrumental investigation of the phonetic characteristics of these variants in BrE.

The variety we examine in this chapter, Tyneside, is distinctive in its pattern of glottal allophony on the following two counts:

1. Distribution—unlike other varieties, glottalised variants of /t/ (and also of /p/ and /k/) are common in intervocalic contexts; on the other hand, glottal stops as a realisation of /t/ occur only rarely in intervocalic contexts (Docherty et al., 1997). A further striking constraint on the occurrence of both glottal and glottalised variants in Tyneside English is that they are not usually found prepausally, a context which strongly favours glottal variants in other varieties of BrE. In this context, fully released stops are more typically found instead (see Docherty & Foulkes, 1999b; Docherty et al., 1997, for more details of this).

2. Realisation—Tyneside English seems to have a particular type of glottal reinforcement not found in other varieties of BrE. It is described by Wells (1982, p. 374) as 'glottal masking of the oral plosive burst.' Unlike in other varieties, the glottal occlusion is sustained until *after* the release of the supralaryngeal occlusion, thus rendering the oral release inaudible. Interestingly, an earlier description of this variety of BrE by O'Connor (1947) referred to the reinforced variants as being equivalent to a 'very weak [b,d,g]' without further explanatory comment. Harris & Kaye (1990) refer to the production of /t/ in *'city'* and *'Peter'* as a 'pre-glottalised tap' ([ˀɾ])in the "northeast of England," but do not elaborate further

on these phonetic characteristics. Thus, it seems then that even within the very limited accounts which have appeared in respect of this variety of BrE, there is a degree of uncertainty about the precise characteristics of these variants.

ESTABLISHING THE PHONETIC PROFILE OF GLOTTAL VARIANTS

In seeking to provide an account of the phonetic characteristics of a sample of glottal variants from Tyneside English, we have adopted a methodology which we refer to as 'acoustic phonetic profiling.' This involves auditorily identifying glottal variants of /p t k/ and classifying and quantifying the acoustic features which are found at these sites. The initial stage of the analysis was unconstrained in the sense that we simply recorded all of the properties that we observed (within the constraints of our spectrographic analysis; see discussion later for further details). As the analysis progressed it became clear which were the recurrent and defining features for these sounds in this particular variety, and this subset of features was then quantified across the whole database. By adopting this style of analysis, we have avoided being constrained by any preconceived views of what glottal variants might 'look like' in acoustic terms, and we have been able to build up a profile of those features that most commonly reflect the realisation of these variants by the subjects as well as an indication of the variability present in their realisation. The obvious limitations of an acoustic analysis of a remote laryngeal articulatory gesture are counterbalanced by the fact that this form of analysis is conducive to the study of a relatively large number of speakers, something which is effectively ruled out with invasive, multichannel, articulatory techniques.

The profiling approach to acoustic analysis was also driven by a second feature of the study, namely that the material should be analysed in a way which would permit the investigation of the impact of a range of social factors on patterns of speaker performance. This was motivated by the overall goal of the *'Phonological Variation and Change'* project to combine instrumental phonetic methods and sociolinguistic analysis to track systematic variation in a contemporary variety of English. Instrumental analysis of social-indexical properties of phonetic realisation has long been established within the dominant Labovian paradigm of sociolinguistic investigation (Labov 1986, 1994; Labov, Yaeger, & Steiner 1972;

Thomas, 2002), but the bulk of this work has focused on variability in the production of vowels. One of the goals of our current work, reflected in this chapter, is to demonstrate the theoretical insights which can also be gained from an analysis of variation in consonant realisation across a socially-stratified sample of speakers. This effectively ruled out anything but acoustic analysis, but more importantly, it was a strong driver for the profiling approach because our goal was to see what variable aspects of performance characterised the particular groups that were the object of our study without making *a priori* assumptions about what we might find.

METHOD

Sample and Recording Context

In each of two Tyneside neighbourhoods, a judgment sample of 16 speakers was drawn to include equal numbers of men and women. Half of the speakers were between the ages of 15 and 27, and half were between the ages of 45 and 67. The neighbourhoods were differentiated on broad socioeconomic grounds (for convenience, we refer to these neighbourhood groups as working class 'WC' and middle class 'MC,' but these labels should not be interpreted as providing anything more than a broad denotation of the socioeconomic differences between the communities). This design allowed us to consider the effects of age, gender, and 'class' on patterns of linguistic variation and change. To obtain sufficient speech in a reasonably casual style, speakers were recorded conversing in self-selected pairs for about 50 min with minimal fieldworker intervention. A carefully structured 138-item word list was also recorded (listed in the Appendix). The word list was designed to elicit the production of a significant number of glottal variants in a common set of environments. Audio recordings were made using a portable Sony TCD–D10 Pro II DAT recorder. As a result of elimination by the fieldworker of as much ambient noise as possible and careful microphone positioning, the recordings were of sufficiently high quality to enable relevant acoustic measures to be made.

Acoustic Analysis

The results presented later are derived from analysis of the word-list recordings in order to obtain consistent material across the speakers, but the characteristics observed are entirely representative of glottal tokens found in our analysis of conversational data.

There is only sporadic guidance to be found in the literature regarding the acoustic characteristics that might be associated with tokens of stops being perceived as glottal or glottalised. Pierre-humbert (1995, p. 46) cites irregular periodicity as the prime acoustic correlate of glottal allophones, noting that spectral correlates which might have been expected (such as narrow formant bandwidths, especially in the region of F1, or an adjustment of spectral balance toward high frequencies 'in glottalized regions') were frequently not observed. She also mentions (p. 56) that in cases of glottal-reinforced [t], it is not always possible to tell if a coronal closure occurred. In their study of glottalised onset–offset of vowels in American English, Redi and Shattuck–Hufnagel (2001) track four key acoustic features (aperiodicity, creak, diplophonia, and what they refer to as 'glottal squeak,' the latter being defined (p. 414) as 'a sudden shift to relatively high sustained fo, which was usually very low amplitude'). In the context of BrE, Gimson (1980, p. 167) asserts that 'there is no acoustic manifestation of the glottal plosive other than the abrupt cessation or onset of the adjacent sounds.'

In this study, we proceeded as follows. Word-list tokens were first assessed auditorily as belonging to one of three general categories: (a) released, (b) glottal or glottalised, or (c) other. The 'released' category encompassed oral stops produced in 'canonical' fashion with an oral occlusion and noisy release burst, as well as those which were spirantised (see Docherty & Foulkes, 1999b). The 'other' category included cases where /t/ was produced as an approximant or very occasionally as a tap. A number of tokens were not analysed either due to mispronunciations or interference on the recording. In the very small number of cases where the auditory judgement was difficult to make with any confidence, a conservative path was taken and these were assigned to the nonglottal category. No attempt was made to auditorily differentiate glottaled and glottalised variants. All subsequent analysis was carried out on tokens assigned to the glottal variant category (b).

For all speakers, wide-band, spectrographic analysis (using a Kay Elemetrics CSL system) was carried out of /p t k/ word-list items auditorily judged to be produced with a glottal variant. This gave a total of 549 tokens: 98 of these were variants of /p k/, and the other 451 were variants of /t/. The vast majority of these tokens consisted of /t/ in within-word and across-word ['V_ (#) V] environments (e.g., *daughter*, *beat it*). In Tyneside English, these represent the key environments in which glottal variants are found (as already pointed out, in prepausal position, voiceless stops are only rarely glottalised, usually being clearly released instead). The sample of data did, however, include a small number of tokens in other environments, including ['V_ syllabic l] (e.g., *bottle, brittle*), and ['V _ nasal] (e.g., *jumper, hunter*). In all cases, however, the criterial stops were located between two voiced segments, either vowels, approximants, or nasals, and were in a *strong–weak* prosodic environment. Table 8.1 shows how the sample of glottal variants identified auditorily was distributed across the different groups making up the sample of speakers. Of the 32 subjects, 10 failed to produce a single glottal token (4 × OMC–F, 2 × OMC–M, 3 × YMC–F, 1 × OWC–F), and a further 8 produced less than 10 tokens—leaving only 14 whose sample of glottals reached double figures. Note that the skewing of these figures is not only due to the sociolinguistic factors applying to a particular cell but also to the fact that in more formal styles (such as reading a word list, as in this study), it seems that certain groups do tend to produce fewer localised variants such as glottal allophones of /t/.

An acoustic profile was then constructed to analyse the key characteristics of the glottal/ised variants. As mentioned earlier, the analysis was based on the quantification of acoustic parameters which our spectrographic observations suggested are the most important,

TABLE 8.1

Distribution of Glottal/ised Plosives Across the Sample of Speakers

	y. WC	o. WC	y. MC	o. MC	Total
Men	176	143	79	20	418
Women	111	15	5	0	131

Note. y. = young, o. = old, WC = working class, MC = middle class.

defining the phonetic properties of this category of sound. For these purposes, we focus on three of these properties:

1. Periodicity—Each token was categorised as being fully voiced, partially voiced, or completely voiceless. Full voicing was assigned when there was no break in voicing corresponding to the plosive. 'Voiceless' was assigned when there was a period of voicelessness broadly coterminous with the end of the preceding segment and the onset of the following segment. For this purpose, we ignored any small incursion of less than 20 msec into an otherwise totally voiceless stop slot. 'Partial voicing' was assigned to any case where there was an interruption in voicing during the production of the stop but not of sufficient duration for the stop to be labelled as fully voiceless.

2. Formant Transitions—To gauge whether the token was glottal or glottalised, we recorded the presence or absence of a supralaryngeal gesture, as evidenced by any F2 transitions characteristic of the appropriate supralaryngeal place of articulation (on the assumption that such transitions would be absent in the case of an intervocalic glottal stop produced without an accompanying supralaryngeal articulation).

3. Transient—The presence or absence of a release burst was noted for each token—as well as being evidence of the presence of an occlusion, this parameter would also be revealing in respect of articulatory coordination given that the Tyneside glottalised variants are claimed to have the release masked by the glottal articulation (Wells, 1982). It could be objected that visual identification of a release burst in this way would not discriminate between the burst arising from oral occlusions and the burst which would be found on the release of a canonical glottal stop. However, in the very few canonical tokens that we encountered, the onset of the vowel following [ʔ] was marked by a sudden onset of energy across the complete frequency range which looked quite different from that which is typically found for oral stops, each of which have their own particular spectral characteristics which are readily distinguishable (Stevens, 1998).

We reiterate that this study cannot make any claims to exhaustiveness in respect of the phonetic description which it provides, but the acoustic features tracked in the analysis, as well as being relatively prominent within the spectrographic images, do enable a description of some important characteristics of glottal variants, which, in the absence of previous studies of this sort, goes some way to filling the gaps in our knowledge of this area.

RESULTS

Table 8.2 gives a description of the overall frequency of acoustic patterns which we tracked. Each of the three main acoustic parameters is now considered in turn.

1. Periodicity—Seventy percent of tokens were characterised by unbroken periodicity, signalling that they were fully voiced. Only 3% of tokens had a canonically voiceless interval with the appearance of a voiceless stop occlusion. The intervals of voicing in the fully- and partially-voiced tokens were usually characterised by some degree of laryngealisation. In some cases, remarkably little laryngealisation indeed was observed, and the only acoustic correlate of the audible production of a glottal variant was the misalignment of two or three vertical striations bounded by the two adjacent vowels (see examples in Figures 8.1 and 8.2).

TABLE 8.2

Frequency of Different Patterns of Voicing, F2 Activity in Glottal Variants, and Release Burst Activity

| | | Pattern of Voicing | | | |
		Fully Voiced	Partially Voiced	Fully Voiceless	Total
F2	Supralaryngeal gesture present	284	139	13	435 (79%)
	Supralaryngeal gesture absent	100	10	3	114 (21%)
		384 (70%)	149 (27%)	16 (3%)	549
Release	Release burst absent	286	108	13	406 (74%)
	Release burst present	98	41	3	143 (26%)
	Total	384 (70%)	149 (27%)	16 (3%)	549

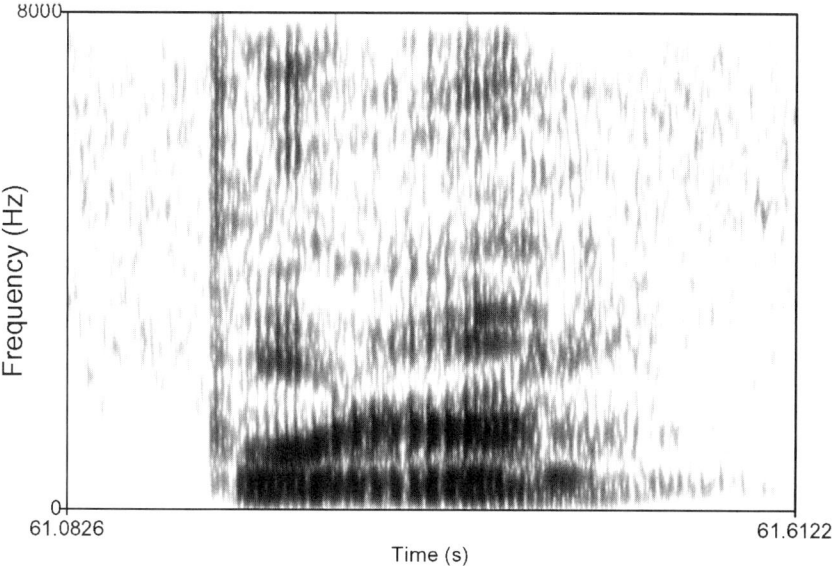

FIG. 8.1. Spectrogram of the word "Bootle" produced by an old WC male speaker, showing unbroken voicing with medial laryngealisation (but no indication of stop release).

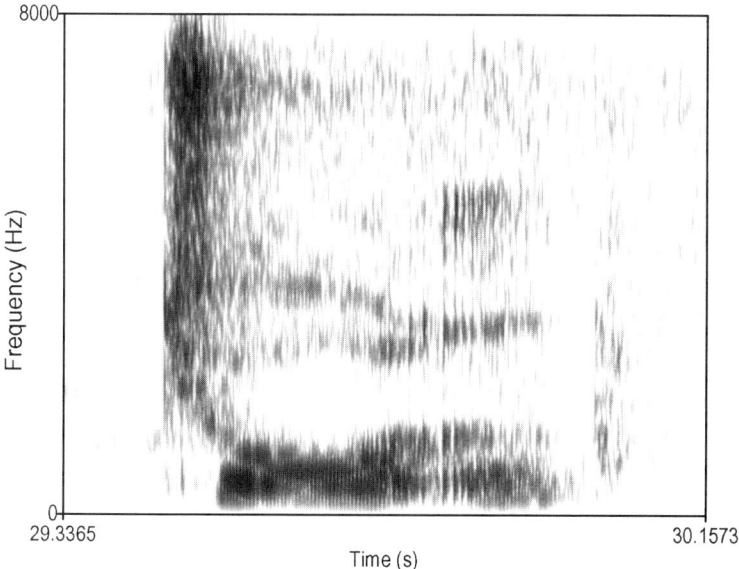

FIG. 8.2. Spectrogram of the word "chortle" produced by a young WC female speaker showing unbroken voicing with medial laryngealisation (but no indication of stop release).

2. F2 Transitions—In 79% of the tokens, F2 transitions into or out of the stop were indicative of the presence of an oral gesture. The exceptions to this (i.e., [ʔ]) were largely found in /t/ occurring before a syllabic /l/.

3. Release Burst—The co-occurrence of release burst and occlusion is shown in Table 8.3. A release burst was observed in 32% (141 out of 435) of the glottalised tokens analysed (see Fig. 8.3 for an example). This could be considered rather a high figure given the claims (referred to earlier) that in the Tyneside variety of English, the glottal gesture masks the oral release.

4. Interspeaker Variability—The nature of the data sample permits consideration of the distribution of the various acoustic features across the different groups of speakers. Table 8.4 shows the frequency of occurrence of the five most frequently found phonetic realisations as a function of the three speaker variables of age, sex, and 'class.'

Although most of the large differences in frequency of occurrence can be accounted for by reference to the overall frequencies of glottal variants (as shown in Table 8.1), there is at least one aspect of this which seems to warrant a different explanation. Older men (especially older WC men) show a relatively high presence of release burst in their glottalised tokens. This is reflected in Fig. 8.4, which shows the percentage of all tokens produced with a release burst by age, sex, and 'class.' A chi-square test suggests that there is a significant difference in the distribution of bursts across old versus young WC men ($p <$

TABLE 8.3

Frequency of Different Patterns of F2 Activity in Glottal Variants, and Release Burst Activity

	F2 Evidence of Supralaryngeal Gesture Present	F2 Evidence of Supralaryngeal Gesture Absent	
Release burst absent	294	113	407
Release burst present	141	0	141
	435	113	

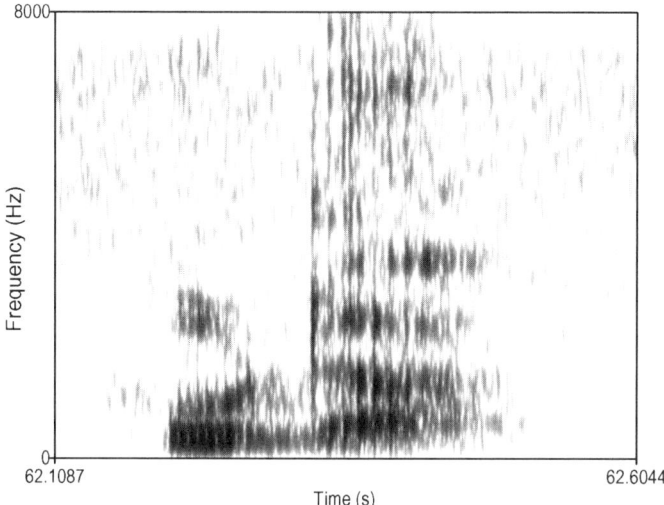

FIG. 8.3. Spectrogram of the word "hooter" with an auditorily-distinct glottalised variant of /t/ produced by an old WC male speaker, showing the presence of a release burst and formant transitions arising from an oral occlusion.

0.001). This would seem to indicate that older men have a tendency to time their oral and laryngeal gestures such that the former lags behind the latter (making the release audible), much as is found in other varieties of English (although not necessarily in the same environments). By contrast, on the whole, the glottalised variants produced by other speakers generally show the pattern of temporal coordination previously reported for Tyneside with the oral release masked by the sustained glottal gesture. This pattern of results points to a subtle (although auditorily very distinct) difference in articulatory coordination across different speakers of the 'same' accent.

DISCUSSION

A striking feature of the results is the virtual absence of 'canonical' glottal stop or glottalised stop articulations in any of the data. Although we cannot comment directly on the actual articulatory gestures produced by our speakers, the vast majority of our tokens are produced with full or partial voicing. The irregularity observed in

TABLE 8.4

Frequency of Occurrence of the Five Most Frequently Found Phonetic Realisations as a Function of the Three Speaker Variables of Age, Sex and 'Class'

		Social Group				
		YWC	OWC	YMC	OMC	Total
		M: $n = 165$	M: $n = 133$	M: $n = 77$	M: $n = 17$	
		F: $n = 108$	F: $n = 15$	F: $n = 5$	F: $n = 0$	
	Fully voiced, glottalised, no release					
	M	57	29	31	7	124
	F	55	3	4	—	62
						186
	Fully voiced, glottalised, released					
	M	21	49	8	8	86
	F	9	2	1	—	12
						98
Variant	Fully voiced, glottaled, no release					
	M	37	20	10	1	68
	F	23	9	0	—	32
						100
	Partially voiced, glottalised, no release					
	M	42	17	18	0	77
	F	20	1	0	—	21
						98
	Partially voiced, glottalised, released					
	M	8	18	10	1	37
	F	3	0	0	—	3
						40

the pattern of vertical striations suggests that speakers are producing a creaky voice quality which in turn suggests that there is a degree of constriction of the vocal folds (compared to that found in modal voice), but no sustained occlusion. Indeed, in some cases, clear glottal percepts arise merely from the presence of very slight perturbations in the vertical striations (and hence vocal fold vibration) in the middle of what appears to be a smooth transition from the voiced segment preceding the underlying stop to the following vowel segment. Note that similar findings have emerged from a parallel study which we have carried out of the Derby variety of English (Docherty & Foulkes, 1999b), suggesting that this is not a feature that is peculiar to Tyneside English.

The majority of the tokens in our current dataset also bear a strong resemblance to the examples of [ʔ] in Lebanese Arabic and [*] in Gimi given by Ladefoged and Maddieson (1996), the latter of which is described as a creaky-voiced glottal approximant characterised by an interval of attenuated energy between two vowels. They are also reminiscent of the patterns of realisation noted from word-initial glottaling in American English (Redi & Shattuck–Hufnagel, 2001) and German (Kohler, 1994, 1999). Thus, our findings are consistent with the reports of other investigators that variants which readily give the auditory impression of involving a glottal stop either as a primary or secondary articulation are commonly produced without a sustained glottal stop articulation (as conventionally described). Our results are also in line with previous findings that, at least in some varieties of some languages, the most typical laryngeal characteristic associated with these sounds is an interval of laryngealised voice quality.

Our results support the claims in the literature that, as with other varieties of BrE, there are two types of glottal variant to be found in the Tyneside variety: with and without an accompanying supralaryngeal gesture. The latter is a variant of /t/, whereas the former is found as a realisation of /p t k/. Where Tyneside English differs from other varieties, however, is that the glottaled variant appears to have a more restricted pattern of occurrence. It is found most commonly in the environment of a following syllabic lateral, and, much less commonly than in other varieties, in word-medial position or in word-final intersonorant position. With regard to the observation from previous work that Tyneside

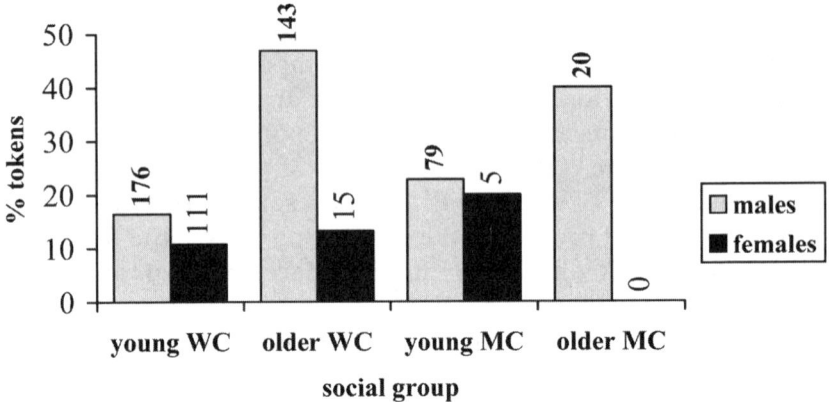

FIG. 8.4. % tokens with release burst (absolute figures shown above each bar).

English has a particular type of glottal reinforcement (such that the stop release is masked), our results paint a rather mixed picture. The more localised form of glottalisation is found to predominate for the subjects who produced glottalised forms, with the exception of older men (especially older WC men) who produce a significantly greater proportion of glottalised variants with an audible oral release (i.e., with the laryngeal–supralaryngeal timing adjusted such that there is no masking of the oral release). Thus, the phonetic properties of glottalised stops in the Tyneside variety of English must be described as being variable, both in the sense that all of the individual speakers produce tokens of preglottalised and postglottalised forms, but also in the sense that older male speakers appear to make significantly greater use of the former variant. Nevertheless, the variety is clearly different from other varieties of English in the use by many speakers of an auditorily-distinct postglottalised form masking the oral release of the oral articulation.

Our capturing of the complex pattern of glottal articulations in Tyneside English has clearly been facilitated by the size of our sample and the profiling technique which was used to analyse the recordings. The results underline the general finding of the *Phonological Variation and Change*' project (explored in more detail in Docherty et al., 1997) that it is unlikely that a systematic account of the phonetic properties of any particular variety of a language can be provided without some account being taken of the social and stylistic dimensions along which speakers' performance can vary. As pointed out by Docherty and Foulkes (2000), Docherty, Foulkes, Tillotson, and Watt (in press), and Docherty (2003), it is a concern that so much theoretical modelling has proceeded in the absence of this being taken into consideration. Evidence such as that reported in this chapter emphasises the need for investigators to be as sensitive to the socially-correlated dimensions of variability within their data as they are to the contextual and prosodic dimensions (Foulkes, 2003; Ladefoged, 2003).

The acoustic profiling approach which we applied in this study has made it very clear that tokens which we hear as glottal/ised stops may often not be so. It has further allowed us to identify the key acoustic parameters which are associated with glottal variants in this variety of English and how they vary across individuals and groups of speakers. However, the importance of taking an approach of this sort, as opposed to relying on impressionistic auditory-symbolic representations, goes much further. Browman and Goldstein (1992) point out that

> there is much systematic, quantitative variation of speech gestures that has never been captured in a narrow allophonic transcription of the conventional sort, and could not easily be described in this way ... [it has been argued that] ... this intermediate allophonic transcription does not contribute in a useful way to the complete description of the variability. It is either unnecessary, or gets in the way of stating the generalisations. Thus it seems that many allophonic differences are just quantitative differences that are large enough that phoneticians/ phonologists have been able to notice them, and to relate them to distinctive differences found in other languages. (p. 164ff)

Browman and Goldstein would presumably argue that the auditory analysis which has dominated previous work on glottal variants has been 'getting in the way' of an understanding of the real nature of speakers' performance and would advocate a more detailed acoustic or preferably articulatory analysis. This is a view which we would endorse and the results of our study have gone some way to unpacking the complexities behind the use of the impressionistic symbol [ʔ] in phonetic and phonological accounts of one variety of English.[7]

CONCLUSION

Two of the hallmarks of John Laver's contribution to the field of phonetics are the promotion of rigorous phonetic taxonomy and, in line with his unfailing ability to discern and illuminate 'the bigger picture,' an abiding interest in the broad indexical functions of speech communication. Our aspiration is that in contributing to our understanding of the nature of glottal variants in English and in highlighting the social-indexical dimension to their distribution, this study will have made a helpful contribution to both of these aspects of phonetic theory.

ACKNOWLEDGMENTS

We'd like to acknowledge the contribution made to this work by our co-investigators Lesley Milroy, Jim Milroy and Dom Watt. We are grateful to Penny Oxley for carrying out our field recordings and to our subjects for their time and energy.

NOTES

[1] A brief account of these findings has previously appeared in Docherty & Foulkes (1999a).

[2] The large-scale project referred to was entitled *'Phonological Variation and Change in Contemporary Spoken English,'* and was funded by the UK Economic and Social Research Council, award No. R0000234892.

[3] The terms *creaky* and *laryngealised voice* are being used interchangeably here, as in Ladefoged and Maddieson (1996).

[4] Byrd's (1993) data include all tokens transcribed as [ʔ], irrespective of their context, with 49% of these occurring in *word-initial* position (ie., as a hard-attack to a word-initial vowel) and a further 29% in an 'unaffiliated' environment defined by the author as 'between vowels at a word-boundary' (p. 14).

[5] See Byrd (1993, 1994), Dilley, Shattuck–Hufnagel, and Ostendorf (1996), Kohl and Anderson (2000), and Redi and Shattuck–Hufnagel (2001), for a discussion of patterns of glottalisation in North American English, and Tollfree (1996) and Holmes (1995) for Australian and New Zealand English, respectively.

[6] There are a number of environments in which these variants can be found, but a good deal of variability in terms of which environments are active for particular speakers. Wells (1982) points out that in British English, glottalisation is found in syllable-final stops preceded by a vowel, liquid, or nasal in the following environments:

1. ____ # True C
2. ____ # L or S
3. ____ # V (unstressed)   True C = obstruents and nasals
4. ____ Pause   L = non-syllabic liquid
5. ____ True C   S = semi-vowel
6. ____ No. L or S
7. ____ Syllabic [m, n, Î]
8. ____ V or syllabic [l]

However, Wells notes that for some speakers, preglottalisation is found to occur in most or all of these environments, but for others it only occurs in environments (1), (2), and (5), and some speakers will not produce glottal stops in any of these environments. Studies which are particularly focused on accounting for the environments in which these variants are found include Gussenhoven (1986), Roach (1973), and Carr (1991).

[7] In pursuing the question of what exactly is the mapping between the auditory categories represented as [ʔ] or [ʔt] and acoustic parameters such as those investigated in this study, it would be interesting, for example, to see what the minimum amount of intervocalic laryngealisation might be to generate a percept of a V[ʔ]V (but this falls outside the scope of this chapter and is a matter for future work).

REFERENCES

Andrésen, B. S. (1968). *Pre-Glottalization in English standard pronunciation.* Oslo, Norway: Norwegian Universities Press.

Browman, C., & Goldstein, L. (1992). Articulatory phonology: An overview. *Phonetica, 49,* 155–180.

Byrd, D. (1993). 54,000 American stops. *UCLA Working Papers in Phonetics, 83,* 1–19.

Byrd, D. (1994). Relations of sex and dialect to reduction. *Speech Communication, 15,* 39–54.

Carr, P. (1991). Lexical properties of post-lexical rules: Postlexical derived environment and the elsewhere condition. *Lingua, 85,* 255–268.

Catford, J. C. (1977). *Fundamental problems of phonetics.* Edinburgh, Scotland: Edinburgh University Press.

Chirrey, D. (1999). Edinburgh: Descriptive material. In P. Foulkes, & G. J. Docherty, (Eds.), *Urban voices: Accent studies in the British Isles* (pp. 223–229). London, England: Arnold.

Christopherson, P. (1952). The glottal stop in English. *English Studies, 33,* 156–163.

Clark, J., & Yallop, C. (1995). *An introduction to phonetics & phonology.* Oxford, England: Blackwell.

Collins, B., & Mees, I. (1996). Spreading everywhere? How recent a phenomenon is glottalisation in received pronunciation? *English World-Wide, 17,* 175–187.

Dilley, L., Shattuck–Hufnagel, S., & Ostendorf, M. (1996). Glottalization of word-initial vowels as a function of prosodic structure. *Journal of Phonetics, 24,* 423–444.

Docherty, G. J. (2003). Speaker, community, identity: Empirical and theoretical perspectives on sociophonetic variation. *Proceedings of the XVth International Congress of Phonetic Sciences, Barcelona, Spain,* 11–16.

Docherty, G. J., & Foulkes, P. (1995). Acoustic profiling of glottal and glottalised variants of English stops. *Proceedings of the XIIIth International Congress of Phonetic Sciences, University of Stockholm, Sweden, 1,* 350–353.

Docherty, G. J., & Foulkes, P. (1999a). Sociophonetic variation in 'glottals' in Newcastle English. *Proceedings of the XIVth International Congress of Phonetic Sciences, University of California, Berkeley, USA,* 1037–1040.

Docherty, G. J., & Foulkes, P. (1999b). Newcastle and Derby: Instrumental phonetics and variationist studies. In P. Foulkes & G. J. Docherty (Eds.), *Urban voices: Accent studies in the British Isles* (pp. 47–71). London, England: Arnold.

Docherty, G. J., & Foulkes, P. (2000). Speaker, speech & knowledge of sounds. In N. Burton–Roberts, P. Carr, & G. J. Docherty (Eds.), *Phonological knowledge: Conceptual & empirical issues* (pp. 105–129). Oxford, England: Oxford University Press.

Docherty, G. J., Foulkes, P., Milroy, J., Milroy, L., & Walshaw, D. (1997). Descriptive adequacy in phonology: A variationist perspective. *Journal of Linguistics, 33,* 275–310.

Docherty, G. J., Foulkes, P., Tillotson, J., & Watt, D. (in press). On the scope of phonological learning: Issues arising from socially structured variation. In L. Goldstein, D. Whalen, & C. Best (Eds.) Papers in Laboratory Phonology, 8. Berlin; Germany: Mouton de Gruyter.

Esling, J. (1996). Pharyngeal consonants and the epiglottal sphincter. *Journal of the International Phonetic Association, 26,* 65–88.

Esling, J., Fraser, K., & Harris, J. (in press). Glottal stop, glottalized resonants, and pharyngeals: A reinterpretation with evidence from a laryngographic study of Nuuchahnulth (Nootka). *Journal of Phonetics.*

Fabricius, A. (2000). *T-glottaling: Between stigma and prestige: A sociolinguistic study of modern RP.* Unpublished doctoral dissertation, Copenhagen Business School, Copenhagen, Denmark.

Fabricius, A. (2002). Ongoing change in modern RP: Evidence for the disappearing stigma of t-glottalling. *English World-Wide, 23,* 115–136.

Foulkes, P. (2003). Fieldwork for studies of phonological variation. *Proceedings of the XVth International Congress of Phonetic Sciences*, Barcelona, Spain, 211–214.

Foulkes, P., Docherty, G. J., & Watt, D. (1999). Tracking the emergence of sociophonetic variation. *Proceedings of the XIVth International Congress of Phonetic Sciences, University of California, Berkeley,* 1625–1628.

Gimson, A. C. (1980). *An introduction to the pronunciation of English* (3rd ed.). London, England: Arnold.

Gussenhoven, C. (1986). English plosive allophones and ambisyllabicity. *Gramma, 10,* 119–141.

Harris, J., & Kaye, J. (1990). A tale of two cities: London glottalling and New York tapping. *The Linguistic Review, 7,* 251–274.

Henton, C., Ladefoged, P., & Maddieson, I. (1992). Stops in the world's languages. *Phonetica, 49,* 65–101.

Higginbottom, E. (1964). Glottal reinforcement in English. *Transactions of the Philological Society,* 129–142.

Holmes, J. (1995). Glottal stops in New Zealand English: An analysis of variants of word-final /t/. *Linguistics, 33,* 433–463.

Jones, D. (1967). *The pronunciation of English* (4th ed.). Cambridge, England: Cambridge University Press.

Kingsmore, R. K. (1995). *Ulster Scots speech. A sociolinguistic study.* Tuscaloosa: Alabama, USA. University of Alabama Press.

Kohl, A., & Anderson, A. (2000). *Glottalization as a sociolinguistic variable in Detroit.* Paper presented at the 29th NWAV (New Ways of Analyzing Variation) Conference, Michigan State University, East Lansing. Retrieved 1/7/03 from http://www.lsa.umich.edu/ling/detroit/akbanwav00.pdf

Kohler, K. (1994). Glottal stops and glottalisation in German. *Phonetica, 51,* 38–51.

Kohler, K. (1999). Articulatory prosodies in German reduced speech. *Proceedings of the XIVth International Congress of Phonetic Sciences, University of California, Berkeley, USA,* 89–92.

Labov, W. (1986). Sources of inherent variation in the speech process. In J. Perkell, & D. Klatt, (Eds.), *Invariance and variability in speech processes* (pp. 402–425). Hillsdale, NJ, USA: Lawrence Erlbaum Associates, Inc.

Labov, W. (1994). *Principles of linguistic change: Volume 1—Internal factors.* Oxford, England: Blackwell.

Labov, W., Yaeger, M., & Steiner R. (1972). *A Quantitative study of sound change in progress.* Philadelphia, USA: US Regional Survey.

Ladefoged, P. (2003). Phonetic fieldwork. *Proceedings of the XVth International Congress of Phonetic Sciences, Barcelona, Spain,* 203–206.

Ladefoged, P., & Maddieson, I. (1996). *The sounds of the world's languages.* Oxford, England: Blackwell.

Lindqvist, J. (1969). *Laryngeal mechanisms in speech.* (Rep. No. 2–3). Stockholm, Sweden: Royal Institute of Technology, Speech Transmission Laboratory.

Macaulay, R. (1977). *Language, social class and education: a Glasgow study.* Edinburgh, Scotland: Edinburgh University Press.

Macaulay, R. K. S. (1991). *Locating dialect in discourse: The language of honest men and bonnie lasses in Ayr.* Oxford, England: Oxford University Press.

Maddieson, I. (1984). *Patterns of sounds.* Cambridge, England: Cambridge University Press.

Mees, I. M. (1987). Glottal stops as a prestigious feature of Cardiff English. *English World-Wide, 8,* 25–39.

Mees, I. M., & Collins, B. (1999). Cardiff: A real-time study of glottalisation. In P. Foulkes & G. J. Docherty (Eds.), *Urban voices: Accent studies in the British Isles* (pp. 185–202). London, England: Arnold.

Milroy, J., Milroy, L., Hartley S., & Walshaw, D. (1995). Glottal stops and Tyneside glottalization: Competing patterns of variation and change in British English. *Language Variation & Change, 6,* 327–357.

Milroy, L., Milroy, J., & Docherty, G. J. (1997). *Phonological variation and change in contemporary spoken British English.* Final report to the ESRC (Economic and Social Research Council) UK (Research grant No. R000234892).

Milroy, L., Milroy, J., Docherty, G. J., Foulkes, P., & Walshaw, D. (1999). Phonological variation and change in contemporary English: Evidence from Newcastle upon Tyne and Derby. *Cuadernos de Filología Inglesa de la Universidad de Murcia, 8,* 35–46.

Newbrook, M. (1986). *Sociolinguistic reflexes of dialect interference in West Wirral.* Bern, Switzerland: Peter Lang.

Nolan, F. J. (1995). The role of the jaw—Active or passive: Comments on Lee. In B. Connell & A. Arvaniti (Eds.), *Phonology and phonetic evidence: Papers in laboratory phonology IV* (pp. 361–367). Cambridge, England: Cambridge University Press.

O'Connor, J. D. (1947). The phonetic system of a dialect of Newcastle upon Tyne *Le Maître Phonétique, 87,* 6–8.

O'Connor, J. D. (1973). *Phonetics.* Harmondsworth, England: Pelican.

Pierrehumbert, J. (1995). Prosodic effects on glottal allophones. In O. Fujimura & M. Hirano (Eds.), *Vocal fold physiology: Voice quality control* (pp. 39–60). San Diego, CA, USA: Singular.

Przedlacka, J. (2002). *Estuary English? A sociophonetic study of teenage speech in the Home Counties.* Bern, Switzerland: Peter Lang.

Redi, L., & Shattuck–Hufnagel, S. (2001). Variation in the realization of glottalization in normal speakers. *Journal of Phonetics, 29,* 407–429.

Reid, E. (1978). Social and stylistic variation in the speech of children: Some evidence from Edinburgh. In P. Trudgill (Ed.) *Sociolinguistic patterns in British English* (pp. 158–171). London, England: Arnold.

Roach, P. (1973). Glottalization of English /p/, /t/, /k/ and /tʃ/—a re-examination. *Journal of the International Phonetic Association, 3,* 10–21.

Stevens K. (1998). *Acoustic phonetics.* Cambridge, MA, USA: MIT Press.

Stoddart, J., Upton, C., & Widdowson, J. (1999). Sheffield dialect in the 1990s: Revisiting the concept of NORMs. In P. Foulkes, & G. J. Docherty (Eds.), *Urban voices: Accent studies in the British Isles* (pp. 72–89). London, England: Arnold.

Stuart–Smith, J. (1999). Glottals past and present: A study of T-glottalling in Glaswegian. *Leeds Studies in English, 30,* 181–204.

Thomas, E. (2002). Sociophonetic applications of speech perception experiments. *American Speech, 77,* 115–147.

Tollfree, L. (1996) *Modelling phonological variation and change: Evidence from English consonants.* Unpublished doctoral dissertation, University of Cambridge, Cambridge England.

Tollfree, L. (1999). South–East London English: Discrete versus continuous modelling of consonantal reduction. In P. Foulkes & G. J. Docherty (Eds.), *Urban voices: Accent studies in the British Isles* (pp. 163–184). London, England: Arnold.

Trigo, L. (1991). On pharynx–larynx interactions. *Phonology, 8,* 113–116.

Trudgill, P. (1974). *The social differentiation of English in Norwich.* Cambridge, England: Cambridge University Press.

Wells, J. C. (1982). *Accents of English* (3 vols.). Cambridge, England: Cambridge University Press.

APPENDIX

Word List and Read Sentences
From the Phonological Variation and Change Project

sheet	boat	lap it	half-cut
beetle	total	apron	automatic
metre	motor	matron	Jupiter
I beat it	I wrote it	micro	epileptic
gate	put	metro	sheet
paint	footer	leprosy	read
fatal	put it in	petrol	breeze
later	boot	acrid	key
I hate it	Bootle	atlas	gate
eighty eight	hooter	hopper	made
bet	bite	butter	may
bent	title	hacker	boat
felt	mitre	topple	load
fettle	pint	bottle	go
better	bite it	hackle	boot
I met him	out	whisper	brood
hat	fount	custard	booze
ant	outer	after	brew
battle	pit	whisker	out
batter	bitter	doctor	loud
drat it	brittle	chapter	cow
cart	print	jumper	sight
can't	I hit it	hunter	side
carter	hilt	bunker	size
pot	beak	appear	sigh
totter	wreck	attend	sighed
bottle	back	occur	knife
font	I seek it	appearance	five
salt	I wreck it	attendance	knives
I got it	I back it	occurrence	dive
caught	bank	alpine	dial
daughter	lamp	alter	Friday
chortle	leap	polka	diary
haunt	cap	staircase	
I bought it	steep it	half-past	

198

I've got to do it tomorrow
I had to put it off
He meant what he said
He's booking separate tables for supper
A simple sentence
Pick up a packet of firelighters
Pack it in or beat it
He's putting it off
He put in a bid
Jump up on the tractor
He won't do that in a hurry
Put a comma in it

Chapter 9

Exploring the Phonetics of Spoken Narratives in Australian Indigenous Languages

Janet Fletcher
University of Melbourne, Australia

The research described in this chapter addresses two aspects of phonetic theory examined by John Laver. The first question is more broad, and focuses on the phonetic description of speech sounds in little studied languages (e.g., Laver, 1967). The second considers the importance of discourse context in the study of connected speech (e.g., Laver, 1980, 1991). Laver claims (1994) that both questions should play a critical role in shaping phonetic theory. I examine these questions with particular reference to a group of North Australian languages—Kayardild, Dalabon, and Mayali—which are among the few remaining spoken Australian indigenous languages. Although many Australian languages have been the focus of a great deal of grammatical description in the last 30 or more years, (e.g., Blake, 1981; Dixon, 2002), there have been relatively few large-scale linguistic phonetic analyses of their segmental properties. Moreover, it is only recently that the intonational features of some of these languages have been systematically examined. In the sections that follow, I examine vowel inventories in the three Australian languages, in the spirit of Laver's thesis that one of the goals of phonetic theory is to explain "the phonetic regularities that serve to ... make each language sound different from other languages" (Laver, 1995, p. 95). In the second part of this chapter, I examine pitch range and its role as one of the "cues that are conventionally used to claim and yield the floor in the control of speaking-turns and conversational interaction" (Laver, 1994, pp. 95–96) in two of the three languages. In particular, I investigate the contribution of pitch variation to the signaling reported speech in spontaneous narratives.

VOWEL DISPERSION IN THREE NORTH AUSTRALIAN LANGUAGES

The phonetic properties of Australian languages are of interest to phoneticians in a number of ways. Most of them have complex consonant inventories in the place dimension, relatively few consonant manner contrasts, and small vowel inventories (Evans, 1995b). An example of a language with all these traits is Kayardild (Evans, 1995a), one of the languages analysed in this chapter, whose consonant and vowel inventories are reproduced in Table 9.1. Kayardild is a member of the Tangkic family (non-Pama-Njungan), spoken in the south Wellesley Islands, southern Gulf of Carpentaria. Fewer than 10 people now speak Kayardild. It is quite unrelated to Dalabon, or

TABLE 9.1

Consonant and Vowel Phoneme Inventory of Kayardild (After Evans, 1995b)

		Consonants—Place of Articulation				
Manner of Articulation	Bilabial	Lamino- Dental	Apico- Alveolar	Retroflex	Lamino- Palatal	Velar
Short stop	p	t̪	t	ʈ	c	k
Nasal	m	n̪	n	ɳ	ɲ	ŋ
Lateral			l	ɭ		
Trill			r			
Approximant	w			ɻ	j	
		Vowels				
		Front		Back		
Close		i iː		u uː		
Open			a aː			

Mayali, the two other languages investigated in this chapter. These two languages are members of the Gunwinjguan family (non-Pama-Nyungan) and are still spoken in northern Arnhem land. Mayali has over a thousand remaining speakers, and is spoken in Kakadu national park, whereas Dalabon has only a few remaining speakers, living in and around Maningrida. The segmental phonologies of all three languages are relatively similar, although both Dalabon and Mayali have an additional length contrast in the stop series, and a contrastive glottal stop. The basic syllable structure in Kayardild is C V (Liquid or Glide; Nasal) and in both Dalabon and Mayali, it is C V (Liquid or Glide; Nasal; Stop), where the bracketing means optional.

As mentioned earlier, vowel systems in Australian languages are generally small, and around 50% have triangular vowel spaces. The languages examined here illustrate this distribution. As we can see from Table 9.1, Kayardild is a three-vowel language with a vowel length contrast. Mayali is one of the 9% of Australian languages that has a five-vowel inventory (after Busby, 1979), and Dalabon has been analysed as a six-vowel language (Alpher, 1982). The sixth vowel has been impressionistically described as close central, or close central rounded. The vowel inventories from these two languages are shown in Table 9.2. They are identical except for the additional central vowel

TABLE 9.2

Vowel Inventory of Dalabon and Mayali

	Front	Central	Back
High	i	(ɨ)	u
Mid	e		o
Low		a	

in Dalabon. The sixth vowel of Dalabon is the high central vowel which is represented by "v" in the practical orthography for the language. This convention is retained in this chapter.

Although the unusual typological features of consonant systems of Australian languages have been noted in the literature (e.g., Ladefoged & Maddieson, 1996), few studies have examined the vowel systems of Australian languages with reference to theories of vowel distribution, with the exception of a small study by Butcher (1994). According to Johnson (2000, p. 1) among others, most notably Liljencrants & Lindblom, 1972, and Lindblom, 1986, "the distinctive sounds of a language tend to be positioned in phonetic space so as to maximise perceptual contrast." Furthermore, dispersion theory (DT) predicts that vowel contrasts are essentially systemic and relational, not absolute or local. When applied to vowel inventories of languages, DT or adaptive dispersion theory suggests that each vowel acts as a repeller in a dynamical system. This is usually cited as the reason why three vowel systems tend to consist of /i/, /a/, /u/, and five vowel systems tend to consist of /i/, /e/, /a/, /o/, and /u/. The original hypothesis of DT suggested that vowels are maximally dispersed through the vowel system, although this hypothesis has been modified to suggest that vowels may be sufficiently, rather than maximally, dispersed. Articulatory economy counterbalances the perceptual demands for a contrast (Lindblom, 1986). In their survey of UCLA Phonological Segment Inventory Database (UPSID), Schwartz, Boe, Vallee, and Abry (1997b) found that if languages include at least one nonperipheral close vowel in their vowel inventory, the favoured combination tends to be /i ɨ u/. DT predicts exactly this distribution, as these three vowels are maximally contrastive in the close dimension. On the basis of impressionistic vowel transcriptions of Dalabon by Alpher (1982), for example, this language appears to fit this pattern, with three vowels in the close series (Table 9.2). The phonemic vowel inventories of Mayali and Kayardild also pattern in ways that would be predicted by dispersion theories.

With the original hypothesis of maximum dispersion in mind, Butcher (1994) analyzed vowel formant patterns of a number of Australian indigenous languages, including Arrernte, Warlpiri, and Burarra. These languages have two, three, and five contrastive vowels, respectively. Burarra, like Dalabon and Mayali, is spoken in the Northern Territory of Australia. He found that rather than illustrating maximum dispersion relative to size of vowel inventory, the acoustic vowel spaces of these languages tend to be "compact" compared to languages with large vowel inventories like English or Swedish, for example, thus illustrating the principle of sufficient, as opposed to maximum, dispersion. Butcher also claims that although one of the presiding principles of dispersion theories in general is that the close vowels of three vowel languages (and of five vowel languages, for that matter) are phonetically [i] and [u], the close series in many Australian languages is often realized phonetically as somewhere between close to close-mid. A recent study of the four-vowel languages of Shipibo, Paiwan, and San Carlos Apache, by Maddieson (2003), also shows that the back rounded vowels, in particular, tend to be close-mid rather than close, with some variability as to the nature of the fourth vowel (ranging from central back to mid central), whereas the two vowels /i/ and /a/ are somewhat dispersed in the vowel space. The results of both of these studies suggest, then, that the vowels of the languages under investigation in this chapter may well be less dispersed than indicated by the phonemic transcriptions shown in Tables 9.1 and 9.2.

A second issue in relation to dispersion theories is that many of them are based on phonemic databases like UPSID. It is probable that vowel transcriptions in these databases are also based on impressionistic analyses of paradigmatic vowel contrasts in isolated words, for the most part (as well as from connected speech). It might be useful, then, to consider the effects of different prosodic contexts (e.g., stress, phrasal position) on vowel dispersion within languages. It might also be of interest to consider vowel patterns in different kinds of spoken discourse, other than isolated citation forms, to get a sense of the degree of phonetic variation that might occur for each contrastive vowel category of a language. For example, previous studies have shown that in English, vowel targets are sharpened in words in focus, and in clear speech in general (e.g., de Jong, 1995; Harrington, Fletcher, & Beckman, 2000; Moon & Lindblom, 1994). Furthermore, one can consider the notion of "setting" in this context. According to Laver (1994), settings can

> also form part of the manifestations of higher-level units of language, such as the morph, the word, and the phrase ... it (setting) can be used as a theoretical device to explain the basis of phonetic similarity between segments. Any two segments that share a given setting are thereby phonetically more similar to each other than two segments that display no setting in common. (pp. 115–116)

In other words, we might also assume that prosodic effects, like presence of a focal accent, effectively acts like a setting because its effects are seen throughout the entire syllable, foot, or word, and not just on the phonetic characteristics of an individual segment. This has been in English, where the effects of focal accentuation are evident throughout the stressed foot, and not just localized on the primary stressed syllable associated with the focal pitch accent (e.g., Harrington, Beckman, Fletcher, & Palethorpe, 1998; Palethorpe, Beckman, Fletcher, & Harrington, 1999). One of the aims of this chapter, then, is to consider the potential role of these prosodic factors in determining vowel formant patterning in Mayali, Dalabon, and Kayardild.

All three languages have been analyzed previously as stress languages, with postlexically determined intonational pitch accents located on metrically strong syllables in earlier work (Evans, 1995a; Fletcher & Evans, 2002; Fletcher, Evans, & Round, 2002). Although the phonemic vowel inventories of the languages are well described, only some preliminary analysis of Dalabon and Mayali vowels has previously been carried out (Fletcher & Evans, 2002). Neither Dalabon, Kayardild, nor Mayali, are associated with strong vowel reduction in metrically weak syllables, although all three languages elide vowels in these contexts in connected speech. One might predict, therefore, that sufficient contrast among vowels is achieved in all contexts where vowels are fully articulated, because there is no attested reduction to "schwa" in unstressed syllables, unlike stress languages like English, for example. On the other hand, even nonvowel reducing languages like French show some vowel centralization in unaccented syllables, particularly in the F1 domain

(Delattre, 1969), so it is not unreasonable to presume that some effect of prosodic context on vowel quality may be apparent in these Australian languages. Recent analysis of Creek vowels (Johnson & Martin, 2001) also suggests that phonemically short vowels are centralized relative to phonemically long vowels, reflecting a pattern observed in many languages with contrastive vowel length (e.g., Engstrand & Krull, 1994). Johnson and Martin (2001) also found that vowels in intonational phrase-final position are centralized slightly, showing "positional reduction," providing further support for the need to consider local syntagmatic, as well as global paradigmatic, factors in any study of vowel formant patterning.

To see whether the acoustic vowel spaces of Mayali, Dalabon, and Kayardild show sufficient rather than maximum dispersion, as has been suggested by Butcher (1994) for a range of other Australian languages, a corpus of spoken narratives from each of the aforementioned languages was analyzed. As mentioned previously, the vowel formant patterns of two of the languages, Dalabon, and Mayali, have already been already partially described, but are reanalyzed here to take into account additional prosodic factors, like phrase-final context. A corpus of connected speech rather than isolated tokens was chosen, in keeping with Laver's belief that a phonetic theory should deal with all types of spoken interactive discourse. Furthermore, given the fragility of two of the languages, Dalabon and Kayardild, it was not possible to obtain a corpus of isolated forms for this study. Obviously, factors like speaking rate variability, consonant context, and possibly lexical frequency effects, have to be taken into consideration in any theoretical conclusions.

A further aim is to see if the sixth vowel of Dalabon is a central close vowel as would fit with predictions of DT, or whether in fact it has formant patterns more like "schwa," which is the more common central vowel observed by Swartz et al. (1997) in their UPSID survey. The effects of local as well as global factors on vowel dispersion are also of interest here; so phrasal and prosodic context was controlled for in this study. Moreover, Kayardild, like Creek, has a phonemic length contrast, which has never been analyzed acoustically. This is another factor taken into consideration in the analysis.

The corpus consisted of approximately 6 min of spontaneous discourse from Dalabon and Mayali, from two male speakers, recorded in northern Arnhem land. The Kayardild corpus consisted of two separate narratives from a male and female speaker. These narratives were 9 and 12 min long, respectively. Vowel and consonant segments were identified from acoustic waveforms and wideband spectro-grams, and labelled using Emu (Cassidy & Harrington, 2001). A total of 2,484 vowel tokens were labelled in the corpus. A fundamental frequency signal was also extracted, and the texts were annotated intonationally, using conventions outlined in previous studies of the three languages (Fletcher & Evans 2000; Fletcher & Evans, 2002; Fletcher et al., 2002). On the basis of an intonational analysis from the earlier studies, syllables were identified as accented (i.e., where a syllable was associated with a postlexical pitch accent, usually located in the vicinity of a lexically stressed syllable), or unaccented (absence of a pitch accent), and phrase-final syllables were identified as those which occurred at the end of an intonational phrase (irre-spective of accentuation). All three languages have one major high pitch accent type ("H*") according to our earlier analyses of these languages. Lexically stressed syllables, not associated with pitch accents, were classified as unaccented. The location of phrasal stress in all three languages is usually on the penultimate syllable of an intonational phrase.

Vowel targets (i.e., where there was evidence of a steady-state in formants 1 and 2) were visually identified from the spectrograms, and labelled separately. If a steady state was not readily identifiable, the label was placed at the vowel midpoint. F1 and F2 values were extracted at the labelled vowel target points for each vowel in the corpus using EMU (Cassidy & Harrington, 2001). The values in HZ were converted to the auditory bark scale (Zwicker, 1961) using the following formula:

$$F_{bark} = 13\tan^{-1}(0.0076f_{HZ}) + 3.5\tan^{-1}(fHZ^2/7500) \qquad (1)$$

Fig. 9.1 shows ellipse plots in the F1–F2 formant plane for vowels produced by the Mayali speaker in this corpus. All vowels are plot-ted, irrespective of prosodic context, and each ellipse includes at least 95% of measured vowel data. Fig. 9.3 shows similar formant plots for the two Kayardild speakers. Fig. 9.2, by contrast, shows mean F1–F2 formant values for Dalabon, as well as mean F1–F2 for-mant values for a range of vowels produced by five male speakers of general Australian English (from Harrington & Cassidy, 1994). The size of the ellipses for the Mayali and Kayardild vowels (Figures 9.1 and 9.3) shows that there is a large amount of variation and overlap

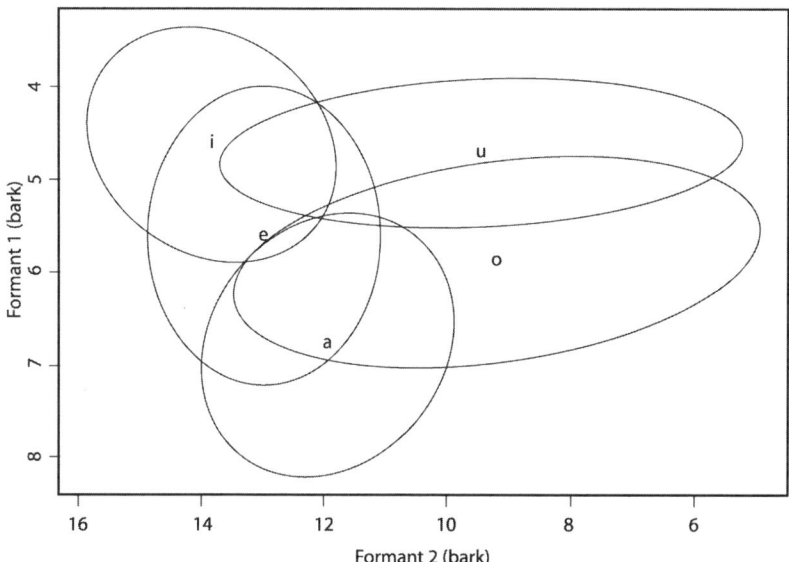

Vowel ellipses: Gun-djeihmi Mayali

FIG. 9.1. Average F1 and F2 values (bark) and ellipse plots of vowels produced by a male speaker of Mayali.

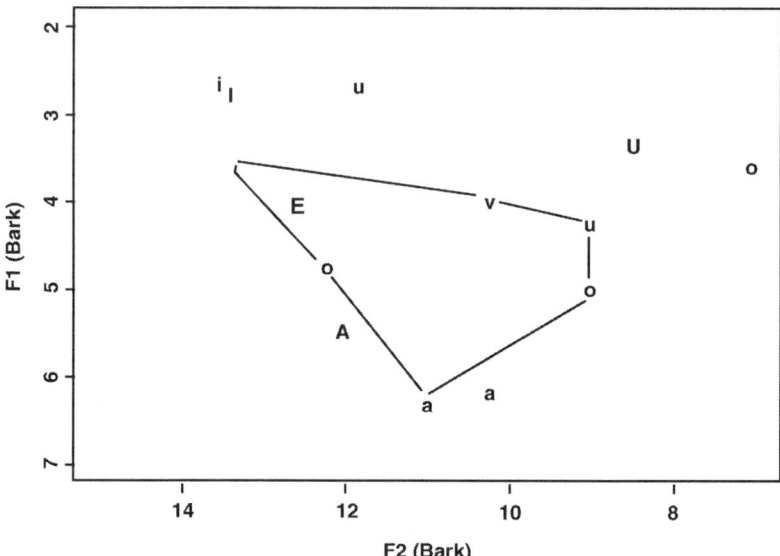

Average Formant Frequencies (Bark) - Dalabon & Male Speakers of Australian English

FIG. 9.2. Average F1 and F2 values (bark) in Dalabon (linked by solid lines), including the vowel /é/, plotted with mean F1 and F2 values of selected vowels for five male Australian English speakers (from Harrington & Cassidy, 1994).

209

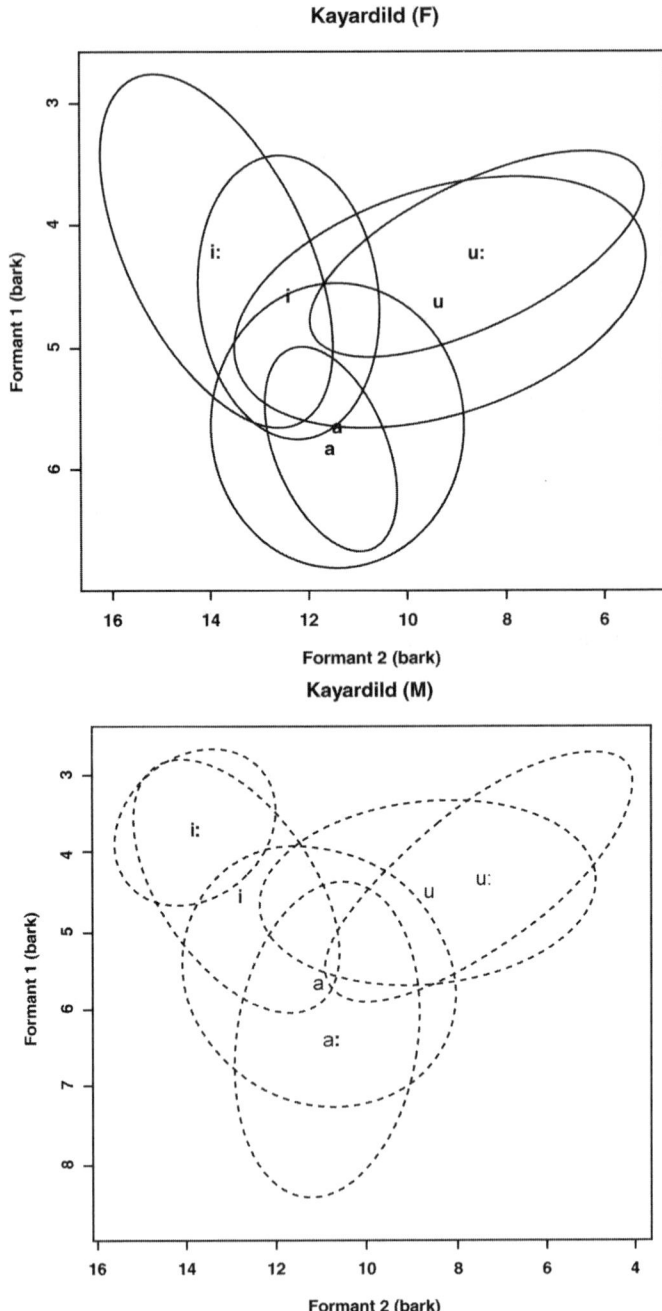

FIG. 9.3. Average F1 and F2 values (bark) and ellipse plots of vowels, in Kayardild for two speakers (male and female). Long vowels are plotted separately from short vowels.

210

within each vowel category. In Mayali, for example, the front vowels show a lot of variation in the F1 dimension, whereas in the back dimension, there is more variation in F2. This is largely due to coarticulatory effects of surrounding consonants. A similar degree of variation also occurs in Dalabon, although the ellipses are not shown in Fig. 9.2. Kayardild (Fig. 9.3) also shows a large amount of overlap among vowel categories, with variation in both the F1 and F2 dimension, although the short back vowel /u/ shows more variation in F2 than its long counterpart.

The amount of spread and overlap of ellipses is to be expected given the nature of the corpus (free, spontaneous speech) and we would expect there to be effects of consonant context, as well as potential effects of prosodic context on vowel formant patterning. It is still possible, however, to draw a number of inferences from these formant plots. The vowel spaces of the three languages are reasonably similar, in spite of the slightly different sizes of their vowel inventories. The acoustic vowel space in all three languages is somewhat compact, as suggested by Butcher (1994) for other Australian languages. The vowel spaces are also fairly symmetrical. This is clearly apparent in the case of Mayali (Fig. 9.1) and Kayardild (Fig. 9.3). The compactness of the vowel spaces is also very apparent, when one compares the Dalabon vowel space with Australian English, as shown in Fig. 9.2. The most similar vowel in the F1 dimension is /a/. Given the relatively less open and central quality of the low vowel in Australian English (i.e., the typical realization of the vowel in "car" is [ɐ]), this is not that surprising. The rest of the vowel space in Dalabon is somewhat compressed, with higher F1 values for the "close" series, compared to the Australian English /i/ and /ʊ/ values, also plotted in Fig. 9.2. This suggests that this series is really between close-mid to close, rather than close. A similar observation can be made with respect to both the Mayali and Kayardild data, with the phonemic close series /i/ and /u/ being realized as more mid-close, than close. I discuss effects of phonemic vowel length on formant patterns in Kayardild presently.

With respect to the "sixth" vowel in Dalabon, the vowel is located in the central-back dimension, with similar mean F1 values to the front and back vowel of the series, so the distribution of the "close" series does not necessarily refute the predictions of DT, that is, where contrasts are relational rather than absolute. As mentioned earlier, however, in the six-vowel languages included in UPSID, the favoured combination of six vowels usually includes "schwa" as a sixth vowel. The neighbouring language to Dalabon, Rembarrnga, is reported to have a more "schwa"-like vowel in its six-vowel inventory. Dalabon, by contrast, has a vowel that is not a true "schwa," but the acoustic analysis here shows that it is less close than the phonemic value /ɨ/ given it by field linguists. In this instance, it becomes relevant to consider what effects prosodic context has on vowel quality in these three languages. Schwartz et al. (1997) consider that the reason why "schwa" might be the favoured sixth vowel in languages is that it is often an "unstressed" version of other vowels in the phonemic vowel inventory of these languages. However, in the Australian languages examined in this chapter, prosodic context does not prove to have a significant effect on vowel formant patterning, with a few exceptions. Only the open vowel /a/ in Dalabon and Mayali, and the long vowel /a:/ in Kayardild, are affected by presence of accentuation ($p < 0.05$). In Mayali and Dalabon, /a/ tends to be realized as a more raised variant of [ɐ] in unaccented contexts, largely due to F1 lowering. Phrasal position also has a limited effect in these two languages. There is a significant difference in F2 between accented and final /a/ in Dalabon, with F2 slightly higher in intonational phrase-final position, suggesting slight positional reduction of this vowel. However, /i/ in both languages is more dispersed when it occurs in intonational phrase final position (Dalabon: $F = 4.157$, $p < 0.02$; Mayali: $F = 5.25$, $p < 0.01$). This is particularly apparent with lower F1 in Dalabon, and a lower F1 and higher F2 in Mayali. Phrase-final midfront vowels in Mayali have a higher F2 ($F = 6.489$, $p < 0.01$), but there are no significant effects of phrasal position on this vowel in Dalabon. Midback rounded vowels show no significant differences according to phrasal context in either language.

With respect to the close vowel /u/, F2 is significantly lower in intonational phrase-final syllables in Mayali ($F = 3.837$, $p < 0.02$), resulting in a more peripheral realization of /u/, but there are no significant effects of prosodic context on this vowel in Dalabon. Of note is that there are also no significant F1–F2 differences between phrase-final or unaccented versions of /ɨ/ and /u/ in Dalabon, yet the difference between accented productions of these vowels approaches significance ($p < 0.06$). This suggests that the position of the vowel "v" in Fig. 9.2 does not give a true reflection of the range of quality differences observed in different contexts. Interestingly, the contrast is not produced by all of the remaining speakers of Dalabon (believed to be less than 10).

In Kayardild (Fig. 9.3), prosodic context does not significantly affect F1 or F2 of (mid) close vowels for either speaker, although vowel length is a significant variable for the male speaker (F1: $F = 6.6756, p < 0.05$; F2: $F = 6.3164, p < 0.05$), and there is a significant interaction between vowel length and prosodic context for the female speaker (F1: $F = 5.1731, p < 0.001$; F2: $F = 8.03, p < 0.05$). In other words, short close vowels are more centralized in unaccented contexts, and long close vowels more dispersed in final contexts. With respect to back rounded vowels, prosodic context ($F = 4.06, p < 0.01$) and vowel length ($F = 2.97, p < 0.05$) have a significant effect on F1 for the male Kayardild speaker. Final long vowels are more back than all other close back rounded vowels, with long accented back vowels slightly more dispersed than unaccented back vowels. There are no significant effects of prosodic context or vowel length on back vowels for the female speaker, although long vowels tend to be more peripheral than short vowels.

Finally, for the open central vowels, there are clear effects of prosodic context ($F = 11.816, p < 0.0001$) and phonemic vowel length ($F = 35.97, p < 0.0001$) on F1 for the male speaker. The long vowel /a:/ in final contexts is the most open, with unaccented /a/ being the least open of the low vowels. This pattern is less evident for the female speaker although both prosodic context ($F = 5.497, p < 0.01$), and vowel length ($F = 3.71, p < 0.05$) have a significant effect on F1. Short vowels show significant centralization relative to long vowels, although there is no significant difference between final and unaccented short vowels, and accented short vowels are more open.

In summary, the acoustic vowel spaces of the three Australian languages do not differ significantly in their overall patterning, compared to earlier acoustic descriptions of other Australian languages (Butcher, 1994). Moreover, they are not significantly expanded under conditions of accentuation, except in the case of the low central vowel, although Mayali shows greater *tendency* for accented vowels to be more peripheral than unaccented vowels, compared to Dalabon or Kayardild. Vowel length in Kayardild is a more consistent predictor of "peripherality," with phrase-final long vowels for the most part, occupying more extreme positions in the vowel space (Fig. 9.3). There is also some evidence of some final vowels (in the front dimension) being more peripheral in the other two languages, although this is not consistent for all vowels. Phrase-final syllables in all three languages are lengthened relative to nonfinal syllables, and short vowels tend to be centralized in Kayardild, as in other quantity languages (e.g., Engstrand & Krull, 1994; Johnson & Martin, 2001). This suggests that a relatively simple model of duration-related "expansion" is possibly in operation (after Lindblom, 1963). However, intonational phrase-final position appears also to be a prosodically salient position in all three languages. Although all three have been described as stress accent languages, the prosodic typology appears to be more "phrasal," which is possibly why we observe no strong effect of positional reduction. It is also well known that vowel spaces are more compressed in nonlaboratory versus laboratory speech (e.g., Lindblom, 1986). It could be argued that the results of the vowel analysis might have been different if a segmentally controlled corpus of laboratory-style speech had been analyzed. However, earlier analyses of vowels in isolated words in the three-vowel language Warlpiri, (Harrington, Butcher, & Palethorpe, 2000) recorded under laboratory conditions, show that this language exhibits patterns of acoustic dispersion of [ɪ ɐ u] that are similar to the patterns observed for point vowels in the languages examined in this chapter.

All three languages examined here clearly exhibit the principle of sufficient contrast rather than maximum dispersion, whether their vowel systems consist of three, five, or six vowels. As suggested by Butcher (1994), vowel spaces in Australian languages are compact, and anchored around an open central vowel. The relatively high F1 of the close series does not necessarily suggest that vowels traditionally transcribed as /i/ act as an additional anchor, although the relatively close /i/ and relatively open /a/ may define some "polarity" in the vowel spaces of these languages, for the reason put forward by Maddieson (2003, p. 2331), with the relatively close vowels exhibiting "diffuse versus compact mid-frequency spectral energy" compared to the open vowel. Clearly more detailed analyses for a larger number of Australian languages will contribute more to our understanding of the phonetics of small vowel systems. The results reported here suggest that minimal distinctiveness is maintained in a variety of prosodic contexts in connected speech in Mayali, Dalabon, and Kayardild, with the exception of the unstable close-mid, close-central vowel in Dalabon.

PITCH RANGE VARIATION IN SPOKEN NARRATIVES

In this part of the chapter, I investigate a second aspect of the phonetics of Australian languages that relates to another area of phonetic theory, championed by Laver (1994), namely, the importance of discourse context in the phonetic description of spoken communication. Specifically, I examine the role of pitch range and the potential role of voice quality in narrative discourse in Australian languages. I pay particular attention to the role of pitch range variation in signaling of reported speech, building on preliminary research by Evans, Fletcher, Birch, Bishop, and Mushin (1999) and Fletcher and Evans (2000) on pitch range in Australian languages. Reported speech can be defined as when the speech or thoughts of others, or of the speakers themselves, is represented in spoken or written discourse (e.g., Klewitz & Couper–Kuhlen, 1999). This can be achieved through the use of overt lexico-syntactic framers, such as "(s)he said," or some other quotative expression. Impressionistic observations by field linguists suggest that many Australian languages often dispose of overt framers of quoted speech, and rely purely on prosodic cues, particularly intonation, to signal the transition from narrated action to reported speech or thought (Evans et al., 1999). Although this is also possible in other languages, it is deemed to be the norm for signaling reported speech in the narrative genre in these languages.

A number of studies of English have shown that there is a link between overall pitch range, intonational phrasing, and directly reported speech. Klewitz and Couper–Kuhlen (1999) found that reported speech is demarcated by shifts into and out of high pitch register, relative to surrounding talk. Hirschberg and Grosz (1992) also found that quoted intonational phrases in their corpus of spoken American English were realized in a higher pitch range than surrounding phrases, and nonsentence initial quoted intonational phrases also differed in pitch range compared to nonsentence initial unquoted phrases. Following on from Klewitz and Couper–Kuhlen, Jansen, Gregory, and Brenier (2001) investigated the prosodic differences between directly reported speech and indirectly reported speech in a corpus of American English, and found that direct quotes signal speech demonstrations or actions, whereas indirect quotes are used for "descriptions." They found that pitch range and pitch reset of indirect–direct quotes could be distinguished, marking the difference between speech demonstrations and speech descriptions. They also found that pitch range shift aids in the prosodic distinction between the two quote types, with more overall pitch range change for direct quotes (47 Hz vs. 19 Hz) than for indirect quotes, and significant degrees of pitch reset for direct quotes, with no significant pitch reset for indirect quotes. Like Hirshberg and Grosz, Klewitz and Couper–Kuhlen also found there were additional prosodic cues to reported speech. Reported speech was more "loud," of slower tempo, and more stylistically "rhythmic," with use of frequent, regularly placed pitch accents on focal elements, compared to surrounding talk. They also claimed that the pitch range shifts could coincide with changes in voice quality.

Previous studies of some Australian languages indicate that a similar range of phonetic parameters to those outlined by Klewitz and Couper–Kuhlen (1999) may be in operation in these languages. For example, Sharpe (1972), in her description of Alawa, claims the following: "Quoted speech, symbolised by enclosure between /" "/ marks, is sometimes marked by greater stress on the quoted matter, sometimes by an effect of greater pitch variation (often this can be correlated with the question intonation /?/), or the exasperation modification /#~/, or conversation intonation variants ... " (p. 38).

Where there are quotative framers in Alawa, she goes on to say the following:

> "The quotation is marked by a word such as /namuban/ 'he said', inserted after (occasionally before) the quoted speech; this quotation marker is usually less loud than the quoted speech." (Sharpe, 1972, p. 38).

Thus, earlier impressions of reported speech in Australian languages suggest that overall pitch range is expanded, as well as an upward shift in pitch key. In the remainder of this chapter, I outline the results of a quantitative investigation of pitch range variation in two of the languages investigated earlier, Kayardild and Dalabon. This analysis builds on, and extends a very preliminary impressionistic examination of quotation in Australian languages (Evans et al., 1999). Three aspects of pitch range are quantitatively investigated in this section; (a) pitch key or "topline" pitch, (b) pitch reset between reported speech and surrounding talk, and (c) overall or global pitch range. I also examine whether there are any additional changes to the tone of voice in reported speech. Both narratives contain many long fragments of reported speech (15 in the Kayardild text, 20 in the Dalabon text). In many cases, the reported speech fragments consist of several intonational phrases (IPs). Of note is the lack of quotative framer in the example from Kayardild, which is typical of reported speech in this language (Evans et al., 1999)

Part of the same corpus, described earlier, also served as the corpus for this study. As mentioned earlier, the two narratives were transcribed intonationally for accentuation and phrasing. The Tones and Break Indices (ToBI) convention for measuring pitch range or pitch topline was also adopted, and an additional tonal label "hiF0" was used in the tonal transcription of the two texts (Beckman and Ayers–Elam, 1997). According to ToBI labelling conventions, the hiF0 of a phrase corresponds to the highest observable pitch value associated with a high tone pitch accent, discounting segmental perturbation effects. For the purposes of this study then, pitch topline was equated with the f_o maximum (Hz) associated with an accented syllable, and the f_o values at the label point were measured for successive intonational phrases. It was, thus, also possible to calculate topline reset between preceding or following talk, and reported speech. I also investigated global pitch range for the speakers of the two languages by calculating the range of high pitch values (measured by hiF0) and low pitch values in each phrase. If an intonational phrase terminated with an L% low tone boundary, the f_o value (Hz) associated with this target was taken to be a rough indicator of the pitch baseline. This method is not ideal as it was not possible to get a measure of the lowest pitch value for all phrases, if not all of them ended with a low tone. Furthermore, some intonational phrases in the corpus also exhibited final lowering, that is, where there was a further drop in pitch at the end of a larger stretch of discourse, usually preceding a shift in topic. A similar phenomenon has been observed in many languages (see Ladd, 1996, for a summary). Where there was no L% boundary, I extracted the fo for all measured vowels in the intonational phrase, and took the lowest value to indicate the lowest pitch for that particular phrase. Recall that all vowels had been previously labelled segmentally, so it was relatively straightforward to extract pitch information for each vowel. Once again, all data analyses were carried out using EMU+Splus, as described earlier.

Fig. 9.4 shows two typical examples of reported speech from the corpus. Example "a" from the male Dalabon speaker consists of a fragment of quoted speech, followed by a quotative framer, /kaʔjiniɲ/ "he said." Looking at the f_0 contour, it is clear that there is a clear drop in pitch at the start of the framer, relative to the preceding quoted fragment. The latter is realized in an elevated pitch key, relative to the framer. Example "b" from the female speaker of Kayardild shows a stretch of preceding talk, followed by a quoted fragment. In this case, there is no quotative framer. The stretch of reported speech

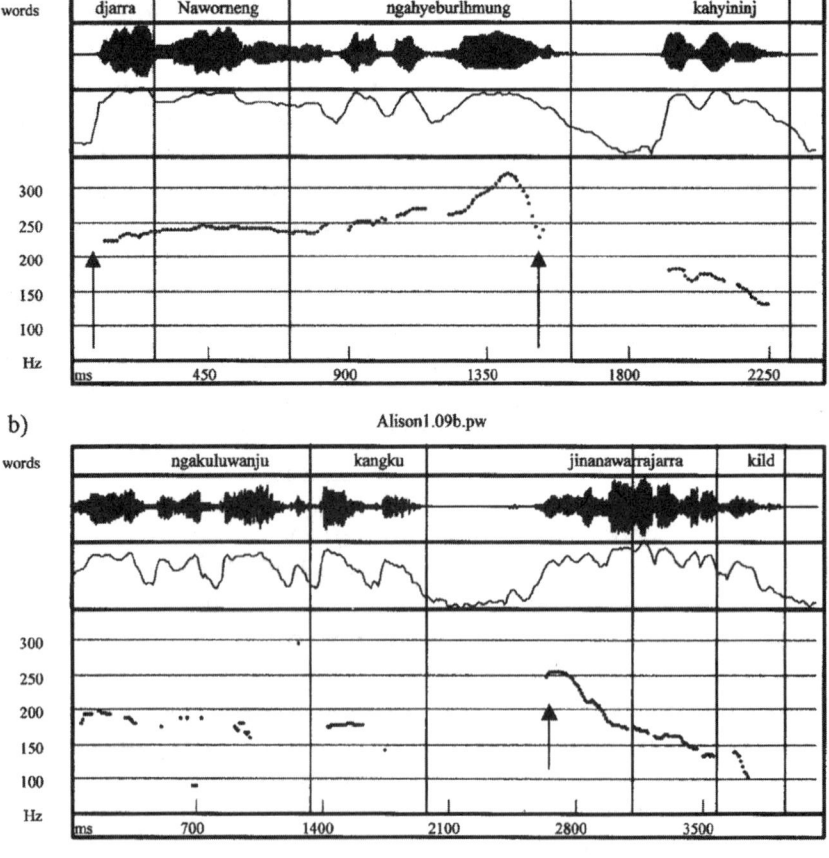

FIG. 9.4. Waveforms and fo contours of two examples of reported speech in (a) Dalabon, and (b) Kayardild.

commences with a sharp upward reset of pitch of around 50 Hz or more, relative to the preceding talk.

To get a sense of general pitch range characteristics of either speaker, the median pitch of all measured vowels in the Dalabon narrative is 213 Hz, whereas the Kayardild female speaker actually has a somewhat lower tone of voice, which is reflected in the median pitch value of around 170 Hz for all measured vowels in her narrative. With these values in mind, it is useful to see how the pitch topline (hiF0) patterns throughout each narrative. Fig. 9.5 plots the pitch topline for 50 successive intonational phrases in the two narratives. The mean pitch topline value for the Dalabon speaker's narrative is 247 (Hz) whereas the female speaker of Kayardild actually has a lower mean topline value of 207 (Hz). However, the elevated value for the Dalabon speaker could well be due to the extensive amount of quoted material in his narrative. There are a large number of intonational phrases in this narrative, where the highest f_0 value is

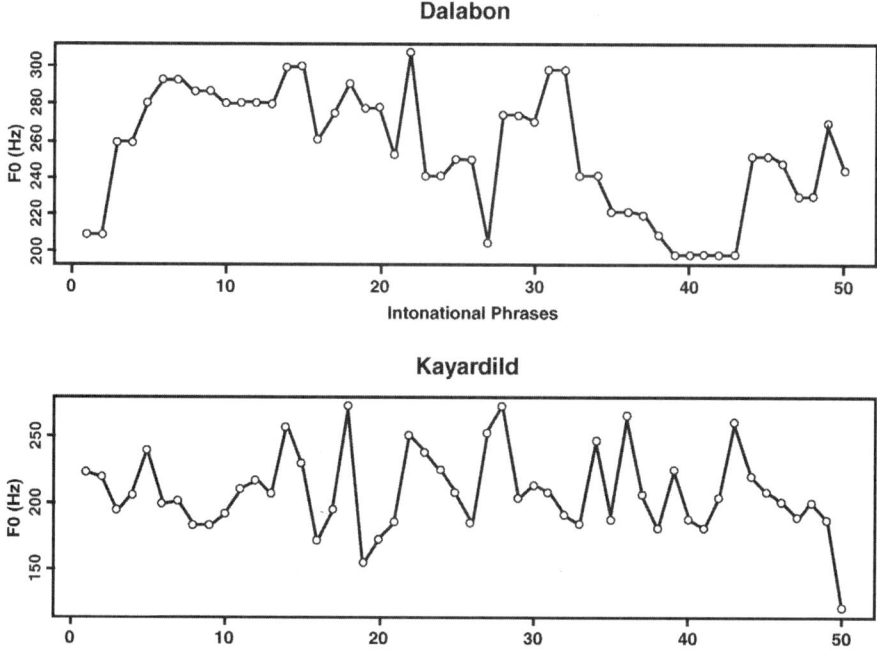

FIG. 9.5. Pitch topline (hiF0) values (Hz) plotted for the first 50 intonational phrases in the Kayardild and Dalabon narratives.

well in excess of 250 (Hz), often exceeding 300 (Hz) at the most lively points of the narrative. It is also clear from Fig. 9.5 (bottom plot) that there are a number of intonational phrases produced by the Dalabon speaker, where the highest pitch value is around 220 (Hz). These intonational phrases tend to correspond with parts of the narrative, where he continues to tell his story without the use of reported speech. The Kayardild speaker (Fig. 9.5, top plot) also utters a number of intonational phrases where the highest pitch values range between 220Hz and 270 Hz. There are a large number of examples of extreme pitch reset of 50 Hz or more between successive phrases. The Dalabon speaker also uses similar kinds of resets, although he utters a number of successive phrases in similar high-pitch register, at various times during his narrative. This is quite evident from the sixth intonational phrase in Fig. 9.5 (bottom plot). However, not all sharp upward resets in pitch necessarily correspond to reported speech, in either narrative. Some also signify topic change or topic initiation. This is an informational use of pitch topline reset that has been well recorded for other languages (e.g., Gussenhoven, 2002; Ladd, 1996).

To test the amount of pitch topline reset associated with quoted speech, I extracted hiF0 values associated with quoted fragments from the corpus. These were then compared to hiF0 values of immediate surrounding talk in the Dalabon and Kayardild narratives. The results are shown in Fig. 9.6. The boxplots show the simplified distribution, outliers, and median pitch topline f_o (Hz) for reported fragments and surrounding talk. It is clear that there is a significant reset of pitch associated with reported speech in both cases, supporting impressionistic observations. These differences are highly significant [Kayardild: $df(1, 22)$, $F = 27.451$, $p < 0.0001$; Dalabon: $df(1, 63)$, $F = 48.516$, $p < 0.0001$] and are of around 52 (Hz) in magnitude for the Kayardild text, and 65 (Hz) in the Dalabon text. There is, however, no significant difference between the amount of upwards pitch reset from preceding surrounding talk to reported fragments, compared to pitch reset from reported fragments to following talk. Furthermore, although more quotative framers are used by the Dalabon speaker than the Kayardild speaker, there are no obvious differences in patterns of pitch topline variation relating to presence or absence of framer.

The amount of global pitch range variation (i.e., between pitch topline and low f_o values in each phrase) also varies significantly

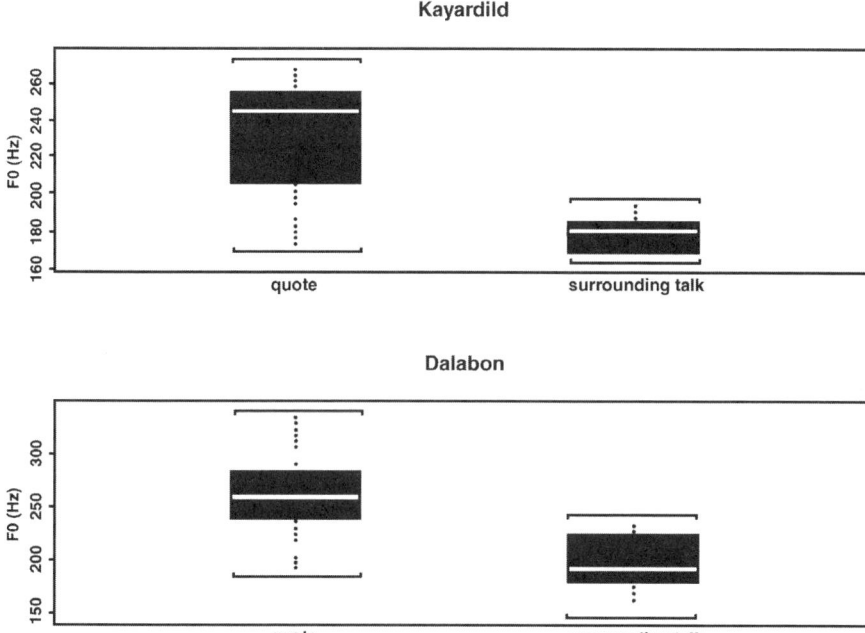

FIG. 9.6. Boxplots comparing the simplified distribution, median values, and outliers of pitch topline values associated with reported speech intonational phrases, and intonational phrases in immediately surrounding talk for the Kayardild and Dalabon narratives.

between reported fragments and surrounding talk (97 Hz vs. 38 Hz) in Dalabon, and in Kayardild (110 Hz and 78 Hz). A comparison of the low pitch targets in reported stretches (associated with any final falls in the final IP of a reported stretch), and those of surrounding talk does not reveal any significant differences in pitch baseline between the two. This might suggest, initially, that for Dalabon, at least, the difference in global pitch range between reported speech and surrounding talk, is largely accounted for by an upward reset of the pitch topline. However, it should be noted that only 11 out of the 44 reported speech IPs terminate with low pitch boundaries, suggesting that at least three quarters of reported speech IPs are realized in a high pitch key or register. The Kayardild narrative shows a similar pattern with no significant difference between pitch baselines and between quoted fragments and surrounding talk, also suggesting that any differences in global pitch range are due to pitch topline reset. One interesting additional feature of the two narratives is that sometimes the speakers enact a conversation between two talkers, within the reported speech fragments. For example, the Kayardild speaker shifts the pitch topline substantially to indicate there are two participants in the conversation. The Dalabon speaker also uses this device. This manipulation of pitch topline, as well as the use of final lowering of pitch at the end of the IP, helps signal a turn change in the reported conversation.

In fact, the same patterns of final lowering are observed at the end of a significant number of the quoted stretches, and many of the final IPs in quoted stretches in the Kayardild narrative end in creaky voice. Like the speaker of Dalabon, a significant proportion of reported speech IPs (32 out of 70 IPs) are also realized in high pitch register, terminating with a sustained or high level pitch, although to a lesser extent than in Dalabon. However, these patterns are also evident in surrounding talk also, when the speaker is not using reported speech. Interestingly, the Kayardild speaker sometimes uses a sustained mid-high pitch register during preceding fragments of surrounding talk, compared to following stretches of reported speech. In other words, in addition to resetting the pitch topline upward in the reported fragment, a more "lively" tune is often employed, by contrast with the preceding talk. This is most apparent in the earliest part of his narrative.

Other phonetic cues to reported speech are less consistent. Changes in dB values are observed at certain times throughout the two narratives, but this is not at all consistent. Of the two speakers, the Dalabon speaker is most likely to utter reported stretches more "loudly" than surrounding talk. Also, as Heath (1984) observed for Gunwinjku, the Dalabon speaker sometimes changes tempo during reported speech, with quoted speech fragments uttered at more rapid tempo compared to surrounding talk. Both speakers also display voice quality characteristics that are not unusual in Australian languages (e.g., Sharpe, 1972).

However, there are no systematic changes in voice quality associated with reported speech of the Kayardild speaker, although she has a somewhat "harsh" voice quality, apparent in both high and low registers (Laver, 1979). As mentioned earlier, the Dalabon speaker has a higher overall pitch topline in general, and he exploits a very high register during reported speech. His voice quality in general is best described as raised larynx voice (Laver, 1979), producing an auditory effect that sounds strained. This could also account for some of the vowel formant patterns observed for this speaker (discussed earlier). However, during reported speech there appears to be additional manipulation of the laryngeal musculature by both speakers, to produce the excessive pitch variations, shown in Figures 9.5 and 9.6. As suggested in earlier work, it appears that pitch range variation, particularly manipulation of the top register, is the major device used to signal reported speech in these Australian languages.

CONCLUSION

In this chapter, I have chosen to examine two aspects of the phonetics of three North Australian languages that relate to some of the topics examined by John Laver during his long career. This work is by no means complete. For example, more quantitative research is clearly necessary to characterize voice quality features in Australian languages in general, and Laver's work in this area will be of great assistance to achieve this end. I have attempted to show that Laver's ideal, that a phonetic theory should provide a vocabulary to deal with the prosodic as well as segmental features of spoken communication, has inspired a new era of research on the phonetics of seldom studied languages, like the ones examined here.

REFERENCES

Alpher, B. J. (1982). Dalabon dual-subject prefixes, kinship categories and generation skewing. In J. Heath, F. Merlan, & A. Rumsey,)Eds.), *Languages of kinship in aboriginal Australia* (pp. 19–30). Sydney, Australia: Oceania Linguistic Monographs.

Beckman, M. E., & Ayers–Elam, G., (1999). *Guide to ToBI Labelling—Version 3.0.* Retrieved 3/1/2001 from http://ling.ohiostate.edu/Phonetics/E_ToBI/ eToBI_homepage.html.

Blake, B. J. (1981). *Australian aboriginal languages.* Sydney, Australia: Angus and Robertson.

Busby, P. A. (1979). *A classificatory study of phonemic systems in Australian Aboriginal languages.* Unpublished mater's thesis, Australian National University, Canberra.

Butcher, A. (1994). On the phonetics of small vowel systems. *SST–94, 1,* 28–33.

Cassidy, S., & Harrington, J. (2001). Multi-level annotation in the EMU speech database management system. *Speech Communication, 33,* 61–77.

de Jong, K. (1995). The supraglottal articulation of prominence in English: Linguistic stress as localized hyperarticulation. *Journal of the Acoustical Society of America, 97,* 491–504.

Delattre, P. (1969). An acoustic and articulatory study of vowel reduction in four languages. *International Review of Applied Linguistics, 4,* 295–325.

Dixon, R. M. W. (2002). *Australian languages: Their nature and development.* Cambridge, England: Cambridge University Press.

Engstrand, O., & Krull, D. (1994). Durational correlates to quantity in Swedish, Finnish, and Estonian: Cross language evidence for a theory of adaptive dispersion. *Phonetica, 51,* 80–91.

Evans, N. (1995a). *A grammar of Kayardild. With comparative notes on Tangkic.* Berlin, Germany: Mouton de Gruyter.

Evans, N. (1995b). Current issues in the phonology of Australian languages. In J. Goldsmith (Ed.), *The handbook of phonological theory* (pp. 723–761). Oxford, England: Blackwell.

Evans, N., Fletcher, J., Birch, B., Bishop, J., & Mushin, I. (1999). *The sound of one quotation mark: Intonational cues to quotation in five north Australian languages.* Abstract retrieved 10/7/2003 from http://www.arts.uwa.edu.au/LingWWW/als99/abs_frame.html.

Fletcher, J., & Evans, N. (2000). Intonational downtrends in Mayali. *Australian Journal of Linguistics, 20,* 23–38.

Fletcher, J., & Evans, N. (2002). An acoustic phonetic analysis of intonational prominence in two Australian languages. *Journal of the International Phonetics Association, 32,* 123–140.

Fletcher, J, Evans, N., & Round, E. (2002). Left-edge tonal events in Kayardild (Australian): A typological perspective. In. B. Bel & I. Marlien (Eds.), *Proceedings of Speech Prosody 2002* (pp. 295–298). Aixeen-Provence, France: Université de Provence, Laboratoîre de Parve et Langage.

Gussenhoven, C. (2002). Intonation and interpretation: Phonetics and phonology. In B. Bel & I. Marlien (Eds.), *Proceedings of Speech Prosody 2002* (pp. 47–57). Aixeen-Provence, France: Université de Provence, Laboratoire de Parole Langage.

Harrington, J., Butcher, A., & Palethorpe S. (2000). *An acoustic analysis of word stress in Warlpiri.* Retrieved 10/7/2003 from http://www.shlrc.mq.edu.au/~jmh/SEMINAR/WARL.

Harrington, J., & Cassidy, S. (1994). Dynamic and target theories of vowel classification: Evidence from monopthongs and diphthongs in Australian English. *Language and Speech, 37,* 357–373.

Harrington, J., Fletcher, J., & Beckman, M. E. (2000). Manner and place conflicts in the articulation of accent in Australian English. In M. B. Broe & J. Pierrehumbert (Eds.), *Acquisition and the lexicon: Papers in laboratory phonology V.* (pp. 70–87). Cambridge, MA: Cambridge University Press.

Heath, J. (1984). *Functional grammar of Nunggubuyu.* Canberra, Australia: Australian Institute for Aboriginal Studies.

Hirschberg, J., & Grosz, B. (1992). Intonational features of local and global discourse structure. *Proceedings of the DARPA Workshop on Spoken Language Systems. Proceedings of the Speech and Natural Language Workshop, Harriman, NY,* 23–26.

Jansen, W., Gregory, M., & Brenier, J. (2001*). Proceedings of the ISCA Workshop on Prosody in Speech Recognition and Understanding,* Red Bank, New Jersey, October 22–24, 2001.

Johnson, K. (2001). Adaptive dispersion in vowel perception. *Phonetica, 57,* 181–188.

Johnson, K., & Martin, J. (2001). Acoustic vowel reduction in Creek: Effects of distinctive length and position in the word. *Phonetica, 58,* 81–102.

Klewitz, G., & Couper–Kuhlen, E. (1999). The role of prosody in the contextualisation of reported speech sequences. *Pragmatics, 9,* 459–485.

Ladd, D. R. (1996). *Intonational phonology.* Cambridge, England: Cambridge University Press.

Ladefoged, P., & Maddieson, I. (1996). *The sounds of the world's languages.* Oxford, England: Blackwell.

Laver, J. (1967). A preliminary phonology of the Aywele dialect of Etsako. *Journal of West African Languages, IV, 2,* 53–56.

Laver, J. (1979). The description of voice quality. *Edinburgh University Department of Linguistics Work in Progress, 12,* 30–52

Laver, J. (1980). *The phonetic description of voice quality.* Cambridge, England: Cambridge University Press.

Laver, J. (1991). *The gift of speech.* Edinburgh, Scotland: Edinburgh University Press.

Laver, J. (1994). *Principles of phonetics.* Cambridge, England: Cambridge University Press.

Liljencrants, J., & Lindblom, B. (1972). Numerical simulation of vowel quality systems: The role of perceptual contrast. *Language, 48,* 839–862.

Lindblom, B. (1963). Spectrographic study of vowel reduction. *Journal of the Acoustical Society of America, 35,* 1773–1781.

Lindblom, B. (1986). Phonetic universals in vowel systems. In J. Ohala & J. Jaeger (Eds.), *Experimental Phonology* (pp. 13<@15044). New York: Academic.

Maddieson, I. (2003). Vowel spacing in four-vowel systems. *Journal of the Acoustical Society of America, 113,* 2331.

Moon, S–J., & Lindblom, B. (1994). Interaction between duration, context and speaking-style in English stressed vowels. *Journal of the Acoustical Society of America, 96,* 40–55.

Palethorpe, S., Beckman, M., Fletcher, J., & Harrington, J. (1999). The contribution of schwa vowels to the prosodic accent contrast in Australian English. *Proceedings of the XIVth International Congress of Phonetic Sciences, 1,* 695–699.

Schwartz, J–L., Boe, L–J., Vallee, N., & Abry, C. (1997a). Major trends in vowel system inventories. *Journal of Phonetics, 25,* 233–253.

Sharpe, M. (1972). *Alawa phonology and grammar.* Canberra, Australia: Australian Institute of Aboriginal Studies.

Zwicker, E. (1961). Subdivision of the audible frequency range into critical bands (Frequenzgruppen). *Journal of the Acoustical Society of America, 33,* 248.

Chapter 10

Deepening or Lessening the Divide Between Diphthongs: An Analysis of the Queen's Annual Christmas Broadcasts

Jonathan Harrington
Institute of Phonetics and Digital Speech Processing (IPDS),
University of Kiel, Germany

Sallyanne Palethorpe
Macquarie Centre for Cognitive Science (MACCS),
Macquarie University, Sydney, Australia

Catherine Watson
Macquarie Centre for Cognitive Science (MACCS),
Macquarie University, Sydney, Australia

This study is about the changes that have taken place in the last 50 years to one variety of English, Received Pronunciation (RP), the so-called standard accent of Britain. It is also about defining some of the pronunciation characteristics of Her Majesty Queen Elizabeth II. Close to the time of writing, Professor John Laver CBE has accepted the Queen's Anniversary Prize, on behalf of Queen Margaret University College, Edinburgh, for its pioneering contributions to speech science. Just over 2 years before this, in a thoughtful and well-reasoned article on a paper we had just published entitled 'Does the Queen still speak the Queen's English', Philip Hensher, writing in *The Independent*,[1] noted that our study could hardly seem anything but disrespectful to the point of *lèse-majesté*, whereas *The Times*,[2] labelling us as 'three Australian phoneticists' [*sic*] in its editorial of December 21st, 2000, entitled 'Our Common Queen: Rougher Talk from her Majesty,' thundered the following: 'We are not amused—oh no we ain't.' We feel, then, that we have a duty to explain our motives for going down this potentially treacherous research path.

Part of the answer is to be found in the multiple strands of speaker characteristics and variability that have been so carefully documented and modelled by John Laver in his many writings on these subjects over the last 30 years. As discussed in both *Principles of Phonetics* (Laver, 1994), and the *Phonetic Description of Voice Quality* (Laver, 1980), those aspects of vocal performance that define the characteristics of a speaker are due to considerably more than the anatomical and physiological properties of the vocal organs (although these, of course, play a considerable role as well). Within the same speaker there can be variations along a number of dimensions. The formality of speaking style can vary resulting in a greater or lesser tendency to reduce and assimilate speech. There can be variation in the paralinguistic tone of voice in which the loudness, pitch, and segment duration can change according to a speaker's mood and emotional state. Articulatory settings can vary between speakers: there may be short-term differences, as in the tendency for some speakers of British English RP to produce /s/ with lip-rounding (Laver, 1994); or there may be long-term effects if, for example, a speaker habitually produces speech with hyponasality. Beyond these issues, there are the well-known differences in speakers due to dialect and social status, a factor that is especially relevant to the standard accent of England, RP. However, the general point, as summarised by Laver (1994), follows:

It will be apparent on reflection that the phonetic realizations of every phoneme of every speaker have the potential of being slightly different from those of many other speakers even of the same general accent. A lifetime of settling to a habitual mode of speaking has given the personal accent of every speaker an individualizing realizational flavour, within the overall systemic, structural and selectional conventions of his or her own accent-group. (p. 66)

The variability in the speech signal due to speaker differences poses a considerable problem if we wish to provide an experimental basis for how sounds have changed in time. Typically, in what has come to be known in sociolinguistics as an '*apparent time*' study (Chambers & Trudgill, 1980; Labov, 1994), pronunciation change is inferred by comparing the speaking characteristics of two different agegroups of the same community. However, any such study is confronted with the difficulty that the many dimensions on which speakers can differ may mask the changes in pronunciation that we seek to validate experimentally, especially if—as is so often the case in sociophonetic analyses—we wish to base our comparison on continuous, or even completely spontaneously, produced speech. A further potential difficulty may lie in the assumption that underlies apparent time studies that the spoken characteristics of, say, present-day 60-year-old speakers is equivalent to those of 20-year-old speakers from the early 1960s (Chambers & Trudgill, 1980). As Labov (1994) comments, 'apparent time studies may understate the actual rate of sound change, since older speakers show a limited tendency towards communal change, participating to a small extent in the changes taking place around them'. A similar view is held by Laver and Trudgill (1979) who, in discussing the four major ways in which accents between two speakers can differ, state the following:

'These comments about accent differences between speakers make the assumption that a speaker's accent is fixed and unchanging. It seldom is, of course, and a further area where linguistic concepts can help us to refine our analysis of social markers in speech concerns certain aspects of the notion of *linguistic variability*.' (their emphasis, p. 19)

Laver and Trudgill's (1979) view about the changing accent within the same speaker as well as Labov's (1994) caveat are consis-

tent with a few so-called 'real-time' analyses which have found pronunciation changes in the same adult speakers recorded at
intervals of between 15 and 20 years in Montreal French
(Yaegor–Dror, 1994) and RP (Bauer, 1985).

On Christmas day in 1952, Queen Elizabeth II first adopted a tradition that was started by her grandfather King George V in 1932
and then continued by her father King George VI who had broadcast a message to his people in all parts of the world. Since that
time, the Queen has made broadcasts annually on Christmas Day
and since 1957 these have been televised. From the point of view of
studying sound change, the Christmas broadcasts are unique: as far
as we know, there are no other spoken materials recorded annually
for over a 50-year period from the same person reading a text with a
broadly similar communicative intent (a message to people in all
parts of the world) in any variety of English. The advantages of analysing the Christmas broadcasts for studying sound change are not
only that we eliminate many of the confounding influences due to
variation in spoken language between speakers, but also those due
to variation within a speaker, because neither the speaking style
nor the communicative purpose of the Christmas broadcasts vary a
great deal from year to year. For these reasons, experimental evidence that points to sound change in the Christmas broadcasts can,
in all likelihood, be attributed to a phonetic change, rather than to
an artifact of variation due to speaker-characteristics or changes in
speaking style. To make use of a metaphor from Laver (1980), in
which the relation between voice quality and the linguistic-phonetic content of vocal performance is likened to that between a figure and the ground against which it is set, a very detailed study (in
our case almost 3,000 vowels and diphthongs) of one speaker over
a 50-year period clarifies the figure (the phonetic content) precisely because ground (the speaker-specific aspects) becomes so
sharply delineated.

There is another reason why the Christmas broadcasts are of
great interest to phonetics and its relation to sociolinguistics: they
can tell us something about the extent to which adults can resist
pronunciation changes that are taking place in the community. We
can be in no doubt that RP has changed in the last 50 years (Crystal,
1988; Laver, 1994) and it is also likely that at least some of these
changes are linked to the considerable change that took place in
the social structures and hierarchies in the second part of the 20th

century. In the 1950s, the demarcation between the social classes was sharp, but throughout the 1960s, there was a progressive blurring between the class boundaries (Cannadine, 1998). Many professions, which in the 1950s would have been exclusively the preserve of the Establishment and those educated at public schools, have been increasingly pursued by those from a variety of different class backgrounds. The weakening of the boundaries that define the class system has a corollary in the change in accent in England and the attitude toward RP, a label first used by Alexander J. Ellis (1869, p. 23) to refer to the accent of the Establishment: that is, an educated pronunciation of the metropolis, of the court, the bar, the pulpit, and one that did not differ across regions in England (see also Parsons, 1998, for a comprehensive review of RP). In the 1950s, RP was still very much a prestige accent associated with the middle and upper classes, who had typically been educated in Britain's public schools. It was perhaps unthinkable to most living in the 1950s that RP and the stigmatised Cockney English, associated with the working classes, had very much in common at all (beyond the fact that both were accents of the same language). But in the 1980s and 1990s, the situation is very different. The form of RP spoken by the upper classes is declining according to Gimson and Cruttenden (1994) whereas a greater proportion of the educated middle classes now apparently speak *Estuary English*, a term first used in 1984 by David Rosewarne. Estuary English is an accent of the South East of England (spoken around the Thames Estuary, hence the name), whose foundation is RP but which has considerable influences from London Cockney (but see Maidment, 1994, for a critique of Estuary English). Wells (1994) provides evidence that RP has been influenced by Cockney in recent times and Crystal (1995) notes that Estuary English is increasingly heard in public domains and has begun to penetrate the Establishment. The rise of Estuary English has also occurred over a period which has seen a change in the attitude toward RP: whereas in the 1950s, RP enjoyed prestige status and Cockney was stigmatised, since at least the 1970s, many younger speakers have rejected RP (Burridge, 1998; Gimson, 1966) precisely because of its unfashionable association with the Establishment. Indeed, a form of RP associated with the upper classes is in more recent times often regarded as affected and its speakers have for many 'become a figure of fun' (Gimson & Cruttenden, 1994). It is against this backdrop of the collapsing hierarchical social structures accompanied by the blurring between accents that mark social class as well as change in attitude to RP that the question of changes to the pronunciation in the Christmas broadcasts over a period of time are of great interest. As the representative of the very pinnacle of the Establishment as well as both the preeminent speaker and personification of the Queen's English, a form of English upheld and defended by many against 'debasement, ambiguity and other forms of misuse,[3]' we can reasonably speculate that the Queen might be resistant to accent change from below. From another perspective, if we find further evidence for a shift in the Queen's accent in the direction of changes that have taken place in the wider community, then such a finding lends support to the view that adults throughout their lives cannot be immune from accent change that is taking place around them and it would also give credence to Labov's (1994) comment that the rate at which pronunciation changes may well be underestimated in apparent time studies.

Our investigation is principally concerned with the relation between what has been termed *upper-class, upper-crust,* or *U-RP* and *mainstream RP* (Wells, 1982). The distinction between "U" and "non-U" goes back to Ross (1954) and Mitford (1956) and U-RP is described and partly caricatured by Wells (1982) as the accent of a dowager duchess, a Noel Coward sophisticate, a Terry Thomas cad, or an upper-class army officer. This description of U-RP is more or less equivalent to *refined RP* used by Gimson & Cruttenden (1994). *Conservative RP* is defined by Gimson (1966) as a form of RP used by the older generation and, traditionally, by certain professions or groups and it is distinguished from *advanced RP*, a form of RP used by the younger generations (Gimson, 1964). Mainstream RP, which is also sometimes known as *Standard Southern British* (SSB; Deterding, 1997) is, according to Wells (1982), spoken by the majority of RP speakers. It is the type of accent that is characteristic of many of the professional middle classes in England and is still exemplified by many nonregional BBC news presenters:[4] it is closest to what is sometimes described as *BBC English*, which is the term used in the later editions of Daniel Jones's *English Pronouncing Dictionary* (1924), instead of RP (Roach & Hartman, 1997). Mainstream RP is distinct from *Estuary English* which, as discussed earlier, is a form of RP that is coloured by a London accent and Cockney (Coggle, 1993; Parsons, 1998; Rosewarne, 1994, 1996; Wells, 1994, 2003).

Auditory impressions suffice to show that the Queen's accent of both the 1950s and 1980s is not the same as mainstream RP. There are certainly some aspects of the Queen's accent that are characteristic of U-RP, such as a markedly back /u/ (in the 1950s broadcasts at least), a noticeably intervocalic /r/ in words like 'very,' an open-mid realisation of /æ/ (typical of 'conservative RP'), and some lexically-specific U-RP characteristics such as a high back /ɔ/ vowel in 'lost' (to rhyme with 'forced').

In Harrington, Palethorpe, and Watson (2000a, 2000b) we suggested that there had been a shift in the Queen's monophthongal vowel space toward that of 1980s mainstream RP. We reached this conclusion by analysing the Christmas broadcasts from the 1950s and 1980s and demonstrating that the Queen's vowels from the 1980s were closer (in an auditorily transformed formant space) than those from the 1950s broadcasts to the averaged vowel space of five mainstream RP female BBC presenters from the 1980s. The main change was in the direction of a 'vertical' expansion of the vowel space, so that between the 1950s and 1980s, the high vowels had become higher and the open vowels had become more open. We also found a much smaller tendency for a 'horizontal' change, such as a marginally (but significantly) more fronted /u/ in the 1980s than in the 1950s broadcasts. The changes were in all cases in the direction of the vowels of 1980s mainstream RP speakers, *without actually attaining those vowel positions*: for example, the Queen's 1980s /æ/ was shown to be intermediate in phonetic openness (as judged from formant data) between the Queen's 1950s /æ/ and the /æ/ of the 1980s mainstream RP speakers, whereas the Queen's 1980s /u/ was not as front as the 1980s mainstream RP /u/, but more advanced than in the 1950s broadcasts.

In our present contribution, we aim to extend this analysis to the front and back rising diphthongs /aɪ eɪ aʊ oʊ/ in the same corpora (see Table 10.1 for the system of RP transcription used in this chapter). As a precursor to the experimental analyses, we begin with a brief summary of some of the reported phonetic characteristics of these RP diphthongs, and of the way in which they are distinguished in some of the RP varieties. We also report whenever possible on the phonetic changes that may have taken place to these RP diphthongs in the last 50 years or so. Because, with the exception of some formant frequencies in /hVd/ words in Gimson and Cruttenden (1994), there are, as far as we know, no systematic

TABLE 10.1

Number of Vowels and Diphthongs in the Three Corpora

Corpus		Q50	Q80	SSB
Lax Monophthongs				
ɪ	(hid)	103	123	60
ɛ	(head)	138	156	62
æ	(had)	96	77	68
ʌ	(run)	80	83	62
ɒ	(pod)	62	64	51
ʊ	(hood)	8	21	26
Tense Monophthongs				
ɪ	(heed)	82	82	57
ɜ	(herd)	37	33	42
ɑ	(hard)	35	42	68
ɔ	(hoard)	78	82	55
u	(who'd)	24	17	42
ju	(few)	31	37	
Diphthongs				
aɪ	(hide)	90	78	198
eɪ	(hay)	89	118	276
aʊ	(how)	24	19	128
oʊ	(hoe)	75	64	214

Note. The number of accented vowel and diphthong tokens analysed in the Q50, Q80, and SSB corpora. In the SSB corpus, there is no differentiation between /u/ and /ju/ which are collapsed in the /u/ (n = 42) category.

experimental studies of RP diphthongs, this brief review is necessarily based on auditory analyses.

According to Gimson and Cruttenden (1994), RP /aɪ/ extends from a position midway between cardinal vowels 4 and 5 toward RP /ɪ/, although the second target is typically undershot and therefore more open and centralised compared with RP /ɪ/. In refined or U-RP, the first target of /aɪ/ has 'a very back starting point' (Gimson & Cruttenden, 1994). A back first component may also occur in Cockney (Wells, 1982) which, as in a broad Australian English accent (Bernard, 1970, 1980; Harrington, Cox, & Evans, 1997), may also be rounded. There is some evidence that the first component of mainstream RP /aɪ/ has retracted since the early to midpart of the 20th Century (Wells, 1982), which would then correspond to a diachronic shift in the direction of a Cockney accent.

RP /eɪ/ extends from somewhere between cardinal vowels 2 and 3 (close to RP 'head') toward RP /ɪ/. Both Gimson and Cruttenden (1994) and Wells (1982) note that a phonetically close first target of /eɪ/ is old-fashioned and characteristic of older RP speakers. In U-RP, the first target of /eɪ/ is more open (presumably than in mainstream RP) and the entire diphthong may be monophthongised. Wells (1982) also comments that a London variety of RP has a backer first target whereas in London Cockney (as in Australian English) it is noticeably more open.

The phonetic definition of /oʊ/ is complex and there seems to be a good deal of variation both across RP varieties and age groups. There is some agreement that the first target of RP /oʊ/ has a central position and that the movement is in the direction of RP /ʊ/. The first component is raised and further back for older speakers whose first component starts near RP /ɔ/ (Wells, 1982). Refined RP has a fronted first target relative to mainstream RP (Gimson & Cruttenden, 1994) whereas in Cockney, the first component is more open than in mainstream RP and the second component may be completely unrounded.

There is some agreement that the first component of RP /aʊ/ has a starting position close to RP /ɑ/ and is therefore somewhat further back than the first component of RP /aɪ/. The movement of the diphthong is in the direction of RP /ʊ/ although it is often undershot to a midposition (Gimson & Cruttenden, 1994). There are few comments about changes to RP /aʊ/ in the last 50 years, although Wells (1982) has suggested that the first component is becoming backer whereas Gimson and Cruttenden (1994) list the increasing convergence of the first targets of /aɪ/ and /aʊ/ as a current RP change.

The experiments of this study are designed to test the hypothesis that the Queen's accent between the 1950s and 1980s has changed in the direction of a 1980s mainstream RP or SSB accent. If this is so, then we should be able to predict more or less the positions of the diphthongs in the 1980s Christmas broadcasts by an extrapolation (in an F2 × F1 auditorily transformed space) between the diphthong positions in the

1950s Christmas broadcasts and those in a corpus of 1980s SSB speakers: that is, the 1980s Christmas broadcast diphthongs should be located in a space that is intermediary between the 1950s Christmas broadcast and 1980s SSB corpora, if our hypothesis is tenable.

To test this hypothesis, the experiments are divided into two parts. First (section 2), we establish and compare the positions in an F2 × F1 space of the diphthongs and monophthongs in the 1980s SSB and 1950s Christmas broadcast corpora. Second, we form a set of predictions (discussed later) about where in this space the 1980s Christmas broadcast diphthongs should be located, based on the hypothesis that they are located in approximately intermediary positions between those of the 1950s Christmas broadcasts and 1980s SSB positions. The predictions are then tested by comparing the relative proximity of monophthongs and diphthongs in these three spaces using classifications based on Bayesian distances.

METHOD

Q50 and Standard Southern British Corpora

The materials included the diphthongs /aɪ aʊ oʊ eɪ/ in subsets of the same two Christmas broadcasts and SSB corpora that were analysed in Harrington et al. (2000a, 2000b). The Christmas broadcast corpora in this study included six broadcasts, three from the 1950s (henceforth the 'Q50 corpus') and three from the 1980s (henceforth the 'Q80 corpus'). The analysed vowels and diphthongs in the Q50 corpus are from 1952, 1954, and 1957, and in the Q80 corpus, they are from 1983, 1985, and 1988. Harrington et al. (2000a, 2000b) also analysed broadcasts from the late 1960s and early 1970s, but we do not include these in this study, because our analyses had shown a minimal change in the vowels between them and the broadcasts from the 1980s. For the Standard Southern British corpus (henceforth the 'SSB corpus'), we analysed the same five female BBC broadcasters from the 'Machine Readable Spoken English Corpus' (Roach, Knowles, Varadi, & Arnfield, 1994) that were also the subject of the analysis in Deterding (1997). These speakers were recorded in the 1980s and they are described by Deterding (1997) as having a 'Standard Southern British accent,' (p. 48) a style of speech that 'may be familiar … through listening to the BBC World Service' (p. 47).

We segmented and labelled in these three corpora all rising diphthongs /aɪ/, /eɪ/, /aʊ/, /oʊ/ that occurred in prosodically accented words from acoustic displays including a waveform, spectrogram, superimposed formant tracks, and occasionally an amplitude contour using the EMU speech database analysis system (Cassidy & Harrington, 2001). (We did not include /ɔɪ/ because there were too few tokens in any one corpus). We marked the first target either in the most steady-state part of roughly the first half section of the diphthong trajectory or when F1 reached a maximum in /aɪ/ and /aʊ/. The formant trajectories were occasionally manually corrected in the case of obvious formant tracking errors. The segmentation and labelling were carried out by the first two authors of this chapter. The formant values were also converted to the Bark scale (Zwicker, 1961) and all statistical analyses were applied to values in Bark. The numbers of tokens for each diphthong category in the three corpora are shown in Table 10.1. The monophthong data in Table 10.1 are taken from Harrington et al. (2000a, 2000b) and include the SSB monophthongs from Deterding (1997). In the Queen's data, we differentiated between /u/ that followed /j/ (as in 'few' and marked as /ju/ in Table 10.1) from those that did not follow /j/ (marked as /u/ in Table 10.1) because /j/ has a marked influence on the formants of this vowel.

Various plots of the diphthongs in an F2 × F1 Bark space were derived by linearly time-normalising all diphthong trajectories to the same 20 equally spaced intervals on the time-axis between their acoustic onset and offset (Fig. 10.1b) and then averaging the trajectories separately for each diphthong category (Fig. 10.1c) and plotting averaged time-normalised F2 against F1 (Fig. 10.1d). In the SSB corpus, the averages were calculated across the five female SSB speakers without applying any speaker-normalisation techniques.

RESULTS

Standard Southern British Diphthongs

Fig. 10.2 shows the average positions of the monophthongal vowels in the F2 × F1 Bark space of the five 1980s SSB speakers as reported in Harrington et al. (2000a, 2000b) and Deterding (1997) with superimposed, linearly, time-normalised and then averaged trajectories for the four separate diphthong categories. The figure shows a separation

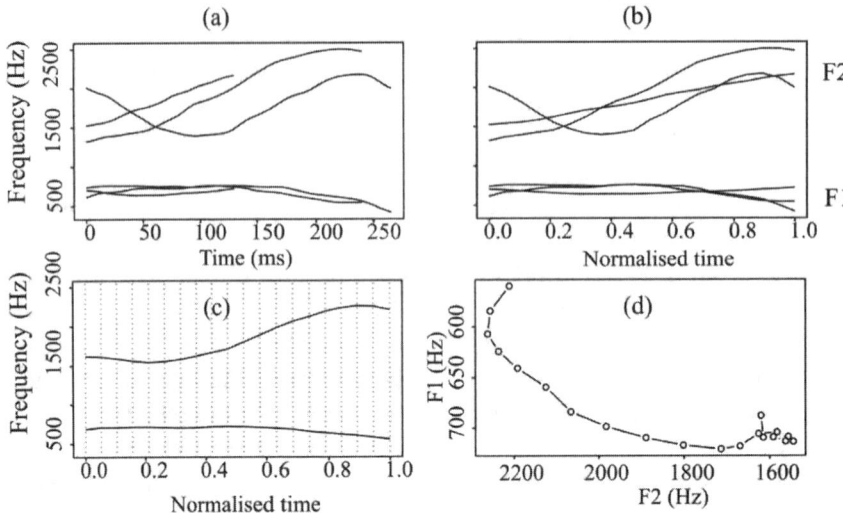

FIG. 10.1. (a) F1 and F2 trajectories of three /aɪ/ diphthongs. In (b) these trajectories are linearly time-normalised and in (c) the time-normalised trajectories in (b) are averaged at 20 equally spaced time intervals [shown by dotted lines in (c)]. (d) is a plot of the averaged F1 against the averaged F2 derived from (c).

between the front-rising /aɪ eɪ/ and back-rising diphthongs /aʊ oʊ/ and there is also a separation in this F2 × F1 Bark space between /eɪ ou/ and /aɪ aʊ/ based on the first formant frequency.

The positions of the SSB diphthong trajectories in the F2 × F1 space are consistent with only some of the auditory analyses of mainstream RP reviewed earlier. There is an elbow (and hence a first target) for both /aɪ/ and /aʊ/ between /æ/ ('had') and /ɑ/ ('hard') supporting the interpretation that these diphthongs originate between these two vowels. The F2 × F1 trajectories are also consistent with auditory interpretations that the diphthongs end at positions which are phonetically somewhat higher than /ɛ/ ('head') and /ɒ/ ('pod') respectively. Fig. 10.2 also shows that the trajectories point toward /ɪ/ /ʊ/ and this, together with some evidence that the direction in which the diphthong points (rather than the final target attained) is the main factor that determines the phonetic identity of the second component (Gottfried, Miller, & Meyer, 1993; Nearey & Assmann, 1986; Pols, 1977), may underlie the auditory impression

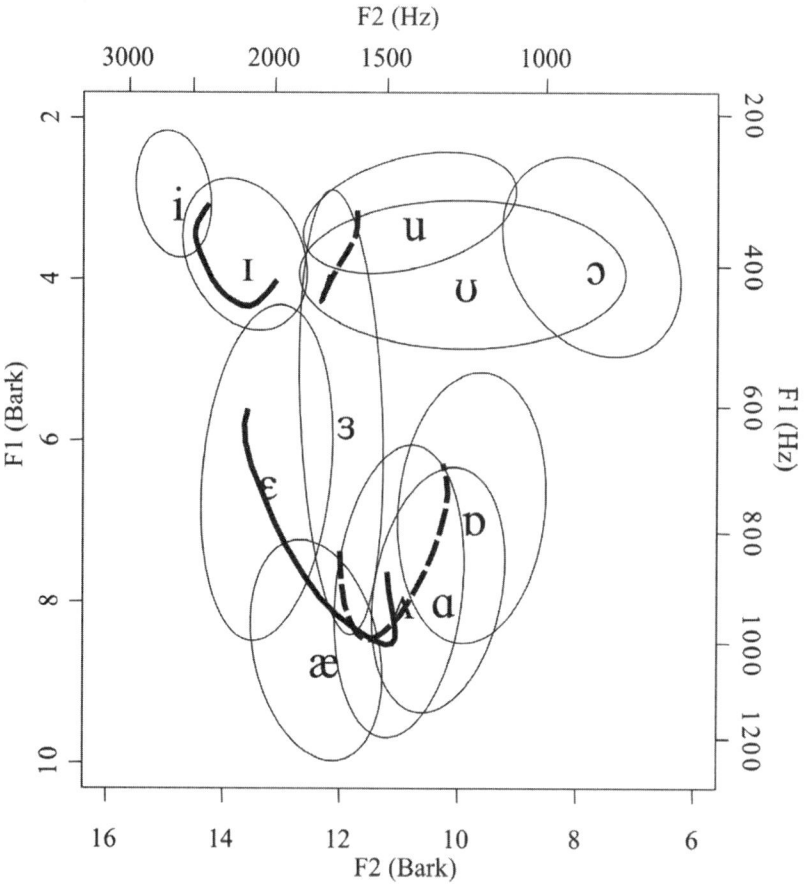

FIG. 10.2. Averaged Standard Southern British diphthong trajectories for /aɪ/ /eɪ/ (solid: /aɪ/ is below /eɪ/) and /aʊ/ /oʊ/ (dashed: /aʊ/ is below /oʊ/) superimposed on the SSB vowel monophthongs in an F1 × F2 Bark space. The vowel symbol is plotted at the centroid (mean) and the ellipses include 2 standard deviations around the mean.

that the second components of /aɪ/ and /aʊ/ are phonetically close to /ɪ/ and /ʊ/ respectively.

At first sight, there seems to be little support for the auditory impressions that the first target of /aʊ/ is phonetically more back than that of /aɪ/ because the elbow and therefore the targets of these diphthongs both originate from similar positions between the /æ/ and /ɑ/ spaces. However, although both diphthongs have their starting point in a similar location in the F2 × F1 space, it is also clear that /aɪ/ and

/aʊ/ pass predominantly through the /æ/ and /ɑ/ ellipses, respectively (Fig. 10.2). The movement of the trajectories through these separate vowel spaces may give rise to the percept that the first components of these diphthongs differ in backness with /aɪ/ being predominantly associated with /æ/ and /aʊ/ with /ɑ/.

For the first part of the /eɪ/ and /oʊ/ diphthong trajectories, F1 is low and considerably lower than the centroids of /ɛ/ ('head') and /ɜ/ ('herd') with which the first component of these diphthongs is assumed to be most closely associated in auditory impressions of mainstream RP. A separate analysis of each speaker (Fig. 10.3) shows that the starting trajectory of /eɪ/ is nearer to /ɪ/ than to /ɛ/ for 4 out of 5 speakers whereas for one speaker (S1) it is about midway between /ɪ/ and /ɛ/. Fig. 10.3 also confirms that /oʊ/ originates from a position that is above /ɜ/ (i.e., with a lower F1) for 4 out of 5 speakers.

As far as the second component is concerned, /eɪ/ moves through the /ɪ/ ellipse in the direction of /i/ for all five speakers (Fig. 10.3) without attaining the /i/ centroid. Fig. 10.3 also shows that /oʊ/ ends nearer to the centroid of /u/ rather than /ʊ/.

Q50 Diphthongs

The averaged diphthong trajectories superimposed on a mono-phthongal vowel space from the Queen's 1950s broadcasts in Fig. 10.4 show some similarities but also some very clear differences in comparison with the SSB vowels and diphthongs in Figures 10.2 and 10.3. One of the most striking differences is that there is consider-ably more compression along the F1 dimension so that in the Q50 data, the end of the /aɪ aʊ/ trajectories overlap with the beginning of the /eɪ oʊ/ trajectories whereas in the SSB data they do not. Another is that the Q50 diphthongs are confined to the front-central part of the F2 × F1 space and do not extend into, or come as close to, the space occupied by the rounded vowels and /ɑ/.

We consider first the acoustic structure of the Q50-/aɪ aʊ/ diph-thongs. Fig. 10.4 shows that the first components of these diph-thongs originate between Q50-/æ/ and Q50-/ɑ/. As in the SSB corpus, there is no evidence that the first 'target' (corresponding to the elbows of the diphthong trajectories in Fig. 10.4) is phoneti-cally more retracted in /aʊ/ than in /aɪ/; however, as in the SSB cor-pus, /aɪ/, but not /aʊ/, passes through the Q50-/æ/ space on its way

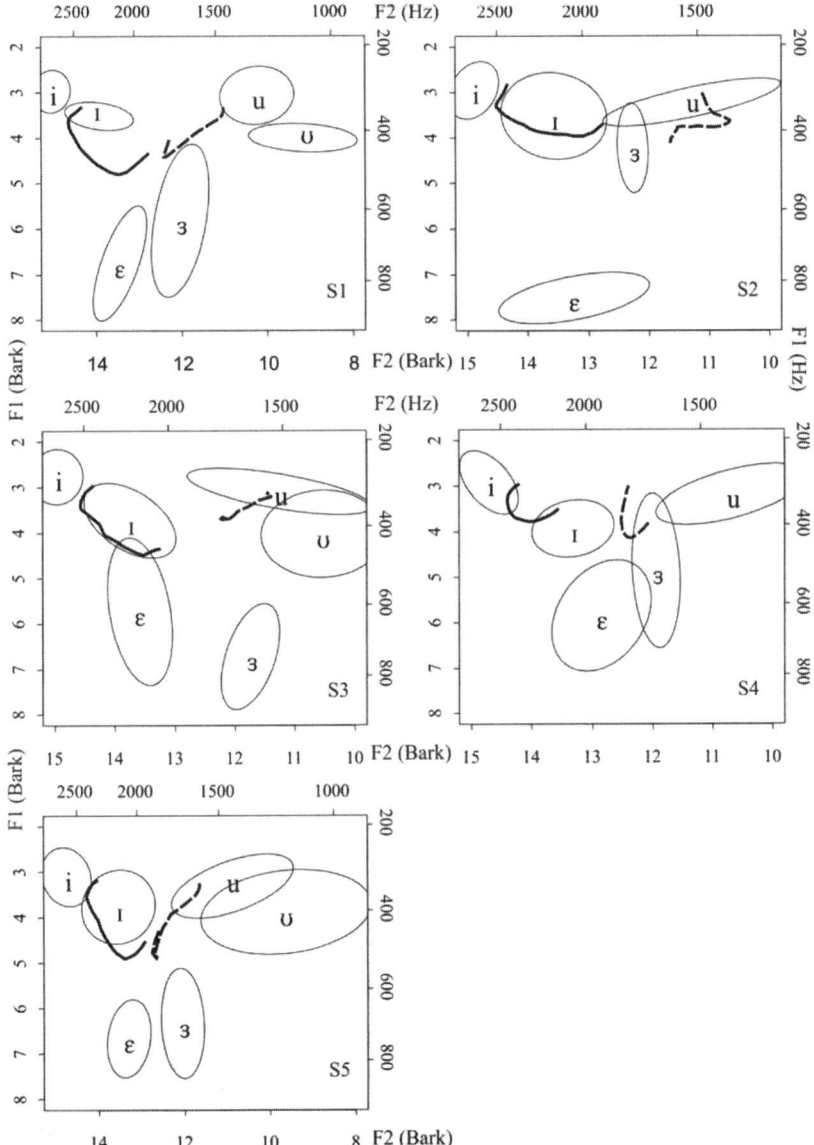

FIG. 10.3. As Fig.10.2, but plotted separately for the five (S1–S5) speakers and showing only /eɪ/ (solid) and /oʊ/ (dotted). (There are no /ʊ/ tokens for S2 and S4 because the number tokens was too small to form an ellipse).

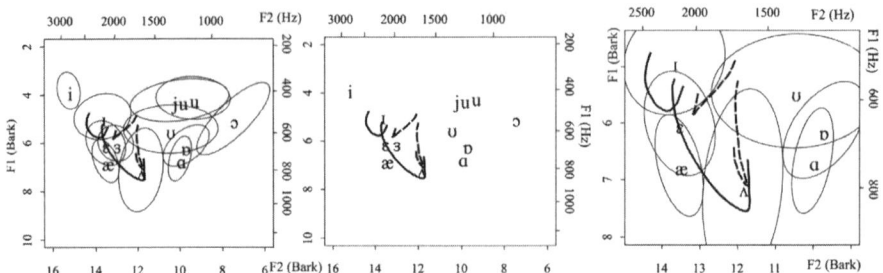

FIG. 10.4. Averaged Q50 diphthong trajectories for /aɪ/ /eɪ/ (solid: /aɪ/ is below /eɪ/) and /aʊ/ /oʊ/ (dashed: /aʊ/ is below /oʊ/) superimposed on the Q50 vowel monophthongs in an F1 × F2 Bark space with (a) and without (b) 2 standard deviation ellipses around the monophthongal means. (c) is an enlarged version of (a) but showing only the lax vowels and /ɑ/.

toward Q50-/ɪ/ (Fig. 10.4). On the other hand, whereas the SSB-/aʊ/ trajectory actually passes through SSB-/ɑ/, Q50-/aʊ/ has a higher F2 than Q50-/ɑ/ along its entire trajectory: this suggests that Q50-/aʊ/ is phonetically more front relative to Q50-/ɑ/ than SSB-/aʊ/ is to SSB-/ɑ/.

It is also evident from a comparison of Figures 10.2 and 10.4 that Q50-/aɪ aʊ/ start around one Bark lower than SSB-/aɪ aʊ/. This difference parallels the findings for the open monophthongs in Harrington et al. (2000a, 2000b) which showed that F1 of /æ ɑ ʌ/ in the Q50 corpus were all significantly lower than in the SSB-corpus. In general, these data are consistent with the view that open vowels, including both open monophthongs as well as diphthongs with an open first component, are phonetically closer in the Q50 compared with those in the SSB corpus. But by far the most marked open vowel difference between these corpora is in /æ/. Its F1 is almost 2 Bark lower in the Q50-corpus and, as discussed in Harrington et al. (2000a, 2000b), this lends strong support to the phonetic impressions that /æ/ has become more open since the 1950s. Because the extent of F1 difference between the Q50 and SSB data is greatest for /æ/, it follows that the relation between /æ/ and the first component of the /aɪ aʊ/ diphthongs is also slightly different in the two corpora: in the Q50 corpus, F1 of the first components of /aɪ/ and /aʊ/ are higher than F1 of /æ/, whereas in the SSB corpus, the first components of /aɪ aʊ/ and the monophthong /æ/ have quite similar F1 values. Taken together, these findings suggest first that the Q50-/aɪ aʊ/ diphthongs are phonetically more open than Q50-/æ/; second, that all the open monophthongs and /aɪ aʊ/ are phonetically more open in the SSB than in the Q50 corpus; and third, that the extent of the openness differences between these two corpora is more pronounced in /æ/ than in /aɪ aʊ/.

As far as the second component of these diphthongs is concerned, Q50-/aɪ/ passes through the middle of the Q50-/ɛ/ ellipse and extends into the Q50-/ɪ/ space, terminating just below (i.e., with a higher F1) than the Q50-/ɪ/ centroid. Q50-/aʊ/ passes from the Q50-/ʌ/ into the Q50-/ʊ/ space, ending within the Q50-/ʊ/ ellipse at a position roughly between the Q50-/ɪ/ and Q50-/ʊ/ centroids. The extent of the diphthong trajectories through the F2 × F1 space is quite comparable in the two corpora, but because all the phonetically close vowels in the SSB corpora are shifted upward in the F2 × F1 space, as inferred by the lower F1 values for SSB-/i ɪ ʊ u ɔ/, the SSB-/aɪ aʊ/ diphthongs terminate well short of SSB-/ɪ ʊ/ and near SSB-/ɛ ɒ/, as discussed earlier. Another important difference is in the direction of the /aʊ/ trajectory. In the SSB data, /aʊ/ bends toward the back of the F2 × F1 space as it passes through SSB-/ɑ/, ending slightly above SSB-/ɒ/ and pointing toward SSB-/u ʊ/. In the Q50-corpus, by contrast, the trajectory moves almost vertically upward through the F2 × F1 space and is well forward (i.e., with a higher F2) of any of the Q50 rounded vowels. In general, these data suggest that /aɪ/ and /aʊ/ are a good deal less differentiated in the Q50 than in the SSB corpus.

Turning now to /eɪ/, in the Q50 corpus this diphthong originates between the Q50-/ɛ/ and Q50-/ɪ/ centroids and then extends in an arc around the high-F2 part of the Q50-/ɪ/ ellipse ending about midway between the Q50-/ɪ/ and Q50-/i/ centroids, but well within the Q50-/ɪ/ ellipse. In the Q50 and SSB corpora, the relation between /eɪ/ and /ɪ/ is therefore quite similar. On the other hand, both the /eɪ/ trajectory and the /ɪ/ ellipse are acoustically much nearer to /i/ and further from /ɛ/ in the SSB than in the Q50 corpus.

The first component of the /oʊ/ diphthong is within the /ɜ/ and /ɛ/ ellipses in the Q50 corpus, but a good deal further from these monophthongs in the SSB corpus. The differences are evident both in the positional relation between /oʊ/ and these monophthongs and in terms of absolute values (F1 and F2 of the first component of /oʊ/ are lower in the SSB corpus). These data suggest that the first component of /oʊ/ and /ɜ/ are phonetically fronted in the Q50 compared with the SSB corpus (see also Fig. 10.3 which shows that the starting trajectory of /oʊ/ does not extend into /ɛ/ for any of the SSB speakers). Considering now the second target, /oʊ/ extends through the edge of the /ʊ/ ellipse and points toward /u/ rather than /ʊ/ in both the Q50 and SSB corpora. Whereas /oʊ/ extends into the /u/ space for 3 out of 5 SSB speakers, it reaches the edge of, but does not extend into, the /u/ ellipse in the Q50 corpus.

Q80 CORPUS

Predictions for Q80

We can make a number of predictions about the positions of the Q80 vowels in the F2 × F1 space based on a comparison between the Q50 and SSB corpora: that is, if the Queen's accent of the 1980s has shifted in the direction of a more mainstream 1980s RP, as Harrington et al. (2000a, 2000b) have proposed, we should expect the Q80 diphthongs to be at approximately intermediate locations between those in the Q50 and SSB corpora. For example, because the first component of /aɪ/ and /æ/ are acoustically nearer to each other in the SSB corpus than in the Q50 corpus, we predict (see P1 later) that the first target of /aɪ/ will be acoustically nearer to /æ/ in the Q80 corpus. A summary of predictions about the differences in the positions of the diphthong in the F2 × F1 spaces between the Q50 and Q80 corpora based on an extrapolation from the Q50 to the SSB corpora is as follows. All these predictions are statements about the position of the Q80 diphthongs relative to those in the Q50 corpus:

Q80 /aɪ/:

    P1. The 1st target will be nearer to /æ/.
    P2. The 2nd target will be further from /ɪ/.
    P3. F1 of the 1st target will be higher.
    P4. F2 of the 1st target will be lower.

Q80 /aʊ/:

P5. The 1st target will be nearer to /æ/.
P6. F1 of the 2nd target will be further from /ʊ/.
P7. F1 of the 1st target will be higher.
P8. F2 of the 2nd target will be lower.

Q80 /eɪ/:

P9. The 1st target of /eɪ/ will be further from /ɛ/.
P10. The 2nd target will be nearer to /i/.
P11. F1 of the 1st target will be lower.
P12. F1 of the 2nd target will be lower.

Q80 /oʊ/:

P13. The 1st target will be further from /ɜ/.
P14. The 2nd target will be closer to /u/.
P15. F1 of the 1st target will be lower.
P16. F1 of the 2nd target will be lower.

Some additional predictions can be made about how the diphthongs have changed relative to each other. The predictions are once again to do with the positional change of the diphthongs in the Q80 corpus relative to the Q50 corpus:

P17. The 2nd target of /aɪ/ will be further from the 1st target of /eɪ/.
P18. The 2nd target of /aɪ/ will be further from the 1st target /oʊ/.
P19. The 2nd targets of /oʊ/ and /aʊ/ will be further from each other.
P20. The 2nd targets of /aɪ/ and /aʊ/ will be further away from each other.

METHOD

We used a Gaussian probabilistic technique to quantify the extent to which two vowel types, let us call these /X/ and /Y/, overlapped with each other in the F2 × F1 Bark space. We did this by calculating the probability that a given token of /X/ could be a member of type /Y/; and we also calculated the probability that a given token of /Y/ could be a member of type /X/. We did this for all tokens of /X/ and for all tokens of /Y/ so that each token from /X/ and each token from /Y/ is associated with a probabilistic distance (that it could be a member of type /Y/ and /X/, respectively). We compared two sets of probabilistic distances, one set obtained for /X/ and /Y/ in the Q50 corpus and one set obtained for /X/ and /Y/ in the Q80 corpus. The probabilistic distances are, in fact, Bayesian distances which are derived from the density function of the normal curve with a known mean, variance, and (in the multidimensional case) covariance matrix (Harrington & Cassidy, 1999, p. 252).

These steps are illustrated in Fig. 10.5 with reference to the first prediction, P1, that /æ/ and (the first target of) /aɪ/ overlap to a greater extent in the Q80 corpus. First, a two-dimensional Gaussian model is fitted to the distribution of Q50-/æ/, which essentially converts every data point in the Q50 F2 × F1 space into a Bayesian distance that quantifies the likelihood that it could be a member of /æ/. Equal Bayesian distances form ellipses that are proportional to standard deviations away from the mean, or centroid, of /æ/ in the F2 × F1 space (Fig. 10.5b). The Bayesian distances to /æ/ can therefore be obtained for all the individual tokens (data points) of /aɪ/ (Fig. 10.5c). The process is then repeated, but now the Gaussian model is calculated for /aɪ/ (Fig. 10.5d) and the Bayesian distances are obtained from the tokens of /æ/ to /aɪ/ (Fig. 10.5e). The two sets of Bayesian distances (Figs. 10.5c, and 10.5e) thus obtained are combined in a single distribution (Fig. 10.5f). The more the values in Fig. 10.5f tend to zero, the greater the overlap between /aɪ/ and /æ/ in the Q50 corpus, whereas increasingly negative values imply a greater separation between these vowel types. The same methodology is used to derive a Bayesian distance distribution for /æ/ and /aɪ/ in the Q80 corpus. That is, we derive two versions of Fig. 10.5f: one distribution shows the pooled Bayesian distances between /æ/ and /aɪ/ in the Q50 corpus, and another shows the pooled Bayesian distances between /æ/ and /aɪ/ in the Q80 corpus. These two distributions are then compared statistically.

The null hypothesis for all the predictions is that these two distributions are not significantly different, which we would interpret to mean that the overlap in the F2 × F1 space between the two vowel types we are testing is about the same in the Q50 and Q80 corpora. Tests of significance in comparing these distributions of Bayesian distances are carried out using the nonparametric Wilcoxon rank

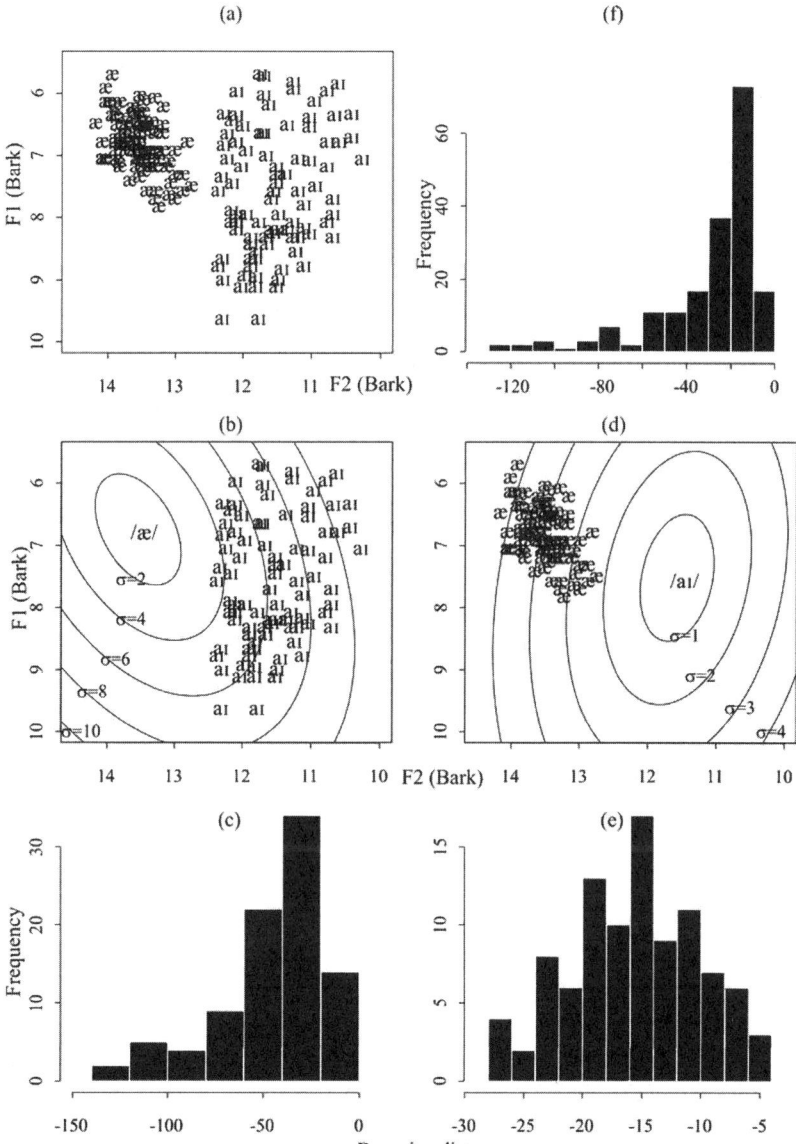

FIG. 10.5. An illustration of the technique for comparing the extent to which two vowel categories [here /æ/ and /aɪ/ in panel (a)] overlap in the F2 × F1 Bark space in the Q50 corpus. Panel (b)—/aɪ/ tokens superimposed on ellipses at s standard deviations away from the centroid of /æ/. Panel (c)—the Bayesian distances of the /aɪ/ tokens to /æ/ calculated using the model in (b). Panels (d) and (e)—as panels (b) and (c) respectively, but in which Bayesian distances are calculated from the tokens of /æ/ to /aɪ/. Panel (f)—a combination of the distributions in panels (c) and (e).

sum test because (as subsequently confirmed by the Shapiro–Wilk W-statistic on these data) distributions of the kind shown in Fig. 10.5f are not Gaussian.

The aforementioned test of significance was used when we wanted to quantify the extent of overlap between two vowel types. When we wanted to compare the change in F1 or F2 Bark values between the Q50 and Q80 corpora, we applied a (parametric) Welch two-sample t test. Finally, when comparisons were made with the second diphthong target, we obtained a notional second target by averaging the final 20% of the diphthong trajectory. We did this because finding a reliable second target for a diphthong is very difficult in view of the strong tendency for it to be undershot (Gay, 1968, 1970; Jha, 1985; Nâbélek & Dagenais, 1986; Pols, 1977).

RESULTS: Q80 VOWEL POSITIONS

In general, the results strongly support the hypothesis that the Queen's diphthongs have shifted in the direction of the corresponding 1980s SSB positions. Both Fig. 10.6 and in particular Fig. 10.7 show that the linearly time-normalised Q80 trajectories occupy positions in the F2 × F1 Bark space that are intermediate between those in the Q50 and SSB corpora; the statistical analysis confirmed that 16 out of 20 predictions were significant, most of these well below $p < 0.01$ (Table 10.2).

Considering now the predictions in further detail, the results show that /æ/ is acoustically closer to the first targets of /aɪ/ and /aʊ/ (Table 10.2: P1 and P5) and that F1 of the first targets of /aɪ/ and /aʊ/ (P3 and P7) are higher in the Q80 corpus. These findings support the interpretation that all the vowels that can be characterised as phonetically open have become more open in the Q80 corpus. The extent of the shift has been greatest for /æ/; however, because /æ/ starts in the Q50 data from a phonetically higher position than /aɪ aʊ/, the net effect is a convergence so that /æ/ and the first components of /aɪ/ and /aʊ/ are less differentiated in the Q80 (and SSB) than in the Q50 corpus.

Whereas the first targets of /aɪ aʊ/ have become phonetically more open, those of /eɪ oʊ/ are associated with a lower F1, suggesting phonetic raising in line with the predicted changes from the Q50 to the SSB corpora (Table 10.2: P11 and P15). Because the shift in the

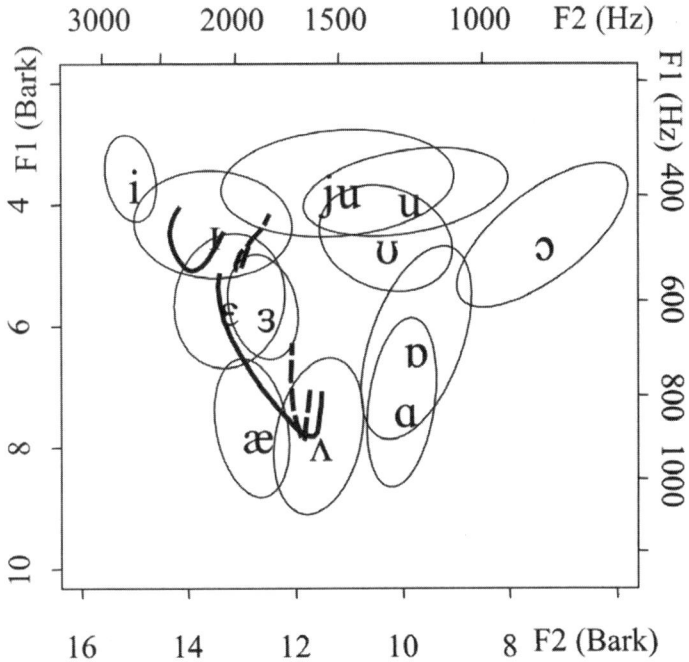

FIG. 10.6. Averaged Q80 diphthong trajectories for /aɪ/ /eɪ/ (solid: /aɪ/ is below /eɪ/) and /aʊ/ /oʊ/ (dashed: /aʊ/ is below /oʊ/) superimposed on the Q80 vowel monophthongs in an F2 × F1 Bark space. The vowel symbol is plotted at the centroid (mean) and the ellipses include 2 standard deviations around the mean.

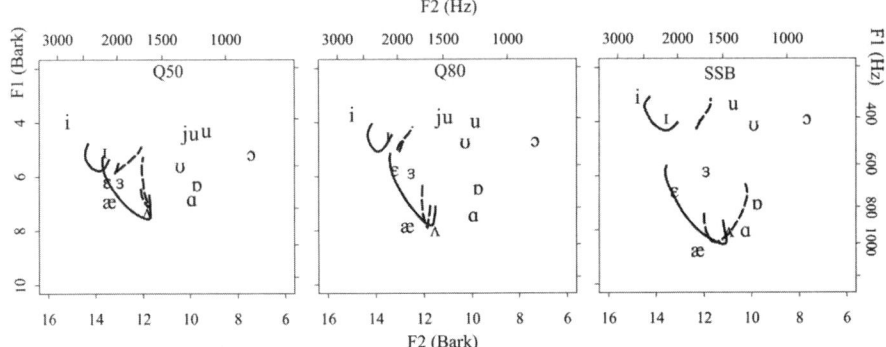

FIG. 10.7. Q50 (left), Q80 (middle), and Standard Southern British (right) averaged diphthong trajectories superimposed on the vowel centroid positions from the corresponding corpora. /aɪ eɪ/ are the solid trajectories (/aɪ/ is below /eɪ/) and /aʊ oʊ/ are the dotted trajectories (/aʊ/ is below /oʊ/).

TABLE 10.2

Predicted Changes to the Q80 Corpus

Code	Prediction	Result
	/aɪ/	
P1	1st target of /aɪ/ is closer to /æ/	W = 5978, p < 0.00001
P2	2nd target of /aɪ/ is further from /ɪ/	W= 25268, p < 0.00001
P3	F1 of the 1st target of /aɪ/ is higher	t = –2.00, df = 164.6, p < 0.05
P4	F2 of the 1st target of /aɪ/ is lower	NS
	/aʊ/	
P5	1st target of /aʊ/ is closer to /æ/	W = 3329, p < 0.00001
P6	2nd target of /aʊ/ is further from /ʊ/	W = 1263, p < 0.00001
P7	F1 of the 1st target is higher	t = –2.81, df = 40.6, p < 0.001
P8	F2 of the 2nd target is lower	NS
	/eɪ/	
P9	1st target of /eɪ/ is further from /ɛ/	W = 44232, p < 0.00001
P10	2nd target of /eɪ/ is closer to /i/	W = 13275, p < 0.0001
P11	F1 of the 1st target of /eɪ/ is lower	t = 10.36, df = 198.2, p < 0.00001
P12	F1 of the 2nd target of /eɪ/ is lower	t = 9.83, df = 164.2, p < 0.00001
	/oʊ/	
P13	1st target of /oʊ/ is further from /ɜ/	W = 8056, p < 0.00001
P14	2nd target is of /oʊ/ is closer to /u/	W = 4599, p < 0.00001
P15	F1 of the 1st target of /oʊ/ is lower	t = 10.4, df = 198.2, p < 0.00001
P16	F1 of the 2nd target of /oʊ/ is lower	t = 8.00, df = 134.2, p < 0.00001
	Interdiphthong Comparisons	
P17	2nd target of /aɪ/ is further from the 1st target of /eɪ/	W = 25558, p < 0.00001
P18	2nd target of /aɪ/ is further from the 1st target /oʊ/	W = 15404, p < 0.00001
P19	2nd target of /oʊ/ is further from the 2nd target of /aʊ/	NS
P19	2nd target of /oʊ/ is further from the 2nd target of /aʊ/	W = 6440, p < 0.00001
P20	2nd target of /aɪ/ is further from the 2nd target of /aʊ/	NS

Note. Results of the statistical analysis of 20 predicted changes in the Q80 corpus relative to the Q50 corpus. W = Wilcoxon rank sum test with continuity correction; t = T statistic of Welch Two-Sample *t* test.

midvowels /ɛ ɜ/ from the Q50 to the Q80 corpora is small, these monophthongs are acoustically further from the first targets of /eɪ ou/ respectively, in the Q80 corpus, which is a predicted change (Table 10.2: P9 and P13) in the direction of the SSB positions.

Turning now to the diphthongs' second targets, /aɪ/ and /au/ terminate near the midvowels /ɛ/ and /ɜ/ in the Q80 corpus (Figures 10.6 and 10.7) and they are significantly further in the F2 × F1 Bark space from /ɪ/ and /ʊ/, respectively, than in the Q50 corpus, in accordance with the predicted changes in the direction of SSB (Table 10.2: P2 and P6). The second target of /aɪ/ is also acoustically further from the first targets of /eɪ/ and /ou/ (Table 10.2: P17 and P18), partly because the entire /eɪ ou/ trajectories have shifted upward in the F2 × F1 Bark space in the Q80 compared with the Q50 corpus. This shift is not only in absolute terms, confirming various predictions (Table 10.2: P11 and P12, P15, P16), but also relative to most of the other vowels and diphthongs: as a result, the second targets of /eɪ/ and /ou/ are acoustically nearer to /i/ and /u/, respectively, in the Q80 than in the Q50 corpus, in accordance with the predicted shift in the direction of SSB (Table 10.2: P10 and P14). Because /ou/ has shifted upwards in the F2 × F1 Bark space and because the second target of /au/ falls acoustically well short of the phonetically high vowels in the Q80 corpus, the second targets of /ou/ and /au/ are also acoustically further apart from each other in the Q80 corpus, in accordance with the predicted shift in the direction of SSB (Table 10.2: P19).

There is, however, one major nonsignificant change which is associated with F2 of /au/. In the Q50 data, F2 of /au/ is noticeably higher than in the SSB corpus; indeed, in the SSB corpus, /au/ extends very clearly into the space associated with back vowels. There is no suggestion that F2 of /au/ has lowered in the Q80 corpus (Table 10.2: P8) and the trajectory extends more or less vertically upward in the F2 × F1 space as in the Q50 corpus. Therefore, there is no evidence from this data to suggest that the second targets of /aɪ/ and /au/ have become more divergent, in contrast to the prediction based on the interpolation from the Q50 to the SSB spaces (Table 10.2: P20).

DISCUSSION

The acoustic analysis of the four diphthongs that we have investigated shows a very clear F1-dependent separation between /aɪ au/ on the one hand and /eɪ oʊ/ on the other. For the 1980s SSB speakers, /aɪ aʊ/ both originate between SSB-/æ/ and SSB-/ɑ/. Phoneticians may have associated the first components of these diphthongs with open front and open back vowels respectively because, whereas SSB-/aɪ/ passes predominantly through the SSB-/æ/ space, the trajectory of SSB-/aʊ/ bends in the opposite direction through SSB-/ɑ/, as these diphthongs extend upward in the F2 × F1 formant plane. Their trajectories terminate at positions corresponding approximately to phonetically mid in the SSB space, and they end well below the first components of SSB-/eɪ oʊ/. For all five SSB speakers, the first components of SSB-/eɪ oʊ/ generally start above the spaces associated with SSB-/ɛ/ and SSB-/ɜ/. The second component of SSB-/eɪ/ is about midway between the SSB-/ɪ/ and SSB-/i/ spaces and the second component of SSB-/oʊ/ is nearer to SSB-/u/ than to SSB-/ʊ/.

As reported in Harrington et al. (2000a, 2000b), there has been a 'vertical expansion' of the Queen's monophthongal vowel space between the 1950s and 1980s as evidenced by an F1-raising of the open monophthongs /ɑ ʌ æ ɒ/ and an F1-lowering of the half-close and close monophthongs /ɪ ʊ ɔ i u/. In light of these and other changes which were shown to be in the direction of the SSB-monophthongal vowels, we were interested to know whether there would be an analogous shift in the diphthong trajectories.

The results of this study show a change from the 1950s to the 1980s Christmas broadcast corpora such that the diphthongs with an open first component, /aɪ aʊ/, have moved downward in the F2 × F1 space with /ɑ ʌ æ ɒ/, whereas the diphthongs with a midhigh first component, /eɪ oʊ/, have shifted upward with /ɪ ʊ ɔ i u/. Since the extent of the trajectory between the first and second targets within the same diphthong category is about the same across the two sets of years, /aɪ aʊ/ overlap a good deal with (the first components of) /eɪ oʊ/ in the 1950s broadcasts, but they do not in the broadcasts of the 1980s. For the same reason, /aɪ aʊ/ extend well into the /ɪʊ/ spaces in the 1950s broadcasts, but they do not in those of the 1980s; and the first components of /eɪ oʊ/ start within the /ɛ ɜ/ spaces in the 1950s broadcasts, but they are on the upper edge of them in 1980 broadcasts.

These are precisely some of the changes that are predicted to occur by extrapolating between the acoustic vowel spaces of the 1950s Christmas broadcast and 1980s SSB corpora. Moreover, we can see that, as for the monophthongs, the diphthongs have shifted toward

1980s SSB positions, but without actually attaining them. These data would seem to corroborate the interpretation in Harrington et al. (2000a, 2000b) that between the 1950s and the 1980s, the Queen's accent has shifted toward, but not attained, a 1980s SSB accent.

However, there is also evidence that the Queen's accent has not changed in some respects. Consider, for example, /aʊ/. The trajectory rises vertically up through the F2 × F1 space in both the 1950s and 1980s Christmas broadcast data, whereas in the 1980s SSB data, /aʊ/ very clearly bends toward the back of it. As a result, the /aɪ/ and /aʊ/ trajectories have not become more divergent in the 1980s Christmas broadcast data, contrary to the predicted change based on their extrapolation toward the SSB positions. It has been suggested[5] that the lack of divergence in the F2 × F1 space between /aɪ/ and /aʊ/ may provide experimental evidence for the popular impression that these diphthongs are less distinct in U-RP, giving rise to the caricature that the pronunciation by some members of the Royal Family of 'house' and 'trousers' is close to 'hice' and 'trisers' (Wales, 1994). Perhaps the fronting of the second component of /aʊ/ has come to be identified as an especially salient marker of the U-RP and SSB distinction, in the same way that glottal stop is a perceptually dramatic marker of London Cockney. We can speculate that if U-RP speakers (and the Queen) choose to set themselves apart from those with a mainstream RP accent, then they may do so precisely by resisting change in those attributes that provide especially prominent cues to the U-RP and SSB distinction.

Although the changes to both the diphthongs reported in this chapter as well as to the monophthongs in Harrington et al. (2000a, 2000b) can be interpreted as evidence for *phonetic* changes in the direction of SSB, we must also consider the following alternative explanations: that they are attributable to *age-related* or *speaking-style* changes.

In Harrington et al. (2000b), we rejected an age-related explanation because the formant differences in the positions of the 1950s and 1980s Christmas broadcast monophthongs were not compatible with some recent experimental findings by Rastatter, McGuire, Kalinowski, and Stuart (1997), who examined formant differences between a young and old age group producing similar materials. It is, however, clear from the data in Table 10.3 that there are global changes to the formant positions between the 1950s and the 1980s broadcasts. These data were derived by calculating means and standard deviations across all the frames of data from vowel onset to vowel offset in the same monophthongs that were analysed in Harrington et al. (2000b). Turning first to the means, Table 10.3 shows that all the F1 to F4 means have decreased in the 1980s Christmas broadcasts relative to those from the 1950s by up to 0.4 Bark (in F4). Interestingly, this decrease in predicted by Laver and Trudgill (1979) who suggest, based on remarks by Luchsinger and Arnold (1965), that the entire respiratory system and digestive tract are in a lower position with increasing age. Such a lowering would cause the vocal tract to lengthen resulting in the well-known downward shift in the formant frequency ranges (Laver & Trudgill, 1979, p.10). We also see in Table 10.3 an age-related change in fundamental frequency which is reported to be lower in older women (Helfrich, 1979): as Table 10.3 shows, the mean F0 in the 1980s broadcasts is some 0.5 Bark lower in the 1980s than in the 1950s broadcasts. However, although we recognise that some of the formant displacement may be due to maturation of the vocal tract, there is no evidence of a general lowering of F1 and F2 in the Queen's 1980s monophthongs and diphthongs relative to those of the 1950s (Fig. 10.7). In particular, the dramatic F1-rise in open monophthongs and diphthongs with an open first component as well as the F2-increase in /u/ are not compatible with such an age-related expla-nation Nevertheless, we cannot entirely rule out an age-related com-ponent in the F1-lowering of the first component of both the /eɪ oʊ/

TABLE 10.3

Means and Standard Deviations of the Formants and Fundamental Frequency

	F1		F2		F3		F4		f0	
	m	s	m	s	m	s	m	s	m	s
Q50	5.5	1.1	12.0	2.3	15.5	0.5	17.5	0.6	2.8	0.6
Q80	5.3	1.6	11.8	2.2	15.4	0.5	17.1	0.6	2.3	0.5
Change	−0.2	0.5	−0.2	−0.1	−0.1	0	−0.4	0	−0.5	−0.3

Note. Means (m) and standard deviations (s) of the first four formants (F1–F4) and of the fundamental frequency (f0) in the Q50 and Q80 corpora in Bark (the third row shows the difference in the mean and standard deviation values between the two corpora). The means and standard deviations were calculated across all the frames (Q50: n = 20429 frames; Q80: n = 17972 frames) from acoustic onset to offset of the monophthongs in Harrington, Palethorpe, and Watson (2000a, 2000b). The values are corrected to one dec-imal place.

diphthongs and of some of the close monophthongs, but there are three points that need to be considered with regard to such an inter-pretation. First, the relation between formant lowering and increasing age needs to be investigated further: the study by Rastatter et al. (1997), for example, suggests that the formants may *rise* from younger to older speakers in some vowels. Second, the F1 decrease in /eɪ oʊ/ in the 1980s Christmas broadcasts relative to the 1950s broadcasts is somewhat greater than the average F1 change between these two cor-pora: in particular, there is approximately a 0.75 Bark decrease in the first targets of /eɪ oʊ/ whereas the data in Table 10.3 show an average 0.2 Bark decrease between these two time periods. Third, we would have to reconcile a purely age-related explanation with our evidence that the changes to the vowel and diphthong positions between the two sets of Christmas broadcast materials are very clearly in the direc-tion of the 1980s SSB corpus. An age-related explanation of the F1-changes in /eɪ oʊ/ would then lead us to the conclusion that the 1980s SSB speakers must have been a good deal older than the Queen (ages 57–62 between 1983 and 1988) given that the SSB F1-values for these diphthongs and close vowels are even lower than those in the 1980s Christmas broadcasts. Deterding (1997) does not list the ages of the SSB speakers, but we have no reason to believe from our auditory impressions of them that they are all considerably older than 57–62. For all these reasons, we continue to reject an age-related explanation for the formant changes we have presented in this study and in Har-rington et al. (2000a, 2000b).

The influence of speaking-style changes is another matter, how-ever. One interpretation that was considered in Harrington et al. (2000a, 2000b) is the following: Newsreaders and broadcasters, such as those analysed in this 1980s SSB corpus, are likely to have a particularly clear speaking style. The Queen may have learned to increase the clarity of the delivery of the broadcasts over the 30-year period we have examined; the incremental shifts in the Queen's Christmas broadcast data toward the 1980s SSB values would (under this interpretation) simply be the consequence of an increase in the clarity of speaking style, not of changes to the phonetic quality of vowels. An expansion on the F1-dimension, of the kind that we have found, could be the acoustic consequence of an increased phonetic height differentiation: that is, an increase in clarity might be effected by a 'vertical hyperarticulation' in which phonetically high vowels are produced with a more raised jaw position and greater vocal tract narrowing and phonetically low vowels are produced with a lower jaw position and greater vocal tract opening (resulting in an expansion along the F1 dimension, given the well-known articulatory-acoustic relation demonstrated by, e.g., Lindblom & Sundberg, 1971, between a greater vocal tract opening and jaw lowering, and F1-raising). Certainly, there is very clear evidence for a change in the range (standard deviation) of the formants from the 1950s to the 1980s Christmas broadcasts: in the 1980s broadcasts, the standard deviation of F1 is 0.5 Bark higher than in the 1950s broadcasts (Table 10.3). On the other hand, we also reasoned in Harrington et al. (2000a, 2000b) that a hyperarticulation of the vowel space with the goal of increasing communicative clarity has been shown to affect F1 *and* F2: that is, hyperarticulated and more clearly produced vowels become more *peripheral*, that is, are produced further from the centre of the F2 × F1 vowel space (de Jong, 1995; Harrington, Fletcher, & Beckman, 2000; Moon & Lindblom, 1994). However, there is no evidence for an F2-expansion in the vowels of the Queen's Christmas broadcasts or of a global increase in the standard deviation of formants above F1 (Table 10.3). In fact, F2 is lowered in many of the front vowels from the 1950s to the 1980s Christmas broadcasts whereas F2 of /u/ is raised (i.e., there is a modest *compression* along much of the F2 dimension) and both of these changes are in the direction of the F2 positions in the 1980s SSB vowel space. A hyperarticulation of the vowel space also does not seem to be compatible with global changes to the vowel duration between the 1950s and 1980s broadcasts: a subsequent analysis has shown that the average vowel duration in the 1980s Christmas broadcasts is significantly less than the 1950s for almost all of the monophthongal and diphthongal vowel types, which suggests that the rate at which the Christmas broadcasts is delivered has increased in the later years. An explanation couched in terms of a general hyperarticulation of the vowel space between the 1950s and 1980s broadcasts would also need to reconcile an expansion along the F1-dimension in monophthongs with a nonsignificant F1-change that we have also established in the *extent* of the diphthong trajectories between their first and second components. That is, if there were global changes of speaking style from the 1950s to the 1980s Christmas broadcasts resulting primarily in a 'vertical' hyperarticulation and F1-expansion, we might expect the extent of F1-change from the first to the second components of /aɪ/ and /aʊ/ to increase from the 1950s to the 1980s broadcasts, but the data are not consistent with this interpretation.

However, on the other hand, if we abandon completely an interpretation of the results of this chapter in terms of speaking-style changes, then we are forced into an explanation based on phonetic changes (assuming that we can generally discount the age-related explanation). Under a purely phonetic interpretation, we would have to conclude that speakers of U-RP from the 1950s compress their vowels a good deal on the phonetic height dimension and expand them slightly on the phonetic backness dimension in comparison with 1980s SSB speakers. Certainly, there are many reported phonetic changes from an older and more conservative variety RP to its more modern usage that are entirely compatible with such a general interpretation, including the following: the lowering of /æ/ (Gimson, 1966; Ramsaran, 1990; Wells, 1982); the fronting of /u/ (Gimson, 1966); the fronting of the second component of /oʊ/ (Wells, 1982), the fronting of /ʌ/ (Gimson, 1964—although, like Bauer, 1985, we have found no evidence for this change in our data), the raising of /ɪ/ (Bauer, 1985, but see Wells, 1982, for a different interpretation), the raising of /ɔ/ (Gimson, 1966; Wells, 1982), and the possible convergence of the first targets of /aɪ/ and /aʊ/ (Wells, 1982). Yet some of the changes we have found, such as the upward shift in the $F2 \times F1$ space of the entire /eɪ/ and /oʊ/ trajectories, find scant support in impressionistic analyses of RP change in the literature.

It seems, then, we must come back to John Laver's most apt metaphor, that even after our analyses of almost 3,000 vowels and diphthongs from the same speaker producing speech with a similar communicative intent, we have not yet quite managed to delineate sufficiently the figure from the ground against which it is set. The matter of what is phonetic and what is speaker-specific and more generally the characterisation of speakers should "rest on a scientific base, and not rely on impressionistic description which is idiosyncratic to the individual analyst" (Laver, 1980, p. 7). Extending the range of available large-scale speech corpora for the 'real time' longitudinal analysis of many other types of speakers of RP and other varieties of English will help us to achieve this important aim.

NOTES

[1] "Don't be fooled: the Queen is not speaking our language," P. Hensher, 2000.
[2] *The Times,* 2000.
[3] From the Queen's English Society.
[4] For example, Julian Marshall, presenter of Newshour on the BBC World Service.
[5] My thanks to Francis Nolan for this observation.

ACKNOWLEDGMENTS

We thank Buckingham Palace for granting permission to analyse the Christmas broadcasts and the BBC for providing us with the recordings from their archives. This chapter has benefited from the comments from a number of Colleagues at the Institut für Phonetik und Sprachliche Kommunikation, Munich; the Department of Linguistics, Cambridge University; the Istituto di Fonetica e Dialettologia, del CNR, Padua; and the Institute of Phonetics; and Saarland University, where earlier versions of this research were presented in 2002.

REFERENCES

Bauer, L. (1985). Tracing phonetic change in the received pronunciation of British English. *Journal of Phonetics, 13,* 61–81.

Bernard, J. R. L. (1970). Towards the acoustic specification of Australian English. *Zeitschrift fur Phonetik, 2/3,* 113–128.

Bernard, J. R. L. (1981). Australian pronunciation. In A. Delbridge (Ed.), *The Macquarie dictionary* (pp. 18–27). Sydney, Australia: Macquarie Library.

Burridge, K. (1998). *English in Australia and New Zealand: An Introduction.* Melbourne, Australia: Oxford University Press.

Cannadine, D. (1998). *Class in Britain.* New Haven, CT: Yale University Press.

Chambers, J. K., & Trudgill, P. (1980). *Dialectology.* Cambridge, England: Cambridge University Press.

Cassidy, S., & Harrington, J. (2001). Multi-level annotation in the Emu speech database management system. *Speech Communication, 33,* 61–77.

Coggle, P. (1993). *Do you speak Estuary?* London: Bloomsbury.

Crystal, D. (1988). *The English language.* The Hague, Netherlands: Mouton.

Crystal, D. (1995). Estuary English. In D. Crystal (Ed.), *Cambridge encyclopaedia of the English language* (p. 327). Cambridge, England: Cambridge University Press.

de Jong, K. (1995). The supraglottal articulation of prominence in English: Linguistic stress as localized hyperarticulation. *Journal of the Acoustical Society of America, 97,* 491–504.

Deterding, D. (1997). The formants of monophthong vowels in standard southern British English pronunciation. *Journal of the International Phonetic Association, 27* 47–55.

Ellis, A. J. (1869). *On early English pronunciation.* London: English Early Text Society.

Gay, T. (1968). Effect of speaking rate on diphthong formant movement. *Journal of the Acoustical Society of America, 44,* 1570-1573.

Gay, T. (1970). A perceptual study of American English diphthongs. *Language & Speech, 13* 65–88.

Gimson, A. C. (1964). Phonetic changes and the RP vowel system. In D. Abercrombie, D. Fry, P. MacCarthy, N. Scott, & J. Trim (Eds.), *In honour of Daniel Jones* (pp. 131–136). London: Longman.

Gimson, A. C. (1966, 1970, 1980). *An introduction to the pronunciation of English* (1st ed.). London: Edward Arnold.

Gimson, A. C. and Cruttenden, A. (1994). *Gimson's pronunciation of English* (5th ed., Revised by Alan Cruttenden). London: Edward Arnold.

Gottfried, M., Miller, J. D., & Meyer, D. J. (1993). Three approaches to the classification of American English diphthongs. *Journal of Phonetics, 21* 205–229.

Harrington J., & Cassidy S. (1999). *Techniques in speech acoustics.* Dordrect, The Netherlands, Kluwer.

Harrington, J., Cox, F., & Evans, Z. (1997). An acoustic phonetic study of broad, general, and cultivated Australian English vowels. *Australian Journal of Linguistics, 17,* 155–184.

Harrington, J., Fletcher, J., & Beckman, M.E. (2000). Manner and place conflicts in the articulation of accent in Australian English. In M. Broe (Ed.), *Papers in laboratory phonology, 5* (p. 40–55). Cambridge, England: Cambridge University Press.

Harrington, J., Palethorpe, S., & Watson, C. (2000a). Does the queen speak the queen's English? *Nature, 408,* 927–928.

Harrington, J., Palethorpe, S., and Watson, C. (2000b). Monophthongal vowel changes in received pronunciation: An acoustic analysis of the queen's Christmas broadcasts. *Journal of the International Phonetic Association, 30,*63–78.

Helfrich, H. (1979). Age markers in speech. In K. Scherer & H. Giles (Eds.), *Social markers in speech* (pp. 63–107). Cambridge, England: Cambridge University Press.

Jha, S. K. (1985). Acoustic analysis of Maithilli diphthongs. *Journal of Phonetics, 13,* 107–115.

Jones, D. (1924). *English pronouncing dictionary* (2nd ed.). London: J. M. Dent & Sons.

Labov, W. (1994). *Principles of linguistic change*. Cambridge, MA: Blackwell.

Laver, J. (1980). *The phonetic description of voice quality*. Cambridge, England: Cambridge University Press.

Laver, J. (1994). *Principles of phonetics*. Cambridge, England: Cambridge University Press.

Laver J., & Trudgill, P. (1979). Phonetic and linguistic markers in speech. In K. Scherer & H. Giles (Eds.) *Social markers in speech* (pp. 1–26). Cambridge, England: Cambridge University Press.

Lindblom, B., & Sundberg, J. (1971). Acoustical consequences of lip, tongue, jaw, and larynx movement. *Journal of the Acoustical Society of America, 42,* 830–843.

Luchsinger, R., & Arnold, G. E. (1965). *Voice-speech-language*: Belmont, CA: Wadsworth.

Maidment, J. A. (1994, August). Estuary English: Hybrid or hype? Paper presented at the 4th New Zealand Conference on Language & Society, Lincoln University, Christchurch, New Zealand.

Mitford, N. (1956). *Nobless oblige: Enquiry into identifiable characteristics of English aristocracy*. London: Penguin.

Moon, S.-J., and Lindblom, B. (1994). Interaction between duration, context, and speaking style in English stressed words, *Journal of the Acoustical Society of America, 96,* 40–55.

Nâbélek, A. K., & Dagenais, P. A. (1986). Vowel errors in noise and in reverberation by hearing-impaired listeners. *Journal of the Acoustical Society of America, 80,* 741–748.

Nearey, T. M., & Assmann, P. F. (1986). Modeling the role of inherent spectral change in vowel identification. *Journal of the Acoustical Society of America, 80,* 1297–1308.

Parsons, G. (1998). *From "RP" to "Estuary English": The concept 'received' and the debate about British pronunciation standards*. Unpublished master's thesis, University of Hamburg.

Pols, L. C. W. (1977). *Spectral analysis and identification of Dutch vowels*. Unpublished doctoral dissertation, University of Amsterdam, Netherlands.

Ramsaran, S. (1990). RP: Fact and fiction. In S. Ramsaran (Ed.), *Studies in the pronunciation of English* (pp. 178–190). London: Routledge.

Rastatter, M., McGuire, R., Kalinowski, J., & Stuart, A. (1997). Formant frequency characteristics of elderly speakers in contextual speech. *Folia Phoniatrica, 49,* 1–8.

Roach, P., & Hartman. J. (1997). *English pronouncing dictionary* (15th ed.). Cambridge, England: Cambridge University Press.

Roach, P., Knowles, G., Varadi, T., & Arnfield, S. (1994). MARSEC: A machine-readable spoken English corpus. *Journal of the International Phonetic Association, 23,* 47–54.

Rosewarne, D. (1984). Estuary English. *Times Educational Supplement, 19.*

Rosewarne, D. (1994). Pronouncing Estuary English. *English Today, 40, 10,* 3–6.

Rosewarne, D. (1996). Estuary as a world language. *Modern English Teacher, 5,* 13–17.

Ross, A. S. C. (1954). Linguistic class indicators in present-day English. *Neuphilologische Mitteilungen, 16,* 171–185

Wales, K. (1994). Royalese: The Rise and Fall of "The Queen's English". *English Today 39, 10* 3–10.

Wells, J. (1994). English accents in England. In P. Trudgill (Ed)., *Language in the British Isles* (pp. 55–69). Cambridge, England: Cambridge University Press.

Wells, J. C. (1982). *Accents of English.* Cambridge: Cambridge University Press.

Wells, J. C. (2003). Web documents relating to Estuary English. Retrieved 3/1/2004, from http://www.phon.ucl.ac.uk/home/estuary/home.htm

Yaeger–Dror, M. (1994). Phonetic evidence for sound change in Quebec French. In P. A. Keating (Ed.), *Phonological structure and phonetic form: Papers in laboratory phonology III* (pp. 267–292). Cambridge, England: Cambridge University Press.

Zwicker, E. (1961). Subdivision of the audible frequency range into critical bands (Frequenzgruppen). *Journal of the Acoustical Society of America, 33,* 248.

Chapter 11

On the Interactional and Phonetic Design of Collaborative Completions

John Local
Department of Language & Linguistic Science
University of York

The natural home of spoken language is 'talk-in-interaction.' However, despite an upsurge in interest in 'connected speech' in recent years, we still know surprisingly little in detail about the ways in which ordinary people *use* the phonetic resources of language in everyday talk to undertake interactional tasks (e.g., handling turn-transition and entry to and exit from talk; configuring their talk as a continuation of some prior, abandoned talk or as a new departure; showing that they are now correcting some trouble in prior talk; signalling that they are willing to yield a turn-at-talk, treating some talk, which overlaps their own, as interruptive but other overlapping talk as supportive).

Talk-in-interaction relies on complex, highly structured, rule-governed behaviour of a semiotic richness that throws into sharp contrast the minimalist approach to the description of speech in spoken language favoured by recent generations of linguists and phoneticians (Laver, 2003). A key aspect of this richness is that information relevant to the identity of 'units of speech,' and to pragmatic intent more generally, is distributed and embedded in sequences of turns-at-talk.

This chapter is part of ongoing work which seeks to explicate this richness and to understand the ways in which speakers and listeners manipulate phonetic detail and phonetic variability in structuring and interpreting the moment-to-moment flow of everyday conversation (French & Local, 1983; Local, 1986, 1992, 1996; Local & Kelly, 1986; Local, Kelly, & Wells, 1986; Ogden, 2001; Walker, 2001). The work attempts to integrate detailed parametric phonetic analysis with the rigorously empirical methodology of Conversation Analysis (CA; see e.g., the articles in Atkinson & Heritage, 1984; Sacks, 1992; Sacks, Schegloff, & Jefferson, 1974; Schegloff, 1979, 1984, 1991, 1996, 1998). In consequence, the work differs from many other approaches to the functioning of phonetic parameters in speech in four respects:

- The data derives *entirely* from naturally occurring talk-in-interaction interaction.
- The approach is one which seeks to locate and identify specific interactional activities and to state the general phonetic parameters which speakers use to accomplish them.
- The CA-informed methodology takes it as axiomatic that it should be interactional categories which provide the basis for the analysis and such categories must be arrived at from, and grounded in, the data. These categories must be shown to be relevant to the participants in their talk and not be derived ultimately from the analyst's intuitions as a speaker of the language under analysis.
- The approach demands that the analysis prejudges as little as possible the relevance of particular phonetic details and particular phonetic parameters.

The work attempts to develop an interactionally-grounded analysis of the phonetics of everyday talk with the goal of elaborating a 'phonology of talk-in-interaction.'

THE PHENOMENON: COLLABORATIVE COMPLETION

Once we begin to examine systematically naturally-occurring talk-in-interaction, it becomes clear that the phonetic detail of everyday talk is thoroughly saturated and shaped by ongoing interactional activities. Consider, for example, the following two stretches of talk produced in the course of everyday conversation. The first occurs during a telephone call, the second occurs in face-to-face interaction:

but when we walk out of the class nobody knows what went on

and he and his wife obviously thought he'd had a heart attack

There is nothing particularly remarkable about these two stretches of natural coherent speech except that they are jointly accomplished by two speakers, rather than one. Fragments (1) and (2) provide the sequential context. The relevant turns are indicated by arrows[1]:

(1) Two Girls:5

```
1 Bee:    ['hhh [an' w]e no:d when he wants us to say ye:s?
2         (h)e[n ]'hhh
3 Ava:        [Ye ]ah,=
4 Bee:    =We raise our ha:nds when he wantsuh take a po:ll?=
5 Bee:    ='n[ : : ]
6 Ava:        [Ye:h]
7 Bee:    'hh Yihknow buh when we walk out of the cla:ss.=
8 Ava:→   =nobody knows what [wen' on,]
```

(2) C&M Xmas83.10

```
1 C:    it happened it was in the middle of the night he woke up in bed
2       with this (0.6) excruciating pain in his chest (1.0) staggered
3       out of bed and collapsed and went unconscious on the floor (.)
4       and he and his wife obviously thought he'd had a [heart attack]
```

5 K: →   [heart attack]
       yeh

In Fragment (1), Bee is complaining about one of her teachers and is in the course of constructing something like a three-part list (line 1, line 4, and line 7). Bee's turn at line 7 syntactically and pragmatically projects more talk from her (*class* carries the major accent of the turn with a prominent rising-falling pitch which ends some 4.4 semitones from her baseline). At line 8, Ava provides a possible (syntactic, pragmatic, and prosodic) completion of Bee's turn, timing her start-up rather precisely to latch onto the end of prior talk. In Fragment (2), K has been talking about her father's health and whether some 'attacks' he's been suffering are to be attributed to indigestion or something more serious. As part of the ongoing talk, C recounts a story about a neighbour who similarly suffered 'terrible attacks' which turned out simply to be indigestion. At line 4, as she is moving to the denouement of her telling, K joins with her to complete the turn (*heart attack* is coproduced with high to low falling pitch). Cases such as Fragment (1), where the talk which is a possible completion is produced by a single speaker, have been termed *collaborative productions* (e.g., Sacks, 1992: Fall Lecture 3, 1965; Fall Lecture 4, 1967) or *collaborative completions* (Lerner, 1991, 1996). Lerner (1996, 2002) has termed join-talk such as that in Fragment (2) *choral co-production.*

In what follows I present a preliminary description of some of the phonetic and sequential characteristics of collaborative completions such as that in Fragment (1). In such sequences, we find that in the course of a not-yet-completed turn-in-progress, a second speaker produces talk which is syntactically, pragmatically, and phonetically fitted to the prior talk as a 'continuation' of that talk. This incoming talk brings the turn-in-progress, begun by the first speaker, to a possible (syntactic, pragmatic, and prosodic) completion point. Characteristically, following the completion, the speaker whose prior talk has been collaboratively completed does further talk which 'receipts' and attends to the import of the collaborative.[2]

The fragments I present are drawn from a data-set of some 180 cases which represent all the occurrences of collaborative completions in approximately 18 hr of recordings of talk-in-interaction. The material includes telephone conversations, radio phone-ins, and face-to-face interaction. A range of speakers are represented (in terms of age and sex) in a range of varieties of British and American English (including a number of nonstandard varieties).

Fragments (3) to (9) provide further illustration of the phenomenon and give some sense of the sequential environments in which collaborative completions may occur.

(3) C&MXmas83

```
K:          o:nce those cameras start flashing particularly with the infants
                    (0.2)
C:    →     'hhh it puts them off
K:          it puts them of [f and i[t it's such a[s h a m   e]
C:                          [yeh   [yeh uh(.)   [people were] doing
            that last Wednesday
K:          oh they always do it (0.9) they always do it
```

(4) Kons.enough.beer

```
A:          er:m tomorrow or Sunday I shall be weighed again and then:
            I shall say: (0.3) [m:: ingress] = (0.4)
BE:   →                       enough is enough.
A:          no more (0.2) no more barley wine
                    (0.4)
BE:         oh de [ar
A:                [no more Wally's beer (0.7) because before we went
            away we had a good session on it for weeks
```

(5) Holt.2.2.2.3

```
Car:        When she went back she wz feeling a bit °calmer by nex'da:y
            [(and uh)° (.) she did see the doctor she's used to=
Les:        [Mm:.
Car:        =up the:re.
Les:        Yes.
Car:        A:nd so by the evening she'd made up her mind,
Les:  →                       To stay.
Car:        Well he'd told her not t'come °back (any ra[te),°
Les:                                                   [Yes.=
Car:        =°C'z 'ee[wanted t'see her again. ° [Yes.=
```

(6) C&M.dresses.see-him120

```
C:          and I thought my God.
M:          yeh
C:          if I can see him,
                (.)
M:    →     he can see you.
                (0.2)
C:          and I don't always just get undressed in my living room.
```

(7) HoltJ86.2.1.2-4

```
Fos:        [No: we:'re going away'n coming back on the tenth. of
            September.=
Les:        =D'you fly: (.)°o:[r (.) g[o (.)°with°
Fos:                          [.hhh [We go by helicopter fr'm
            Penzanc[e to: to Tresco: yes.=
Les:        [Yes.
Les:        =Yes.=
Fos:        ='t's only a (0.4) quarter'v'n hour fli:ght °but uh°
                (0.2)
Les:   →    .hhhh expens[ive.
Fos:                    [interesting .hhhh     (0.2)
Fos:        We[ll I yes I    s]poze ih-i-it's: uh:: it's about forty=
Les:          [ehh heh heh]
Fos:        =pou:nds retu:rn.
Les:   →                      Yes:. Yes.
```

(8) Szc-World

```
B:          she didn't have any
                (0.3)
Mal:        (cou[gh)
B:              [hard ambitions to go out and see the world
                (0.9)
B:          she'd been to Paris she'd been to Belgium s h [e'd
Mal:                                                       [.hiuhh hhiuh
            hhiuh
F2:    →    seen the world. huhm huhm huhm [huhm
```

```
B:                                          [she'd seen=
F2:        =hah hah [hah hah
B:                    [the world (.) as far as she was concerned
```

(9) Szc-Cranky

```
MI:        they're making progress they always have that until they
           reach adulthood (.) in which case
              (0.4)
PE:   →    they get old and cra(hh)nky [like the rest of us]
MI:                             [i t  s t o p s:  [ :  ]:
PE:                                          [iuhhuh .heh heh
           heheh
```

Environments for Collaborative Completions

Collaborative completions can occur in a wide range of sequential environments and may be fitted to a variety of interactional activities. For instance, in Fragments (1) and (5), the collaboratives formulate or complete upshots of 'tellings-in-progress.' In Fragment (3), C's completion formulates a reason for the complaint begun by K. BE's completion in Fragment (4) is fitted to A's defensive (posttease) description of how she intends to get back to her diet. In Fragment (7), Lesley completes Foster's talk by solving his word-search (Foster's treatment of it suggests the she gets it wrong). In Fragment (8), F2 provides a humorous third-part summative completion of the list which B has been constructing. Similarly, in Fragment (9), PE provides a humorous completion to MI's serious observations.

In the current data-set, collaborative completions may occur both at places where speakers are experiencing some problem formulating their talk (77% of the cases),[3] and at places where there is no such evidence of trouble. For example, in Fragment (7), there is overt evidence in the talk preceding the collaborative that Foster is having difficulties with managing the progressivity of his talk (*but uh*). In such a case, the disruption to the movement of the turn toward completion provides an opportunity for a coparticipant to take up the talk. By contrast, in Fragments (3), (5), and (8), there do not appear to be any such indications of trouble in the precollaborative talk.

In cases where there are no apparent 'hitches' in the production of the turn, collaboratives may be initiated at a place where the syntax or the interaction clearly projects more talk from the current speaker and the design of the turn up to that point provides a basis for seeing what it would take to bring the talk to completion (Lerner, 1991, 1996). So, for instance, in Fragments (1), (3), (5), and (6), the collaboratives are done as the second part of a projected two-parted structure (e.g., 'if-then,' 'when-then' type constructions), and in Fragment (4), the collaborative is done after a 'quotation-maker' which '(1) projects an upcoming utterance, (2) provides a place for that utterance, and (3) proposes the form that utterance will take—a quote' (Lerner 1991, p. 446). Fragment (8) combines aspects of both such projected completion and disruption to the temporal progression of the turn to completion. In (8), B is clearly in the process of constructing a list as part of a description of an individual's 'lifestyle' aspirations. Her formulation *she'd been to Paris she'd been to Belgium*, is done with rhythmic parallelism and pitch parallelism (the two versions of *been to* are produced within 0.5 semitones of each other and the rising pitches on *Paris* and *Belgium* begin within 0.6 semitones of each other and rise 11.6 and 12.5 semitones, respectively). To this extent, coparticipants can find that on the production of another *she'd*, that either another list item is due or a list-completer is due. The incipient laughter by Mal, placed in overlap with the end of B's ongoing turn, disrupts the turn's progression and provides an opportunity for F2 to start up her completion.

On those occasions where the turns-in-progress cease at a place which is prosodically 'incomplete-for-lexico-syntax,' we find a variety of pitch characteristics coincident with the final stressed syllable of the turn. For instance, Fragments (3) and (6) have prominent falling–rising pitch with the rise ending above mid in the speaker's range (the low point of the fall to the peak of the rise is 4 and 5 semitones, respectively), and Fragments (4), (5), and (9) have relatively level pitch (low in the case of (4), around 1.5 semitones up from the speaker's baseline; and mid in the case of (5), around 10 semitones up from the speaker's baseline).[4] Local and Kelly (1986) have shown that on occasion, speakers may 'design' their talk to be prosodically or syntactically 'incomplete' to yield their turn to a coparticipant. However, none of these prosodically 'incomplete-for-lexico-syntax' instances show the other 'trail-off' phonetic characteristics which

Local and Kelly document. All are hearable as designedly projecting more talk from the same speaker.

Treatment of Collaborative Completions by Coparticipants

On finding that his or her talk is being collaboratively completed, a participant is confronted with a number of problems. One is that the completion might not turn out to be what the speaker 'was going to say.' For instance, the collaborative completer might show by his or her talk that he or she has not appropriately understood the gist of the talk, for example, in Fragment (7). Alternatively, the collaborative completion could be specifically designed to undercut the direction of the talk to that point by providing a humorous or incongruous completion. Another problem generated by the production of a collaborative completion is that not only is the incoming speaker bringing the turn to a syntactic and prosodic completion, but he or she is also potentially bringing the activity which the turn-in-progress was undertaking to a completion. Fragments (3) to (9) provide some indication of the characteristic ways in which prior speakers (whose talk is being collaboratively completed) treat the collaborative productions and deal with the problems they pose.

A first observation is that, in the data-set, collaborative completions are predominantly allowed to run to completion in the clear. Where the prior speaker produces talk-in-overlap with the collaborative, for example, Fragments (7) and (9), we observe two things: (a) such talk routinely proposes a different version of the collaborative, even if the morphosyntactic category is the same as in (7); and (b) the incoming speaker regularly produces more talk beyond the end of the collaborative. In Fragment (9), although MI's overlapping talk does not extend beyond the end of the collaborative, he produces a noticeably long fricative at the end of *stops* (at least 500 msec), which allows his talk to be coextensive with PE's collaborative. Talk-in-overlap by the prior speaker, which proposes a different version, is typically produced to be pitch, loudness, and tempo integrated with his or her own precollaborative talk (i.e., it is designed with the characteristics of 'continuation' of his or her prior talk; Auer, 1996; Local; 1992, Selting, 1996). So, for instance, in Fragment (7), although Foster produces talk which provides quite a different completion to Lesley's, it has none of the phonetic characteristics of overtly correcting talk.[5] Different versions produced in the clear are also constituted phonetically (and often lexically) as a continuation of prior talk.

In Fragments (3) and (8), we see that one possible treatment is a redoing of the collaborative itself. In such cases, the redoing forms the first component of the turn and the speaker produces more on-topic talk, thereby, of course, treating the collaborative as not having brought the precollaborative talk to a completion. In cases such as this, lexically exact redoings of collaboratives by the prior speaker are timed so that they are placed after, and not in overlap with, the collaborative [Fragments (3) and (8)]. On occasion, as in Fragment (6), the postcollaborative talk may simply build on the collaborative itself. In such cases, the postcollaborative talk is regularly designed, as in Fragment (6), with some kind of explicit 'connective' marker at its beginning. Notice again that this treatment works to keep open the sequence which the collaborative potentially closed. In (4), following the collaborative, A produces a different, more specific completion to the generic, idiomatic one offered by BE and goes on to account for her reasons for dieting. Again, this serves to abrogate the closing implicativeness of the collaborative. In Fragment (5), Carol's *Well he'd told her not to come back* treats Lesley's collaborative as having formulated part of the gist (Carol's daughter, although ill, is not coming home) but clarifies the basis for her daughter's decision not to return home.

Phonetic Design of Collaborative Completions

Although the phonetic detail of collaborative completions differs across the data-set, there are a number of systematically deployed prosodic phonetic resources which characterise them and may serve to discriminate them from other kinds of completions.

Tempo.—In terms of the pace of their production, collaborative completions are typically faster than surrounding talk (or than any redoing of the collaborative talk by a coparticipant). On occasion, collaborative completions may not be faster, but they are typically not slower than surrounding talk. They are also typically timed to begin 'in the clear' (where there is overlap it is rarely more than 1 syllable or 1 'segment').

There is no universally agreed approach to the analysis of the tempo and rhythm of naturally occurring talk which corresponds to the percepts of lay and professional analysts (see, however, Couper–Kuhlen, 1993, for some suggestions). Here I reflect overall speech-rate by giving gross measures of average syllables per sec (syll/sec). So for example, K's talk prior to the collaborative incoming in Fragment (3) falls into two intonational phrases: *once those cameras start flashing* and *particularly with the infants*. The first of these phrases is paced at 3.5 syll/sec, with a mean stressed syllable rate of 2.5 syll/sec. Her second phrase is faster with an overall rate of 5.4 syll/sec, with a mean stressed syllable rate of 4.6 syll/sec. C's collaborative, *it puts them off*, is produced at a faster rate than either of these phrases: 6.7 syll/sec, with the mean of the two stressed syllables *puts* and *off* being 5.8 syll/sec. K's subsequent redoing of *it puts them off* is noticeably slower at a mean rate of 3.0 syll/sec (mean stressed syllable rate of 2.4 syll/sec). In Fragment (4), A's precollaborative talk also falls into two intonational phrases groups: *tomorrow or Sunday I shall be weighed again* (mean syllable rate 4.0 syll/sec, mean stressed syllable rate 3.3 syll/sec), *and then I shall say*, which is delivered at a somewhat slower overall pace (3.6 syll/sec, with a mean stressed syllable rate 2.8 syll/sec). B's collaborative utterance is delivered at a noticeable faster rate (6.7 syll/sec, with a mean stressed syllable rate of 4.3 syll/sec). When A resumes her talk after the collaborative and produces her own version of a completion, the pace is markedly slower than BE's collaborative with a mean rate of 3.6 syll/sec (mean stressed syllable rate 3.5 syll/sec). Even where the talk preceding the collaborative is relatively fast, the collaborative typically gets done faster. For instance in Fragment (8), B's talk, *she'd been to Paris she'd been to Belgium she'd*, is produced at around 4.7 syll/sec. F2's completion, *seen the world* is delivered at 6.2 syll/sec. B's redoing of *seen the world* is produced at a very much slower pace (1.9 syll/sec).

Loudness.—One of the tasks facing a speaker who is producing a collaborative completion is to ensure not only that the lexis and syntax is fitted to the prior talk, but also that the collaborative sounds like a continuation of the talk-in-progress rather than a disjunctive, new contribution. One way in which speakers seem to do this is by not producing the collaboratives at a greater volume than the preceding talk which they complete (Local, 1992; Szczepek, 2000). For example, Ava's collaborative in Fragment (1) is produced at around the same loudness as Bee's preceding talk. In Fragment (3), C's collaborative, *it puts them off*, is produced noticeably quieter than K's preceding talk and K's subsequent talk, which redoes the collaborative and is loudness-matched with C's collaborative. In Fragment (4), BE's collaborative matches the loudness of the precollaborative talk and postcollaborative talk. In Fragment (6), M's collaborative incoming is quieter than C's preceding talk, *if I can see him*. C's talk after the collaborative returns to the loudness level of her precollaborative talk. In Fragment (7), Foster's precollaborative and postcollaborative talk and Lesley's collaborative are all produced at a similar volume. F2's collaborative completion in Fragment (8) is produced slightly more quietly than B's precollaborative talk. PE's collaborative talk in Fragment (9) is produced at the same volume as MI's preceding talk.

Pitch.—The turn-delimiting pitch contours associated with collaborative completions are similar to those which can constitute complete turns and transition relevance places in the appropriate varieties (typically falling pitch). However, the pitch excursion of these falls is regularly less extensive and tends to end higher in the speaker's range than other designed-to-be-complete turn-final falls. The pitch range of the collaborative completions as a whole is also relatively narrow, compared with the functional range of the speaker and that of the talk preceding the collaborative. Impressionistically, the overall pitch of the collaborative appears to be regularly matched to the overall pitch height of the preceding talk, making it hearable as a continuation of that talk (Couper–Kuhlen, 1996; French & Local, 1983; Local, 1992; Szczepek, 2000).

Figures 11.1, 11.2, and 11.3 give a visual impression of some of these pitch characteristics. Figure 11.1 plots F_0 for the precollaborative and collaborative talk in Fragment (1).

The contour corresponding to the collaborative completion is encircled. Pitch is represented in semitones scaled relative to each speaker's baseline. Bee's precollaborative talk, *when we walk out of the class*, has a relatively narrow (4 semitone) pitch range until the 11-semitone (rising)–falling pitch on *class*. Ava's collaborative talk, *nobody knows what went on*, has a narrow pitch range of 3.0 semitones. The major accented syllable of the collaborative, *on*, has a barely falling (1.0-semitone fall) contour compared with the average of 9.2 semitones for Ava's typical turn-final falls. Notice that the precollaborative and collaborative talk is produced in a similar part of the speakers' pitch range: the precollaborative talk is around 4 semitones up from Bee's baseline and the overall pitch of Ava's collaborative completion is some 4 semitones up from her baseline.

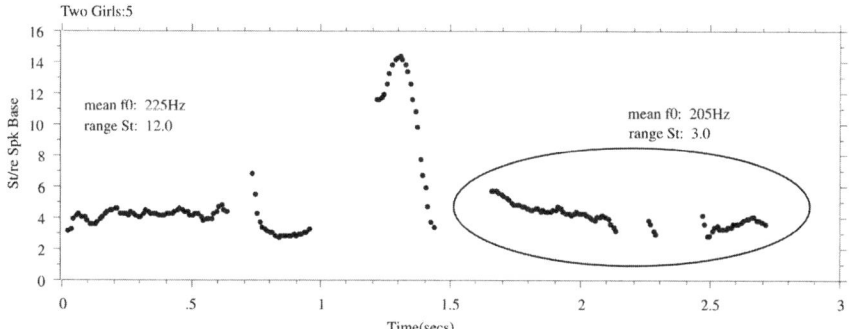

FIG. 11.1. F_0 in semitones relative to the speakers' base for the precollaborative and collaborative talk (encircled) in Fragment (1).

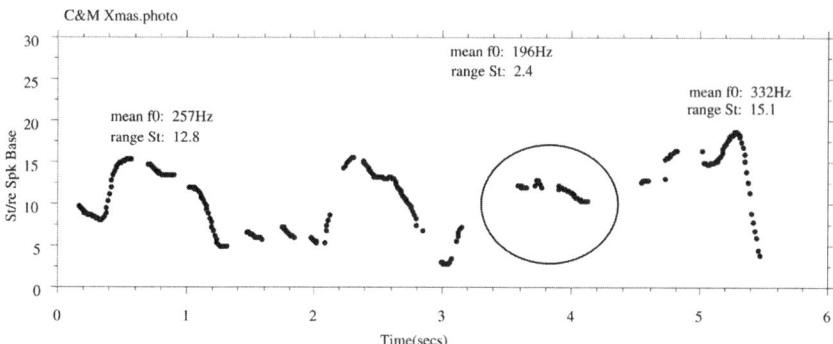

FIG. 11.2. F_0 in semitones relative to the speakers' base for the precollaborative talk, collaborative talk (encircled), and postcollaborative talk in Fragment (3).

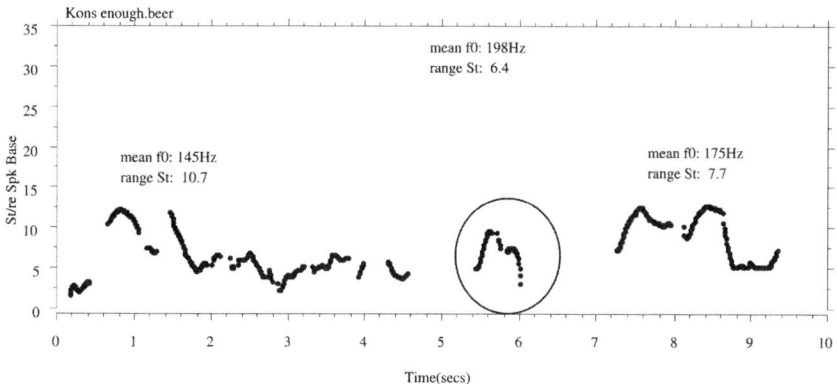

FIG. 11.3. F_0 in semitones relative to the speakers' base for the precollaborative talk, collaborative talk (encircled), and postcollaborative talk in Fragment (4).

Figure 11.2 plots the F_0 contours for Fragment (3). The pitch range of C's collaborative completion, *it puts them off*, has a narrow pitch range of 2.4 semitones and contrasts dramatically with the pitch range of the preceding talk (which has a 12-semitone range). The talk following the collaborative, which redoes the words *it puts them off*, is also markedly different with a falling pitch of 11.4 semitones on *off*. The falling pitch on C's *off* (1.7 semitones) is considerably less than that associated with her typical designed-to-be-complete falls which average 10 semitones. Despite these differences, the overall pitch of the collaborative completion is again located in a similar part of the speakers' pitch range: K's pre-collaborative talk is, on average, 10.5 semitones up from her baseline whereas C's collaborative talk is, on average, 11.4 semitones up from her baseline.

The pitch characteristics around the collaborative in Fragment (4) are illustrated in Fig. 11.3. Again we can see that the pitch range of the precollaborative and postcollaborative talk is wider than that of the collaborative. The precollaborative (*'tomorrow or Sunday I shall be weighed again and then: I shall say'*) has a range of 10.7 semitones compared with 6.4 semitones for the collaborative completion itself (*'enough is enough'*). The major accentual pitch excursion on the second token of *'enough'* in the collaborative is 4.4 semitones. The average for turn-final pitch falls found elsewhere in BE's speech is 11 semitones. There is overall pitch-matching again between the precollaborative and the collaborative completion itself: A's precollaborative talk is around 6 semitones up from her baseline, whereas BE's collaborative is, on average, 7 semitones up from her baseline.

'Competitive' Collaborative Completion

On a few occasions in the data-set, the phonetic design of the collaborative completion is rather different from the general pattern observed for Fragments (3) to (9). Fragment (10) is one such case.

(10) NB.IV.10.R.52

Emma: hhh Oh::

Lottie: An' it's oh it's rea:l ni:ce so they ha:d a sale so hhh you could
            get the co:mpa:ct in some mo:re crea-ea- crea::m (.) an: u-an
            uh: nother: (.) t-uh lipSTICK
Emma:→   for fiv[e d]o:[llar [s.] (or)
Lottie: [for-] [for: [f]I : V E DO:LLars
Emma: I know it 't's what somebody told me

In Fragment (10), Lottie is embarking on a 'news telling' about a sale
at a local store. She has enumerated some of the things that are on
offer—*you could get the compact and some more crea- cream and an-
uh nother uh- lipstick.* At this point, Emma comes in and provides a possible completion (upshot or punchline) for Lottie's talk. In terms of
tempo, Emma's collaborative completion, *for five dollars,* patterns in
the same way as the collaboratives in Fragments (3) to (9). Lottie's
precollaborative talk is delivered at around 3.0 syll/sec with a mean
stressed syllable around 3.3 syll/sec. Emma's collaborative is produced
at a noticeably faster rate (5.7 syll/sec, with a mean stressed syllable rate
of 4.7 syll/sec). However, unlike the collaborative completions considered up to this point, Emma's collaborative is produced with markedly
greater volume than Lottie's preceding talk. It also has a markedly wider
pitch range than Lottie's preceding talk: Lottie's precollaborative talk
has a mean F_0 of 202 Hz and a range of 8.5 semitones. Emma's collaborative talk has a mean F_0 of 228 Hz and a range of 10.3 semitones.
Emma's completion comes off as prosodically designed to preemp-
tively deliver the news punchline (its phonetic shape can be compared
with the way in which incoming speakers design 'competitive interruptions;' French & Local, 1983). Emma's talk here might be said to constitute a 'competitive completion.' In designing her completion in this
way, Emma effectively usurps Lottie's news and renders it 'no news.' In
this context, the design of Lottie's subsequent talk is also interestingly
different from the typical postcollaborative talk described to this point.
As in Fragments (3) and (8), the collaborative is redone. Here, however,
Lottie's redoing begins in overlap with the ongoing collaborative itself.
Although Emma sets out on a completion, Lottie does not let her finish
it in the clear. In all other cases in the data-set where a prior speaker
begins his or her talk in overlap with the collaborative, they produce a
different version and extend the talk beyond the end of the collaborative [e.g., Fragment (7)]. Although Lottie's talk is not lexically different,
it is certainly phonetically different. It is noticeably louder than Emma's
collaborative and produced at a much slower rate than Emma's version

(2.9 syll/sec, with a mean stressed syllable rate of 2.5 syll/sec). It is also produced relatively high in Lottie's pitch range and terminates with a 17-semitone fall in pitch to Lottie's baseline over *'dollars.'* Unlike other cases where the postcollaborative talk provides a different version, these pitch and loudness features do not serve to design Lottie's talk as a 'continuation' of her precollaborative talk. Indeed, these characteristics are very like those which French and Local (1983) describe for 'fight-backs' to competitive interruptions. I suggested earlier that where a speaker begins talking again during the production of a collaborative version [e.g., Fragment (7)], there is evidence that they are designing their talk to display that the collaborative was inadequate or inappropriate in some respect. By placing her talk in the course of Emma's collaborative, and designing it as she does, Lottie can be seen as displaying the inappropriateness of Emma's action.

CONCLUSION

One central outcome of CA research has been the finding that 'no order of detail can be dismissed, a priori, as disorderly, accidental or irrelevant' (Heritage, 1989, p. 23). Work on the analysis of everyday talk indicates that this is particularly true in the phonetic domain (e.g., Jasperson, 2002; Local, 1986, 1996; Local & Kelly, 1986; Local et al., 1986; Ogden, 2001; Walker 2001; Wright, 2001). The phonetic design (particularly its patterns of variation) of talk is one of the orderly 'details' of interaction. It provides a resource which speakers use to accomplish social action and guide its interpretation. The design of collaborative completions reveals some of the ways in which participants systematically deploy such phonetic resources.

As well as trying to understand how talk-in-interaction works and how particular phonetic features operate in its constitution, the kind of work I have reported here is also concerned with an attempt to reconfigure understanding of the conventional categories of description employed in linguistic-phonetics and phonology. This ongoing work indicates that *a priori* assumptions about the putative importance or otherwise of particular phonetic parameters and what their function(s) might be are likely to be problematic. It takes serious interactional and phonetic analysis to show not only that something is present and systematic in talk, but also that it is relevant to the participants. When, or if, we wish to say things about the work that phonetic detail does in talk, it is necessary to start with a sequentially-grounded account of action and not with our intuitions (no matter how refined they may be). By doing this, we can begin to reconfigure our understanding of the constitutive elements of phonetics and phonology and begin to explicate in a serious fashion the different systems of phonological contrast which operate at different places in sequential organisation. Such an approach should significantly enhance our ability to give a cogent account of the polysystemic and multistructural linguistic constitution of talk-in-interaction and of phonetic detail in particular.

ACKNOWLEDGMENTS

Parts of this chapter were written when the author was in receipt of a British Academy Research Readership. Versions of this chapter have been given to audiences at the Universities of Essex, Manchester, Newcastle, Sheffield, and Boulder, Colorado, and at the Euroconference on interactional-linguistics held in Spa, Belgium, 2000. I thank everyone at these presentations who clarified my thinking. Particular thanks to Beatrice Szczepek for giving me access to her collection of collaboratives. All errors are my own.

NOTES

[1] The transcriptions of interaction given here are based on the conventions used in Conversation Analysis (Atkinson and Heritage, 1984, pp. ix–xvi). Those in plain orthography are my own. Those which employ modified spelling are adapted from transcriptions by Gail Jefferson. Turns at talk are shown sequentially down the page. Speakers are identified, by initial, at the beginning of a line. Audible out-breaths are indicated by sequences of 'h,' audible in-breaths by ''hh.' Increased duration is indicated by ':.' Intervals of no talk are timed in seconds and durations are shown within parentheses; '(.)' indicates a brief no-talk interval of around 0.1 sec. Vertically aligned left square brackets indicate the start of talk from one speaker which overlaps that of another. Vertically aligned right square brackets indicate the point of offset of overlapping talk. Jefferson's transcriptions employ punctuation and arrows to give an indication of pitch movement.

[2] Note that 'collaborative' here refers to the design of the turn (i.e., co-produced) and not to the interactional status of the activity the collaborative producer is doing. As well as showing understanding of, and

alignment with, the turn in progress, these collaboratives can, for instance, be used incursively to undercut the seriousness of prior talk by providing a humorous completion.

[3] See, however, Schegloff (1993), on the problems associated with the interpretation of such figures.

[4] Impressionistically, the level pitch of *which case* in Fragment (9) sounds low (mean F_0: 110 Hz), but I do not have enough speech data to calculate the speaker's pitch-range or be confident about a baseline.

[5] Lesley treats Foster's precollaborative talk about the shortness of a helicopter flight as formulating an assessment or complaint about how expensive it is. Foster's own, in-overlap, completion treats his prior talk as formulating an appreciation of the pleasure of the flight, despite its shortness.

REFERENCES

Atkinson, J. M., & Heritage, J. (1984). *Structures of social action.* Cambridge, England: Cambridge University Press.

Auer, P. (1996). On the prosody and syntax of turn-continuations. In E. Couper–Kuhlen & M. Selting (Eds.), *Prosody in conversation: Interactional studies* (pp. 57–100). Cambridge, England: Cambridge University Press.

Couper–Kuhlen, E. (1993). *English speech rhythm: Form and function in everyday verbal interaction.* Amsterdam: Benjamins.

Couper–Kuhlen, E. (1996). The prosody of repetition: On quoting and mimicry. In E. Couper–Kuhlen & M. Selting (Eds.), *Prosody in conversation* (pp. 366–405). Cambridge, England: Cambridge University Press.

French, P., & Local, J. (1983). Turn-competitive incomings. *Journal of Pragmatics, 7,* 701–715.

Heritage, J. (1989). Current developments in conversational analysis. In D. Roger & P. Bull (Eds.), *Conversation* (pp. 21–47). Clevedon, England: Multilingual Matters.

Jasperson, R. (2002). Some linguistic aspects of closure cut-off. In C. E. Ford, B. A. Fox, & S. A. Thompson (Eds.), *The language of turn and sequence* (pp. 257–287). Oxford, England: Oxford University Press.

Laver, J. (2003). Three semiotic layers of spoken communication. *Journal of Phonetics, 31,* 413–415.

Lerner, G. (1991). On the syntax of sentences-in-progress. *Language in Society, 20,* 441–458.

Lerner, G. H. (1996). On the "semi-permeable" character of grammatical units in conversation: Conditional entry into the turn space of another speaker. In E. Ochs, E. A. Schegloff, & S. A. Thompson (Eds.), *Interaction and grammar* (pp. 238–276). Cambridge, England: Cambridge University Press.

Lerner, G. H. (2002). Turn-sharing: The choral co-production of talk-in-interaction. In C. E. Ford, B. A. Fox, & S. A. Thompson (Eds.), *The language of turn and sequence* (pp. 225–256). Oxford, England: Oxford University Press.

Local, J. (1986). Patterns and problems in a study of Tyneside intonation. In C. Johns–Lewis (Ed.), *Intonation in discourse* (pp. 181–198). London: Croom Helm.

Local, J. (1992). Continuing and restarting. In P. Auer & A. di Luzio (Eds.), *The contextualization of language* (pp. 272–296). Amsterdam: Benjamins.

Local, J. (1996). Some aspects of news receipts in everyday conversation. In E. Couper–Kuhlen & M. Selting (Eds.), *Prosody in conversation* (pp. 177–230). Cambridge, England: Cambridge University Press.

Local, J., & Kelly. J. (1986). Projection and silences: Notes on phonetic and conversational structure. *Human Studies, 9,* 185–204.

Local, J., Kelly, J., & Wells, W. H. G. (1986). Towards a phonology of conversation: Turntaking in Tyneside English. *Journal of Linguistics, 22,* 411–437.

Ogden, R. (2001) Turn-holding, turn-yielding and laryngeal activity in Finnish talk-in-interaction. *Journal of the International Phonetics Association, 31,* 139–152.

Sacks, H. (1992). *Lectures on conversation. Volumes I & II. (1965-1972).* (G. Jefferson, Ed.). Oxford, England: Blackwell.

Sacks, H., Schegloff, E. A., & Jefferson, G. (1974). A simplest systematics for the organization of turn-taking for conversation. *Language, 50,* 696–735.

Schegloff, E. A. (1979). The relevance of repair for syntax-for-conversation. In T. Givon (Ed.), *Syntax and semantics 12: Discourse and syntax* (pp. 261–288). New York: Academic.

Schegloff, E. A. (1984). On some questions and ambiguities in conversation. In J. M. Atkinson & J. Heritage (Eds.), *Structures of social action: Studies in conversation analysis* (pp. 28–52). Cambridge, England: Cambridge University Press.

Schegloff, E. A. (1991). Conversation analysis and socially shared cognition. In L. Resnick, J. Levine, & S. Teasley (Eds.), *Perspectives on socially shared cognition* (pp. 150–171). Washington, DC: American Psychological Association.

Schegloff, E. A. (1993). Reflections on quantification in the study of conversation. *Research on language and social interaction, 26, 1,* 99–128.

Schegloff, E. A. (1996). Turn organization: one intersection of grammar and interaction. In E. Ochs, E. A. Schegloff, & S. A. Thompson (Eds.). *Interaction and grammar* (pp. 52–133). Cambridge, England: Cambridge University Press.

Schegloff, E. A. (1998). Reflections on studying prosody in talk-in-interaction. *Language and speech, 41,* 235–263

Selting, M. (1996). On the interplay of syntax and prosody in the constitution of turn-constructional units and turns in conversation. *Pragmatics, 6,* 357–388.

Szczepek, B. (2000). Formal aspects of collaborative productions in English conversation. *InLiSt* (Interaction and Linguistic Structures) No. 17. Universität Konstanz.

Walker, G. (2001). *A phonetic approach to talk-in-interaction—Increments in conversation.* Unpublished master's thesis, University of York, UK.

Wright, M. (2001). *Conversational phonetics: The case of 'and' and 'but'.* Unpublished master's thesis, University of York, UK.

PART IV
Voice Quality

Chapter 12

Perceptual Analysis of Voice Quality: The Place of Vocal Profile Analysis

Janet Mackenzie Beck
Queen Margaret University College, Edinburgh

The main focus of phonetics, throughout its history, has been upon segmental features of speech. Although this focus is understandable, given that a primary motivation for development of phonetics as an academic discipline was a wish to understand the way in which linguistic units are realised, it still seems somewhat surprising that voice quality has not received more attention. Voice quality was described by Abercrombie (1967) as " ... those characteristics which are present more or less all the time that a person is talking ... a quasi-permanent quality running through all the sound that issues from his mouth.", (p. 91), and I will apply this definition in its broadest sense, taking the view that the whole of the speech production apparatus may contribute to voice quality. This is an important divergence from narrower definitions that equate voice with phonation, but is probably quite consistent with the usual lay-person's usage of the word "voice". The importance of voice quality in human interaction is hard to overstate, and is apparent in almost any description, academic or otherwise, of social interaction and communication. Its salience is evident in the huge range of descriptive terms for voice which can be found in accounts of interactions and personal characteristics, be they factual or fictional, and oral or written (Laver, 1991).

Voice quality functions in social interaction both communicatively and informatively. Following the definitions offered by Lyons (1977), communicative functions of voice quality encompass any phonetic modifications of voice intended by the speaker to convey information. These may range from the short-term modifications, acting over a few syllables, which are used systematically to regulate discourse, through the types of modification which are generally classed as "tone of voice", to the longer-term modifications which are used to signal emotion or mood. To a greater or lesser extent, communicative functions of voice are coded within linguistic, paralinguistic, and cultural frameworks. Voice quality may also be informative, in the sense that listeners may be able to make inferences about a speaker's physical, psychological, or social attributes on the basis of their voice, without the speaker intending this information to be conveyed. A fuller discussion of communicative and informative functions of voice can be found in Laver (1991).

The communicative versus informative dichotomy is related, to some extent, to two interacting sources of voice quality. The voice quality of a speaker at any given time is the combined product of his or her organic state and of any phonetic adjustments to the vocal apparatus. Phonetic adjustments of the muscles controlling the vocal apparatus are potentially under voluntary control, and thus can be used by the speaker in a communicative manner. We do not have the same level of control over our organic state, however, so voice quality features which derive from organic state contribute to the informative power of voice quality. An example of an organically determined voice quality feature would be the denasal quality of a child with chronically inflamed adenoids, where a physical blockage prevents normal nasal resonance. Although voice quality features derived directly from organic factors are necessarily informative rather than communicative, it may not necessarily be true that all phonetic adjustments are necessarily communicative. This is because most speakers acquire habitual patterns of voice quality which are appropriate for their particular accent and speech community. Although these accent-related voice quality features are theoretically manipulable by the speaker, in practice they may be so deeply ingrained that speakers have very limited ability to exercise conscious control over them. This takes us into a somewhat grey area, but I would argue that, for many speakers, it may be better to view these voice quality features as being informative rather than communicative, even though they are the result of phonetic adjustments of the vocal apparatus.

Some aspects of organic state, such as the basic anatomy of muscle and bone which forms the architecture of the vocal apparatus, will be relatively constant for each person. Although there will be changes during the life cycle, especially during the periods of rapid growth and development, these changes take place over a relatively long time span. Other organic factors may fluctuate over a much shorter time span. For example, level of hydration is thought to have an effect on the mucosal lining of the whole of the vocal tract (e.g., Pannbacker, 1998). The pattern of vocal fold vibration is extraordinarily sensitive to very minor changes within the mucosa, so that dehydration may have perceptible effects on phonation. Extreme versions of this may be portrayed in the stereotypical "hoarse" voice of the film character emerging from the desert, but many people are aware of subtle voice changes associated with less severe levels of dehydration. Similarly transient changes in voice quality are commonly associated with allergic responses such as hay fever. Within a very short period of exposure to an allergen, susceptible individuals may suffer from significant inflammation within the nasal cavity, pharynx, and larynx, with clearly audible consequences for nasal resonance and phonation.

One of the most interesting issues to arise from the study of the role of voice quality in social interaction is the potential for misinterpretation that may arise if a listener believes that a speaker is modifying their voice with communicative intent, when they are not, or vice versa. Such misattributions arise from the fact that very similar, if not indistinguishable, voice quality features may be caused by either organic variations or phonetic adjustments. For example, harsh voice, the auditory correlate of irregular vocal fold vibration, may be produced by any speaker with normal vocal fold anatomy by increasing certain parameters of laryngeal tension, and is conventionally recognised as a signal of aggression or anger (e.g., Scherer, 1986). Alternatively, it may result from altered vocal fold structure, such as that associated with a vocal fold polyp or laryngeal carcinoma. Given an auditory equivalence between harshness adopted as a phonetic adjustment to communicate anger, and organically derived harshness associated with laryngeal disorder, it is easy to see how listeners may misinterpret what they hear. The speaker with a vocal fold disorder may be misjudged by an unfamiliar listener to be either temporarily angry or habitually aggressive. Similar misattributions may also occur within organically derived voice quality features, if transient organic factors are interpreted as reflecting long-term organic factors, or vice versa. For example, the fundamental frequency of a speaker with a laryngeal infection may be lowered temporarily as a result of the increased mass of the inflamed vocal folds. An unfamiliar listener, during a telephone conversation, might assume that the low pitch is associated with permanently heavier or longer vocal folds. This could lead them to believe that the speaker is physically larger than is actually the case, or that they have the type of chronic vocal fold inflammation often seen in heavy smokers. On the other hand, people with chronic voice disorders such as vocal fold paralysis are sometimes asked if they have a cold, so it seems that the voice quality resulting from a longer-term organic change is being wrongly attributed to a more common transient organic change.

The richness of voice quality as a source of information and a tool for communication means that it is of interest not just to phoneticians and speech scientists, but also to a wide range of other disciplines and professionals. Among these are singing and acting teachers, who may be concerned to maximise the efficiency of voice production and to utilise the voice effectively in expressing emotion or depicting a character. Laryngologists and speech and language therapists share an interest in understanding how physical changes within the larynx, or abnormal patterns of muscle activity, can affect voice quality. This understanding is essential in informing clinical assessment and treatment of people with voice problems. Therapists working with voice difficulties also need to understand the way in which psychological state can be a factor in the generation of voice disorders, and, conversely, how difficulties with voice production can impact on social interaction and psychological state. Psychologists may be interested in voice quality as an indicator of affective state or as a regulator of social interaction, forensic phoneticians may use voice quality in assessing speaker identity, and there are many more disciplines that could be mentioned here.

Research in all of these areas has one thing in common: a need for sensitive and efficient tools for analysis of voice quality. The scarcity of appropriate tools has probably been a significant factor in inhibiting voice quality research until relatively recently. This chapter focuses on one approach to auditory perceptual assessment of voice quality, Vocal Profile Analysis (VPA), placing it within a broader context of possible approaches to voice quality description and showing how it has facilitated research over the last two or three decades. Many questions about the nature and role of voice quality remain unanswered, however, so the chapter includes a brief discussion of some of the research areas which remain relatively unexplored. Before discussing VPA in any detail, however, it may be worth considering some more general issues relating to the role of perceptual analysis of voice quality.

THE ROLE OF PERCEPTUAL ANALYSIS IN DESCRIPTION OF VOICE QUALITY

Among the academics and professionals who share an interest in voice, there has been a long and ongoing debate about the relative merits of perceptual and instrumental approaches to voice analysis. The last 20 years of the 20th century saw a proliferation of instrumental techniques for voice measurement, facilitated by the extraordinary growth in affordable computing power available to researchers. Instrumental techniques include those which rely on the acoustic signal and those, such as laryngography, which measure some aspect of physiological function. Development of such techniques has been accompanied by a real optimism about their ability to provide truly objective measurement systems with the potential to negate the need for what some view as the unacceptable subjectivity of perceptual judgments. Although there is no doubt that the detail offered by many instrumental techniques has greatly enhanced our understanding of the mechanics and acoustics of voice production in general and phonation in particular, and some extraordinary advances have been made, the initial optimism has been somewhat tempered by a growing appreciation of some of the difficulties associated with collecting and interpreting instrumental data. There are a number of useful summaries of instrumental techniques for measurement of voice quality, including Baken and Orlikoff (2000), Hirano (1981), and several chapters in Kent and Ball (2000). It would not be appropriate to replicate these here, but a discussion of some general issues which need to be considered when selecting appropriate tools for investigation of voice quality may help to explain the continuing need for perceptual analysis, whether this be as a primary approach to analysis or as an adjunct to instrumental techniques.

Objective Versus Subjective Assessment

The tendency for instrumental techniques to be viewed as 'objective' and perceptual techniques to be viewed as 'subjective' has been touched on earlier and is unsurprising. The belief that use of any automated or mechanical equipment will avoid subjectivity is very seductive, but experience in using instrumentation rapidly exposes the dangers inherent in such a belief. One difficulty is that all instrumental techniques involve human operators or interpreters, who may bring their own judgments to bear at various stages in the process of analysis. For example, initial selection of the speech data recorded may depend on an operator's judgment. It is not uncommon, for example, for voice clinics to rerecord speech data for acoustic analysis until the operator judges the sample to be the 'best' that the subject can produce. This immediately invites a major element of subjectivity, which affects any attempt to standardize and objectify the process. Similarly, after recording, some procedures may involve further selection of data for analysis. A fairly typical illustration of this is provided by a clinical evaluation of an automatic system for acoustic analysis and airflow measurement, carried out in Edinburgh, Scotland (EC-VALUE Project, 1994). Technical aspects of the system were of a high standard, and the evaluation was very positive, but it did show very clearly the potential for results to be affected by operator judgment. The analysis procedure specified that F0 analysis should be based on a 1-sec sample of speech selected manually by the operator to exclude the perturbed part of the waveform at voice onset. Repeated analyses of the same speech samples showed that minor variations in judgment about the appropriate placement of the analysis window could result in markedly different analysis outputs. Test-retest variation was of the same order as interspeaker variation. Many instrumental techniques also involve subjective judgments about the data output. For example, although the Laryngograph system (Abberton, Howard, & Fourcin, 1989; Fourcin, 2000) includes a number of valuable automated data analysis packages which reduce the need for operator judgment, some subjective interpretation is nonetheless involved. Subjectivity may also come into play when operators are making judgments about whether equipment is functioning normally, when it needs recalibration, and so forth. Whatever the value of an instrumental measure may be, any assumptions about objectivity therefore require critical and cautious evaluation.

Breadth Versus Depth of Information

There is no doubt that instrumental analysis may be extremely valuable in providing detailed information about specific aspects of voice. Ultrahigh speed video imaging of laryngeal vibration, for example, has allowed fine-grained analyses of both normal and abnormal patterns of vocal fold vibration, thus greatly enhancing our understanding of the relationships between laryngeal structure and function (Kiritani, 2000; Švec & Schutte, 1996). Equally important insights into aerodynamic aspects of phonation have stemmed from instrumental measurement of subglottal and supraglottal airflow and pressure (Baken & Orlikoff, 2000; Hillman & Kobler, 2000). These examples are typical of the majority of instrumental measurement, in that they focus quite narrowly on one part of the vocal apparatus or one aspect of voice production. Although this kind of detailed measurement is clearly of enormous benefit in informing theories of voice production, it is difficult to use instrumental analysis techniques to get a complete overview of the complex interplay of respiratory, phonatory, and articulatory activity which influences the overall voice quality of a speaker in natural situations. This is in direct contrast with perceptual analysis, where the listener's task is to analyse the auditory result of the coordinated activity of the whole of the voice production system. Although this makes it much easier to gain an overview of a speaker's voice quality, the challenge lies in developing skills in perceptual discrimination of the auditory features associated with specific strands of voice production.

ISSUES RELATING TO CHOICE OF PERCEPTUAL ANALYSIS APPROACH

The approach chosen for perceptual judgment of voice depends, at least in part, on the motivation for its use. Common motivations for undertaking perceptual voice quality descriptions include the following: rating of degree of abnormality or of differences between speakers, measurement of change associated with therapeutic intervention or disease progression, assessment of organic state and function, differentiation between qualities within the "normal" range. (e.g., in forensic phonetics or in tracking "tone of voice" fluctuations), and as an aid to planning therapy goals in voice disorder.

A review in 1993 of perceptual voice analysis schemes identified 57 different schemes in the United States alone (Kreiman, Gerrat, Kempster, Erman, & Berke, 1993), and there are many more that are in use around the world. Decisions regarding the most appropriate scheme for any given purpose may require consideration of a number of cross-cutting parameters. Bearing in mind that what any listener hears is the combined auditory result of a complex, multistranded process of production, one choice facing any potential judge of voice quality relates to whether they are concerned more with the overall voice quality, or with the strands of performance which feed into it. Descriptive systems for voice vary along a continuum from holistic approaches to componential systems. Holistic approaches assign a single label or scalar value to the overall voice quality, and literature on this topic indicates a fairly rich variety of holistic systems for voice quality description. One example, designed for clinical voice assessment, is the system devised and tested by Wynter and Martin (1981), which provided a numbered set of "cardinal" voice qualities as referents against which any voice could be compared. The task of the listener was thus to decide which of these referent qualities was most similar to the voice being described. The difficulty with such approaches is that the number of referent qualities which can be memorized is very small by comparison with the wide range of voice qualities which may occur, and this limits their discriminatory power. Simple ordinal or visual analogue scales for judging the degree of "abnormality" could also be classed as holistic approaches, and these have been fairly widely used within clinical settings (Kreiman et al., 1993; Yu, Revis, Wuyts, Zanaret, & Giovanni, 2002).

Although holistic systems of description may be useful for some purposes, it is often more productive to be able to identify more precisely the component parameters which contribute to the overall voice quality. In fact, identification of these components is an essential step toward understanding the phonetic adjustments and organic factors that determine habitual voice quality and "tone of voice" adjustments. A review of componential procedures for voice description shows considerable variation in the scope and choice of terminology used. Some, such as the GRBAS (Hirano, 1981), consider only laryngeal aspects of voice quality, whereas others, such as the Buffalo III Voice Profile (Wilson, 1987), extend the scope to include nasal resonance and breath supply. There are very few that include explicit comment on vocal tract and articulatory parameters, but the VPA scheme includes more than 20 parameters, allowing analysis of the contribution of the whole of the vocal apparatus to voice production. There is, of course, a trade-off between the scope and number of parameters included and ease of use. Widening the scope and increasing the number of parameters increases the sensitivity of a scheme and the ability to differentiate between voices, but at the cost of increased complexity, the need for more extensive training, and the risk of decreasing reliability. If the motivation for voice description is primarily to provide a simple rating of abnormality, or difference from some standard referent, then a holistic scheme, or one with very few components, may be most appropriate. If, however, the motivation is to fully analyse the nature of voice quality in order to plan appropriate therapy for a client with a voice disorder, then a multicomponent scheme may be more valuable. Much of the disagreement and misunderstandings between different authorities about how best to approach perceptual voice judgment probably stems from a failure to fully consider individual motivations for making the judgments.

Choice of terminology is also a vexed issue, and a comparison of schemes suggests that in some cases different labels may be used to describe the same quality. Conversely, the same label may be used to describe different qualities. We are therefore faced with a situation where, although it is probably safe to assume that the terms *creak* and *glottal fry* refer to the same quality, other terms are much less consistently defined, if, indeed, they are defined at all. We cannot, for example, assume that a term such as *hoarse* is being used by different authors to refer to the same auditory quality. The rationale for choice of labels is not always clear, although some authors, such as Hammarberg (1986), have applied careful experimentation and statistical analysis to the selection of appropriate terminology. The VPA scheme takes a different approach, by drawing on general phonetic principles, so that most of the labels used should be familiar to anyone with a comprehensive education in phonetics.

THE VOCAL PROFILE ANALYSIS SCHEME

Having raised some general issues relating to perceptual analysis of voice quality, it may be useful to give a rather fuller account of the VPA approach to voice quality analysis.

The Historical Context

The VPA approach to voice description has grown out of some early work by John Laver on the phonetic analysis of voice quality (Laver, 1968, 1980). In this primary work, Laver drew on general phonetic principles to provide a systematic phonetic framework for the description of speakers' habitual voice quality. The term *voice quality* was used in this context to encompass all the nonsegmental features of speech which characterise an individual's habitual speech patterns, to include adjustments of any part of the vocal apparatus. It is true that there was already a long history of efforts to pin down voice quality description, but Laver took these efforts to a different level and his 1980 text presents a highly innovative synthesis of concepts from phonetics and biological sciences. Laver acknowledges some significant influences on his conceptual development in this area, including Honikman (1964) and Abercrombie (1967), but he provided a much more comprehensive and theoretically motivated framework for voice quality analysis than had existed previously. A major strength of Laver's approach to voice quality description is the articulation of an explicit theoretical link between perceived quality, anatomical and physiological factors, and acoustic measurement. The pervasive influence of Laver's descriptive framework is evident in many areas, including the conventions for voice quality transcription proposed by Ball, Code, Rahilly, and Hazlett (1994) for the International Phonetic Association; these follow very closely the symbols and diacritics proposed in Laver's 1980 book.

Laver's principles for voice quality description formed the basis for a very precisely defined system for clinical assessment for voice, the Vocal Profile Analysis Scheme (VPAS; Laver, Wirz, Mackenzie, & Hiller, 1991; Wirz & Mackenzie Beck, 1995). This was the main outcome of a 3-year project funded by the Medical Research Council, which aimed to develop a formal assessment procedure which could be used for both clinical and research purposes. The historical context for this project was one in which there was no national or international standard terminology for voice description, and a general tendency within both speech and language therapy and phonetics to consider only phonation, and perhaps nasal resonance, as being components of habitual voice quality. Even where attempts had been made to formalize voice quality assessment, labels used tended to be quite subjective, and not clearly related to either the organic bases of speech production or the acoustic characteristics. The VPAS thus addressed a real need within speech and language therapy, not only providing a formalized and comprehensive procedure for voice quality assessment, but also providing a theoretical framework for management of speech and voice disorder. The project also evaluated the procedure in assessment of speakers with a range of speech and voice disorders.

The remainder of this chapter treats VPA as a particular approach to analysis, rather than as a single precisely specified procedure. This is because during the 20 years or so since the inception of the VPAS as a clinical and research tool for voice analysis, a number of slightly different protocols have evolved. They all draw on the same basic concepts and principles, however, and the various protocol forms can be seen as minor variations in presentation of the same analytical principles.

General Principles of Vocal Profile Analysis

Fuller descriptions of the approach can be found elsewhere (Laver 1991; Laver, 2000; Mackenzie Beck, 1988, Wirz & Mackenzie Beck, 1995), but it may be useful to identify some key features of VPA which, when taken together, differentiate it from other commonly used approaches:

1. VPA considers the whole of the vocal apparatus as contributing to an individual's characteristic voice quality. This is consistent with Laver's view, mentioned earlier, that the auditory colouring of a speaker's voice is as likely to stem from modifications of the vocal tract as from phonation (Laver, 1980, 1991, 2000), but is in marked contrast to voice rating scales such as the GRBAS, which consider only phonation type.

2. Voice quality is seen as being made up of a number of more or less independent components, or 'settings' (Honikman, 1964), which can be combined in a multitude of ways. Three basic types of setting are considered.

- Configurational settings relate to long-term-average configuration of the vocal apparatus, around which the moment-to-moment movements required for segmental performance are made.
- Range settings relate to the typical range of movement a speaker utilizes.
- Overall tension settings relate to the overall level of muscular tension used during speech production.

3. The scheme does not compare voices to a 'normal' baseline, but rather to a clearly defined 'neutral' setting. The auditory perceptual quality of the neutral setting baseline is associated with a clearly specified configuration and range of activity of each part of the vocal apparatus, and with predicted acoustic correlates (Laver, 1980). The avoidance of a 'normal' baseline as a referent addresses the difficulty in defining what is 'normal' voice quality (Mathieson, 2000) and obviates the need to consider an 'ideal' target manner of voice production (Hollien, 2000). There is evidence of significant

variation in voice quality between languages and accent groups (e.g., Esling 1978, 2000; Stuart–Smith, 1999), which means that listeners and speakers from different language or speech communities will have different intuitions about what can be judged to be 'normal'. This makes it extremely difficult for listeners from different accent or language backgrounds to reach agreement about how a normal baseline should be described. The use of a neutral baseline, however, means that judgments should be independent of judges' intuitions about 'normality', and differentiates the scheme from most others, including the Buffalo III Voice Profile and the GRBAS. The only disadvantage with this approach may be that judges do have to be trained to recognize the auditory characteristics of the neutral setting.

4. Deviations from neutral are quantified, thus allowing quantitative as well as qualitative judgments to be made. The maximum scalar degree for each setting corresponds to the most extreme deviation from neutral that is achievable by a speaker with a normal vocal apparatus. A general working rule is that judgments in the lower half of the setting scale (i.e., scalar degrees 1–3 for most settings) represent qualities which are typical of habitual voice quality in normal populations, whereas more extreme scalar degrees are usually found only in speakers with voice or speech disorder. This working rule is neither foolproof nor fully adequate, however, and it is supported by specific phonetic guidelines for assignment of scalar degrees for each setting, as illustrated in Table 12.1. This extract from a handout provided at VPA training workshops summarizes the neutral baseline for this category of setting and the key segments affected by this setting, and then details phonetic cues associated with specific scalar degrees. Key segments are those that are most susceptible to the performance effects of a given setting or those on which the auditory perceptual effects are most perceptually salient. This very explicit phonetic definition of scalar degree qualities is intended to increase the objectivity of voice quality description.

5. The approach explicitly acknowledges the possibility of auditory equivalence between phonetic and organically derived settings. The full range of settings that may be described using the VPA approach can all be produced by anyone with a fairly standard vocal apparatus, by making phonetic adjustments to their vocal performance, and the labels used reflect the type of

TABLE 12.1

Guidelines for Judging Labial Settings, Taken From a Vocal Profile Analysis Training Handout

Setting	Key Segments and Phonetic Consequences	Scalar Degree Conventions
Lip rounding/ protrusion	[s], [θ] → low 'pitch' [i] → unspread or rounded	1–3 = open rounding 4–6 = close rounding
	/r, ʃ, tʃ, ʤ/ → rounded	3 = LTA position as for [ɔ]
		4 = LTA position as for [o]
		6 = LTA position as for [u]
Lip spreading	[s], [θ] → high 'pitch'	4 = LTA position as for [e]
	/w/ + rounded vowels → unrounded	6 = LTA position as for overspread [i]
Labiodentalization	[s] → low 'pitch'	1–3 = labiodental onset and offset of labials
	/p, b, m/ → labiodental involvement	6 = /p, b, m/ → labiodental stops

Note. Labial: Neutral = long-term average (LTA) position as for [ə].

adjustment used. For example, to produce a fronted and raised tongue body setting, most speakers would need to adjust their habitual tongue position forward and upward, thus constricting the vocal tract in the palatal area. An equivalent auditory quality might, however, be produced by someone with an anatomically narrow or low hard palate without an equivalent phonetic adjustment of the tongue. Similarly, although a habitual labiodental lip setting might be due to active retraction of the lower lip toward the upper teeth, it could also be the direct consequence of anatomical state in a speaker with an undershot jaw (i.e., an Angle Class II malocclusion; Mackenzie Beck, 1988, 1997). Since the descriptive labels used reflect the phonetic adjustments that a speaker with a typical vocal apparatus would need to make in order to produce a given voice quality setting, it follows that labels may be misleading where speakers with nonstandard vocal apparatuses are concerned and auditory judgments must always be interpreted in the light of information about the speaker's physical characteristics.

Protocols for Vocal Profile Analysis

An important factor in development of a clinical and research assessment tool based on Laver's earlier work was the design of a protocol which could structure the listening process, reflect the underlying phonetic theory and provide a graphic representation of a speaker's overall vocal profile. A vocal profile, in this context, is the composite result of all the settings, neutral and otherwise, which contribute to the overall quality of a speaker's voice. The protocol has passed through a number of evolutionary stages, but a central aim has always been to allow a clear, graphic representation of the way in which any speaker relates to the neutral setting on more than 20 separate setting scales. As mentioned earlier, any deviation from neutral is quantified by the assignment of scalar degree values to non-neutral settings. The protocol form shown in Fig. 12.1, dating from 1983, has been modified a number of times, most significantly in 1991 (as reproduced in Koschkee & Rammage, 1997, p. 81), and 2000 (Laver, 2000, pp. 44–45). Although there are some minor differences between the forms in terms of sequence and layout, all encourage a structured and systematic approach to auditory analysis and allow the magnitude of any deviations from neutral to be recorded. Revisions have been driven partly by theoretical considerations and partly by growing experience in application of the scheme. For example, in the earliest published version of the VPA protocol shown here, 6 scalar degrees were allowed for each setting scale, but subsequent versions of the protocol have reduced the number of scalar degrees for a small number of settings. For close jaw, this was because it became obvious that the potential range of phonetic adjustment between neutral and the maximum possible expression of the setting is too small to allow accurate differentiation of 6 scalar degrees. For other settings, such as tongue body settings, the reduced number of scalar degrees is a response to consistent findings that newly-trained judges showed poorer differentiation of tongue body settings than of most other setting categories (see discussion of agreement figures later).

Vocal Profile Analysis Protocol

Speaker: .... Sex: .... Age: .... Date of Analysis: .... Tape: .... Judge: ....

I VOCAL QUALITY FEATURES

CATEGORY	FIRST PASS			SECOND PASS						
	Neutral	Non-neutral		SETTING	Normal				Abnormal	
		Normal	Abnormal		Scalar Degrees					
					1	2	3	4	5	6
A. Supralaryngeal Features										
1. Labial				Lip Rounding/Protrusion						
				Lip Spreading						
				Labiodentalization						
				Extensive Range						
				Minimised Range						
2. Mandibular				Close Jaw						
				Open Jaw						
				Protruded Jaw						
				Extensive Range						
				Minimised Range						
3. Lingual Tip/Blade				Advanced						
				Retracted						
4. Lingual Body				Fronted Body						
				Backed Body						
				Raised Body						
				Lowered Body						
				Extensive Range						
				Minimised Range						
5. Velopharyngeal				Nasal						
				Audible Nasal Escape						
				Denasal						
6. Pharyngeal				Pharyngeal Constriction						
7. Supralaryngeal Tension				Tense						
				Lax						
B. Laryngeal Features										
8. Laryngeal Tension				Tense						
				Lax						
9. Larynx Position				Raised						
				Lowered						
10. Phonation Type				Harshness						
				Whisper(y)						
				Breathiness						
				Creak(y)						
				Falsetto						
				Modal Voice						

"VOCAL PROFILES OF SPEECH DISORDERS" Research Project. (M.R.C. Grant No. G978/1192) Phonetics Laboratory, Department of Linguistics, University of Edinburgh.

II PROSODIC FEATURES

CATEGORY	FIRST PASS			SECOND PASS						
	Neutral	Non-neutral		SETTING	Normal				Abnormal	
		Normal	Abnormal		Scalar Degrees					
					1	2	3	4	5	6
1. Pitch				High Mean						
				Low Mean						
				Wide Range						
				Narrow Range						
				High Variability						
				Low Variability						
2. Consistency				Tremor						
3. Loudness				High Mean						
				Low Mean						
				Wide Range						
				Narrow Range						
				High Variability						
				Low Variability						

III TEMPORAL ORGANIZATION FEATURES

CATEGORY	FIRST PASS		SECOND PASS			
	Adequate	Inadequate	Scalar Degrees			
			Inadequate			
			1	2	3	
1. Continuity						Interrupted
2. Rate						Fast
						Slow

IV COMMENTS

	Adequate	Inadequate	1	2	3	
Breath Support						
Rhythmicality						

	Present	Absent
Diplophonia		

Other Comments:

© 1981.

FIG. 12.1. Vocal Profile Analysis Protocol (1981).

Data for Vocal Profile Analysis

Analysis is usually based on high quality recordings of at least 40 sec of connected speech. The quality of the recording is of paramount importance, as some common recording faults can have a marked effect on the perception of voice settings. For example, any nonperiodic, high frequency background noise may mimic the perceptual characteristics of whisperiness or audible nasal escape. Adequate sample duration is also important. Although it may be possible to judge phonation settings from samples shorter than 40 sec, experience suggests that longer samples are necessary to allow abstraction of long-term-average vocal tract settings from the segmental fluctuations of speech. This is consistent with experiments using data samples of different durations for measurement of related acoustic parameters. Results suggest that some measurements only stabilise when sample duration exceeds 35 to 45 sec (Hiller, Laver, & Mackenzie, 1984). The need to base analysis on longer samples is backed up by a study by Vieira (1997), which showed rather poor interjudge and intrajudge agreement for phonation settings when analysis was based only on isolated vowels.

Although spontaneous speech data may provide the most realistic representation of habitual voice quality, many studies use standard read texts to elicit speech data, so as to standardize the phonetic context and facilitate comparison between speakers.

Reaching Agreement

Just as segmental analysis of speech requires extensive practical training, so does VPA. Evaluation of reliability of voice quality assessment is notoriously complex (Kreiman & Gerratt, 2000), and these complexities have not yet been fully addressed in relation to VPA. The primary motivation in design of successive VPA protocols has been to reflect the underlying phonetic principles and to accommodate varying types of setting (configurational, range of movement, and overall tension). Although this may make sense in terms of the analysis process and allows judgments to be presented in a systematic manner which corresponds to the process of speech production, this does pose some problems for anyone attempting to undertake statistical analysis of reliability of the overall system.

For people with preexisting skills in practical phonetics, intensive courses of 18 to 24 hr (usually within 3–4 days) seem to be adequate, with trainees typically achieving low average error scores and at least 70% agreement on most settings by the end of a course (Laver et al., 1991; Mackenzie Beck, 1988; Wirz, 1987). Agreement figures do vary from setting to setting, and it does appear that it is easier for newly trained judges to reach agreement with skilled judges on some settings, such as phonation settings, tip/blade settings, and range of articulation, than on others, including configurational settings of the tongue body and larynx position. Not surprisingly, agreement seems to improve with continued use of the scheme, and more experienced users of the scheme may reach agreement figures well above 85% (Mackenzie Beck, 1988; Wirz, 1987; Wirz & Mackenzie Beck, 1995). Table 12.2 shows agreement figures for judges with a high level of experience judging two groups of speakers (normal young Scottish adults and older speakers with Parkinson's disease). The finding that agreement is less good for the speakers with neurological impairment may be due to the fact that some aspects of their speech are characterized by fluctuating patterns of speech production, so that it is less easy to abstract long-term-average tendencies.

APPLICATIONS

Since its inception in the 1980s, the VPAS has supported a range of clinical and research applications. This section is by no means exhaustive, but aims to give some indication of the diversity of the research supported by VPA. The VPA approach can be used to support either detailed single case studies, or group studies, where group characteristics can be defined in terms of means, range, and standard deviations for each setting scale.

Defining Normal Baselines

As indicated earlier, one of the limitations to voice quality research has been a lack of information about normal interspeaker and interlanguage variation in voice quality. VPA has facilitated a number of normative studies which have highlighted the level of normal interspeaker and intergroup variation in voice quality, and some of these are summarized in Table 12.3. John Esling's (1978) sociophonetic study of voice quality in Edinburgh is included here, even

TABLE 12.2

Interjudge and Intrajudge Agreement for Skilled Judges

Setting Scale	Interjudge Agreement Judge 1 versus Judge 2				Intrajudge Agreement Judge 1 versus Judge 1				Intrajudge Agreement Judge 2 versus Judge 2			
	Absolute		Within 1 SD		Absolute		Within 1 SD		Absolute		Within 1 SD	
Lip rounding/spreading	**40**	*46*	**84**	*62*	**40**	*30*	**90**	*70*	**40**	*40*	**80**	*60*
Labiodentalization	**100**	*100*	**100**	*100*	**100**	*100*	**100**	*100*	**90**	*100*	**100**	*100*
Labial range	**76**	*62*	**100**	*85*	**70**	*40*	**100**	*80*	**70**	*80*	**100**	*100*
Close/open jaw	**68**	*15*	**96**	*62*	**60**	*30*	**100**	*70*	**50**	*0*	**90**	*40*
Protruded jaw	**100**	*62*	**100**	*85*	**100**	*80*	**100**	*80*	**100**	*30*	**100**	*100*
Mandibular range	**84**	*39*	**96**	*69*	**80**	*0*	**100**	*70*	**50**	*20*	**100**	*70*
Tongue tip/blade	**36**	*15*	**72**	*69*	**20**	*10*	**90**	*80*	**60**	*20*	**70**	*60*
Fronted/backed T. body	**28**	*31*	**88**	*54*	**30**	*70*	**80**	*100*	**20**	*20*	**80**	*50*
Raised/lowered T. body	**64**	*39*	**96**	*62*	**30**	*50*	**70**	*80*	**50**	*30*	**100**	*80*
Lingual range	**96**	*39*	**100**	*77*	**80**	*50*	**100**	*70*	**100**	*30*	**100**	*100*
Nasal/denasal												
Nasal/denasal	**52**	*54*	**100**	*85*	**40**	*50*	**100**	*90*	**80**	*80*	**100**	*90*
Pharyngeal constriction	**80**	*23*	**100**	*39*	**50**	*30*	**100**	*60*	**50**	*20*	**100**	*90*
Supralaryngeal tension	**56**	*23*	**100**	*54*	**50**	*30*	**90**	*90*	**70**	*30*	**100**	*50*
Laryngeal tension	**48**	*8*	**92**	*39*	**30**	*10*	**100**	*80*	**60**	*30*	**90**	*70*
Larynx position	**56**	*46*	**92**	*92*	**80**	*70*	**100**	*80*	**40**	*40*	**100**	*100*
Harshness	**84**	*31*	**96**	*69*	**100**	*40*	**100**	*60*	**80**	*50*	**100**	*80*
Whisperiness	**48**	*46*	**100**	*85*	**60**	*50*	**100**	*100*	**60**	*60*	**90**	*100*
Creakiness	**60**	*46*	**84**	*85*	**30**	*70*	**80**	*100*	**50**	*60*	**80**	*70*
Mean	**65**	*46*	**94**	*72*	**58**	*45*	**98**	*82*	**62**	*40*	**93**	*79*

Note. Percentage levels of interjudge and intrajudge agreement for two judges for 25 normal adult speakers (in bold) and 13 speakers with Parkinson's disease (in italics). Two levels of agreement are shown: absolute agreement and agreement within one scalar degree (Adapted from Mackenzie Beck, 1988).

TABLE 12.3

A Summary of Voice Profile Analysis Studies of Scottish Speakers

Authors and Date	Subjects	Key Findings and Comments
Esling, 1978	Normal males (adults and children) living in two different areas of Edinburgh, Scotland	Demonstrated voice quality differences between socioeconomic groups: • Standard Edinburgh English → creaky voice, close jaw, and moderate nasality • Broad Edinburgh dialect → harsh voice, protruded jaw, and a range of settings associated with pharyngeal tension
Mackenzie Beck, 1988	Normal Scottish adults (all living or studying in SE Scotland)	Demonstrated some general tendencies and clear gender differences: • Both genders → mild to moderate whisperiness and moderate nasality • Males → more harshness and creakiness • Females → more lip spreading, advanced tip/blade, and advanced tongue body
Stuart–Smith, 1999	A small sample of speakers from Glasgow (13–14 years old and 40–60 years old; male and female; middle and working class)	Demonstrated some general tendencies and some age-, gender-, and class-related differences: • General tendencies: advanced tongue tip/blade, laryngeal tension, whisperiness • Teenagers → more vocal tract laxness • Males → more creakiness and nasalization • Working class speakers → more open jaw, raised and backed tongue body, more whisperiness

though it predates the full development of VPA, because it drew on Laver's early work on phonetic description of voice quality.

It is clear that even among speakers of varieties of English spoken within the central belt of Scotland, there is considerable variation in voice quality.

The Role of Voice Quality in Mother–Child Interaction

Voice quality seems to play a critical role in the interaction between mothers and their very young infants. In the very earliest days of life, tone of voice probably has precedence over visual channels of communication such as facial expression, because of a baby's limited ability to focus visually. For a much longer period, until linguistic development is well advanced, it seems reasonable to assume that tone of voice might be more accessible to the child than the linguistic content of a mother's speech. There has been some research showing that young babies are able to recognize their mothers' voices and that they respond differentially to variations in prosody and voice quality (Mehler, Bertoncini, Barrière, and Jassik–Gerschenfeld, 1978; Walker–Andrews, 1997), and informal observations of my own son, at the age of 2 to 3 months, showed that he frequently showed distress when I demonstrated voice quality settings during VPA training workshops. The negative response was especially marked when harshness or extreme degrees of creak were involved.

More systematic research into the coordination of voice quality with other aspects of mother–child interaction is limited, but a pilot project using VPA does suggest that it has the potential to be a valuable tool in this type of research. The pilot project, which is reported in Marwick, Mackenzie, Laver and Trevarthen (1984) and Trevarthen and Marwick (1982), was part of a larger longitudinal study of mothers interacting with their very young children. A sample from an audiotape of an interaction between a mother and her 18-week-old daughter was analysed by two skilled judges, taking the syllable as the unit of analysis, and marking any change in scalar degree or presence or absence of a setting. The voice quality analysis was then aligned with an independent analysis of interpersonal "state" (interpersonal arousal, affect, and intention), carried out by the psychologists on the team on the basis of the video recording of the interaction. A short section of the overall analysis is presented in Fig. 12.2. The resulting close temporal alignment

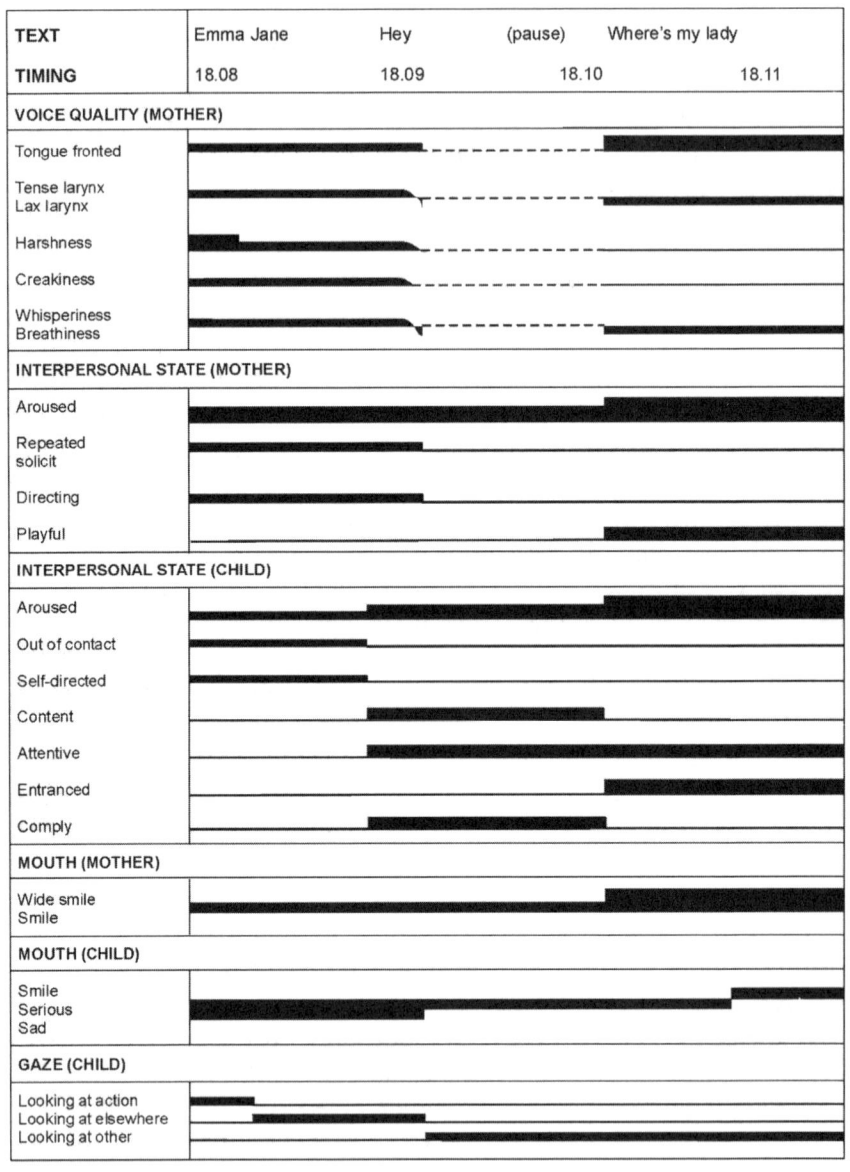

TEXT	Emma Jane	Hey	(pause)	Where's my lady
TIMING	18.08	18.09	18.10	18.11

VOICE QUALITY (MOTHER)

Tongue fronted

Tense larynx
Lax larynx

Harshness

Creakiness

Whisperiness
Breathiness

INTERPERSONAL STATE (MOTHER)

Aroused

Repeated solicit

Directing

Playful

INTERPERSONAL STATE (CHILD)

Aroused

Out of contact

Self-directed

Content

Attentive

Entranced

Comply

MOUTH (MOTHER)

Wide smile
Smile

MOUTH (CHILD)

Smile
Serious
Sad

GAZE (CHILD)

Looking at action
Looking at elsewhere
Looking at other

FIG. 12.2. A representational portion of the analysis of mother–child interaction (adapted from Marwick et al,. 1984).

between changes in communicative intent and changes in vocal setting was very striking, and there were clear associations between patterns of vocal quality change and particular types of interpersonal state (see Tables 12.4 and 12.5). Interpersonal state is defined in terms of level of arousal, affect, and intention. Changes in voice quality seemed to be more consistently associated with changes in interpersonal state than changes in facial expression, gaze behaviour or action and gesture. This gives strong support to the notion that voice quality is a key factor in reflecting or controlling interpersonal state in interactions with preverbal infants. This type of temporal alignment of voice quality variations with other aspects of interactional behaviour is labour intensive, but may still be the most effective approach to research into the role of voice quality and tone of voice in regulating interaction.

TABLE 12.4

The Relationship Between Voice Quality Changes and Changes in Interpersonal Intention and Affect (Adapted From Trevarthen & Marwick, 1982)

Interpersonal Intention and Affect	Voice Quality		
	Setting Change	Momentary Within Setting Change	No change
Change	16	3	2
No change	—	2	—

TABLE 12.5

The Relationship Between Changes in Interpersonal 'State' and Changes in Expressive Mode (Adapted From Trevarthen & Marwick, 1982)

Expressive Mode	Percentage of Interpersonal 'State' Changes Accompanied by a Change in Expressive Mode
Voice quality	90% (excluding 'state' changes not accompanied by any utterance)
Facial expression	57%
Gaze direction	11%
Action and gesture	54%

Voice Quality and Affect

The role of voice quality in carrying information about psychological state has been the topic of considerable interest, as indicated by the wide range of literature sources relating to this topic (see Scherer, 1986, for a review). Most studies on voice quality and emotion, including recent work by Ryan, Ní Chasaide, and Gobl (2003) and the work reported in the chapter by Ní Chasaide and Gobl in this volume, have relied on acoustic analysis, but this typically allows only a rather partial view of the voice quality variations that may be involved in expression of affect. Much of the published research has focused on acoustic parameters associated with phonation and tension, with much less attention being paid to vocal tract modifications. The few studies which have applied a VPA approach to the study of affect indicate that vocal tract settings are also important indicators of psychological state. For example, van Bezooyen used a modified version of the VPAS as part of a study into the recognition and expression of emotion by Dutch-speaking adults and children (van Bezooyen, 1984).

Attribution Studies

The potential for misattributions by the listener has already been mentioned, but this is still an under-researched area. There is no shortage of anecdotal evidence of the interactional difficulties that may result from listeners misinterpreting the cause or communicative intent of voice quality variations, but few systematic attempts to relate misattributions to specific voice quality characteristics have been made.

There are a few studies where some links can be drawn between VPA and listener judgments about the speaker, but most are very small-scale studies. For example, Thomson (1995) investigated listeners' judgments about social and personality attributes of speakers on the basis of recordings of patients suffering from oral cancer made before and after surgical removal of part of the tongue. These recordings had been subjected to VPA as part of another study (Mackenzie Beck et al., 1998) and, when looked at together, these two studies suggest a strong tendency for changes in voice quality such as increased whisperiness and harshness, increased nasality, and altered tongue body settings to be associated with negative attributions on a range of parameters, even where intelligibility is not affected by surgery. A larger study by van Erp (1991) used VPA, among other measures, to characterize the voice quality of speakers with cleft lip and palate in a study investigating listeners' judgments of personality features. Again, she found that the voice quality features associated with cleft lip and palate had a marked impact on the attributions made by listeners.

Another study, by Irving (1997), compared the voice quality of male-to-female transsexual speakers (most of whom were Scottish) with age- and accent-matched male and female speakers and related her findings to listeners' judgments about vocal, personality, and physical characteristics. The findings raised some interesting questions about the relationship between voice and biological sex and gender, and demonstrated very clearly that listeners may make judgments about femininity versus masculinity independently of judgments about biological sex. Although the transsexuals were generally judged to be biological males, they were judged to have very high levels of femininity and, on average, were perceived to be more emotional and sensitive than the nontranssexual males. In terms of voice quality, the transsexual speakers did seem to be more similar to biologically female speakers in some vocal tract settings, such as fronting and raising of the tongue body, but showed more harshness and pharyngeal constriction than either of the nontranssexual groups. Other studies have found the latter two settings to be more characteristic of males, and it may be that they were occurring in these transsexuals as an unwanted consequence of the tension involved in attempting to raise vocal pitch. It was also notable that some of the voice quality settings that seem to mark female gender in nontranssexual speakers from Scotland, such as advanced tongue tip/blade, lip spreading, and increased whisperiness, did not seem to be utilized by this group. It might be beneficial for these speakers to be taught specific techniques to decrease laryngeal tension and increase the settings I have just mentioned.

Foreign Language Teaching

It has long been recognised that languages may be characterised as much by long-term settings as by segmental and prosodic patterns (Abercrombie, 1967; Esling, 2000; Honikman, 1964; Laver, 1980), and the principles of VPA seem eminently applicable to foreign language teaching. An easily accessible example, demonstrated by John Laver in many VPA training courses, is the immediate increase in "authenticity" of a French accent that results from adoption of a slightly whispery phonation and a rounded and protruded lip setting. Given the power of setting changes to colour overall speech quality, it is, perhaps, surprising that VPA settings have not been used more frequently as a systematic adjunct to foreign language teaching and learning. Apart from a few anecdotal reports, Esling and Wong (1983) seem to be alone in publishing work on the application of voice quality settings to the teaching of pronunciation.

Drama Teaching

A number of acting coaches who have attended courses on VPA have commented on the value of this approach in economizing the effort involved in developing students' ability to manipulate speech output appropriately for a wide range of character roles, and this application very much reflects the previous comments on foreign language teaching. For example, adoption of correct segmental patterns for an unfamiliar accent may be much easier, and may indeed be almost automatic, if appropriate long-term settings can be identified and learned. Similarly, identification of key settings which would be typical of particular age groups, social contexts, or emotional states, may allow more effective teaching of appropriate vocal characteristics for a variety of roles. It is probable that many successful impersonators and actors have an almost intuitive ability to reproduce the most perceptually salient settings which characterize an individual or a type of speaker, but for others a knowledge of VPA may provide a structured approach to the development of performance skills.

Forensic Phonetics

Issues relating to forensic phonetics are explored in much greater depth in the chapter by Nolan in this volume, but it may be worth noting here that VPA has been used on at least one occasion when there was a need to assess the probability of two voice samples having been produced by the same speaker. The approach used here was first to compare full vocal profiles for the two samples, and then to look at a sample of 50 normal speakers in order to see what the likelihood would be of any two adults having equivalent levels of similarity. Examination of 120 pairwise comparisons from a database of vocal profiles for Scottish speakers showed that 14.2% (17) of these comparisons could be described as vocal "twins," in that no settings were judged to differ by more than one scalar degree (Mackenzie Beck, 1988, p. 238). This suggests that it would be extremely dangerous to assume that two near-identical vocal profiles can be taken as evidence that two samples must have been produced by the same speaker.

Clinical Applications

The greatest impact of VPA has probably been in the field of voice pathology. The comprehensive scope of the approach allows therapists to understand the way in which behaviour of all the different parts of the vocal apparatus is integrated in the vocal production of people with voice or speech disorders. This has had a considerable influence on the way in which many therapists assess and treat voice disorders, and on the way in which this topic is taught to speech and language therapy students.

A perennial difficulty faced by clinicians dealing with voice disorder is that it is almost impossible to define the limits of "normal" voice (Mathieson, 2000). This creates an inherent difficulty for most of the available clinical voice assessments, including GRBAS and the Buffalo III Voice Profile, which use "normal" voice quality as the referent baseline. As discussed earlier, VPA involves the use of a clearly defined neutral baseline, which is not language or accent specific, and thus overcomes this difficulty. The VPAS is now in widespread use, both for routine clinical practice and for research into disordered voice quality. Its clinical applications extend well beyond specific "voice disorders", such as those commonly seen in teachers, singers, or call centre employees. It can be used for assessment, treatment, and measuring therapy outcomes in a wide variety of other disorders, including hearing impairment, cleft palate, cerebral palsy, Parkinson's disease, and Down's syndrome. Clinical applications of the VPA can be considered under four main headings: description of vocal characteristics of specific speech disorders, baseline assessment, monitoring change, and planning therapy.

Vocal Characteristics of Speech Disorders. An important clinical skill for any speech and language therapist is the ability to recognise the typical vocal characteristics of a range of speech disorders, but all too often development of this skill depends on extensive personal experience of clients more than on research findings. The comprehensive scope of VPA makes it ideal as a means of building up typical profiles of disorders, in just the same way as it can be used to define the vocal profile characteristics of specific accents and sociolinguistic groups. Once this data is available, it allows therapists to acquire knowledge about vocal profiles of disorders in a more efficient and systematic manner.

The group profiles for a range of subject groups with speech disorder, studied using VPA, show that most of the groups differ from the control group on at least some settings. These differences may be evident from either the mean scalar degree or the standard deviation, or both. Fig. 12.3 provides a fairly graphic representation of the

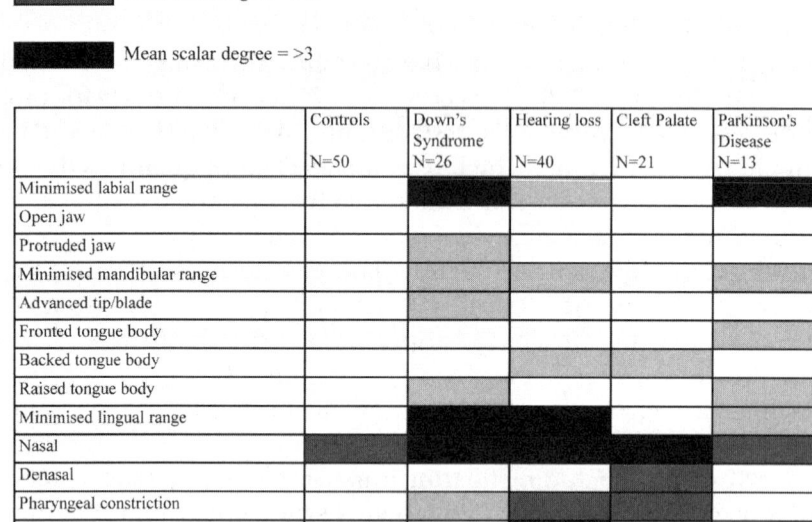

FIG. 12.3. A comparison of mean vocal profile settings for five groups of speakers: Normal adults, adults with Down's Syndrome, adults with profound hearing loss, children with cleft lip and palate, and adults with Parkinson's disease.

average voice quality characteristics of a range of speech disorders, with the shading indicating the extent of deviations from neutral for each setting scale (excluding prosodic and temporal features). In other words, the stronger the shading for a setting, the more that setting may be said to be characteristic of a disorder. Settings where none of the groups showed average deviations from neutral of more than 1 scalar degree (e.g., lip rounding) are not shown. The table illustrates the characteristic vocal profiles of these disorders in a way that can be easily interpreted by anyone familiar with the approach.

The more detailed information about speakers with Down's syndrome included in Fig. 12.4 is an example of a statistical comparison between a specific group of speakers with speech production difficulties and normal speakers.

Baseline Assessment. Baseline assessment is obviously an essential part of the evaluation of any client with speech disorder and a prerequisite for any attempt to monitor change or properly plan treatment. VPA provides a comprehensive overview of habitual voice quality and has been especially useful to clinicians in pinpointing the phonetic sources of abnormal voice quality and in highlighting the ways in which different parts of the vocal apparatus interact in disordered speech production.

Monitoring Change. Financial imperatives in health care have added weight to the need to prove the efficacy of speech and language therapy in the management of communication disorder, but research into outcomes of speech and voice therapy is still relatively sparse. VPA has proved to be a useful tool for measuring outcome, as it can be used systematically to judge whether any changes in voice quality observed after therapy are toward the normal baseline or away from it. An early example of its use in this way was as part of a comparative study into the relative efficacy of two therapy approaches in the treatment of Parkinson's disease (Scott & Caird, 1983). In this case, the use of a simple sign test to evaluate whether there were significant changes in the desired direction after therapy gave strong support for the use of prosodic therapy. VPA has also been used as part of a battery of outcome measures in a major study of voice therapy in the West of Scotland (Mackenzie, Deary, Sellars, & Wilson, 1998) and it is interesting to note that a recent commissioning brief for research into efficacy of treatments for speech disorder

SETTING SCALE	Control subjects (N=16)		Down's Syndrome subjects (N=20)	
	Mean scalar degree	Standard deviation	Mean scalar degree	Standard deviation
Lip rounding (+) → spreading(-)	+ 0.31	0.70	-0.65	1.57
Labial range: minimized (-) → extended (+)	-0.06	0.44	-2.2	1.57
Open (-) → close (+) jaw	+0.36	0.72	-0.75	1.52
Protruded jaw	0.00	0.00	1.60	0.94
Mandibular range: minimized (-) → extended (+)	-0.06	0.25	-1.85	1.42
Advanced (+) → retracted (-) tip blade	+0.75	0.68	+1.45	1.93
Front (+) → back (-) tongue body	+1.00	1.10	+2.60	1.47
Raised (+) → lowered (-) tongue body	+1.19	0.75	+1.50	1.40
Tongue body range: minimized (-) → extended (+)	-0.06	0.25	-3.00	0.65
Nasal (+) → denasal (-)	+2.81	0.40	+3.65	0.49
Audible nasal escape	0.00	0.00	0.40	1.23
Pharyngeal constriction	0.19	0.40	1.40	1.31
Supralaryngeal tension: tense (+) → lax (-)	+0.75	0.68	-0.95	1.67
Laryngeal tension: tense (+) → lax (-)	+1.06	0.93	+1.60	1.70
Larynx position: lowered (-) → raised (+)	-0.31	0.70	-0.75	1.16
Harshness	0.25	0.58	2.65	1.04
Whisperiness	2.63	0.72	3.65	0.67
Creakiness	1.63	1.26	1.10	1.29

FIG. 12.4. A statistical comparison of summated protocols for a group of 20 adult speakers with Down's syndrome and an age- and gender-matched control group. Shading indicates significance levels of $p < 0.02$ (Mann–Whitney U test).

by the UK National Health Service Health Technology Assessment Programme specifically recommended VPA as an outcome measure.

Of course, change in voice quality may not always be in a positive direction, and VPA can sometimes provide evidence of deterioration rather than improvement. The most common circumstance in which this happens is where there is some type of degenerative disease, but it may also be true when therapy is expected to have a beneficial effect.

A clear example of this, where a patient with a traumatically acquired cleft of the palate had undergone surgery and extensive therapy to improve speech and voice quality, and where VPA unfortunately belied the patient's ardent wish to believe that there had been some improvement, was reported by Razzell and Mackenzie (1987).

Planning Therapy. Little has been written about the use of VPA in planning therapy, but my own experience is that by offering a comprehensive view of vocal performance, it often alerts therapists and students to a range of therapeutic approaches that might not be obvious if the assessment focused only on laryngeal features. For example, it is not uncommon for speakers with laryngeal voice disorders associated with excessive muscle tension to present with close jaw and markedly non-neutral tongue body settings. Working on these vocal tract settings often has an immediate and marked effect on laryngeal performance, and may be easier for many patients than working directly on phonation. Koschkee and Rammage (1997, pp. 79–80) present a clear case study showing how VPA findings can have a direct influence on therapeutic management in voice disorder.

FUTURE RESEARCH

Although the development of a systematic and theoretically principled approach to perceptual analysis of voice quality has led to some real advances in knowledge and clinical practice, voice quality remains a relatively unexplored topic within phonetics and our views about the way in which voice functions in human interaction are still based almost as much on intuition as on real data and research.

Normative Data

At a fairly basic level, there is an urgent need for more normative data, providing baseline information about typical voice quality variation within and between different language and accent groups, genders and age groups. Although a number of studies of normal voice quality were described earlier, these focus on a very narrow range of subject groups. A proper understanding of the way in which voice quality functions as a communicative or informative process in social interaction requires a much more comprehensive description of normal voice quality, showing typical age- and gender-related variation across a broad range of language and accent groups.

Tone of Voice and Nonverbal Communication

The use of tone of voice in communication, and its integration with aspects of nonverbal communication such as gesture and facial expression, is another topic which suffers from a lack of empirical research. The complexity of the topic, together with a paucity of appropriate research tools, probably act as something of a deterrent to would-be investigators. John Local's chapter in this volume is an excellent example of research into the phonetic features involved in management of interaction, and there does seem to be a potential role for fuller VPA as an adjunct to such research. The preliminary study of mother–child interaction mentioned earlier (Marwick et al., 1984) does suggest that the principles of VPA can be used to track changes in vocal quality within and between utterances. This approach could be especially productive in the investigation of tone of voice and nonverbal behaviour, if allied with a system for tracking nonverbal behaviour over time as proposed by Laver and Mackenzie Beck (2001). There is a growing body of research showing the high levels of temporal integration between spoken utterances and gesture (McNeill, 2000), and there are some indications that dysfluencies in speech may be associated with suspension of gestural activity (Mayberry & Jaques, 2000; Seyfeddinipur & Kita, 2001) and that inhibition of gesture may result in speech dysfluency (Finlayson, Forrest, Lickley, & Mackenzie Beck, 2003; Graham & Heywood, 1976; Rauscher, Krauss & Chen, 1996). Such observations have been used to support the hypothesis that the central planning and processing of verbal and nonverbal output is coordinated in some way, but little attention has been given to the potential for organic constraints to have concomitant effects on vocal and nonverbal behaviour. This seems surprising, given that physical performance of both vocal and nonverbal behaviours is highly dependent on organic state. It is interesting that most of the descriptive principles which form the basis of the VPAS are equally applicable to the description of nonverbal behaviour, and it seems reasonable to extend a similar analytical framework to the description of gesture and other channels of nonverbal behaviour (Laver & Mackenzie Beck, 2001). The rationale for a common approach to description of voice quality and nonvocal communicative behaviour is strengthened by the observation that some common patterns of organic variation may impact on both vocal and nonvocal performance. This is especially true of factors affecting configuration of the upper spine and shoulder girdle. These structures provide postural support for gestural activity of the arms and hands and their influence on voice production is widely acknowledged by voice teachers and therapists working with voice disorder (Lieberman, 1998; Mathieson, 2001). The communicative consequences of postural constraints can be seen quite clearly in old age, where some of the typical physical changes have the potential to inhibit both vocal and nonvocal performance in ways that may be quite detrimental to social interaction. For example, the alteration in spinal curvature commonly known as "widow's hump" (more properly known as kyphosis), which results from osteoporosis and attrition of the vertebral cartilages, can affect both voice quality and gestural communication. It may have a complex effect on voice quality; breath support may be impaired because the thorax is compressed, vertical laryngeal movement is inhibited because the suspensory muscle system is thrown out of balance by compensatory neck extension, and pitch control may be limited by concomitant inhibition of the cricothyroid visor. In addition, the shelf formed by the collapsed cervical section of the spine may constrict the pharynx (Lieberman, 1998). The range and ease of gestural movement may be constrained because the forward position of the upper spine, together with the effects of gravity, will tend to pull the shoulders downward and inward. A single anatomical change may thus have quite far reaching effects on communication, leading to reduced pitch range and vocal flexibility, pharyngeal constriction, and reduced range of gestural movement. It is easy to see how such physically conditioned changes in communicative behaviour could be misinterpreted as indicators of depression or introversion and have significant implications for social interaction and self esteem. However extrovert and content an individual may initially feel, if physical changes cause that person to behave as if he or she were introverted and depressed, it is quite likely that the responses that person receives from interactional partners may erode his or her self image in a subtle yet damaging manner.

Clinical Applications

Although we have seen a growing body of reports supporting the clinical benefits of the VPA in assessment and management of speech and voice disorder, there is still a need for more rigorous research into its use as a clinical tool. Feedback from therapists using the VPAS is some-what mixed, with some placing considerable value on the comprehensive coverage of the whole vocal apparatus whereas others comment that it is overcomplex for routine use. This dichotomy of views is probably due, in part, to differing levels of training and confidence in its use, but it may also be due to differing expectations and motivations. If a therapist wishes to fully understand the complex interplay of laryngeal and vocal tract performance in determining overall vocal performance as a basis for planning and monitoring intervention, then the VPA has clear advantages. If, however, a clinician wants a simple rating scale for severity of voice disorder, a full VPA may appear unduly complex, even though the process should not, in practice, take more than 5 or 10 min. It may be that there is a place for a more streamlined protocol for partial VPA, designed specifically for rapid clinical rating or screening. The design of an appropriate protocol would need to be informed by some careful research, however. As a starting point, further study of reliability is essential for the selection of robust settings. A systematic survey of the extent of its clinical use, and of therapists' views of its benefits and problems, is also long overdue. Therapists' views on which settings are viewed as most clinically relevant, and on which they feel most (or least) confident about using, should certainly inform the selection of settings. In addition, it would be useful to examine the correlation between VPA settings and patients' own perceptions of the severity of their voice difficulties. This type of multifaceted research could facilitate the design of a streamlined protocol for voice quality description with optimal reliability and clinical relevance and which relates to patients' perceptions of voice problems.

CONCLUSION

I started this chapter with the aim of defining the place of VPA within phonetics and, more specifically, within the area of voice quality analysis. It has become increasingly clear to me that my attempt to define "a place" for VPA was misguided. The concepts developed by John Laver, which underpin VPA, have infiltrated the area in a way that is difficult to quantify, influencing the way in which many phoneticians, clinicians, and speech scientists think about long-term features of speech production. As a descriptive tool, VPA has begun to offer us insights into the way in which voice works in communication, but the potential applications and the unanswered questions about how voice quality works in communication far outweigh the work done so far. Addressing these questions will need complex and creative research methodologies for elicitation of naturalistic interactions and will depend on sensitive instrumental and perceptual tools for assessment of voice quality variations. It is essential that researchers are aware of the ways in which all aspects of verbal and nonverbal output are intertwined in terms both of their physical performance and of their neurological control. The comprehensive, componential nature of VPA seems to me to make it a highly appropriate candidate for inclusion as a core part of such research.

REFERENCES

Abberton, E. R. M., Howard, D. M., & Fourcin, A. J. (1989). Laryngographic assessment of normal voice: A tutorial. *Clinical Linguistics and Phonetics, 3,* 281–296.

Abercrombie, D. (1967). *Elements of general phonetics.* Edinburgh, Scotland: Edinburgh University Press.

Baken, R. J., & Orlikoff, R. F. (2000). *Clinical measurement of speech and voice* (2nd ed.). San Diego, CA: Singular.

Ball, M. J., Code, C., Rahilly, J., & Hazlett, D. (1994). Non-segmental aspects of disordered speech: Developments in transcription. *Clinical Linguistics and Phonetics, 8,* 67–83.

Esling, J. H. (1978). *Voice quality in Edinburgh: A sociolinguistic and phonetic study.* Unpublished doctoral dissertation, University of Edinburgh, Scotland.

Esling, J. H. (2000). Crosslinguistic aspects of voice quality. In M. J. Ball & R. D. Kent (Eds.), *Voice quality measurement* (pp. 25–36). San Diego, CA: Singular.

Esling, J. H., & Wong, R. F. (1983). Voice quality settings and the teaching of pronunciation. *TESOL Quarterly, 17,* 89–95.

Finlayson, S., Forrest, V., Lickley, R., & Mackenzie Beck, J. (2003). Effects of the restriction of hand gestures on disfluency. *Proceedings of DiSS '03 Dysfluency in Spontaneous Speech Workshop, Göteborg University, Sweden,* 21–24.

Fourcin, A. (2000). Voice quality and electrolaryngography. In M. J. Ball & R. D. Kent (Eds.), *Voice quality measurement* (pp. 285–306). San Diego, CA: Singular.

Graham, J. A., & Heywood, S. (1976). The effects of elimination of hand gesture and of verbal codability on speech performance. *European Journal of Social Psychology, 5,* 189–195.

Hammarberg, B. (1986). *Perceptual and acoustic analysis of dysphonia. Studies in logopedics and phoniatrics, No. 1.* Huddinge, Sweden: Huddinge University Hospital.

Hirano, M. (1981). *Clinical examination of voice.* Vienna: Springer–Verlag.

Hiller, S. M., Laver, J., & Mackenzie, J. (1984). Durational aspects of long-term measurements of fundamental frequency perturbations in connected speech. *Work in Progress, University of Edinburgh, Department of Linguistics, 17,* 59–76.

Hillman, R. E., & Kobler, J. B. (2000). In M. J. Ball & R. D. Kent (Eds.), *Voice quality measurement* (pp. 245–256). San Diego, CA: Singular.

Hollien, H. (2000). The concept of ideal voice quality. In M. J. Ball & R. D. Kent (Eds.), *Voice quality measurment* (pp. 13–24). San Diego, CA: Singular.

Honikman, B. (1964). Articulatory settings. In D. Abercrombie, D. B. Fry, P. A. D. MacCarthy, N. C. Scott, & J. L. M. Trim (Eds.), *In honour of Daniel Jones* (pp. 73–84) London: Longman.

Irving, T. (1997). *The vocal characteristics of male-to-female transsexuals and their influence on perceived gender.* Unpublished honours dissertation, Queen Margaret University College, Edinburgh, Scotland.

Kent, R., & Ball, M. J. (2000). (Eds.). *Voice quality measurement.* San Diego, CA: Singular.

Kiritani, S. (2000). In M. J. Ball & R. D. Kent (Eds.), *Voice quality measurement* (pp. 269–284). San Diego, CA: Singular.

Koschkee, D. L., & Rammage, L. (1997). *Voice care in the medical setting.* San Diego, CA: Singular.

Kreiman, J., & Gerratt, B. (2000). In M. J. Ball & R. D. Kent (Eds.), *Voice quality measurement* (pp. 73–102). San Diego, CA: Singular.

Kreiman, J., Gerrat, B. R., Kempster, G. B., Erman, A., & Berke, G. S. (1993). Perceptual evaluation of voice quality: Review, tutorial and a framework for future research. *Journal of Speech and Hearing Research, 36,* 21–40.

Laver, J. (1968). Voice quality and indexical information. *British Journal of Disorders of Communication, 3,* 43–54.

Laver, J. (1980). *The phonetic description of voice quality.* Cambridge, England: Cambridge University Press.

Laver, J. (1991). *The gift of speech.* Edinburgh, Scotland: Edinburgh University Press.

Laver, J. (2000). Phonetic evaluation of voice quality. In M. J. Ball & R. D. Kent (Eds.), *Voice quality measurement* (pp. 37–48). San Diego, CA: Singular.

Laver, J., & Mackenzie Beck, J. (2001). Unifying principles in the description of voice, posture and gesture. In C. Cavé, I. Guaïtella, & S. Santi (Eds.), *Oralité et Gestualité: Interactions et Comportements Multimodaux dans la Communication (Proceedings of ORAGE 2001)* (pp. 15–24). Paris: L'Harmattan.

Laver, J., Wirz, S., Mackenzie, J., & Hiller, S. M. (1991). A perceptual protocol for the analysis of vocal profiles. In J. Laver (Ed.), *The gift of speech* (pp. 265–280). Edinburgh, Scotland: Edinburgh University Press.

Lieberman, J. (1998). Principles and techniques of manual therapy: Applications in the management of dysphonia. In T. Harris, S. Harris, J. S. Rubin, & D. M. Howard (Eds.), *The voice clinic handbook* (pp. 91–138) London: Whurr Publishers Ltd.

Lyons, J. (1977). *Semantics.* Cambridge, England: Cambridge University Press.

Mackenzie Beck, J. (1988). *Organic variation and voice quality.* Unpublished doctoral dissertation, University of Edinburgh, Scotland.

Mackenzie Beck, J. (1997). Organic variation of the vocal apparatus. In W. J. Hardcastle & J. Laver (Eds.), *Handbook of phonetic sciences* (pp. 256–297). Oxford, England: Blackwell.

Mackenzie Beck, J., Wrench, A., Jackson, M., Soutar, D., Robertson, G., & Laver, J. (1998). Surgical mapping and phonetic analysis in intra-oral cancer. In W. Ziegler & K. Deger (Eds.), *Clinical phonetics and linguistics* (pp. 481–492) London: Whurr Publishers Ltd.

Mackenzie, K., Deary, I. J., Sellars, C., & Wilson, J. (1998). Patient reported benefit of the efficacy of speech therapy in dysphonia. *Clinical Otolaryngology, 23,* 280–287.

Marwick, H., Mackenzie, J., Laver, J., & Trevarthen, C. (1984). Voice quality as an expressive system in mother-to-infant communication: A case study. *Work in Progress, University of Edinburgh, Department of Linguistics Work in Progress, 17,* 85–97

Mathieson, L. (2000). Normal-disordered continuum. In M. J. Ball & R. D. Kent (Eds.), *Voice quality measurement* (pp. 3–12). San Diego, CA: Singular.

Mathieson, L. (2001). *Greene and Mathieson's the voice and its disorders* (6th ed.). London: Whurr Publishers Ltd.

Mayberry, R. I. & Jaques, J. (2000). Gesture production during stuttered speech: Insights into the nature of gesture–speech integration. In D. McNeill (Ed.), *Language and gesture* (pp. 199–214). New York: Cambridge University Press.

McNeill, D. (2000). (Ed.). *Language and gesture.* New York: Cambridge University Press.

Mehler, J., Bertoncini, J., Barrière, M., & Jassik–Gerschenfeld, D. (1978). Infant recognition of mother's voice. *Perception, 7,* 491–497.

Pannbacker, M. (1998). Voice treatment techniques: A review and recommendation for outcome studies. *American Journal of Speech-Language Pathology, 7,* 49–64.

Rauscher, F. B., Krauss, R. M., & Chen, Y. (1996). Gesture, speech and lexical access: The role of lexical movements in speech production. *Psychological Science, 7,* 226–230.

Razzell, R, & Mackenzie, J. (1987, August). *Speech quality following surgical repair of acquired cleft palate.* Paper presented at the 1987 meeting of The Craniofacial Society of Great Britain, Edinburgh, Scotland.

Ryan, C., Ní Chasaide, A., & Gobl, C. (2003). The role of voice quality in communicating emotion, mood and attitude. *Speech Communication, 40,* 189–212.

Scherer, K. R. (1986). Vocal affect expression; a review and a model for future research. *Psychological Bulletin, 99,* 143–165

Scott, S., & Caird, F. I. (1983). Speech therapy for Parkinson's disease. *Journal of Neurology, Neurosurgery and Psychiatry, 46,* 140–144.

Seyfeddinipur, M., & Kita, S. (2001). Gesture as an indicator of early error detection in self-monitoring of speech. *Proceedings of DiSS '01, ISCA Tutorial and Research Workshop on Disfluency in Spontaneous Speech, Edinburgh, Scotland,* 29–32.

Stuart–Smith, J. (1999). Glasgow: Accent and voice quality. In G. Docherty & P. Foulkes (Eds.), *Urban voices: Accent study in the British Isles* (pp. 203–222). London: Arnold.

Švec, J. G., & Schutte, H. K. (1996). Videokymography: High speed line scanning of vocal fold vibration. *Journal of Voice, 10,* 201–205.

Thomson, L. (1995). *Listeners' judgments of intra-oral cancer patients (with anterior and posterior sites of tumour/surgical lesion), preoperatively and postoperatively.* Unpublished honours dissertation, Queen Margaret College, Edinburgh, Scotland.

Trevarthen, C., & Marwick, H. (1982). *Cooperative understanding in infants. (Project Report to the Spencer Foundation, Chicago).* Edinburgh, Scotland: University of Endinburgh, Department of Psychology.

van Bezooyen, R. (1984). *Characteristics and recognisability of vocal expressions of emotion.* Dordrecht, The Netherlands: Foris.

van Erp, A. J. M. (1991). *The phonetic basis of personality ratings, with specific reference to cleft-palate speech.* Nijmegen, Holland: Katholieke Universiteit Nijmegen.

Vieira, M. N. (1997). *Automated measures of dysphonias and the phonatory effects of asymmetries in the posterior larynx.* Unpublished doctoral dissertation, University of Edinburgh, Scotland.

Walker–Andrews, A. S. (1997). Infants' perception of expressive behaviours: Differentiation of multimodal information. *Psychological Bulletin, 121,* 437–456.

Wilson, D. K. (1987). *Voice problems of children.* Baltimore: Williams & Wilkins.

Wirz, S. L. (1987). *Vocal characteristics of hearing impaired people.* Unpublished doctoral dissertation, University of Edinburgh, Scotland.

Wirz, S., & Mackenzie Beck, J. (1995). Assessment of voice quality: The Vocal Profiles Analysis Scheme. In S. Wirz (Ed.), *Perceptual approaches to communication disorders* (pp. 39–55). London: Whurr Publishers Ltd.

Wynter, H., & Martin, S. (1981). The classification of deviant voice quality through auditory memory. *British Journal of Disorders of Communication, 16,* 204–210.

Yu, P., Revis, J., Wuyts, F. L., Zanaret, M., & Giovanni, A. (2002). Correlation of instrumental voice evaluation with perceptual voice analysis using a modified visual analog scale. *Folia Phoniatrica et Logopaedica, 54,* 271–281

Chapter 13

On the Relation Between Phonatory Quality and Affect

Ailbhe Ní Chasaide and Christer Gobl
Phonetics and Speech Laboratory, Centre for Language and Communication Studies, University of Dublin, Trinity College, Ireland

The tone-of-voice in which a message is delivered provides a major aspect of the meaning the listener extracts from it, conveying (or betraying) speakers' moods, emotions, how they feel about the interlocutor and about the situation. Tone-of-voice may 'match' the text of the spoken message, reinforcing its textual meaning, or it may mismatch in a variety of ways, a resource we exploit for humor, irony, and numerous other effects. It adds the subtle affective nuances which endow spoken language with its richly human qualities.

Tone-of-voice can largely be equated with phonatory quality, although clearly pitch, speech tempo, and pausing structure, nonspeech interjections, and other factors also play a role in communicating affect. Although the importance of phonatory quality has always been known, we still understand little about how it is used to signal affect, relying mainly on general observations traditionally made by phoneticians associating particular qualities with individual affective states. An overview is presented here of some of our work on phonatory quality, and of some recent perception experiments which aim to explore the mapping between phonation quality and the attribution of affect (reported in Gobl, Bennett, & Ní Chasaide, 2002; Gobl & Ní Chasaide, 2003; Ní Chasaide & Gobl, 2003).

All of our research on phonatory quality has been situated within the conceptual and descriptive framework provided by John Laver's seminal, work *The Phonetic Description of Voice Quality* (1980). We welcome the opportunity this contribution provides of acknowledging our intellectual debt, and hope that our work will complement and extend his. Note that, although in Laver's work voice quality is defined broadly to include supralaryngeal as well as laryngeal aspects, in our work, which has focused uniquely on phonation, the term is used more narrowly in a way that is interchangeable with phonatory quality.

METHODOLOGICAL DIFFICULTIES

Attempting to map between affective state and voice quality is fraught with numerous methodological difficulties. At the meta-theoretical level, there is still no widely accepted system for categorizing and defining affective states or emotions. The discussions concerning what might constitute a 'primary' versus a 'secondary' set of emotions, whether emotions vary in a discrete or continuous fashion, and which emotions are likely to have a universal as opposed to a culturally-specific form of expression, all serve to highlight how far we are from this goal. Consequently, there can be uncertainty in interpreting and comparing the results of different studies. For example, most studies include 'anger' as one of the basic emotions. It seems intuitively obvious that 'anger' may be an umbrella term for underlyingly different emotional phenomena (note that Scherer, 1986, differentiates between two categories of anger: cold anger and hot anger). Additionally, it is likely that a single emotion can have different vocal expressions. Thus, when comparing results of different studies for an emotion such as anger, there may be uncertainty as to whether divergences reflect differences in the underlying phenomenon or in its expression.

A similar problem potentially exists with the use of labels to describe phonatory quality. Most of what is known about the affective coloring associated with voice quality has been passed down as received knowledge, and has involved the use of impressionistic labels such as 'pressed phonation,' 'breathy voice,' etc. For example, breathy voice has been associated with intimacy, whispery voice with confidentiality, harsh voice with anger, and creaky voice with boredom, at least for speakers of English (see comments in Laver, 1980). The problem with impressionistic labels such as 'harsh voice,' 'pressed voice,' etc. is that they can mean different things to different researchers. Consequently, the task of mapping between affective correlates and voice quality can involve a mapping between two states of uncertainty. Fortunately, voice quality is potentially amenable to more precise definitions. As mentioned, the system in Laver (1980), backed by physiological and acoustic data where available, has provided for us a crucial frame of reference. We point out where, on relatively minor details, we deviate from or extend on Laver's usage.

More practical methodological problems arise when it comes to obtaining experimental data for analysis. The desired data for most researchers is emotionally coloured speech; however, to obtain it, the researcher is confronted by a conundrum. If, as is generally the case, emotionally coloured speech is elicited from actors mimicking a range of emotions while producing the same semantically neutral utterances, there is an obvious risk of obtaining exaggerated and stereotypical samples. On the other hand, it is difficult to obtain spontaneously uttered data, and even where such data can be obtained, it lacks the control of the phonetic and semantic content that would enable rigorous comparison.

Finally, there is the difficulty of obtaining reliable analyses of phonatory quality, as appropriate analytical tools have generally not been available. It is not surprising, therefore, that although the importance of voice quality in the signaling of affect is widely acknowledged, virtually all the experimental work to date has been focused on the more readily measured aspects. A great deal of the research in this field has focused on the dynamic variation of f_0. Other features, such as intensity and durational correlates, have also attracted attention. For reviews of the literature, see, for example, Scherer (1986), Murray and Arnott (1993), and Kappas, Hess, and Scherer (1991). For a discussion on methods of voice analysis, see Gobl and Ní Chasaide (1999b).

The approach adopted here tackles the problem from a different perspective, which hopefully will complement other approaches. Rather than attempt to describe the voice quality correlates of affective speech, we explore the expressive dimension through synthesis of phonatory qualities and perceptual testing of the affective associations that ensue.

NONAFFECTIVE VOICE QUALITY VARIATION

Phonatory quality does not only vary to communicate emotions, moods, and attitudes (all of which we intend by the term *affect*). These affect-related variations can be regarded as a layer, which is superimposed as it were, on the speaker's intrinsic voice quality, and is further mediated by those dynamic variations of the voice source which are determined by the segmental and suprasegmental structure of the utterance. These latter sources of variation are outlined briefly here, as a precursor to the exploration of affect-related variation discussed later.

Intrinsic Baseline Voice Quality: Cross-Speaker Variation

Most work on cross-speaker variation has dealt with male–female–child voice differences (e.g., Gobl, 1988; Gobl & Karlsson, 1991; Holmberg, Hillman, & Perkell, 1988; Monsen & Engebretson, 1977). Yet cross-speaker differences include much subtler variation. Each of us has a distinct voice quality: we differ from members of our group (say, women of similar size and with the same accent) in terms of sometimes large, sometimes small and subtle differences in the glottal source signal. Although our baseline voice quality is largely determined by the physical dimensions of our phonatory apparatus, listeners may at times attribute personality features to speakers partially on the basis of such intrinsic voice characteristics.

Within-Speaker, Dynamic Voice Source Variation

There is considerable dynamic variation of the voice source, regardless of the speaker's intrinsic baseline quality. This is governed by many factors, and some of our studies have dealt with aspects of this variation. In analyzing the voice source, our main technique has involved carrying out detailed (typically pulse-by-pulse) inverse filtering of the speech pressure waveform, using interactive software that allows the user to optimize the filter settings in the time and frequency domain. The LF model (Fant, Liljencrants, & Lin, 1985) is then matched to the output of the inverse filter, the differentiated glottal flow. This second procedure is also typically carried out on a pulse-by pulse basis. Details of the analytic procedures can be found in Gobl and Ní Chasaide (1999b). The analytic procedure is labour-intensive and our focus has been on careful examination of very limited amounts of data—a microperspective rather than a macroperspective.

The model matching allows us to extract source parameters, such as those illustrated in Fig. 13.1, for the Swedish utterance, "Han hade legat och skrivit det i en stor sal, … ". The parameters shown here include EE (the excitation strength, measured as the absolute amplitude of the differentiated glottal flow at the main discontinuity of the pulse), RA (a measure that corresponds to the amount of residual airflow after the main excitation, prior to maximum glottal closure, and which affects spectral tilt), RG (a measure of the 'glottal frequency,' as determined by the opening branch of the glottal pulse, normalized to the fundamental frequency), and EE/EI (a measure of glottal pulse skew, defined by the relative amplitudes of EE and EI, where EI is the maximum positive amplitude of the differentiated glottal flow). Finally, RD is a global wave shape parameter proposed by Fant (see Fant 1995, 1997; Fant, Kruckenberg, Liljencrants, & Båvegård, 1994) based on an effective measure of the 'declination time' of the glottal pulse defined as UP/EE where UP is the peak glottal airflow (the amplitude of the pulse). Note that in our data, UP was obtained using an approximate formula suggested by Fant and Lin (1988). For a fuller account of some of these source parameters, see Ní Chasaide and Gobl (1997).

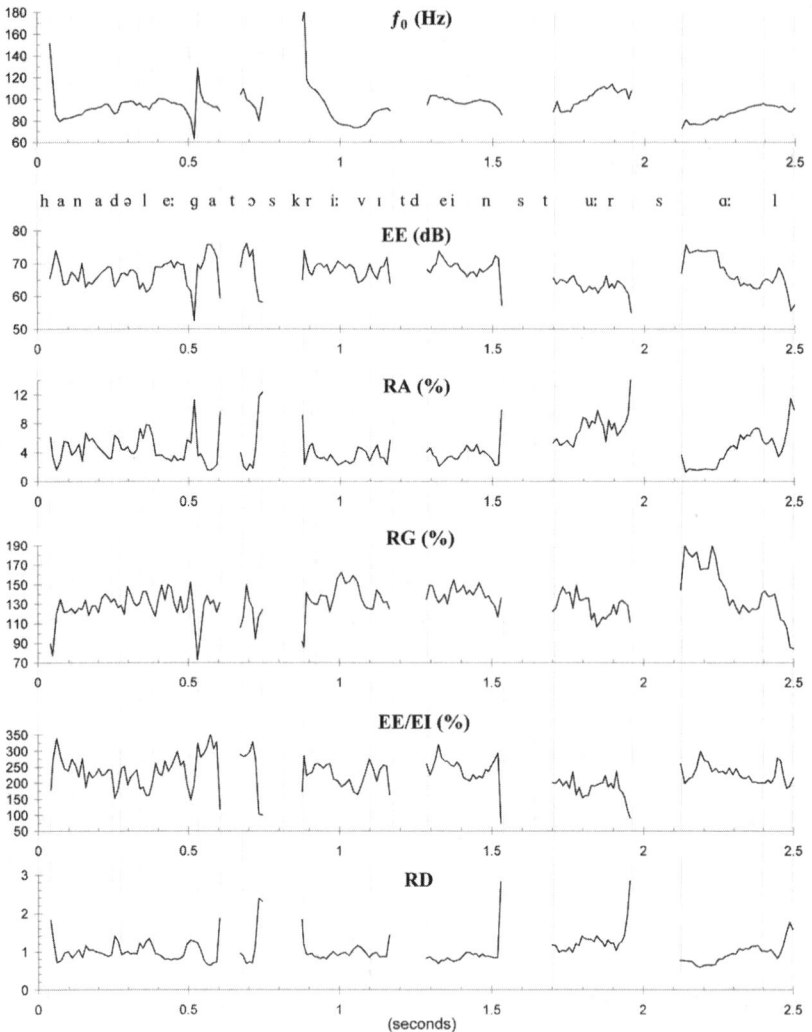

FIG. 13.1. Source parameter variation for the Swedish utterance, "Han hade legat och skrivit det i en stor sal, ... ".

Fig. 13.1 suggests that these source parameters have their own prosodic contour. They are clearly serving part of the signaling function of intonation, for example, differentiation of accented and deaccented syllables, differentiation of terminal and nonterminal boundaries. In Gobl (1988), the source correlates of focal stress in

Swedish are detailed. Pierrehumbert (1989), using this same analysis technique, has analyzed some source correlates of pitch accent in English. This area remains, however, a very underexplored aspect of prosodic structure.

Some striking source variations are related to segmental information: note the perturbations in the vicinity of voiceless consonants in Fig. 13.1. Although not directly inferable from this figure, source parameters also vary as an intrinsic aspect of different segmental articulations. Fig. 13.2 shows source variation associated with voiced consonants with differing manners of articulation (Italian data). These intrinsic types of differences are largely passive effects, resulting directly from the supralaryngeal settings. There may also be some intrinsic variation in the source characteristics as a function of vowel quality, although these differences are typically rather small (Ní Chasaide, Gobl, & Monahan, 1994).

A rather different kind of segment-related source variation arises at the transitions from voiced to voiceless segments. Cross-language studies of vowels in the vicinity of voiced and voiceless consonants (see Gobl & Ní Chasaide, 1999a; Ní Chasaide & Gobl, 1993) indicate that there is considerable cross-language and cross-dialect variation. Whereas in Swedish, source characteristics of a vowel may differ considerably depending on the voiced/voiceless nature of the upcoming stop; in French, such an effect is largely absent. Cross-language differences such as these can sometimes be attributed to differences in the timing of the glottal abduction gesture associated with the voiceless stop. Some of the observed differences cannot be thus explained and appear to arise rather from differences in the laryngeal tension settings associated with voiceless consonants.

Note that the kinds of source dynamics we are discussing here are not likely to be perceived by the listener as involving changes in voice quality per se. Rather, we assume that they are intrinsic aspects of the linguistic differentiation of segments, accented syllables, and so forth. In themselves they have little to do with the expression of affect. This is not of course to say that they are perceptually irrelevant. It is most likely that a failure to capture these in synthesis would affect the perceived naturalness of the speech output.

However, along with the speaker's baseline voice quality, these dynamic variations are the backdrop against which affectively linked

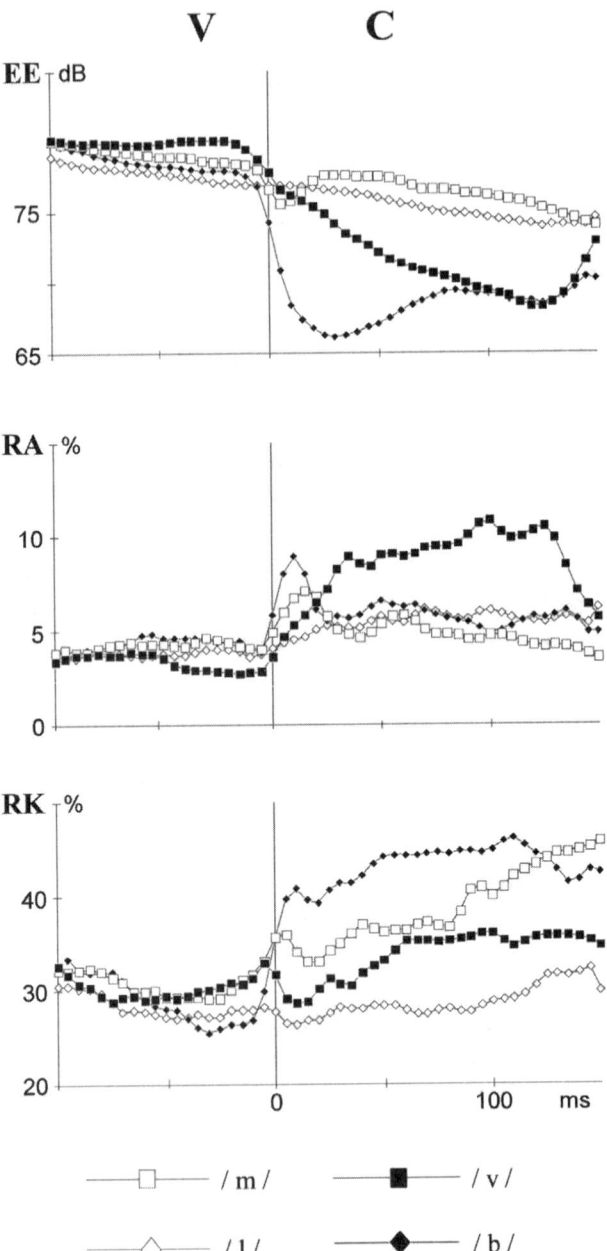

FIG. 13.2. Source data for EE, RA, and RK (for definitions, see text) during the consonants /l(ː) m(ː) v(ː) b(ː)/ and for 100 msec of the preceding vowel, for an Italian. Values are aligned to oral closure or onset of constriction for the consonant (= 0 msec).

phonatory quality changes occur. Given the multiplicity of causes for voice source variation, a major challenge will be to understand the contribution of the different causative elements, to separate the foreground from the background.

VOICE QUALITY AND THE PERCEPTION OF AFFECT

In these experiments, the general idea has been to use utterances synthesized with different phonatory qualities to test listeners on the ensuing changes to the expressive colouring. This approach is largely enabled by earlier experience of analyzing a range of voice qualities, including modal voice, breathy voice, whispery voice, creaky voice, tense voice, and lax voice (e.g., Gobl, 1989; Gobl & Ní Chasaide, 1992). These analyses were based on recordings of a male phonetician, trained in the Laver system.

Much of the research carried out on the vocal expression of affect has focused on a small set of rather strong emotions, such as anger, joy, sadness, and fear. However, phonatory quality contributes greatly to the expressiveness of human speech, signaling to the listener not only information about such strong emotions, but also about milder states, which we might characterize as feelings, moods, attitudes, and general states of being. When eliciting the affective colouring of different phonatory qualities, as in the experiments reported here, we have intentionally allowed for a reasonably wide range of possible affective attributes to include emotions (e.g., *afraid, happy, angry, sad*) as well as speaker states, moods (e.g., *relaxed, stressed, bored*), and attitudes (e.g., *formal, interested, friendly*).

It is worth noting that a broad approach is also potentially more useful for downstream technology applications. A major area of application of this type of research is the provision of expressive voice in speech synthesis. If one wants to aspire to a synthesis that approximates how humans employ their capacity to vary the tone-of-voice, it makes little sense to begin by excluding much of the subject of interest. The voice modifications most frequently sought in specific synthesis applications tend to be ones pertaining to state, mood, and attitude (e.g., relaxed, friendly, polite, etc.), rather than to the 'strong' emotions.

Experiment 1: Can Voice Quality Alone Cue Affect?

In a first experiment (Gobl and Ní Chasaide, 2003), the utterance "ja adjö" ['jɑː aˈjøː] was synthesized with seven different voice qualities: breathy voice, whispery voice, tense voice, harsh voice, creaky voice, lax-creaky voice, and modal voice.

Note that the quality, which is here termed *lax-creaky* voice, is not part of the Laver framework (Laver, 1980). Laver (1980) describes creaky voice as having rather high glottal tension (medial compression and adductive tension). In our earlier descriptive work (Gobl, 1989; Gobl & Ní Chasaide, 1992), it was indeed found that creaky voice has source parameter values tending toward the tense. It was also our auditory impression that creaky voice, as produced by the informant in question, did have a rather tense quality. Yet, we are aware that creaky voice can often sound quite lax in auditory impressionistic terms. It is for this reason that a lax-creaky quality was included, which is essentially based on breathy voice source settings but with no aspiration noise and with added creakiness. Although this lax-creaky voice quality runs counter to the general thrust of Laver's (1980) description for creaky voice, it is worth noting some of the sources he cites imply a rather lax glottal setting (e.g., Monsen & Engebretson, 1977). Clearly more descriptive work on creaky voice is required both at the physiological and acoustic levels.

We would also note that in Laver's (1980) system, tense voice and lax voice involve features both at the laryngeal and supralaryngeal level. In attempting to synthesize these qualities, we have focused on the laryngeal properties. Other than source dependent variation in formant bandwidths, we have not changed filter settings for different synthesized qualities.

The synthesis was carried out using the LF source implementation in KLSYN88a (see Klatt & Klatt, 1990). Our starting point was a copy synthesis of the utterance, produced by a male speaker with a quality which conformed well to Laver's (1980) specification for modal voice. The utterance was analyzed on a pulse-by-basis, and the 'LF parameters' EE, RA, RG, and RG extracted. For the copy synthesis, the latter were transformed into the corresponding 'Klatt parameters': amplitude of voicing (AV), spectral tilt (TL), open quotient (OQ), and speed quotient (SQ). The original 106 glottal pulses were schematized to yield a reduced number for resynthesis (between 7 and 15 per parameter), so that interpolation between these points would capture as much as possible of the dynamic source variation of the original utterance.

In synthesizing the stimuli, 14 parameters in all were varied dynamically: the first five formants, B1 and B2, and three further source parameters, f_0, aspiration noise (AH), and diplophonia (DI, used for the generation of creakiness). Source parameter settings are illustrated in Fig. 13.3 for the different qualities; a full description of the construction of the stimuli is included in Gobl and Ní Chasaide

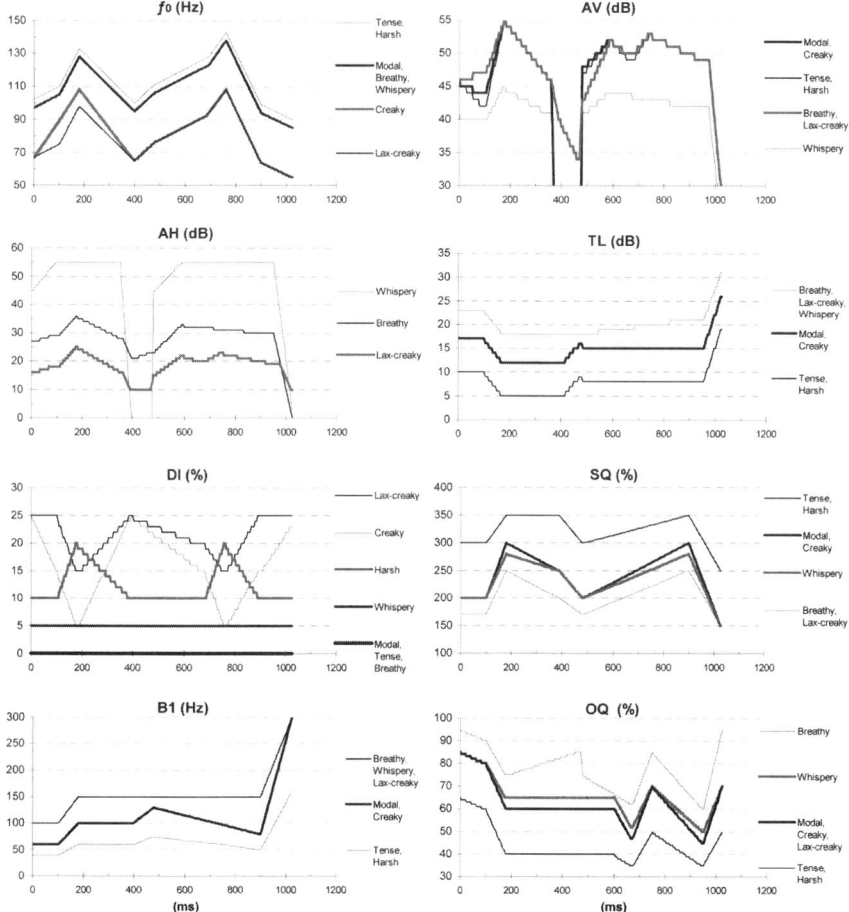

FIG. 13.3. Parameter variation for the synthetic stimuli used in Experiment 1. Note that for the modal, tense, harsh, and creaky stimuli, there was no aspiration noise (AH).

(2003). We simply note here that the deviations from modal were informed by earlier descriptive work, but that the precise settings were ultimately determined by auditory judgment of the effect. This was particularly the case for the parameters AH and DI for which we did not have analytic data. Fundamental frequency was varied only to the extent that was deemed required as an intrinsic voice quality determined characteristic.

The perception test was administered as a series of eight minitests to 12 subjects, speakers of Irish English. In each of these, 10 randomizations were presented, and responses were elicited for a pair of opposite affective attributes (e.g., *bored–interested*) in a way that was loosely modeled on Uldall (1964). Response sheets were arranged with the opposite terms placed on either side, with seven boxes in between, the central one of which was shaded in for visual prominence. Listeners were instructed that they would hear a speaker repeat the same utterance in different ways and were asked to judge for each repetition whether the speaker sounded more *bored* or *interested*, and so forth. In the case where an utterance was not considered to be marked for either of the pair of attributes, they were instructed to choose the centre box. Ticking a box to the left or right of the centre box should indicate the presence and strength to which a particular attribute was deemed present, with the most extreme ratings being furthest from the centre box. The full set of attribute pairs tested included *relaxed/stressed*, *content/angry*, *friendly/hostile*, *sad/happy*, *bored/interested*, *intimate/formal*, *timid/confident*, and *afraid/unafraid*.

Fig. 13.4 illustrates the ratings obtained for each pair of affective attributes across each test. Values for any given voice quality have been joined across the individual tests, to allow the reader to see more readily what might be the affective colouring of particular qualities. Note that 0 in this figure means no affective content, and that the distance from 0 (in the positive or negative direction) indicates the strength with which an attribute was rated.

Results do appear to suggest that voice quality alone can impart an affective colouring to an otherwise neutral utterance. Whereas past comments in the literature might have led us to expect that individual voice qualities would align neatly with single qualities (e.g., boredom with creaky voice, intimacy with breathy voice), this did not emerge in these ratings. Rather, each quality was associated

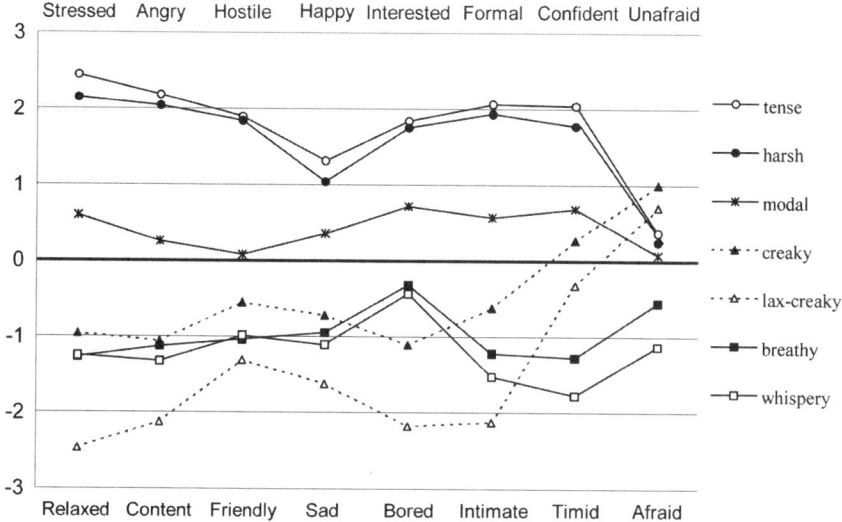

FIG. 13.4. Mean ratings for 12 Irish English subjects of the perceived strength of pairs of attributes for seven voice qualities. 0 = no affective content; +/–3 = maximally perceived.

with more than one attribute, and the differences among qualities had more to do with the strength of the ratings. One possibility suggested by Anne Wichmann (personal communication, 2002) is that the context in which an utterance is produced could determine the interpretation the listener makes of the voice quality (e.g., interpreting lax-creaky voice as *bored* vs. *intimate*).

Interestingly, in this and in further experiments mentioned later, much of the "work" was done by the tense versus lax distinction, and the addition of creakiness appeared to significantly enhance the ratings for the latter. Essentially, tense voice appeared to be associated with high activation and high power states (*stressed, angry, confident, formal*), whereas the lax-creaky voice was associated with low activation states (*relaxed, bored, intimate*). It was also striking that, with the clear exception of *angry,* strong emotions (such as *happy, sad, afraid*) yielded rather low ratings, whereas milder states of being (such as *bored, relaxed, formal*) tended toward higher ratings.

Experiment 2: The Tense–Lax Dimension And Affect Strength

A follow-up experiment (Ryan, Ní Chasaide, & Gobl, 2003) honed in on the tense–lax dimension and addressed the question as to whether affect strength varies in a continuous or in a more discontinuous, categorical fashion with gradient changes to phonatory quality. For example, if exposed to a continuum of qualities ranging from tense to lax, will listeners hear increasing degrees of, say, *anger* or does the attribution of *anger* depend on some threshold value being reached? It was thought at least possible that a quality of moderate tenseness (somewhere between the tense voice and the modal voice settings employed in Experiment 1) could generate a rather different affect, such as *happy*. Note that Scherer (1986) has suggested that tense voice might be associated with angry and happy speech: if this were so, the relatively low ratings for *happy* in Experiment 1 could have to do with the stimulus in question having too extreme a degree of tension.

To test this, an acoustic continuum was generated, that is, a set of stimuli ranging from very tense at one end to very lax at the other extreme. The object was to ensure that for each source parameter, at each timepoint in the utterance, the interstimulus differences involved equidistant steps. Note, however, that the stepsize itself varied from one timepoint to another, depending on the actual value of a given parameter at the specific timepoint in the modal stimulus.

The starting point for the continuum was the modal stimulus used in Gobl and Ní Chasaide (2003), with some minor changes to the AH and AV parameters of the KLSYN88a synthesizer. The full continuum involved 11 stimuli; on the basis of the modal stimulus, 10 more stimuli were generated by manipulating the following parameters of the synthesizer: AV, TL, OQ, SQ, AH, and B1 (first formant bandwidth). Five of the stimuli (Tense5 to Tense1) involved higher levels of 'tenseness' compared to the modal stimulus, and five stimuli (Lax1 to Lax5) involved lower levels of tenseness.

To obtain equidistant steps, a strategy was adopted which is here illustrated for the OQ parameter (Table 13.1 and Fig. 13.5). First, for each parameter in turn, extreme values at the tense and lax ends were established. In the case of OQ, a lax limit of 100% and a tense limit of 30% were chosen. These extreme values were decided on on the basis of suggestions in the KLSYN88a manual, as well as from knowledge about voice production constraints.

TABLE 13.1

OQ (%) for the 11 Stimuli

Time (Msec)	Limit, Lax	L5	L4	L3	L2	L1	M	T1	T2	T3	T4	T5	Limit, Tense	Step Size
0	100	100	97	94	91	88	85	82	79	76	73	70	30	3.0
100	100	100	96	92	88	84	80	76	72	68	64	60	30	4.0
180	100	90	84	78	72	66	60	54	48	42	36	30	30	6.0
600	100	90	84	78	72	66	60	54	48	42	36	30	30	6.0
665	100	64	61	57	54	50	47	44	40	37	33	30	30	3.4
750	100	100	94	88	82	76	70	64	58	52	46	40	30	6.0
945	100	60	57	54	51	48	45	42	39	36	33	30	30	3.0
1025	100	100	94	88	82	76	70	64	58	52	46	40	30	6.0
1195	100	100	94	88	82	76	70	64	58	52	46	40	30	6.0

Note.—OQ values for the 11 stimuli of the continuum, OQ extreme limits, and the calculated interstimulus step size at each timepoint in the utterance are shown. L = Lax; T = Tense.

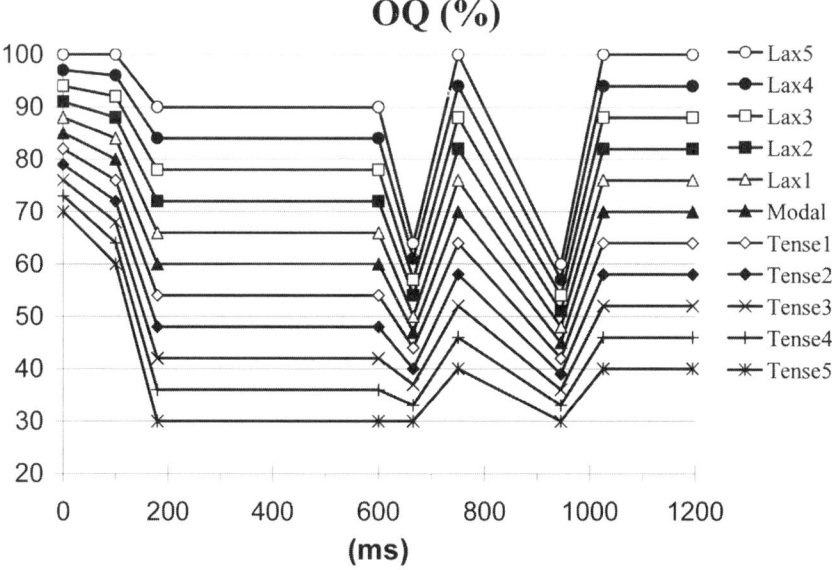

FIG. 13.5. Open Quotient (OQ) variation in the utterance for the 11 stimuli of the tense–lax continuum.

At timepoint 0 in Table 13.1, the OQ value for modal voice is 85%. Thus, OQ may vary by 15 percentage points in the tense direction or by 55 percentage points in the lax. Five equidistant steps would therefore yield steps of 3 percentage points in the tense direction or of 11 percentage points in the lax direction. To ensure equidistant steps between stimuli, the smaller stepsize was always chosen to prevent values from exceeding the limits. This stepsize was recalculated for each timepoint, as illustrated in Table 13.1. Values for TL and SQ were obtained in the same fashion.

Calculations of changes in the B1 parameter follow essentially the same procedure as for OQ. The difference is that the change does not involve a fixed stepsize, but rather a constant multiplication factor. This is motivated by the fact that a constant change in the amplitude level of a formant corresponds more closely to a relative change in the formant bandwidth.

For AH, the original modal stimulus was not taken as the starting point, given that AH was set to zero throughout for this stimulus. Rather, AH values were taken from the breathy voice stimulus of the experiment in Gobl and Ní Chasaide (2003) as the appropriate setting for the Lax3 stimulus. Using Lax3 as a starting point, these AH values were modified for the other stimuli in 2 dB steps, decreasing with increasing degree of tenseness and increasing with increasing degree of laxness.

In the case of the AV parameter, values varied only for vowel onsets and offsets, so as to provide for sharper onsets and offset for the tense stimuli as compared to more gradual onsets and offsets for the lax stimuli. Fundamental frequency variation in the modal stimulus was retained across the continuum.

Manipulations of the SQ parameter in KLSYN88a cause changes in the excitation amplitude (EE) of the glottal pulse generated by the modified LF model of KLSYN88a. Whereas a level difference across a tense–lax continuum of voice qualities would be expected, the AV values were assumed to map closely to variation in the excitation strength (i.e., to the EE values). The indirect changes in EE due to variation in SQ were deemed undesirable and were compensated for as follows.

The overall change to the amplitude level of the stimuli was first measured to be 16.0 dB. Then the changes in EE as a function of the range of SQ variation used here was estimated, by analysing a synthesised utterance with constant AV, but varying SQ. This variation was found to be 8.8 dB. Finally, the overall amplitude of the individual stimuli was adjusted to cancel the variation in EE as function of SQ. The level of the modal stimulus was taken as a reference and was not altered. For a given stimulus, for example, Lax5, the level difference from modal was calculated. The proportion of this difference (8.8:16) was multiplied to the overall level difference to yield the compensation (in dB) that would be required to remove the influence of SQ on EE.

The attributes tested, and the manner in which they were tested, were as for Experiment 1. Some of the results are plotted in Fig. 13.6, for five stimuli over the continuum. Where the tense or lax quality of the voice is relevant to the perception of an affect (e.g., tense voice for anger), the ratings varied in a continuous fashion for the acoustic continuum. From this we conclude that the detection of affect strength is a gradient function, at least as regards the tense–lax dimension of voice quality. Interestingly, the affects *happy–sad* yielded low ratings throughout, and thus did not appear to be associated with the tense–lax dimension of voice quality in any straightforward way. Any expectation that a moderately tense voice quality might yield higher *happy* ratings was not borne out.

Experiment 3: How Do f_0 and Voice Quality Combine?

This experiment (reported in Gobl et al., 2002) was prompted by the results of Experiment 1, particularly the observation that the strong emotions (except *anger*) did not generally yield high ratings as compared to milder states of being. One likely explanation would be that these stimuli did not incorporate large f_0 excursions, which we know from the work of Scherer (e.g., Scherer, 1986) and Mozziconacci (1995, 1998) are typically associated with the signaling of strong emotions. Consequently, in this experiment, two questions are asked: (a) If we match the most likely voice quality candidates for a particular emotion to a more appropriate f_0 contour for that emotion, will we get higher affect ratings? (b) How will the latter stimuli compare to stimuli which incorporate only the f_0 contours for these same affects?

To test this question, the stimuli in Experiment 1 were adapted to yield two sets of stimuli. The first set of stimuli (which we term the f_0 *only* stimuli) were arrived at simply by modifying the f_0 values of the

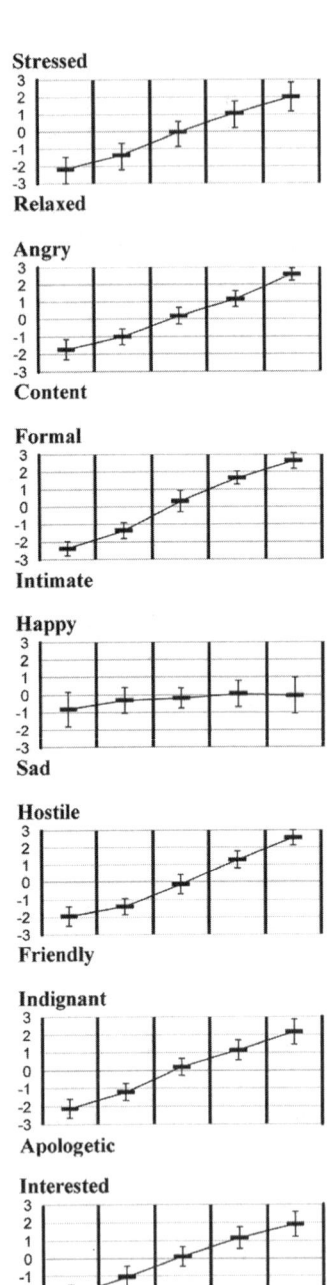

FIG. 13.6. Mean ratings obtained for the subset of stimuli spanning the tense–lax continuum (vertical lines show one standard deviation) for each pair of affective attributes (7-point scale, −3 to +3).

modal stimulus to generate stimuli with a set of f_0 contours, as might be appropriate to specific emotions. These pitch contours were adapted from an experiment by Mozziconacci (1995) and were based on analyses of utterances produced with the following affects: indignation, fear, joy, anger, sadness, boredom, and neutral, and are illustrated in Fig. 13.7. Note that Mozziconacci's basic neutral f_0 contour was rather similar to that of our own modal utterance, and so the latter served as our neutral stimulus. The nonmodal f_0 values were arrived at by a linear scaling of Mozziconacci's values at each of the anchor points in Fig. 13.7. This retained the relative differences with respect to the f_0 values of our neutral stimulus.

The second set of stimuli (which we term the f_0+VQ stimuli) involved matching a particular phonatory quality (e.g., lax-creaky voice as a likely candidate for the *bored* affect) to each of the non-neutral f_0 contours used in the first set of stimuli. The pairings were as follows: the f_0 contour for *boredom* was generated with the lax-creaky voice quality, *sadness* with breathy voice, *anger* with tense voice, *fear* with whispery voice, *joy* with tense voice and *indignation* with harsh voice. These stimuli are referred to as *F0joy+tense*,

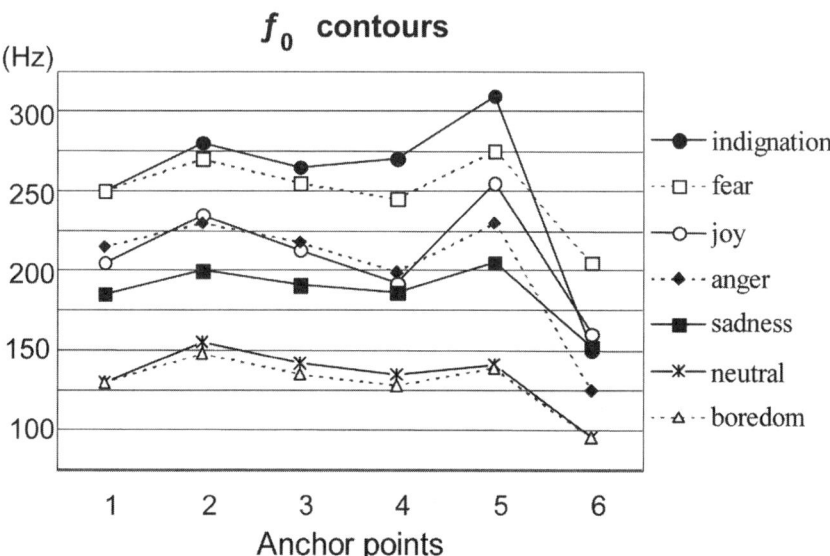

FIG. 13.7. Characteristic fundamental frequency contours for different emotions, based on data from Mozziconacci (1995).

F0indignation+harsh, and so forth. The decision as to which voice quality would be most appropriate for a particular f_0 contour was guided in most cases by the results of Experiment 1.

The test was administered in much the same way as Experiment 1. In addition to the specific targeted affects (i.e., the affects described by Mozziconacci (1995) and for which we had "matched" candidates here), we included tests for some further affect pairs which had been included in Experiment 1: relaxed–stressed and intimate–formal.

Results are shown for both the 'f_0+VQ' and 'f_0 only' stimuli in Fig. 13.8. In answer to the main question posed, the strong emotions did yield relatively higher ratings when these pitch excursions were added to the voice quality differences. It is also clear that the f_0 excursion without voice quality adjustments ('f_0 only' stimuli) yielded rather low ratings in general, strikingly less than obtained for the 'f_0+VQ' stimuli.

CONCLUSIONS AND FUTURE DIRECTIONS

These experiments raise as many questions as they answer. They do suggest unambiguously that voice quality is fundamental to the com-

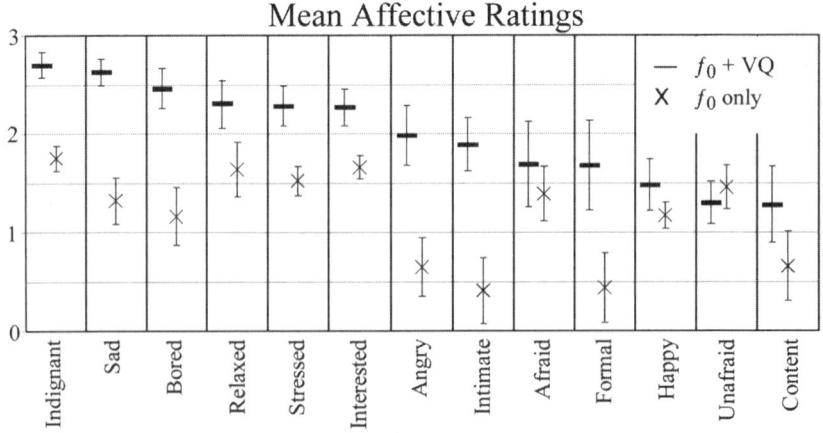

FIG. 13.8. Maximum mean rating and estimated standard error of the mean for each affect: stimuli 'f_0+VQ' (–); 'f_0 only' (x). Affect ratings: 0 = none, 3 = max.

munication of affect. Not surprisingly, the affective rating for different voice qualities is greater when it combines with appropriate pitch excursions. The surprise was how relatively ineffective were the stimuli with large pitch excursions, but without concomitant voice quality shifts.

On reflection, this should perhaps not be so surprising. In nature as opposed to synthesis, large f_0 excursions are unlikely to happen without concomitant shifts in the other voice source parameters. If, as here, we manipulate f_0 alone without changing voice source parameters, we are likely to fail on two accounts: (a) because we are simply failing to capture much of what the listener perceives to be the tone-of-voice, and (b) because we may be introducing artifacts which will in themselves undermine the naturalness of the speech output.

With regard to the tense–lax voice quality continuum, this is a fundamentally important dimension of voice variation, which is likely to be closely linked to the degree of activation of the perceived affect. Where tense or lax voice is linked to specific affective attributes, the perceived strength of the attribute seems to be related in a gradient fashion to the degree of tenseness–laxness (in acoustic terms). Note, however, that the tense–lax dimension is not the only important dimension of voice variation: for example, creakiness appears to yield a major enhancement of the attributes associated with lax voice (for English speakers, at any rate).

The use of voice quality for affect signaling is partially universal and partially language and culture specific. We surmise that the tense–lax voice continuum may be universally linked to the strength (or activation degree) of many affects. Nonetheless, there are likely to be language specific norms concerning where in the continuum a "neutral" quality is located. For certain qualities, such as perhaps lax-creaky voice, the expressive colouring is likely to vary considerably across language groups. Using the synthesis and perception-testing methodology that we have employed in these experiments, we are currently exploring cross-language differences in voice quality to affect mapping.

A particular focus in our future work will be the interaction of f_0 and voice quality. Voice quality and f_0 are integral parts of the voice source, although, for methodological reasons, they are typically treated as independent entities. In terms of speech production and perception, they are, of course, partially independent, but tend to covary.

Increasingly, we are of the view that there is a need to locate the expression of affect within the general workings of prosody. Current intonational analysis tends to focus essentially on what is deemed strictly linguistic phenomena, such as differentiating interrogatives from declaratives, marking broad and narrow focus, and so forth. The expressive functions of prosody of signaling attitude, mood, and emotion are generally regarded as paralinguistic and thus outside the field. Fortunately, the research of psychologists such as Scherer and his colleagues has served to remedy the deficit, and they have over the years explored the latter aspect with extensive analyses of f_0 dynamics, as well as amplitude and tempo. A difficulty arises, however, in that the methodologies are entirely different, so that between linguists and psychologists, we get an artificially fragmented view of prosody. One would be forgiven for thinking that affect expression is an altogether separate entity from the underlying prosody, rather than an enhancement of it. We feel, therefore, that an integrated approach is called for, whereby the prosody of a language is tackled in a way that encompasses the narrowly linguistic and the paralinguistic expressive dimensions within a single framework. To effectively do so, all three phonetic dimensions of prosody should ideally be included, f_0, voice quality, and temporal features, as all three are implicated in both the linguistic and paralinguistic functioning of prosody. We are currently embarking on a project to analyze the prosody of Irish dialects, and it will be a major goal to attempt coverage of this broader canvas in a way that will throw light not only on the interactions of f_0 and other voice source parameters, but also on their combined exploitation in prosody.

REFERENCES

Fant, G. (1995). The LF-model revisited. Transformations and frequency domain analysis. *Speech Transmission Laboratory Quarterly Status and Progress Report 2–3*, Royal Institute of Technology, Stockholm, 119–156.

Fant, G. (1997). The voice source in connected speech. *Speech Communication, 22*, 125–139.

Fant, G., Kruckenberg, A., Liljencrants, J., & Båvegård, M. (1994). Voice source parameters in continuous speech. Transformation of LF-parameters. *Proceedings of the International Conference on Spoken Language Processing, Yokohama, Japan*, pp. 1451–1454.

Fant, G., Liljencrants, J., & Lin, Q. (1985). A four-parameter model of glottal flow. *Speech Transmission Laboratory Quarterly Status and Progress Report 4*, Royal Institute of Technology, Stockholm, 1–13.

Fant, G., & Lin, Q. (1988). Frequency domain interpretation and derivation of glottal flow parameters, *Speech Transmission Laboratory Quarterly Status and Progress Report, 2–3,* Royal Institute of Technology, Stockholm, 1–21.

Gobl, C. (1988). Voice source dynamics in connected speech. *Speech Transmission Laboratory Quarterly Status and Progress Report 1*, Royal Institute of Technology, Stockholm, 123–159.

Gobl, C. (1989). A preliminary study of acoustic voice quality correlates. *Speech Transmission Laboratory Quarterly Status and Progress Report 4,* Royal Institute of Technology, Stockholm, 9–21.

Gobl, C., Bennett, E., & Ní Chasaide, A. (2002). Expressive synthesis: How crucial is voice quality. *Proceedings of the IEEE Workshop on Speech Synthesis, Santa Monica, CA.*

Gobl, C., & Karlsson, I. (1991). Male and female voice source dynamics. In J. Gauffin & B. Hammarberg (Eds.), *Vocal fold physiology: Acoustic, perceptual, and physiological aspects of voice mechanisms* (pp. 121–128). San Diego, CA: Singular Publishing Group.

Gobl, C., & Ní Chasaide, A. (1992). Acoustic characteristics of voice quality. *Speech Communication, 11,* 481–490.

Gobl, C., & Ní Chasaide, A. (1999a). Voice source variation in the vowel as a function of consonantal context. In W. J. Hardcastle & N. Hewlett (Eds.), *Coarticulation: Theory, data and techniques* (pp. 122–143). Cambridge, England: Cambridge University Press.

Gobl, C., & Ní Chasaide, A. (1999b). Techniques for analysing the voice source. In W. J. Hardcastle & N. Hewlett (Eds.), *Coarticulation: Theory, data and techniques* (pp. 300–321). Cambridge, England: Cambridge University Press.

Gobl, C., & Ní Chasaide, A. (2003). The role of voice quality in communicating emotion, mood and attitude. *Speech Communication, 40,* 189–212.

Holmberg, E. B., Hillman, R. E., & Perkell, J. S. (1988). Glottal air flow and pressure measurements for loudness variation by male and female speakers. *Journal of the Acoustical Society of America, 84,* 511–529.

Kappas, A., Hess, U., & Scherer, K. R. (1991). Voice and emotion. In R. S. Feldman & B. Rimé (Eds.), *Fundamentals of nonverbal behaviour.* (pp. 200–238). Cambridge, England: Cambridge University Press.

Klatt, D. H., & Klatt, L. C. (1990). Analysis, synthesis, and perception of voice quality variations among female and male talkers. *Journal of the Acoustical Society of America, 87,* 820–857.

Laver, J. (1980). *The phonetic description of voice quality.* Cambridge, England: Cambridge University Press.

Monsen, R. B., & Engebretson, A. M. (1977). Study of variations in the male and female glottal wave. *Journal of the Acoustical Society of America, 62,* 981–993.

Mozziconacci, S. (1995). Pitch variations and emotions in speech. *Proceedings of the XIIIth International Congress of Phonetic Sciences, Stockholm, 1*, 178–181.

Mozziconacci, S. (1998). *Speech variability and emotion: Production and perception.* Doctoral thesis, Technische Universiteit Eindhoven, The Netherlands.

Murray, I. R., & Arnott, J. L. (1993). Toward the simulation of emotion in synthetic speech: A review of the literature on human vocal emotion. *Journal of the Acoustical Society of America, 93*, 1097–1108.

Ní Chasaide, A., & Gobl, C. (1993). Contextual variation of the vowel voice source as a function of adjacent consonants. *Language and Speech, 36*, 303–330.

Ní Chasaide, A., & Gobl, C. (1997). Voice source variation. In W. J. Hardcastle and J. Laver (Eds.), *The handbook of phonetic sciences* (pp. 427–461). Oxford, England: Blackwell.

Ní Chasaide, A., & Gobl, C. (2003). Voice quality and expressive speech. *Proceedings of the 1st JST/CREST International Workshop on Expressive Speech Processing, Kobe, Japan*, 19–28.

Ní Chasaide, A., Gobl, C., & Monahan, P. (1994). Dynamic variation of the voice source: Intrinsic characteristics of selected vowels and consonants. *Proceedings of the Speech Maps Workshop, Esprit/Basic Research Action No. 6975, Grenoble, France, 2.*

Pierrehumbert, J. B. (1989). A preliminary study of the consequences of intonation for the voice source. *Speech Transmission Laboratory Quarterly Status and Progress Report, 4*, Royal Institute of Technology, Stockholm, 23–36.

Ryan, C., Ní Chasaide, A., & Gobl, C. (2003). Voice quality variation and the perception of affect: Continuous or categorical? *Proceedings of the XVth International Congress of Phonetic Sciences, Barcelona, Spain, 3*, 2409–2412.

Scherer, K. R. (1986). Vocal affect expression: A review and a model for future research. *Psychological Bulletin, 99*, 143–165.

Uldall, E. (1964). Dimensions of meaning in intonation. In D. Abercrombie, D. B. Fry, P. A. D. MacCarthy, N. C. Scott, J. L. M. Trim (Eds.), *In honour of Daniel Jones* (pp. 271–279). London: Longman.

Chapter 14

States of the Glottis: An Articulatory Phonetic Model Based on Laryngoscopic Observations

John H. Esling and Jimmy G. Harris
Department of Linguistics, University of Victoria, Canada

In this chapter, we propose a revised interpretation of the traditional formulation of the states of the glottis and of their relation to each other. We begin with a description of our methodological approach to the investigation of sound quality in the larynx, laryngeal vestibule, and pharynx, then a brief review of early descriptions of states of the glottis, followed by a categorical explanation of our proposed states of the glottis supported by evidence drawn from laryngoscopic observations together with illustrations of cardinal states abstracted from linguistic occurrences in our laryngoscopic research project database.

Our articulatory, auditory, and kinaesthetic approach follows the Bell and Sweet tradition and the further advances made in the second half of the 20th century in the descriptions of states of the glottis, especially in the works of Catford (1964, 1977, 1990), Abercrombie (1967), and Laver (1975, 1980). Our terms defining each category are taken primarily from this background literature. All categories of this catalogue of states of the glottis are understood to be based on articulatory, auditory, and kinaesthetic qualities as identified in the linguistic sound system and as distinguished from other linguistically contrasting sounds. Our primary contributions are the direct visual evidence of what is happening in the larynx, the laryngeal vestibule, and the pharynx, including the action of the aryepiglottic sphincter mechanism. Our objective is to expand the descriptions of states of the glottis to include our interpretation of the direct visual laryngoscopic evidence.

RESEARCH METHODOLOGY

We have obtained direct visual images of the larynx in several languages using the University of Victoria fibreoptic laryngoscope research facility to determine the laryngeal physiology and mechanics involved in the production of a range of glottal, glottalized, phonatory register, and pharyngeal phenomena, including the action of the aryepiglottic sphincter mechanism. Among the languages examined in the project are Nuuchahnulth (Wakashan), Nlaka'pamux (Salish), Yi (Tibeto–Burman), Bai (Sino–Tibetan), Tibetan (Tibeto–Burman), Pame (Oto–Manguean), Arabic (Semitic), Tigrinya (Semitic), Thai (Tai), Sui (Kam–Sui), Cantonese (Sinitic), Korean (Altaic), Somali (Cushitic), and Amis (Austronesian). We have drawn on evidence from these languages as well as from English as a basis for establishing cardinal exemplars of each state of the glottis.

The equipment installation for this research includes the Kay 9100 Rhino-Laryngeal-Stroboscope dual light source and hardware–software system, a Mitsubishi S–VHS video cassette recorder BV–2000 (30 frames per sec) and, in more recent research, a Sony DCR–T4V17 digital camcorder recording simultaneously with the analog S–VHS. Two endoscopes are used for observations: the Olympus ENF–P3 flexible fiberoptic nasal laryngoscope and the Kay 9105 70°-angle rigid oral laryngoscope, both fitted with a 28 mm wide-angle lens to a Panasonic KS152 camera. All language observations were performed nasendoscopically. To illustrate cardinal states of the glottis as abstractions of the sounds observed in linguistically meaningful contrasts, phonetic productions by the first author were recorded by means of the orally inserted endoscope, which permits bilabial closure and prohibits oral articulation beyond a single vowel shape but provides a large bright image of laryngeal activity. Video images were postprocessed with Adobe Premiere 6.5 software.

EARLY DESCRIPTIONS OF STATES OF THE GLOTTIS

Since the development of the laryngoscope by Babington in 1829 and its later perfection by J. N. Czermak and Manuel Garcia in the 1850s, laryngeal function has been observed directly. The development of photographic techniques during the last half of the 19th century and the first half of the 20th century enhanced the ability to view the vocal folds and the states of the glottis. However, we feel there is still a need for a more widely accepted and detailed description of the states of the glottis and of supraglottal adjustments that occur in conjunction with basic cardinal glottal configurations.

In Europe, ever since the research done by Holder (1669, p. 64), a distinction has been made between 'breath' and 'voice.' Melville Bell's (1867) novel organic (iconic) universal alphabet represented 'breath' as an unimpededly open glottis and 'super-glottal passage,' 'voice' as a vibrating glottis, 'whisper' as an open glottis with a contracted super-glottal passage, and 'catch' (i.e., glottal stop) as 'the conjoined edges of the glottis' (p. 46). Bell also defined a compound phonatory category of 'whisper and voice heard simultaneously' which he called 'vocal murmur' (p. 46). The categories 'breath,' 'voice,' and 'whisper' were recognized by Sweet (1877, p.

3), who divided voice into 'chest' and 'head' voice, following Garcia (1855, 1856), with 'falsetto' as the 'shrillest form' of the head register. Sweet also distinguished between different degrees of whisper, and he defined 'glottal catch' as a sudden opening and closing of the glottis (p. 4). These interpretations constituted the basic foundation for the definitions of the states of the glottis until the second half of the 20th century. Catford's (1964, 1968, 1977) now classic works on phonation types and articulatory possibilities are the pioneering systematic treatments of the laryngeal activities involved in different states of the glottis, phonation types, and voice qualities used in the production of human speech. Further important work on voice qualities is that of Laver (1975, 1980).

Sweet (1906, p. 9) defined an open glottis, as in the production of voiceless aspirated stops and affricates, as 'breath.' Sounds made with an open state of the glottis were said to be 'breathed' /brɛθt/. Sweet (1877, p. 75; 1906, p. 3) treated the terms 'voiceless' or 'voicelessness' as simply alternatives for breath. This has led to confusion in the literature. Abercrombie (1967, p. 53) and Ladefoged (1971, pp. 6–9; 1974, pp. 303–304), following the Sweet tradition, defined sounds made with an open glottis as voiceless. They were, therefore, forced to define glottal stop or a closed glottis as neither voiced nor voiceless but as a third category which Catford (1990) called 'unphonated' sounds. The confusion that began with Sweet has been continued by some phoneticians who follow strictly the Sweet tradition. Voiceless or voicelessness is defined as a wide open glottis with air passing through the glottis during the articulatory stricture phase of a sound. Some phoneticians, however, including Noël-Armfield (1931, p. 6), Catford (1939, 1947, 1990), Pike (1943, pp. 142–143), Heffner (1950, pp. 121, 125), and Sprigg (1978, pp. 5–7), did not use the open or breathed state of the glottis as the primary definition of voiceless or voicelessness.

Because definition problems concerning the phonetic terms voiceless and voicelessness are confusing, we propose that the terms voiceless or voicelessness be restricted to mean 'lacking voice,' which conforms to the usual dictionary meaning of the terms. Thus, all breathed sounds are voiceless, but not all voiceless sounds are breathed. All of the traditional basic states of the glottis (except voice) including breath, nil phonation, whisper, unphonated, and creak, as well as prephonation (the state of the glottis for voiceless unaspirated oral stops and affricates), are voiceless. The so-called partially voiced or devoiced sound segments are in fact both voiceless and voiced. The symbols [b̥, d̥, g̊, s̬] represent sound segments that are both voiceless and voiced and could be transcribed as [pb] or [bp], [td] or [dt], [kg] or [gk], [sz] or [zs]. However, sounds made without any type of voiced state of the glottis are by definition voiceless. Thus, all human speech sounds can be classified under two major divisions of phonation: voiceless for those sounds lacking any type of voice and voiced for those sounds containing some type of voice.

BREATH (AND NIL PHONATION)

In his extensive observations of laryngeal function, Catford (1964, pp. 30–31, 1968, p. 319) states that 'breath' and 'nil phonation' are both phonation types of 'voicelessness.' In his definition, both breath and nil phonation have a wide open glottis. The difference between them is in the turbulence of the airflow through the open glottis. According to Catford, breath has a widely opened glottis with turbulent airflow sufficient to be recognized as 'audible breathing.' Nil phonation also has a widely opened glottis but nonturbulent airflow so as to be defined auditorily as 'silent breathing.' The confusing term here is *widely* open glottis. We assume that the widest open glottis is the one used in forced inhalation and that the glottal opening is less wide open during exhalation.

The width of the glottis for an adult male at rest, according to Zemlin (1968, p. 140), is about 8 mm at the vocal processes of the arytenoids, whereas the length of the vocal folds averages 14.5 mm during modal phonation and 16 mm at a pitch one octave higher. Zemlin (1988, pp. 142–143), citing Negus (1929), gives the width of the glottis during normal quiet breathing (nil phonation) as 13 mm. Zemlin shows that glottal width may double during forced exhalation and that it may triple during forced inhalation reaching maximum abduction of the vocal folds. Reviewing the photographs available in the literature suggests that the width of the glottal opening for breath and for nil phonation can vary, but the abduction of the arytenoid cartilages, the lack of displacement of the aryepiglottic folds, the abducted position of the ventricular folds, and the abduction of the vocal folds are characteristics of both breath and nil phonation. It is also well known that prosodic features such as stress can influence the size of the opening of the glottis, so that prosodic environments have to be taken into consideration when making observations on the size and dimensions of laryngeal structures.

Catford (1977, p. 100) comments on the noisy turbulent airflow of (audible) breath at volume velocities above 200 to 350 cm³/s and the smooth nonturbulent airflow of (silent) nil phonation at volume velocities below 200 to 350 cm³/s. For initial [h] and voiceless aspirated oral stops [pʰ,tʰ,kʰ] in stressed syllables in English, there is a high-velocity flow at rates around 1000 cm³/s (Catford, 1977, p. 95). Voiceless fricatives in English, such as [f,s,ʃ], normally have lower velocity flows, which may be at the level of nil phonation at the glottis. We might predict that in languages such as Burmese, with wide-grooving and narrow-grooving lingual contrasts, the width of glottal opening for the fricative with less lingual constriction and wider grooving (often transcribed as an aspirated laminal fricative [sʰ]) is expected to be that of breath (as for aspiration), whereas the fricative with more lingual constriction and a narrower lingual groove ([s]) may have narrower glottal opening. A precedent for relating oral stricture tension to laryngeal tension has been observed in the labial behaviour accompanying lax and tense laryngeal settings in the Tibeto–Burman language Yi (Esling & Edmondson, 2002). Fig. 14.1 illustrates the breath state of the glottis from the aspiration phase of a voiceless aspirated stop. This shape does not appear to differ substantially from the glottal posture for a relatively strongly articulated voiceless bilabial fricative [ɸ], although oral production is limited with the rigid scope, and precise area or distance measurements are problematical with either the oral or nasal laryngoscopic technique.

MODAL VOICE

Holder (1669, p. 64) called voice 'breath vocalized.' According to Sweet (1906, p. 10), voice can be produced in two ways by the action of the breath on the vocal folds. In the first way, the glottis is completely closed so that air can only pass through in a series of rapid puffs. This most sonorous form of voice is what he called 'chest voice' or 'thick register.' In the second way, the vocal folds are stretched and brought close together without making a complete closure of the glottis, which produces a thinner quality of voice known as 'head voice' or 'thin register voice,' the shrillest form of which Sweet (1877, p. 3) called falsetto. The term for chest

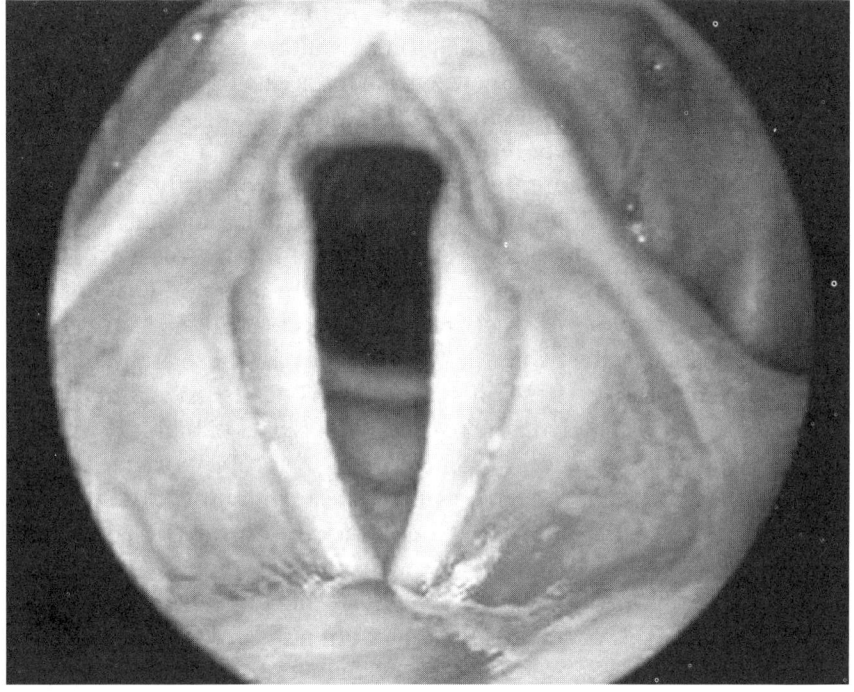

FIG. 14.1. Breath (Nil phonation), during aspiration in the syllable [pʰə].

voice proposed by Hollien (1972) and adopted by Laver (1980, p. 95) is *modal voice.*

Modal voice is widely accepted to be produced through the vibration of the vocal folds, which creates a pulsed output, the frequency of which is the interactive product of muscular and aerodynamic factors. In the aerodynamic-myoelastic model of phonation (Laver, 1980, pp. 95–96), the vocal folds are adducted at their vocal processes, leaving enough space for the pulmonic egressive airstream to pass through the narrowed glottis, accelerating the airstream and causing a drop in air pressure between the folds as a result of the Bernoulli effect, sucking the folds together to initiate the vibratory cycle of closing and opening. The myodynamic components involved in the adduction of the vocal processes of the arytenoids, thereby setting the vocal folds in place medially, are described in detail by Hillel (2001), who finds that minimal but optimal contraction in the interarytenoid muscles is usually sufficient to sustain the approximation of the vocal folds brought about by the initial contraction of the primary adductor muscles. Following aerodynamic theory, the closure of the glottis resulting from the initiation of air flow through the approximated vocal folds causes an increase in air pressure subglottally which rapidly overcomes the myoelastic pressure holding the folds shut, whereon they are blown apart, rapidly diminishing subglottal air pressure, leaving a pressure drop at the glottal borders, and sucking the folds back together again to begin a second cycle. The liminal pressure drop across the glottis in modal voice, according to Catford (1964, p. 31), is of the order of 3 cm of water. Rates of flow vary according to types of voice 'registers,' from about 5 cl/s to a maximum of 23 cl/s for chest voice at 100 Hz. Because these are mean flow rates, rates in excess of these must occur, and because the glottal area is small, the general aerodynamic picture is of a series of high-velocity jets shot into the pharynx. Laver (1994, pp. 193–194) reports that the recurring phonatory cycle for the average adult male is about 120 Hz, within a range of 50 to 250 Hz, and about 220 Hz for the average female, within a range of 120 to 480 Hz. Inverse flow (ingressive voice) is less efficient aerodynamically, producing an irregular effect (Catford, 1968, pp. 318–319), but does occur in speech, essentially paralinguistically. The distinction between sounds made with voice and those made with breath appears to be universal among the world's languages. The voiced glottal state in an initial vowel is illustrated in Fig. 14.2.

PREPHONATION

The articulatory stricture of an oral stop has traditionally been divided into three phases: (a) the closing (or onset) phase; (b) the stricture (or closure) phase, and (c) the release (or offset) phase. Perhaps the best early European descriptions of these three phases were those of Ellis (1874) and Sweet (1877) in the 19th century. They called the three phases the on-glide, the consonant itself, and the off-glide. Abercrombie (1967, p. 140) and Laver (1994, p. 133) give good descriptions of the three phases of a stop. Laver clearly describes the overlap phase between the release (or offset phase) of an initial consonant and the onset phase of a following vowel.

Sweet (1877, p. 74) stated that in the production of a voiceless (unaspirated) stop with voiced offglide, 'in (k[ʌ]a), as in (ga–), the glottis is in the position for voice during the stop, but without any air being forced through it, and consequently the stop is inaudible as in

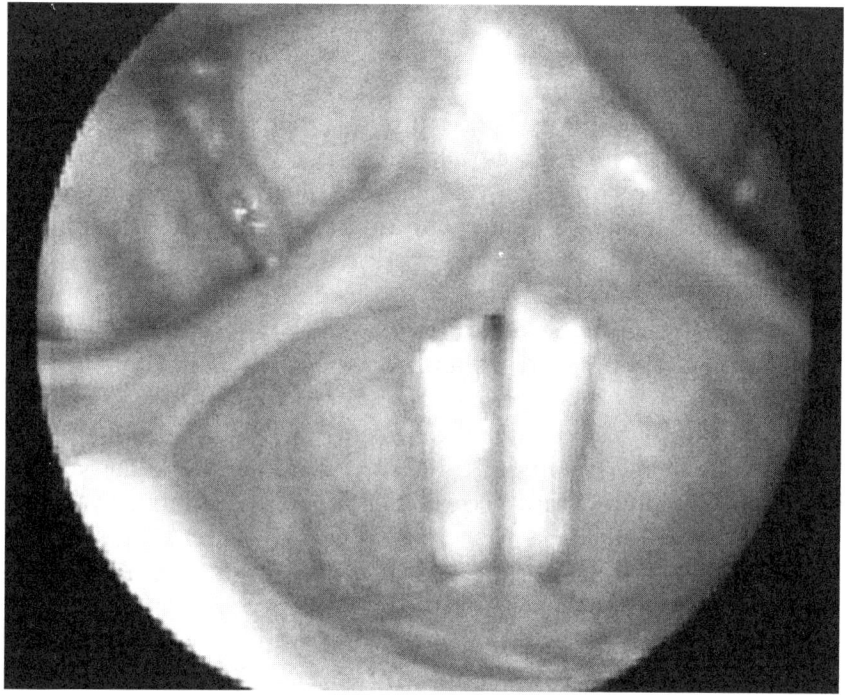

FIG. 14.2. Modal voice, during the middle of the vowel [ə].

the case of (k), but voice begins the moment the stop is loosened, and the glide is therefore voiced.' In English dialects, initial stops written 'b, d, g' are usually pronounced phonetically as partially voiced [b̥, d̥, g̊], and in a few dialects of English, initial stops written 'b, d, g' are pronounced phonetically as voiceless unaspirated stops [p, t, k]. Anyone unaware of these facts would find Sweet's statement, 'k[ʌ]a as in (ga–),' very confusing. However, in Ellis (1874, pp. 1097, 1111), and in his quote in Sweet (1877, p. 75 fn.), he considered initial 'g' as in [ga] to be fully voiced with a voiced off-glide, initial voiceless unaspirated 'k' as in [ka] to be voiceless with a voiced off-glide, and initial aspirated 'k' as in [kha] to be voiceless with a voiceless (breath) off-glide.

Unfortunately, since Ellis and Sweet, the state of the glottis during the articulatory stricture phase of initial voiceless unaspirated oral stops has been frequently confused with either a breathed /brɛθt/ state of the glottis or a complete glottal closure. Harris (1987, pp. 54–56)

used to call it a weak glottal closure or a loosely closed glottis, implying that the glottis was neither completely adducted nor widely abducted. Grammont (1933, pp. 40–41) stated that the state of the glottis for
initial voiceless unaspirated oral stops in French is completely closed.
It is not clear if he meant completely closed like a glottal stop or that
the vocal folds are simply drawn together. Catford (1964, 1968) makes
no specific mention of the state of the glottis for voiceless unaspirated
oral stops and affricates. However, Catford (2001, p. 56), quoting Harris (1999), calls that state of the glottis 'prephonation.'

Acoustic studies by Lisker and Abramson (1964, 1970), following
in the articulatory phonetic tradition of the onglides and offglides of
Ellis and Sweet, have concentrated on the stricture release phase of
initial oral stops and the closing (or onset) phase of the following
voiced vowel. The results of their voice onset time (VOT) studies
have added an important acoustic dimension to the study of the
overlapping stricture release phase of oral stops and the stricture
closing (or onset) phase of following voiced vowels. The results concerning voiceless oral stops point to a direct correlation between the
degree of opening of both the glottis and arytenoids and the amount
of positive VOT lag. The wider open they are, the longer the VOT lag.

In Catford (1977), voiceless unaspirated stops and affricates are
said to have a narrowed although not completely closed glottis that
is restricted in cross-sectional area. Neither Catford's nil phonation
nor his unphonated state of the glottis is appropriate for describing
the state of the glottis for voiceless unaspirated oral stops. Laryngeal observations of the state of the glottis during the articulatory
stricture phase of initial unaspirated oral stops and affricates by
Harris (1999) indicate a state of the glottis different from both nil
phonation and unphonated, referred to as 'prephonation.' Prephonation, as distinct from other voiceless states of the glottis such
as breath, is made with the arytenoid cartilages adducted as for
modal voice, but the vocal folds form a narrowed convex–convex
opening medially in the glottis during which there is presumably
insufficient subglottal air pressure to initiate airflow through the
partially open glottis throughout the closure phase of oral
articulatory stricture. The view of the larynx in Fig. 14.3 shows the
prephonation state of the glottis during [p] oral closure. Our definition of this state of the glottis is a confirmation of Sweet's (1877)
description. Our research has also shown that in North American
English and in Thai, this state of the glottis is one that can precede
an initial vowel in modal voice that is not heavily stressed and does

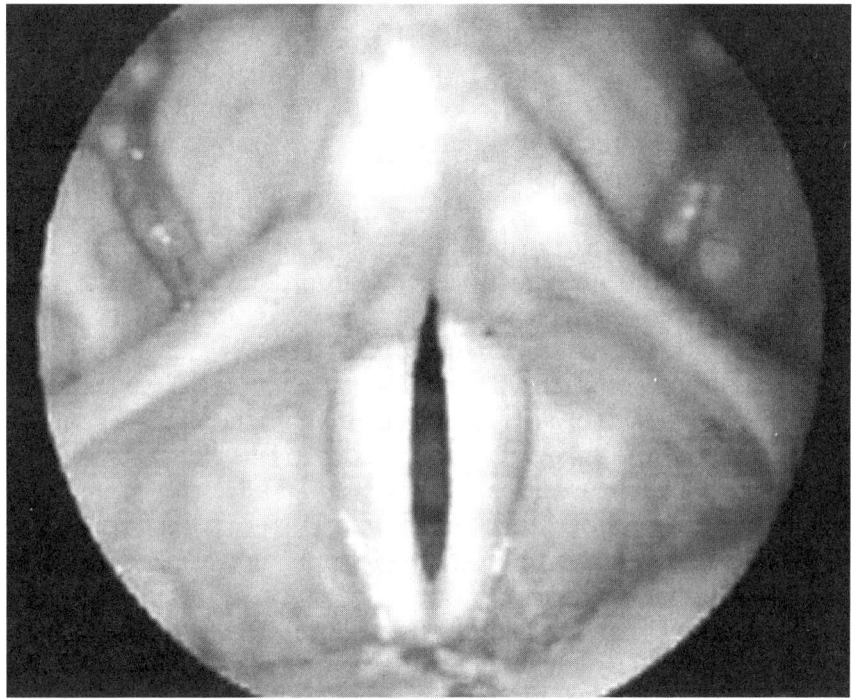

FIG. 14.3. Prephonation, during the stop in unaspirated [pə].

not have a glottal stop before it. We propose that the basic states of the glottis be expanded to include the prephonation state of the glottis used in voiceless unaspirated oral stops and affricates.

UNPHONATED

Glottal Stop

Holder (1669, pp. 60, 72) defined glottal stop as 'a stop made by closing the larynx.' Bell (1867, pp. 46, 60) defined glottal stop as a glottal catch made with the glottis closed and a catch of the breath as in a cough, although he states that the linguistic effect of glottal stop is softer than in a cough. Sweet (1877, pp. 6–7) also called glottal stop a glottal catch and defined it as a sudden opening or closing of the glottis, citing the same example of a glottal catch as in an ordinary cough. Noël–Armfield (1931, p. 107), Heffner (1950, p. 125), and Jones (1956, p. 19) defined glottal stop as a closure and opening of the glottis. Jones added that the glottis must be tightly closed. Ladefoged (1975, p. 46, 1982, p. 50) refers to a glottal stop being made by holding the vocal cords tightly together, also suggesting that glottal stops occur in coughs. Laver (1994, pp. 187–188, 206) defines glottal stop as a maintained complete glottal closure.

Some early visual images of the vocal folds such as the drawings made by A. K. Maxwell from the vocal cords of Stephen Jones of the Phonetics Laboratory, University College London, showed the basic states of the glottis for breath, voice, whisper, and what was called a vigorous glottal stop. The glottal stop that occurs in a cough was called an exaggerated form of glottal stop. The works of both Westermann and Ward (1933, pp. 52–53) and Ward (1929, p. 13) contain these drawings made in the 1920s. The drawing of the so-called vigorous glottal stop closely resembles the laryngoscopic visual images of moderate glottal stop in our research (cf. Esling, 1999a, p. 360). Discussions of the role of the ventricular folds in the production of glottal stop can be found in Lindqvist (1969), whereas an argument against Lindqvist's views on glottal stop can be found in Catford (1977, pp. 104–109).

The unphonated state of the glottis has been described by Catford (1990) as appropriate for describing the state of the glottis for glottal stop and the laryngeal closure used in the glottalic pressure initiation phase of an ejective. Catford suggests that in some glottalic airstream initiation, during the unphonated state of the glottis, there may also be 'some secondary sphincteric compression of the pharynx' (1977, p. 68). Our laryngeal observations have shown the complete closure of the glottis for a moderate glottal stop to include not only the complete adduction of the vocal folds but also a partial incomplete adduction of the ventricular folds (Harris, 1999). The partially adducted ventricular folds apparently reinforce the closure of the true vocal folds. There is also a slight constriction of the whole laryngeal vestibule, which is defined as the supraglottal cavity that extends above the vocal folds upward through the aditus laryngis (Zemlin, 1988, pp. 114–115). The vestibule is delineated anteriorly by the epiglottis, posteriorly by the apices of the arytenoid cartilages, and laterally by the aryepiglottic folds. The sphincteric constriction of this supraglottal cavity is on a continuum beginning with a moderate glottal stop and increasing until the aryepiglottic sphincter mechanism achieves complete closure in an epiglottal stop. This laryngeal constrictor mechanism is a basic component of both glottal stop and epiglottal stop, but differing in degree.

In most modern linguistic literature, glottal stop is usually defined simply as a closed glottis or tightly closed glottis without any reference to the ventricular folds, arytenoid cartilages, or supraglottal cavity activities. Our previous laryngoscopic research, however, has shown that deliberately articulated glottal stops which are part of the articulation component have a complete adduction of the vocal folds and a partial adduction of the ventricular folds, and there is often some narrowing of the laryngeal vestibule through its supraglottic laryngeal sphincter mechanism (Esling, 1996; 1999a; Harris, 1999, 2001). A retraction of the epiglottis and tongue root and a raising of the larynx are also viewed as components of the constriction of the whole laryngeal vestibule. We would venture to resolve the issue of the nature of glottal stop by proposing and seeking evidence for a hierarchical continuum of stricture beginning with a slight adduction of the ventricular folds as a minimum requirement for a glottal stop, further constriction of the sphincter mechanism for a moderate glottal stop, and full engagement of the laryngeal sphincter for an epiglottal stop, which Catford (1977, p. 105) termed a *ventricular (plus glottal) stop*. The image in Fig. 14.4 shows a moderate postvocalic glottal stop. We propose that the description of the unphonated state of the glottis accompanying a glottal stop be expanded to include the partial adduction of the ventricular folds reinforcing vocal fold closure and to include slight sphincteric constriction of the vertical epilaryngeal tube or laryngeal vestibule.

Epiglottal Stop

Sapir and Swadesh described the pharyngeals of Ahousaht Nuuchahnulth (Nootka) as 'laryngealized glottals' (1939, pp. 12–13). Jacobsen (1969, pp. 125) and Stonham (1999, p. 10), both citing Sapir's original description, call Nootka / ʕ/ a 'pharyngealized glottal stop.' Hockett identified a 'pharyngeal catch' (as distinct from a continuant) in some dialects of Arabic (1958, p. 66), and Catford has noted a 'pharyngealized glottal stop' or 'strong glottal stop' in languages of the Caucasus, and a 'pharyngeal stop' in Chechen (Catford, 1983, p. 347). Early work by Stephen Jones at University College London (1934) influenced Catford to draw a relation between pharyngeal constriction and the ventricular phonatory setting, which occurs when 'the ventricular bands are brought

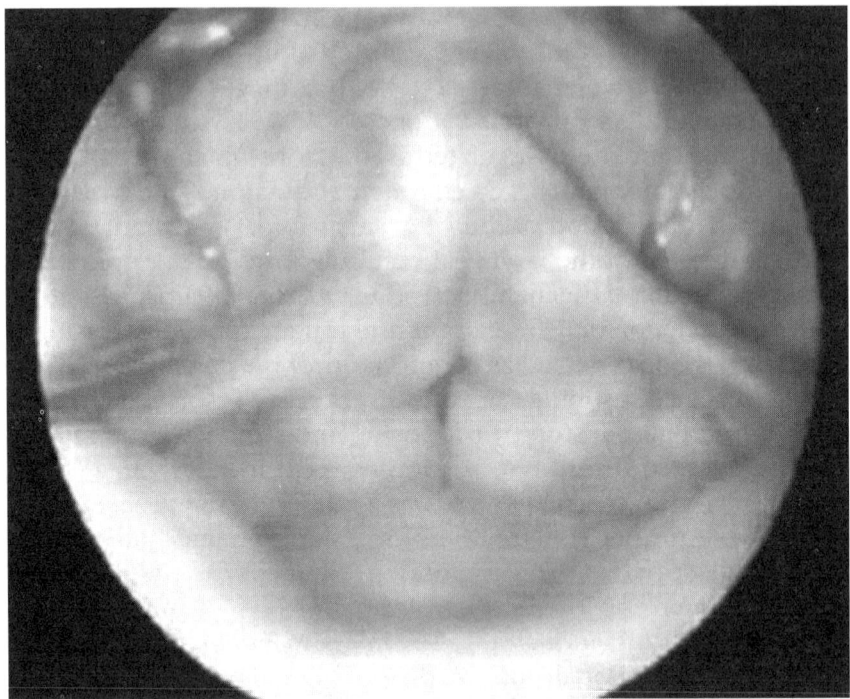

FIG. 14.4. Unphonated: Glottal stop, from the sequence [əʔ].

together... , plus some generalized constriction of the upper larynx and pharynx,' so that 'ventricular or strong glottal stop may be represented by [ʕʔ]' in contrast to [ʔ] (Catford, 1977, p. 163). Gaprindashvili (1966) describes this articulation as a 'pharyngealized glottal stop' (Catford, 1977, p. 163). This strong glottal stop occurs in the Nakh languages and in some Daghestanian languages (Kodzasov, 1987). This sound has been isolated as an 'epiglottal plosive' [ʡ]—inherently voiceless—in the inventory of the International Phonetic Association (1999, pp. ix, 22). Its status in Salish and Wakashan languages has been summarized by Carlson and Esling (2000), Carlson, Esling, and Fraser (2001), and Esling, Fraser, and Harris (in press).

In his 1968 review of articulatory possibilities, Catford advanced the term *'epiglottopharyngeal'* to characterize 'extreme retraction of the tongue, so that the epiglottis approximates to the back wall of the pharynx' (p. 326), but doubted whether a stop articulation could be performed at this location

> since it seems to be impossible to make a perfect hermetic closure between epiglottis and pharynx wall—stop-like sounds produced in this way appear to involve glottal closure as well as epiglottopharyngeal close approximation. However, epiglottopharyngeal *fricative, approximant* and possibly *trill* can be produced. (p. 326)

It should be pointed out that Catford's extensive table of articulatory categories (p. 327) holds open the possibility of epiglottopharyngeal stop and trill (signaled by question marks) in articulatory parallel with fricative and approximant. That a more extreme sound than [ʔ] exists and occurs in phonological contrast to [ʔ] is not controversial. As far as we know, every language said to contain /ʔ/ in its phonological inventory also contains /ʔ/.

In their pioneering applications of laryngoscopic technology, Williams, Farquharson, and Anthony (1975, p. 310) observed a progression of constrictions consisting of 'narrowing of the whole laryngeal vestibule from sphincteric action of the aryepiglottic folds, epiglottis and even the lateral pharyngeal walls.' Roach has observed that 'glottal closure' for certain glottalized consonants 'is in fact made with closure not only of the true vocal folds but also of the false vocal folds and the aryepiglottic folds' (1979, p. 2). Gauffin notes that the protective closure of the larynx is performed by all the sphincter muscles of the larynx to constrict 'larynx tube opening,' and characterizes a glottal stop as a 'reduced protective closure' (1977, p. 308). This very clear reference to a primary anatomical mechanism implies that 'full' protective closure would be associated with an 'extreme' glottal stop, that is, an epiglottal stop.

In 1979, Laufer and Condax used laryngoscopy to observe the activity of the epiglottis in the production of Semitic pharyngeals. They cite and confirm the suspicion of Al–Ani (1970) that Arabic /ʕ/ is sometimes produced as a glide and sometimes as a voiceless stop (Laufer & Condax, 1981, p. 55). They did not observe complete closure between the epiglottis and the pharyngeal wall, but spectrograms showed a voiceless stop and sometimes creak. Laufer and Baer (1988) further demonstrate that pharyngeals /ħ/ and /ʕ/ involve an articulation behind the root of the tongue and between the base of the epiglottis and the top of the arytenoids. Painter (1986, p. 330) describes the components of these physiological 'effort and swallowing gestures' as a sequence of vocal fold adduction, ventricular fold adduction, cuneiform cartilage and aryepiglottic fold approximation, and epiglottis retraction (in conjunction with general tongue retraction). This revised interpretation is consistent with Negus' description of the epiglottis as 'fairly big but degenerate ... because of immobility and lack of function' where 'during swallowing, contraction of the sphincteric muscle fibres contained between the layers of the ary-epiglottic folds closes the aperture of the larynx and prevents inundation' (1949, p. 182). We assume the muscles involved to be initially and primarily the thyroarytenoid muscles.

Ladefoged and Maddieson (1996, p. 37) discuss the many observations of what have been called either 'pharyngeal stops' or 'epiglottal stops' in languages of the world. Catford (1983) conjectured that the 'pharyngeal stop' of Chechen may be produced by the epiglottis as the active articulator folding back and down to meet the arytenoids. Butcher and Ahmad (1987, p. 166) observed that the pharyngeal / ʕ / in Iraqi Arabic sometimes functions as a stop, reporting variable voicing striations in spectrograms. These observations imply some form of what is usually called 'laryngealization,' but which may also be accounted for by trilling occurring at the pharyngeal place of articulation. El–Halees (1985, p. 288) implicates 'a very narrow stricture with the back wall of the pharynx' and illustrates a stop component for / ʕ / without specifying the role of the aryepiglottic folds. Esling (1996) demonstrates that Catford's 'epiglottopharyngeal' category involves the aryepiglottic folds being pulled up and forward underneath the epiglottis as a function of the aryepiglottic laryngeal sphincter mechanism, the third level of closure above the glottis and the ventricular folds, whereby the airway is sealed in an anterior movement against a descending tongue root (Esling, 1999a). As the larynx rises to engage the sphincter, lifting the arytenoids forward to effect an efficient hermetic seal, an epiglottal stop is formed. The result of this action is shown in Fig. 14.5.

FALSETTO

Sweet (1877, p. 3) describes falsetto as the thinnest and shrillest form of 'head' voice or 'thin register,' which he interprets as the vocal folds being brought together only enough 'to enable their edges to vibrate,

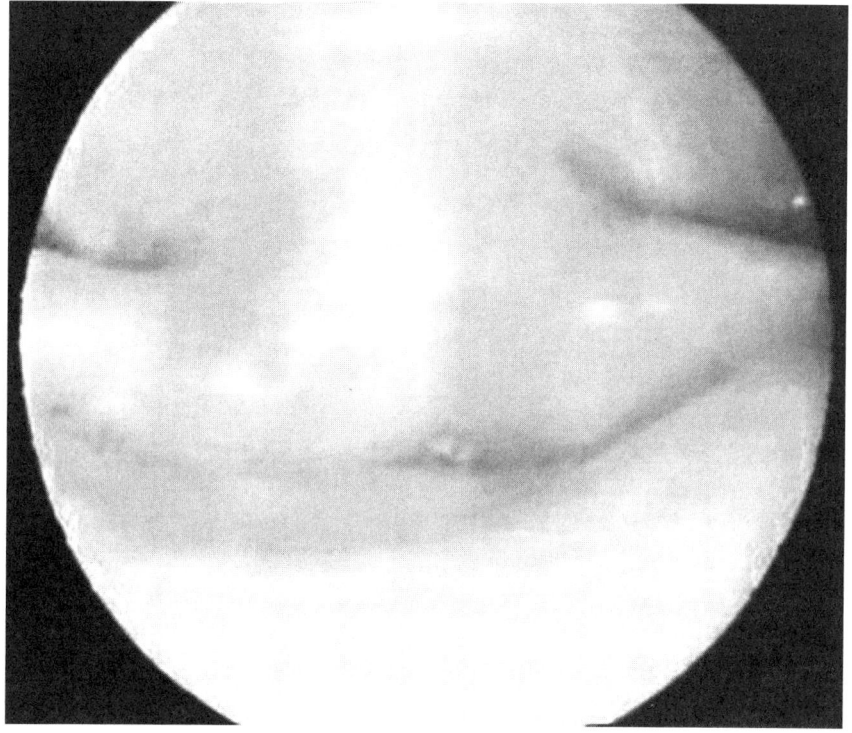

FIG. 14.5. Unphonated: Epiglottal stop, from the sequence [ə?].

without any closure of the glottis.' Laver (1980) reports a wide range of agreement in the literature between 1940 and 1980 in the physiological accounts of the laryngeal mechanisms involving the production of falsetto. The fundamental frequency of falsetto is considerably higher than in modal voice. Hollien and Michel (1968) give the average pitch range of falsetto in the adult male as 275 to 634 Hz, and the average pitch range of modal voice as 94 to 287 Hz. The lower end of the falsetto pitch range overlaps with the high end of the modal range. The vocal folds are adducted and stretched longitudinally so that they are thin at their edges, allowing only a portion to vibrate, whereas the remainder of the length of the vocal folds appears stiff and immobile. Our observations confirm this view. In Fig. 14.6, the vibrating portion of the folds is visible just anterior to the vocal processes. Falsetto is frequently accompanied by a slight breathiness due to the escaping pulmonic airflow through the incompletely closed, nonvibrating portion of the glot-

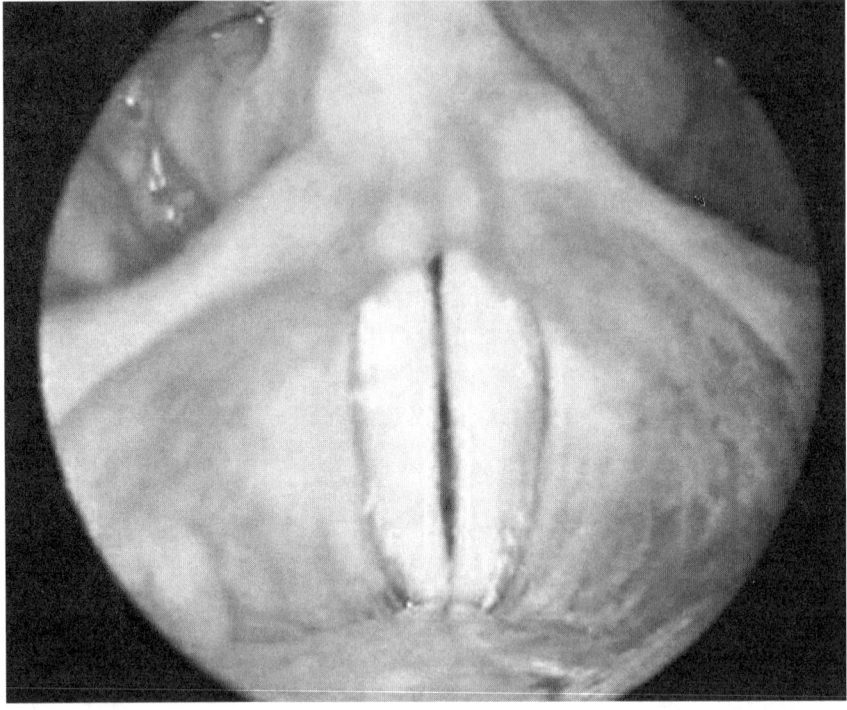

FIG. 14.6. Falsetto, during the middle of the vowel [ə].

tis. As a result of the transglottal leakage, subglottal air pressure is typically lower in falsetto than in modal voice (Laver, 1994, p. 197). Another acoustic characteristic of falsetto is the much steeper slope of the spectrum of the laryngeal waveform for falsetto than for modal voice (Monsen & Engebretson, 1977). Falsetto is not a common linguistic phonation type for languages, but it sometimes has a paralinguistic function. It also appears to occur only on sounds that are voiced. In our articulatory description, falsetto is a glottally adducted state with no supraglottic sphincteric tension.

WHISPER

Laver (1980) reports a lack of controversy in the traditional literature over the physiological description of the 'whisper' state of the glottis. The common form of whisper referred to by Laver is characterized by a triangular opening of the cartilaginous glottis which makes up about a third of the length of the full glottis. This shape has often been referred to as 'an inverted letter Y' (Luchsinger & Arnold, 1965, p. 119). Their reference is to earlier mirror-image views of the glottis with the arytenoids at the bottom. The vocal folds in the ligamental glottis remain slightly abducted. The narrowing of the glottal passage impeding the air flowing through the intercartilaginous gap is said to produce the characteristic soft hissing noise of whisper. Turbulent aperiodic airflow is the major source of what Catford (1977) identifies as a rich hushing sound. The glottal opening for whisper is typically reported to be less than 25% of maximal glottal opening (Catford, 1964, p. 31; 1968, p. 319; 1977, p. 100). As the air flows past the edges of the open cartilaginous glottis, the characteristic whisper sound is produced by 'eddies generated by friction of the air in and above the larynx' (van den Berg, 1968, p. 297). Catford (1964) describes the aerodynamic and acoustic properties of whisper in the following terms. The critical airflow rate is about 2.5 cl/s with an estimated velocity of about 1900 cm/s. The maximum rate of flow is about 500 cl/s. The flow is turbulent with the projection of a high-velocity jet airstream into the pharynx. The acoustic spectrum is said to be similar to breath but with a concentration of acoustic energy into formant-like bands.

Traditionally, other less common types of whisper are also discussed in the literature. Solomon, McCall, Trosset, and Gray (1989) identified three different vocal fold configurations during whisper from 10 videotaped subjects: an 'inverted Y,' an 'inverted V,' and bowing of the anterior glottis. The 'V' shape is the second most common type of whisper referred to in the literature and is usually called soft or weak whisper (Laver, 1980, p. 121). It includes the ligamental as well as the cartilaginous portion of the glottis in the 'V' shape. We assume that weak whisper is more constricted than breath—intermediate between breath and the common form of whisper. Laver cites Zemlin (1964, p. 169) and Heffner (1950, p. 20) in formulating the view that whisper implies adduction of the vocal processes of the arytenoids for medial compression but relaxation of the interarytenoid muscles to maintain intercartilaginous opening. All previous descriptions concentrate on the glottis.

We depart from the traditional literature by defining whisper as a sphinctered laryngeal state. Unlike plain breath, defined at the glottis, the increased turbulence and friction generated in whisper derive not only from the glottal source but in larger measure from the narrowed channel formed by the constriction of the aryepiglottic sphincter. Recent work on the behaviour of voiceless pharyngeals demonstrates the role that the aryepiglottic folds play in the definition of the supraglottic space for the channeling of airflow (Esling, 1999b). Two additional types of whisper are mentioned by Catford (1964): (a) arytenoidal whisper, which he assumes to have a very narrow inter-cartilaginous channel; and (b) ventricular whisper, which implies an even greater narrowing over the glottis. To explain these variations, we take the view that, in addition to aryepiglottic sphincter constriction, larynx height and rate of airflow contribute to the perception of differences in whisper. Whatever these additional adjustments, the cardinal state of whisper, illustrated with supraglottic sphincteric constriction in Fig. 14.7, must generate greater noise than breath. In a study of the preservation of tone in whispered Chinese, Gao (2002) demonstrates the balance between laryngeal sphinctering, pharynx cavity resonance, and airflow in the control of amplitude and of second formant frequency (F2) in whispered tones. In whispered speech, both devoiced

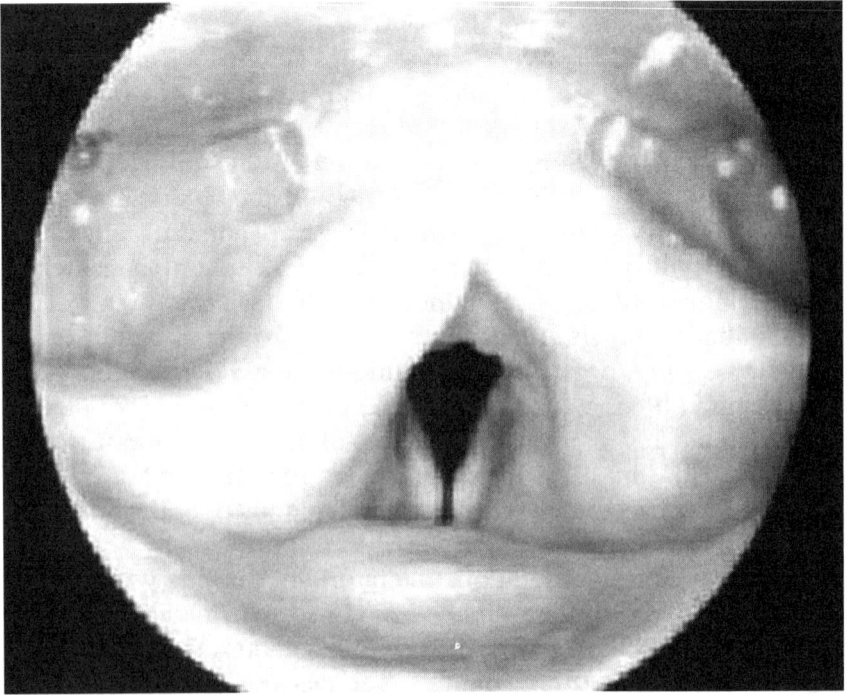

FIG. 14.7. Whisper, during the middle of the vowel [ə].

vowels and voiceless segments such as [h] can be expected to have greater sphincteric turbulence than in the state of breath for plain [h], and the degree of the whispered state can increase depending on prosodic context. In this sense, because the sphincter is essentially the mechanism of the pharyngeal articulator (Esling, 1999b), it could be said that a strongly whispered [h] has the same configurational attributes as a voiceless pharyngeal fricative [ħ] (Esling, 2002).

WHISPERY VOICE

Bell's category of 'whisper and voice heard simultaneously,' which he called 'vocal murmur' (1867, p. 46), persists throughout the literature as 'whispery voice.' Catford's (1964, p. 32) definition— 'whisper + voice: glottis narrowed as for whisper: vocal folds vibrating, but not occluding'—is incorporated in Laver's (1980) voice quality taxonomy. Whisper is a key combinatory element as a noise-producing source in several compound phonation types—the essential characteristic being the inherent degree of constriction required to produce turbulent airflow. Catford (1977, pp. 99, 101) locates the noise-generating source posteriorly between the arytenoid cartilages; but he allows for a second variety of whispery voice for which the location of the opening is less specific and the vocal folds never close completely. He measures average flow from 300 to 400 cm³/s. Although breathiness, due to its greater openness and higher rate of flow, is clearly limited in its combinatory possibilities, whisperiness, as Laver elaborates, combines freely with a range of other phonatory qualities, causing us to postulate that its production mechanism is separate from the glottal mechanism that controls adduction and abduction. Fig. 14.8 illustrates the similarity in the sphinctered posture of the aryepiglottic folds between whisper and whispery voice. In both cases, the cuneiform cartilages of the aryepiglottic folds are pressed tightly against the base of the epiglottis, forming the epilaryngeal vestibule into a narrowed channel with the vertical tube characteristics necessary for increasingly turbulent, noisy airflow.

BREATHY VOICE

Breathy voice is defined by Catford (1964, p. 32) as 'breath + voice: glottis relatively wide open: turbulent airflow as for 'breath' plus vibration of vocal folds.' Two familiar metaphors from Catford's definition are the 'sigh-like' quality and that the vocal folds 'flap in the

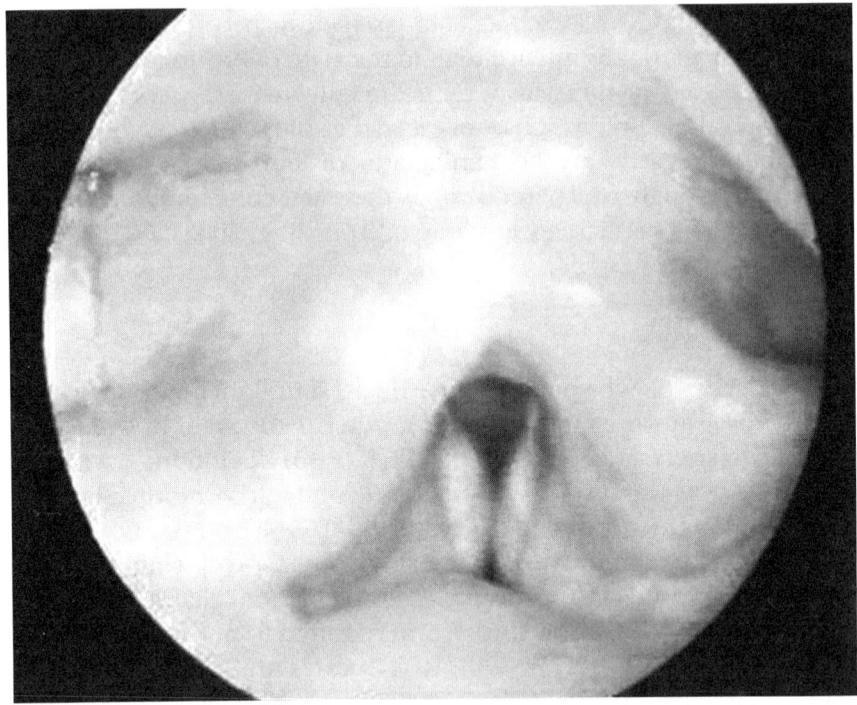

FIG. 14.8. Whispery voice, during the middle of the vowel [ə].

breeze.' Flow is estimated at 900 to 1000 cm³/s, and the glottis is 'not narrowed enough to produce whisper' (Catford, 1977, p. 101). This distinction is crucial, as it implies that breath differs auditorily from whisper as breathy voice differs from whispery voice. This implies in turn that the physiological mechanism responsible for breath and for breathy voice differs in some key respect from the narrowing mechanism required for whisper and for whispery voice. Laver (1980, pp. 132–133) considered that speakers with breathy voices normally have rates of flow lower than Catford's estimates, or at least at the low end of Catford's range, although openness and flow will still be greater than in a whispery voice. Abercrombie (1967, pp. 100–101) pointed out that 'breathy phonation' contrasts maximally with 'tight phonation,' reminding us that the auditory identification of such contrasts is motivated by phonological oppositions in register observed in languages such as Cambodian (Khmer) or Gujarati. Jalapa Mazatec contrasts breathy voice, modal voice, and creaky voice (Ladefoged, Maddieson, &

Jackson, 1988). The many languages of India that have so-called 'voiced-aspirated' (murmured) stops are usually described as being followed by vocalization with breathy voice (Abercrombie, 1967, p. 149; Ladefoged & Maddieson, 1996, pp. 58–62), and the usual designation for murmur in such cases is the voiced glottal fricative [ɦ] or a breathy-voiced diacritic under the vowel [a̤]. It is equally possible for this phonological contrast to be realized phonetically with whispery voice.

Laver (1980, p. 31) makes the crucial observation that breathy voice and lowered larynx are auditorily and physiologically related. The lowering of the larynx and concomitant opening of the airway oppose physiologically the raising of the larynx and concomitant 'tight' phonation which, along with tongue retraction, define the action of the laryngeal sphincter (Esling, 1996, 1999a). Laver (1980, p. 133), citing Fairbanks (1960, p. 179), also points out the relation between breathy voice and low pitch—a parallel which will be of significance in surveying the relation between degrees of harsh voice and pitch. While reviewing the varied and sometimes interchangeable use of the terms *breathy voice* and *whispery voice,* Laver makes it clear that they are part of an auditory continuum. At the same time, Laver ascribes the physiological distinction between them to the presence of increasing medial compression in whispery voice, confining 'the whisper-producing channel ... to the cartilaginous glottis' (1980, p. 134). Based on the relation shown between tightening the airway, raising the larynx, and aryepiglottic sphinctering (Esling, 1999a), we take the view that increasing whisperiness is a function of the laryngeal constrictor mechanism. In our revised interpretation, it is not medial compression at the level of the glottis that accounts for the whisper-producing channel but the tight engagement of the aryepiglottic sphincter superior to the glottis. The difference between the presence and the absence of sphincteric channeling can be seen in the contrast between Fig. 14.8 and Fig. 14.9.

CREAKY VOICE

Creaky voice, also called 'glottal fry' or 'vocal fry,' has long been associated with low pitch (slow vibration) in particular accents (Abercrombie, 1967, p. 101). Zemlin (1968, p. 191) identifies the 'thyromuscularis portion of the thyroarytenoid muscle' as the main mechanism 'to draw the arytenoid cartilage forward, toward the

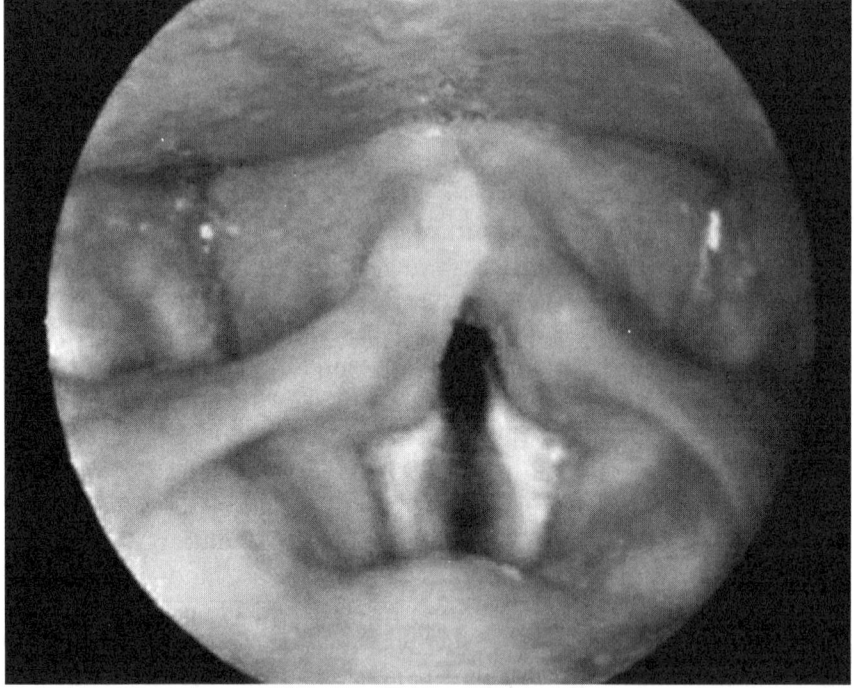

FIG. 14.9. Breathy voice, during the middle of the vowel [ə].

thyroid, and thus shorten and relax the folds.' This results in a pattern where 'the closed phase occupies about 90 per cent of the vibratory cycle, and the opening and closing phases combined occupy about 10 per cent of the cycle' (Zemlin, 1968, p. 197). Although falsetto occupies the highest pitch levels and modal voice occupies mid-pitch range, the literature summarized by Laver (1980, p. 122) agrees that creaky phonation occupies the range below modal voice, typically below 100 Hz. Hollien, Moore, Wendahl, and Michel (1966, p. 247) remarked on the participation of the ventricular folds and their possible influence on the vibrating mass. Hollien (1972, p. 328) illustrated very clearly in a lamingram that vertical compression of the vocal folds and the ventricular folds occurs in creaky voice. Our explanation that the supraglottic space is also reduced as a function of the laryngeal constrictor mechanism and that the laryngeal structures are likely to be elevated during creaky voice is also borne out by his laminagram. Catford's (1964, pp. 32–33) observation that only the ligamental glottis is involved is consistent with Zemlin's physiological description of arytenoid fronting and with Catford's own categories 'ligamental' and 'arytenoidal,' although his table does not admit the possibility that creak is 'ventricular.' All three categories imply an engagement of the aryepiglottic sphincter mechanism, but it is reasonable to exclude creak from the 'ventricular' category, which would probably entail stretching of the vocal folds to achieve higher pitch. The action of the aryepiglottic folds, as in the case of whisper, is a salient feature of the images of creaky voice depicted in Esling (1984), but to the point that the glottis itself is almost completely obscured. The extreme degree of sphinctering required for creakiness is illustrated in Fig. 14.10. Instead of focusing attention only on the size and shape of the glottal opening, it is important to concentrate on the structures immediately superior to the glottis, which have an indirect effect on glottal shape and a direct effect on the airstream. The role of the aryepiglottic constriction mechanism in producing

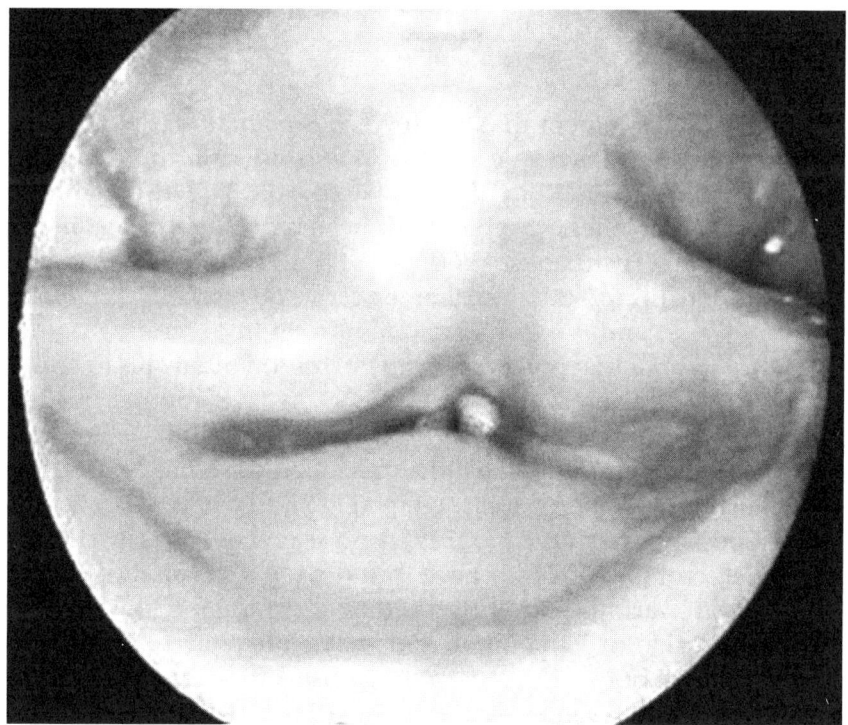

FIG. 14.10. Creaky voice, during the middle of the vowel [ə].

glottal stop and pharyngeal or epiglottal articulations is related to the production of creaky phonation, as often observed when creakiness precedes or follows glottal stop arrest of the airstream.

It should be pointed out that a single isolated burst or set of aperiodic bursts, identified as simple 'creak' phonation in the literature (Catford, 1964, p. 32; Laver, 1980), may differ in timing from creaky voice but not in laryngeal configuration. The pulses of creak that emanate from a tightly constricted sphincter mechanism, as in proximity to glottal closure, are interpreted as creaky voice when a number of them occur in succession. In this broad interpretation, the creaky voice state of the glottis could also be called 'creaky' or 'creakiness.' The combination of a voiceless state (creak) and a voiced state (creaky voice) into one configurational category emphasizes the separation that we believe needs to be made between the glottal control of voicing and the epilaryngeal (sphincteric) control of constriction over the glottis.

HARSH VOICE

There is wide agreement that harsh voice is a function of aperiodic irregularities in the acoustic waveform and noise in the spectrum (Laver, 1980, p. 127). 'Rough' and 'hoarse' voice are also common terms, with hoarseness combining the characteristics of harshness and breathiness (Fairbanks, 1960, pp. 171, 182–183). Kreiman and Garrett (2000, pp. 77–80) note that the terms *hoarseness, harshness* and *roughness,* and *breathiness* are common in describing pathological voices, but that perceptual categorization often fails to correlate with physical measures. Laver (1980, p. 128) points out the anatomical relation between jaw opening and tongue backing and harshness; open vowels being judged as more harsh than close vowels. Acoustic correlates of aperiodicity (e.g., jitter) have been widely researched, but Laver (1980, p. 129) reports that the one physiological correlate of harshness to have found wide agreement is 'laryngeal tension.' Various authors quoted by Laver identify this tension with 'the vocal folds,' 'the throat and neck,' 'the pharynx,' and even with 'the whole body.' The most telling observation is cited by Laver (1980, p. 129) from Van Riper and Irwin (1958); "They quote Russell (1936), to the effect that 'as the voice begins to become strident and blatant, ones sees the red-surfaced muscles which lie above the vocal cords begin to form a tense channel'." We interpret this effect to refer to the action of the laryngeal sphincter. With respect to vibratory frequencies, Van Riper and Irwin (1958, p. 232) report that 'most harsh voices are relatively low in pitch.'

Considering that the mechanism for low pitch invokes the thyroarytenoid muscles for arytenoid fronting (as described for creaky voice) and that tongue retraction as implicated in the correlation of open vowels with harshness is a component of efficient laryngeal constriction, these attributes of harsh voice conform very well with observations of the behaviour of the laryngeal sphincter in our recent research. Adding Abercrombie's (1967) formulation of 'tight phonation' to the equation—allowing little air to escape, in opposition to breathiness (p. 93)—and 'cartilage glottis firmly closed, the rest of the glottis in vibration, and constriction of the upper parts of the larynx' (pp. 100–101)—localizes the mechanism for harsh voice above the glottis to the aryepiglottic sphinctering mechanism for channeling airflow, as in whisperiness, and for introducing tension to the larynx as a whole. It can therefore be hypothesized that the noisy flow generated during harsh voice as well as the irregular periodicity ascribed to various sorts of harsh or hoarse voice can be isolated within the channel formed by the laryngeal sphincter and at its aryepiglottic upper borders. In our revised interpretation, whisperiness as a glottal state and not breathiness is associated articulatorily with harshness. This sphincteric relation between whisperiness and harshness confirms Laver's original compatibility principle (1980, pp. 19–20) in articulatory terms. We speculate that the distinction between creaky voice and harsh voice, both a function of sphincteric constriction, can be attributed either to differences in adjustments of the glottal mechanism at the vocal folds relative to adjustments of the laryngeal sphincter mechanism above it or to varying degrees of contraction in different parts of the thyroarytenoid muscles.

It has been shown that many pitch dependencies exist within the broad terminology of the taxonomy for voice quality (Esling, Heap, Snell, & Dickson, 1994), and it appears that harshness is another complex area of the descriptive scheme which probably deserves to be differentiated by pitch level for effective analysis. One category of 'extreme' harsh voice which may benefit from an elucidation of pitch parameters is what has been called 'ventricular voice' (Laver, 1980, p. 130). Laver identifies adductive tension and medial compression as properties of harsh voice but dismisses longitudinal tension because pitch in harsh voice is not usually high. As the auditory quality previously labeled 'ventricular voice' occupies a higher pitch range than less extreme harsh voice, then longitudinal tension plays a role in its production. Because Laver associates the auditory quality known as 'seal voice'—'very severe compressive effort of the whole larynx' (1980, p. 139)—with 'ventricular falsetto,' there is good reason to investigate the pitch factor in various degrees of 'tight phonation.'

Low Pitch

We propose three categories of harsh voice, based on pitch levels. Harsh voice at low pitch may be difficult to separate auditorily from aspects of creakiness because of the slow speed of vocal fold vibration. To distinguish glottal vibration from a patently harsh vibratory source, the vibrating aryepiglottic folds at the upper border of the laryngeal sphincter are taken as a clear source of harshness at pitches even lower than glottal phonation. Aryepiglottic trilling has been shown to contribute a 50 to 60 Hz signal to the spectrum, at about half the rate of glottal vibration (Esling & Edmondson, 2002). When pitch is low, the laryngeal sphincter is at least moderately engaged, and aryepiglottic trilling is predisposed to occur. When sphincteric constriction and airflow are sufficient to induce trilling, the competing secondary source accounts for the enhanced irregularity or harshness of phonatory quality. In the phonation produced in Fig. 14.11, there are two periodic signals generated, one at a frequency of 110 to 120 Hz and another at a frequency of 50 to 60 Hz.

Mid Pitch

Harshness at mid-pitch range is considered the addition of an irregular component to modal voice. The importance of pitch in qualifying auditory labels for voice qualities has been demonstrated for raised and lowered larynx height settings (Esling et al., 1994). The relevance of pitch to ostensibly intrinsic glottal settings is that antero-posterior stretching of the vocal folds caused by cricothyroid contraction opposes antagonistically the thyroarytenoid contraction that engages

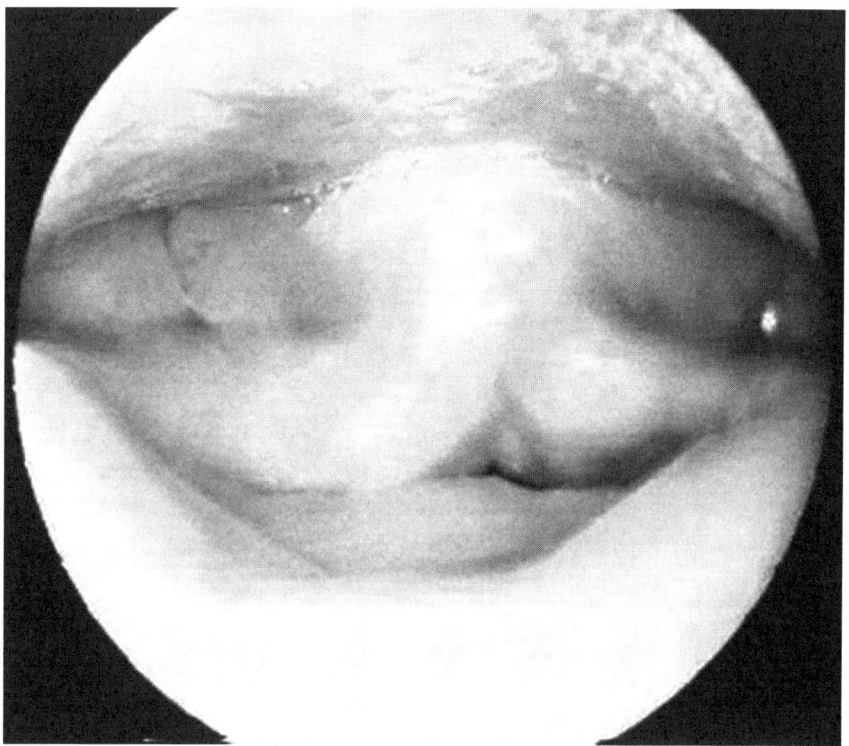

FIG. 14.11. Harsh voice: Low pitch (aryepiglottic trilling).

the sphincter for whispery, creaky, and harsh modes. As pitch increases, the tension in this opposition increases, altering the physical shape of the epilaryngeal tube and the amount of air pressure required to induce vibration. The ability to channel the airstream through a tightly compressed sphincter is compromised as pitch increases, and the epilaryngeal tube is pulled open in a posterior direction. This reduces the possibility of aryepiglottic trilling, unless airflow is increased substantially, and changes the relation between glottal vibration and supraglottic modification of the airstream. Fig. 14.12 shows the slightly opened sphincter at mid-pitch range at a frequency of 100 Hz during the production of auditorily harsh voice. It is reasonable to expect that irregularities of frequency and amplitude in the signal are related to the vibratory and resonance characteristics of the changing shape of the epilaryngeal tube.

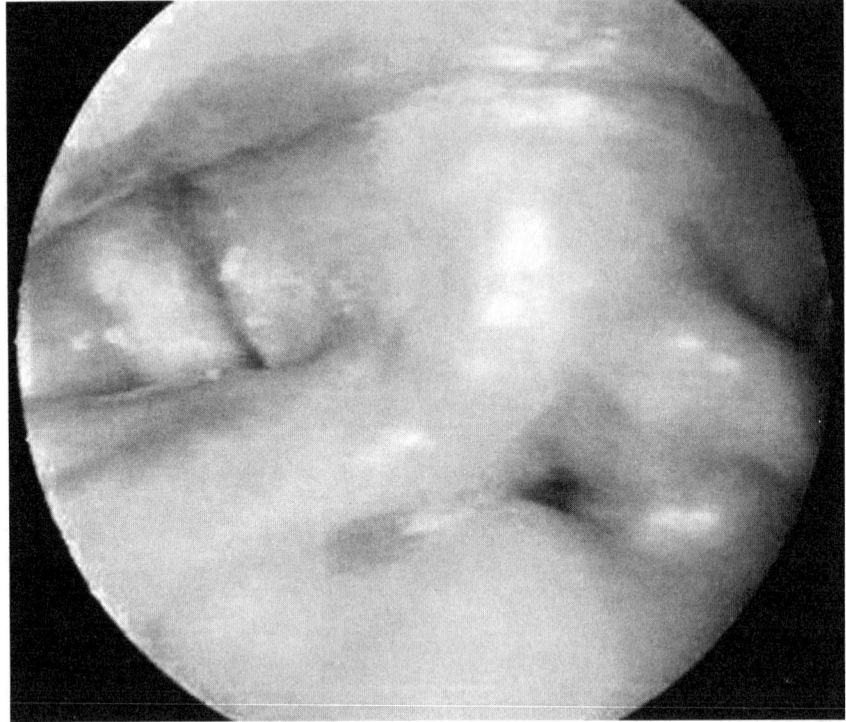

FIG. 14.12. Harsh voice: Mid pitch.

High Pitch

The auditory quality traditionally referred to as 'ventricular voice,' 'extremely harsh voice' (Esling, 1994), or 'pressed voice' (Painter, 1986) is reinterpreted as harsh voice with high pitch. As the vocal folds stretch, vibratory characteristics of falsetto are induced at the same time that constrictive thyroarytenoid tension increases antagonistically. The product is a tightened configuration resembling glottal stop in shape but with increased airflow producing vibration through stretched vocal folds and compressed ventricular folds. The ventricular folds do not actually vibrate in this mode, which is why the label 'ventricular voice' is less appropriate here than in the case of some pathological voice types where the ventricular folds do vibrate. The essence of this state of the glottis is the falsetto-like high pitch that it generates in combination with the irregular waveform related to the sphincteric tension in the immediately supraglottic structures. Fig. 14.13 shows this mode at a frequency of 200 Hz. The extreme version of this mode, 'seal voice' (Laver, 1980, p. 139), generates even higher pitches while under tight sphincteric control. The effect is even more like falsetto, combined with a harsh component as a function of supraglottic compression. We assess its production to be the result of antero-posterior tension of the cricothyroid mechanism acting on the vocal folds at the glottis and, simultaneously, of sphincteric constriction of the thyroarytenoid mechanism acting on the epilaryngeal aryepiglottic folds.

SUMMARY

States of the glottis, therefore, can involve two main levels of laryngeal operation: the glottal level, for adduction, abduction, and stretching, as in prephonation, voice, breath, breathy, or falsetto modes; and the

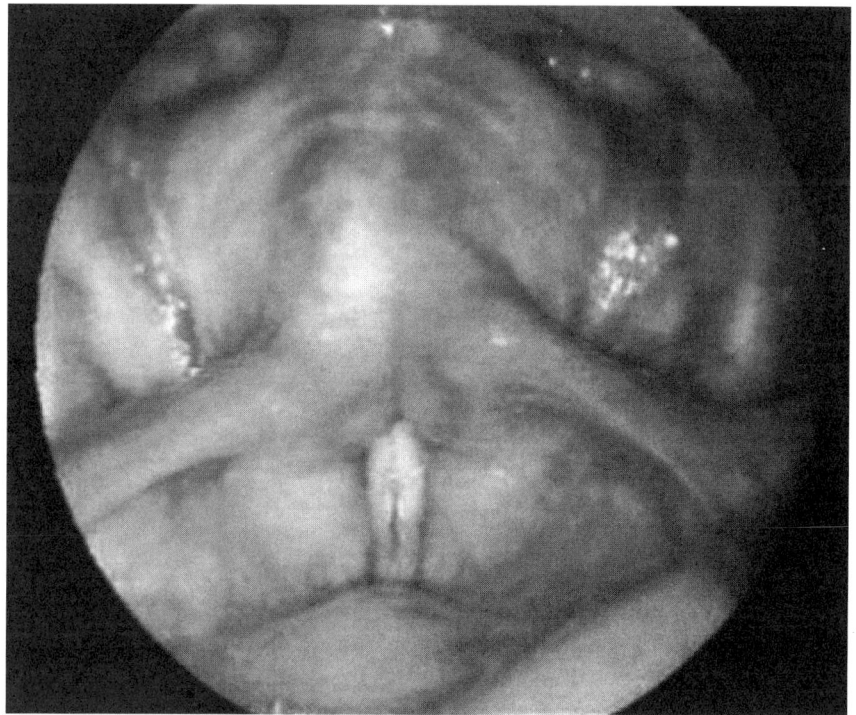

FIG. 14.13. Harsh voice: High pitch. The auditory quality referred to as 'ventricular voice' in many earlier formulations (Esling, 1994; Laver, 1980).

aryepiglottic level, for laryngeal constriction, as in unphonated laryngeal stops, whisper, whispery, creaky, or harsh modes. Prephonation, voice, and falsetto are adducted glottally, but breath is abducted. Breathy voice is partially adducted (and partially open) at the glottis. Prephonation, voice, breath, breathy voice, and falsetto are all open epilaryngeally with no constriction. Glottal stop and epiglottal stop are adducted glottally, with increasing degrees of aryepiglottic constriction. Whisper is abducted glottally, like breath, but constricted aryepiglottally. Whispery voice is partially adducted glottally, like breathy voice, but constricted aryepiglottally. Creaky and harsh phonation require laryngeal constriction and, at low pitch, involve slow vibration of the vocal folds or of the aryepiglottic folds, respectively; but increasing stretching at the glottal level raises pitch, resulting in a stretched adducted glottis together with aryepiglottic constriction. States of the glottis are, therefore, more properly termed 'laryngeal states' rather than states of the glottal level alone.

ACKNOWLEDGMENTS

The equipment and operating expenses for laryngoscopic observation and filming of the larynx and pharynx were made possible through Research Grants 410–93–0539 and 410–2000–0901 from the Social Sciences and Humanities Research Council of Canada to the University of Victoria. We acknowledge the cooperation of Craig Dickson and STR–SpeechTech Ltd. in making their facilities available for laryngoscopic filming. The technical image-processing assistance of Greg Newton is greatly appreciated, as is the collaboration of Dr. Michael Mawdsley, the attending physician.

AUTHORS' NOTE

A preliminary presentation of this research was made at the 3rd International Conference on Voice Physiology and Biomechanics in Denver, CO, in September 2002. Full-motion videos of the illustrations of the states of the glottis represented in Figures 14.1 through 14.13 can be viewed on the University of Victoria Web site: http://www.uvic.ca/ling/research/phonetics

REFERENCES

Abercrombie, D. (1967). *Elements of general phonetics.* Edinburgh, Scotland: Edinburgh University Press.

Al–Ani, S. H. (1970). *Arabic phonology: An acoustical and physiological investigation (Janua Linguarum, 61).* The Hague, Netherlands: Mouton.

Bell, A. M. (1867). *Visible speech: The science of universal alphabetics.* London: Simpkin, Marshall & Co.

Butcher, A., & Ahmad, K. (1987). Some acoustic and aerodynamic characteristics of pharyngeal consonants in Iraqi Arabic. *Phonetica, 44,* 156–172.

Carlson, B. F., & Esling, J. H. (2000). Spokane. *Journal of the International Phonetic Association, 30,* 101–106.

Carlson, B. F., Esling, J. H., & Fraser, K. (2001). Nuuchahnulth. *Journal of the International Phonetic Association, 31,* 275–279.

Catford, J. C. (1939). On the classification of stop consonants. *Le maître phonétique, 3rd Series, 65,* 2–5.

Catford, J. C. (1947). Consonants pronounced with closed glottis. *Le maître phonétique, 3rd Series, 87,* 4–7.

Catford, J. C. (1964). Phonation types: The classification of some laryngeal components of speech production. In D. Abercrombie, D. B. Fry, P. A. D. MacCarthy, N. C. Scott, & J. L. M. Trim (Eds.), *In honour of Daniel Jones* (pp. 26–37). London: Longmans, Green & Co.

Catford, J. C. (1968). The articulatory possibilities of man. In B. Malmberg (Ed.), *Manual of phonetics* (pp. 309–333). Amsterdam: North-Holland.

Catford, J. C. (1977). *Fundamental problems in phonetics.* Edinburgh, Scotland: Edinburgh University Press.

Catford, J. C. (1983). Pharyngeal and laryngeal sounds in Caucasian languages. In D. M. Bless & J. H. Abbs (Eds.), *Vocal fold physiology: Contemporary research and clinical issues* (pp. 344–350). San Diego, CA: College-Hill.

Catford, J. C. (1990). Glottal consonants ... another view. *Journal of the International Phonetic Association, 20(2),* 25–26.

Catford, J. C. (2001). *A practical introduction to phonetics* (2nd ed.). Oxford, England: Oxford University Press.

El–Halees, Y. (1985). The role of F_1 in the place-of-articulation distinction in Arabic. *Journal of Phonetics, 13,* 287–298.

Ellis, A. J. (1874). *On early English pronunciation* (Part IV). London: Trübner & Co.

Esling, J. H. (1984). Laryngographic study of phonation type and laryngeal configuration. *Journal of the International Phonetic Association, 14,* 56–73.

Esling, J. H. (1994). Voice quality. In R. E. Asher & J. M. Y. Simpson (Eds.), *The encyclopedia of language and linguistics* (pp. 4950–4953). Oxford, England: Pergamon Press.

Esling, J. H. (1996). Pharyngeal consonants and the aryepiglottic sphincter. *Journal of the International Phonetic Association, 26,* 65–88.

Esling, J. H. (1999a). The IPA categories 'pharyngeal' and 'epiglottal': Laryngoscopic observations of pharyngeal articulations and larynx height. *Language & Speech, 42,* 349–372.

Esling, J. H. (1999b). Voice quality settings of the pharynx. In J. J. Ohala, Y. Hasegawa, M. Ohala, D. Granville, & A. C. Bailey (Eds.), *Proceedings of the 14th International Congress of Phonetic Sciences: Vol. 3* (pp. 2449–2452). San Francisco, USA.

Esling, J. H. (2002). *The laryngeal sphincter as an articulator: Tenseness, tongue root and phonation in Yi and Bai.* Paper presented at the meeting of the Linguistic Society of America, San Francisco.

Esling, J. H., & Edmondson, J. A. (2002). The laryngeal sphincter as an articulator: Tenseness, tongue root and phonation in Yi and Bai. In A. Braun & H. R. Masthoff (Eds.), *Phonetics and its applications: Festschrift for Jens–Peter Köster on the occasion of his 60th birthday* (pp. 38–51). Stuttgart, Germany: Franz Steiner Verlag.

Esling, J. H., Fraser, K., & Harris, J. G. (in press). Glottal stop, glottalized resonants, and pharyngeals: A reinterpretation with evidence from a laryngoscopic study of Nuuchahnulth (Nootka). *Journal of Phonetics.*

Esling, J. H., Heap, L. M., Snell, R. C., & Dickson, B. C. (1994). Analysis of pitch dependence of pharyngeal, faucal, and larynx-height voice quality settings. In *International Conference on Spoken Language Processing '94: Vol. 3* (pp. 1475–1478). Yokohama, Japan.

Fairbanks, G. (1960). *Voice and articulation drill-book* (2nd ed.). New York, NY: Harper & Row.

Gao, M. (2002). *Tones in whispered Chinese: Articulatory features and perceptual cues.* Unpublished master's thesis, University of Victoria, Victoria, British Columbia, Canada.

Gaprindashvili, Sh. G. (1966). *Fonetika Darginskogo jazyka.* Tbilisi, USSR: Metsniereba.

Garcia, M. (1855). *Observations physiologiques sur la voix humaine.* Paris: Masson.

Garcia, M. (1856). *Nouveau traité sommaire de l'art du chant.* Paris: M. Richard.

Gauffin, J. (1977). Mechanisms of larynx tube constriction. *Phonetica, 34,* 307–309.

Grammont, M. (1933). *Traité de phonétique.* Paris: Librairie Delagrave.

Harris, J. G. (1987). *Linguistic phonetic notes (1969–1979).* Bangkok, Thailand: Craftsman Press.

Harris, J. G. (1999). States of the glottis for voiceless plosives. In J. J. Ohala, Y. Hasegawa, M. Ohala, D. Granville, & A. C. Bailey (Eds.), *Proceedings of the 14th International Congress of Phonetic Sciences: Vol. 3* (pp. 2041–2044). San Francisco, USA.

Harris, J. G. (2001). States of the glottis of Thai voiceless stops and affricates. In K. Tingsabadh & A. S. Abramson (Eds.), *Essays in Tai linguistics* (pp. 3–11). Bangkok, Thailand: Chulalongkorn University Press.

Heffner, R–M. S. (1950). *General phonetics*. Madison: University of Wisconsin Press.

Hillel, A. D. (2001). The study of laryngeal muscle activity in normal human subjects and in patients with laryngeal dystonia using multiple fine-wire electromyography. *The Laryngoscope, 111,* 1–47.

Hockett, C. F. (1958). *A course in modern linguistics*. New York, NY: Macmillan Company.

Holder, W. (1669). *Elements of speech: An essay of inquiry into the natural production of letters*. London: T. N. for J. Martyn Printer to the R. Society.

Hollien, H. (1972). Three major vocal registers: A proposal. In A. Rigault & R. Charbonneau (Eds.), *Proceedings of the 7th International Congress of Phonetic Sciences* (pp. 320–331). The Hague, Netherlands: Mouton.

Hollien, H., & Michel, J. F. (1968). Vocal fry as a phonational register. *Journal of Speech and Hearing Research, 11,* 600–604.

Hollien, H., Moore, P., Wendahl, R. W., & Michel, J. F. (1966). On the nature of vocal fry. *Journal of Speech and Hearing Research, 9,* 245–247.

International Phonetic Association (1999). *Handbook of the International Phonetic Association: A guide to the use of the International Phonetic Alphabet*. Cambridge, England: Cambridge University Press.

Jacobsen, W. H. Jr. (1969). Origin of the Nootka pharyngeals. *International Journal of American Linguistics, 35,* 125–153.

Jones, D. (1956). *An outline of English phonetics* (8th ed.). New York, NY: E. P. Dutton & Co.

Jones, S. (1934). Somali [ħ] and [ʕ]. *Le maître phonétique, 49,* 8–9.

Kodzasov, S. V. (1987). Pharyngeal features in the Daghestan languages. In *Proceedings of the XIth International Congress of Phonetic Sciences: Vol. 2* (pp. 142–144). Tallinn, Estonia, USSR: Academy of Sciences of the Estonian SSR.

Kreiman, J., & Garrett, B. (2000). Measuring voice quality. In R. D. Kent & M. J. Ball (Eds.), *Voice quality measurement* (pp. 73–101). San Diego, CA: Singular.

Ladefoged, P. (1971). *Preliminaries to linguistic phonetics*. Chicago, IL: University of Chicago Press.

Ladefoged, P. (1974). Respiration, laryngeal activity and linguistics. In B. Wyke (Ed.), *Ventilatory and phonatory control systems* (pp. 299–314). London: Oxford University Press.

Ladefoged, P. (1975). *A course in phonetics*. New York, NY: Harcourt Brace.

Ladefoged, P. (1982). *A course in phonetics* (2nd ed.). New York, NY: Harcourt Brace.

Ladefoged, P., & Maddieson, I. (1996). *The sounds of the world's languages*. Oxford, England: Blackwell.

Ladefoged, P., Maddieson, I., & Jackson, M. (1988). Investigating phonation types in different languages. In O. Fujimura (Ed.), *Vocal physiology: Voice production, mechanisms and functions* (pp. 297–317). New York, NY: Raven.

Laufer, A., & Baer, T. (1988). The emphatic and pharyngeal sounds in Hebrew and in Arabic. *Language and Speech, 31,* 181–205.

Laufer, A., & Condax, I. D. (1979). The epiglottis as an articulator. *Journal of the International Phonetic Association, 9,* 50–56.

Laufer, A., & Condax, I. D. (1981). The function of the epiglottis in speech. *Language and Speech, 24,* 39–62.

Laver, J. (1975). *Individual features in voice quality.* Unpublished doctoral dissertation, University of Edinburgh, Scotland.

Laver, J. (1980). *The phonetic description of voice quality.* Cambridge, England: Cambridge University Press.

Laver, J. (1994). *Principles of phonetics.* Cambridge, England: Cambridge University Press.

Lindqvist, J. (1969). Laryngeal mechanisms in speech. *Quarterly Progress and Status Report, 2-3,* 26–32. Stockholm: Speech Transmission Laboratory, Royal Institute of Technology.

Lisker, L., & Abramson, A. S. (1964). A cross-language study of voicing in initial stops: Acoustical measurements. *Word, 20,* 384–422.

Lisker, L., & Abramson, A. S. (1970). The voicing dimension: Some experiments in comparative phonetics. In B. Hála, M. Romportl, & P. Janota (Eds.), *Proceedings of the 6th International Congress of Phonetic Sciences* (pp. 563–567). Prague, Czechoslovakia: Academia Publishing House of the Czechoslovak Academy of Sciences.

Luchsinger, R., & Arnold, G. E. (1965). *Voice—speech—language. Clinical communicology: Its physiology and pathology.* London: Constable.

Monsen, R. B., & Engebretson, A. M. (1977). Study of variations in the male and female glottal wave. *Journal of the Acoustical Society of America, 62,* 981–993.

Negus, V. E. (1929). *The mechanism of the larynx.* London: William Heinemann.

Negus, V. E. (1949). *The comparative anatomy and physiology of the larynx.* London: William Heinemann Medical Books Ltd.

Noël–Armfield, G. (1931). *General phonetics, for missionaries and students of language* (4th ed.). Cambridge, England: W. Heffer & Sons Ltd.

Painter, C. (1986). The laryngeal vestibule and voice quality. *Archives of Oto-Rhino-Laryngology, 243,* 329–337.

Pike, K. L. (1943). *Phonetics: A critical analysis of phonetic theory and a technic for the practical description of sounds.* Ann Arbor, MI: University of Michigan Press.

Roach, P. J. (1979). Laryngeal-oral coarticulation in glottalized English plosives. *Journal of the International Phonetic Association, 9,* 2–6.

Russell, G. O. (1936). Etiology of follicular pharyngitis, catarrhal laryngitis, so-called clergyman's throat; and singer's nodes. *Journal of Speech Disorders, 1,* 113–122.

Sapir, E., & Swadesh, M. (1939). *Nootka texts: Tales and ethnological narratives with grammatical notes and lexical materials.* Philadelphia, PA: University of Pennsylvania, Linguistic Society of America.

Solomon, N. P., McCall, G. N., Trosset, M. W., & Gray, W. C. (1989). Laryngeal configuration and constriction during two types of whispering. *Journal of Speech and Hearing Research, 32,* 161–174.

Sprigg, R. K. (1978). Phonation types: A re-appraisal. *Journal of the International Phonetic Association, 8,* 2–17.

Stonham, J. (1999). *Aspects of Tsishaath Nootka phonetics and phonology. (Lincom Studies in Native American Linguistics, 32).* Munich, Germany: Lincom Europa.

Sweet, H. (1877). *A handbook of phonetics.* Oxford, England: Clarendon Press.

Sweet, H. (1906). *A primer of phonetics.* Oxford, England: Clarendon Press.

van den Berg, J. (1968). Mechanism of the larynx and the laryngeal vibrations. In B. Malmberg (Ed.), *Manual of phonetics* (pp. 278–308). Amsterdam: North–Holland.

Van Riper, C., & Irwin, J. V. (1958). *Voice and articulation.* Englewood Cliffs, NJ: Prentice-Hall.

Ward, I. C. (1929). *The phonetics of English.* Cambridge, England: W. Heffer & Sons Ltd.

Westermann, D., & Ward, I. C. (1933). *Practical phonetics for students of African languages.* Oxford, England: Oxford University Press.

Williams, G. T., Farquharson, I. M., & Anthony, J. K. F. (1975). Fibreoptic laryngoscopy in the assessment of laryngeal disorders. *Journal of Laryngology and Otology, 89,* 299–316.

Zemlin, W. R. (1964). *Speech and hearing science.* Champaign, IL: Stipes.

Zemlin, W. R. (1968). *Speech and hearing science: Anatomy and physiology.* Englewood Cliffs, NJ: Prentice-Hall.

Zemlin, W. R. (1988). *Speech and hearing science: Anatomy and physiology* (2nd ed.). Englewood Cliffs, NJ: Prentice-Hall.

CHAPTER 15

Forensic Speaker Identification and the Phonetic Description of Voice Quality

Francis Nolan
Department of Linguistics, University of Cambridge

A central task in many criminal investigations and subsequent court cases is to establish identity between a suspect and the perpetrator of a crime. An important class of evidence given by ordinary witnesses concerns identity, and much forensic scientific activity has this as its goal. In the most familiar kinds of cases a witness may simply say 'yes, that's the person I saw' on the basis of physical appearance, or a forensic scientist may base an opinion on a fingerprint or on DNA samples, both of which relate directly to the organic make-up of the person(s) involved. However, another kind of case is becoming more and more familiar: the kind in which the basis of the identification is a person's voice. In this event, we enter the realm of forensic speaker identification. We might consider forensic speaker identification evidence under two broad categories: 'naïve,' where it is a matter of a witness identifying a voice; and 'technical,' where an expert brings specialist skills to bear on recorded speech samples (Nolan, 1983, p. 7).

Naïve speaker identification involves the application of our natural abilities as human language users to the identification of a speaker. Given the sophistication of these abilities, the term *naïve* is perhaps inappropriate. The term emphasizes, however, the lack of specific training on the part of the person making the decision. There are several common circumstances which may give rise to such evidence. A witness to a crime may claim to identify a voice heard ('it was "X's" voice making the bomb threat'), a witness may recognize a voice heard without being able to identify it ('it was the anonymous caller who had rung twice the day before'), or a witness may be asked to listen to a 'voice parade' or 'voice line-up' containing the voice of a suspect and a number of foils and to pick out the perpetrator's voice if it is present.

Technical speaker identification is defined by the employment of any trained skill or any technologically-supported procedure in the decision-making process. This applies almost exclusively when there is an incriminating recording (a bomb hoax, a fraudulent bank deal, a wire tap, and so on) and a recording of a suspect. An expert, normally a phonetician, is then asked to assess the likelihood that it is the suspect who is heard on the incriminating tape. The expert, ideally, will apply both auditory skills acquired through phonetic training, and techniques for acoustic visualization and measurement.

In their reports giving their opinion on whether two samples of speech are from the same speaker, forensic phoneticians very often comment on, among other factors, 'voice quality.' Likewise, if witnesses were pressed on the basis of a voice identification, they would quite probably mention something to the effect of 'the quality of the voice' or 'the sound of the voice.' Given the self-evident importance of 'voice quality' to forensic speaker identification, one might expect that descriptive tools for voice quality would loom large in the expert's contribution to the process, whether in technical speaker identification or in the provision of support for naïve speaker identification such as the construction of voice parades. The purpose of this chapter is to examine the extent to which the systematic description of voice quality plays a part in this field. First, however, a summary is given of the most comprehensive descriptive tool for the description of voice quality, the framework set out in Laver (1980).

LAVER'S MODEL FOR THE PHONETIC DESCRIPTION OF VOICE QUALITY

Laver's (1980) descriptive framework provides a means to describe voice quality, understood as 'the characteristic auditory colouring of an individual speaker's voice … a cumulative abstraction over a period of time of a speaker-characterizing quality'(p. 1). The descriptive system is componential, and rather as a consonant can be described in the kind of system on which the International Phonetic Alphabet is based (see, e.g., International Phonetic Association [IPA], 1999) as a 'voiced alveolar plosive,' so a voice can be described as 'palatalized denasal creaky voice.' Terms such as the latter for the description of voice quality are referred to by Laver as 'settings,' these being the descriptive primes of the system. The term *setting* is attributed to Honikman (1964), who wrote in the context of language-learning about 'articulatory settings' as the overall postures of the articulators which is it is necessary to adopt to master the fluent integration of the segments of a particular language. Laver's use of 'setting' as opposed to 'articulatory setting' reflects the fact that he is extending the notion to laryngeal activity, such as 'breathiness,' which is not traditionally referred to by phoneticians as articulation.

Laver's (1980) framework shares with the IPA framework a degree of ambiguity about the domain in which it is operating. When we talk about an 'open back vowel,' the terminology is traditionally seen as reflecting the position of the body of the tongue required to produce such a vowel, but the phonetic category so defined is learned (to a large extent) by reference to an auditory target. Similarly, a setting such as 'palatalized' implies a production in which the average position of the tongue is displaced during the whole of a person's speech somewhat in the direction of the hard palate, but the descriptive prime is defined by a particular auditory quality. As Laver states (1980, p. 7), 'The descriptive system ... stands on an auditory foundation.' On the whole this ambiguity is not problematic—although, for instance Nolan, (1982, pp. 446–447) points out that the auditorily defined parameter 'raised larynx' may actually involve not only raising of the larynx but also constriction of the pharynx—and for the purposes of this discussion we can fairly safely equate a 'setting' and what might be termed a *voice quality component* (Nolan, 1982, p. 444) as respectively the articulatory and auditory reflexes of an abstract descriptive category.

The scope and inclusiveness of Laver's framework is impressive. Laver writes that 'with some forty basic settings available in the descriptive repertoire, a very large number of composite voice qualities can be described' (1980, p. 9). The settings are divided into supralaryngeal and laryngeal settings, which account for the majority, and overall tension settings (limited to 'tense' and 'lax'). All settings are defined relative to an arbitrarily chosen reference setting, the 'neutral' setting. This setting is achieved when the articulatory 'bias' of the vocal tract is toward equal cross-sectional area along its whole length, it is neither lengthened nor shortened at either lips or larynx, nasality is present only on those segments where it is linguistically required, and the vocal folds are vibrating regularly and efficiently. The possibility of describing a voice as having, for instance, 'harsh whispery falsetto, with strong nasalization and mild palatalization,' shows that the framework provides for very precise and detailed specifications of voices.

THE RELEVANCE OF THE VOICE QUALITY FRAMEWORK TO FORENSIC SPEAKER IDENTIFICATION

From what has been said so far, it would seem that a descriptive phonetic framework for voice quality, for 'the characteristic auditory colouring of an individual speaker's voice' (Laver, 1980, p. 1), should be highly appropriate to the task of forensic speaker identification. Although there are those who have proposed (e.g.,

Baldwin, 1979) that, in effect, finer and finer dialect analysis will lead to the definition of a dialect community with just one speaker, I have consistently argued (Nolan, 1991, 1997) that the notion that each speaker has a definable 'idiolect' is unproven and, even if true, impractical given the limited samples available in forensic work. This means that the analysis of (crudely) the vowels, consonants, and intonation of two samples will (very helpfully) narrow the samples down to a dialect community, but not to individual speakers. Such analysis is a linguistic analysis, and what is linguistic is shared between individuals. Rather what is needed is analysis of those properties which are speaker-specific and not shared by even a small community, and these properties comprise 'voice quality' in the general sense.

However, there is a conceptual problem which has to be dealt with before we say unhesitatingly that Laver's framework is relevant to forensic speaker identification. The problem arises from the fact that the nonlinguistic colouring of individuals' voices arises from two sources: their anatomy, and their speaking habits. Often the terms *organic* and *learned* are used for differences between speakers arising from these two sources; Laver himself (1976) has also written equivalently of 'intrinsic' and 'extrinsic' aspects of voice quality. Clearly, much of what differentiates the sound of a man and his 10-year-old daughter stems from the fact that his vocal tract and vocal cords are much larger than hers. The man will also, aside from the difference in overall size of vocal tract, have a proportionately longer pharynx. The same is true less dramatically between two men or between two women; minor differences in size of the vocal tract and the larynx, and a failure of vocal tracts all to be 'isomorphic' (i.e., scaled down or scaled up versions of each other, with everything in proportion), means that any two people will sound different. Laver's framework is not designed to capture this least linguistic, arguably nonphonetic, aspect of how people sound.

What it is designed to do is to provide a descriptive framework, within general phonetic theory, for those aspects of voice quality which are susceptible of imitation by a speaker with a normal vocal apparatus: the settings 'are all capable of being imitated by all anatomically and physiologically normal speakers' (Laver, 1980, p. 9). For instance, everyone whose vocal organs fall within the normal range can choose to adopt breathy voice or creaky voice (either for effect, or as a general habit of speaking), and can choose to lower his or her larynx or position the tongue body on average further down and back in the mouth (pharyngealization). The extent to which these 'choices' are under completely conscious and voluntary control at a particular time may vary from individual to individual, but in the more general sense, whether in acquiring language or under phonetic tuition, these settings are available to a speaker. On the other hand, the man in the earlier example does not have the choice to have the voice of a 10-year-old girl. He might make choices which make him sound less different from her, such as raising his larynx, adopting falsetto phonation, and using a tongue-body setting of palatalization, but by doing so he will sound like a man adopting those parameters, not a little girl. The organic facts underlying personal voice quality impose limits on the variation achievable by a voice.

There are, then, two simplifying assumptions behind Laver's system. First, the majority of the population have equivalent vocal apparatuses (not identical, clearly, but equivalent); and second, the shared vocal apparatus has a 'neutral' configuration which is common. Each of us can then choose to deviate, in terms of long-term trends, from that neutral configuration, thereby adopting various settings. In reality, our vocal apparatuses are not equivalent, as discussed earlier, and their nonequivalence gives rise to important aspects of our vocal identity. It would seem on the face of it that this imposes a serious limit to the applicability of Laver's framework to forensic speaker identification. Only the 'learned' element of personal voice quality is susceptible to description in the framework: 'the descriptive system offered here largely excludes consideration of the ... organic type of influence on voice quality' (Laver, 1980, p. 10).

In fact, the situation is not so clear cut. Adopting the notion of a vocal tract equivalent between all normal speakers as an analytic assumption does not limit us to describing the speech of those whose anatomy closely approximates that abstraction. One of the most successful applications of Laver's framework has been in the description of pathological speech of one kind and another (see chapter in this volume by Mackenzie Beck). A particularly illuminating example is found in the description of the speech of Down's Syndrome speakers (see Beck, 1988, 1997). Voice quality descriptions within Laver's framework found that Down's syndrome speech was associated with high degrees of the tongue-body setting of palatalization. This turns out to reflect an anatomical tendency to an underdeveloped palate relative to the size of the tongue. It is obviously not correct to infer from the description of the speech as palatalized that the Down's syndrome speakers are 'choosing' to palatalize their speech; or, similarly, that a long-term heavy smoker is 'choosing' a harsh whispery setting of the vocal cords. However, it is perfectly feasible descriptively to say that the speech in those examples perceptually replicates the effect of the relevant settings imposed on the descriptive abstraction, the 'equivalent' vocal apparatus.

In like manner, it should be possible to describe forensic samples in terms of 'settings,' always bearing in mind that the production-oriented term (such as palatalized) is a label for a voice quality component in a predominantly auditory classification and not a guarantee about the origin of the voice quality component as either 'chosen' or organically determined. Such an extension of voice quality analysis, as with its application to pathological speech, crosses the border between learned and organic voice characteristics. Having thus established that Laver's framework is in principle applicable in forensic speaker identification, with respect both to 'learned' and (at least some) 'organic' components of voice quality, let us turn to what happens in practice within forensic phonetics.

VOICE QUALITY IN FORENSIC PHONETIC PRACTICE

As a way of getting an overview of how voice quality is treated by phonetic forensic experts, I have looked through the materials in about 30 forensic cases in which I have been involved over the years (1988–2002), all of them in the British Isles. Most of these have been cases where the identity of a speaker has been in question, and where, in principle, a description of voice quality would have been relevant. I discuss first the reports of other experts in these cases. These are 'technical' speaker identification cases, and in all but one instance the other expert's report has been commissioned by the prosecution (the fact that my involvement in technical speaker identification has been for the defence arose originally from my consistently cautious attitude toward what can be determined about identity from speech samples, but by now probably owes more to tradition; notice, however, that in the majority of cases in which I have been asked by the defence to produce a report, my conclusion has broadly agreed with that of the prosecution expert, albeit usually in less definitive terms).

In the British context, the written report of the prosecution expert, by tradition, usually takes the form of a brief statement of opinion couched in relatively simple terms rather than a detailed technical document directed to phonetically trained readers. Because of this, it undoubtedly tends to underreflect the detail with which the analysis has been undertaken. Nevertheless, it is more than a bald statement of opinion, and usually notes what factors have been taken into account. The following quotations (from which identities both of suspects and experts have been omitted) are taken from reports by three different experts, and are typical: (a) 'There were significant similarities between the voice of [the defendant] and that of the person making the telephone calls. These similarities were in vowel and consonant pronunciations, voice quality, and aspects of rhythm and intonation.' (b) 'These [similarities] concern voice quality (speech resonance characteristics), rhythm, intonation and features of consonant and vowel pronunciation.' (c) 'All four samples are characterized by very closely similar voice pitch and voice quality. Furthermore there is a considerable resemblance of accent … '

Some exemplification of the pronunciation similarities in vowels and consonants is usually included in the statement, and sometimes there is a reference to the IPA as a descriptive framework for phonetic analysis. In contrast, in only two of the cases I have reviewed have experts offered anything which could be construed as a reference to a systematic analysis of voice quality, implicitly shown in the following example: 'The slight nasalization of the voice came over consistently in all the recordings and the voice quality was throughout the recordings identified as the same.'

This is also shown quite explicitly in the following example (from a report commissioned by the defence): 'Phoneticians have a number of descriptive categories which may be used to describe voice quality. The type of voice produced by [the defendant] I would best characterize as raised larynx voice whereas the hoax caller does not demonstrate this voice quality.'

The conclusion, then, from a survey of reports of other experts would be that although voice quality is clearly regarded as central to the matter of deciding on speaker identity, there is only occasional evidence in the statements of experts that it is being analysed componentially. It also is not clear whether there is even explicit agreement on what 'voice quality' is. The expert who glossed voice quality as 'speech resonance characteristics' elaborates on this view in another report: ' … Voice quality—the overall impression created by the combination of resonances "overlaid" upon the stream of speech.'

This is fully in sympathy with Laver's view of voice quality, except that it appears to deny a role for laryngeal features to which Laver (1980) accords equal status. I am not sure whether this exclusion is intentional, but I later suggest that there may be a good reason for it. Others do not feel that 'voice quality' needs further explanation, and I would imagine that if pressed they would assume it included laryngeal factors.

It would be elegant at this point to be able to turn to my own reports, and show that my own approach to voice quality has been substantially more analytic. In fact, it turns out that I have rarely commented on individual components of voice quality when doing technical speaker identification. In one report I did comment as follows:

> [The perpetrator] when animated frequently breaks into falsetto, a distinct mode of vibration of the vocal cords. Although from the speech of the other participant [in this conversation] it seems that in this speech community a very wide pitch range is employed at least during heated discussions, such a frequent use of falsetto might be regarded as idiosyncratic.

This comment might be regarded, however, as more about a paralinguistic strategy, a medium-term application of a voice quality component, than a comment about personal voice quality. In another case report, I referred to what sounded like velarization of [s], but this is clearly a matter of a voice quality component operating over only a segment-sized domain.

The only area of forensic phonetic work where I have been more explicit in applying voice quality analysis is in the preparation of two 'voice lineups'—identification parades to test whether it was the suspect whom a witness heard at the time of a crime. This requires the selection of (usually around eight) 'foil' voices, among which the suspect's sample is placed. The foil samples have to be chosen so that the suspect's sample does not stand out, and one aspect of this is voice quality. In my witness statement on the preparation of the parade reported in Nolan and Grabe (1996), I noted explicitly that, although I thought a set of foil samples had been achieved which were appropriate for the suspect, 'none of the potential foils matched the degree of "palatalization" apparent in [the suspect's] voice.' It is never possible, of course, given the multidimensional nature of speech, to place the suspect centrally within the range of a voice parade on all dimensions.

My working notes on the potential foil samples included comments such as 'heavy nasalization,' 'tenser voice than [the suspect],' and 'light voice' (not a term within Laver's framework, but which I would have been using as a cover term for a voice with relatively high pitch and formant frequencies, and possibly phonation tending toward breathy rather than tenser settings). I also rated the distance in terms of voice quality (and separately, accent) between each foil and the suspect on a numerical scale; my voice quality ratings were later shown to be in good agreement with unspecified similarity judgments by a group of subjects (Nolan & Grabe, 1996). Although my numerical rating was a global comparison, in making it I at least had in mind the dimensions of voice quality systematized in Laver's (1980) framework. In another more recent voice parade case, my comments on potential foil samples included the terms *creaky* and *hoarse* (meant in the sense of Laver's term *harsh*), but they focussed more at the level of the cover terms *light* (as above) and *deep* (implying low pitch and formant frequencies in some combination), the reason being the overriding concern to avoid 'deep' voices, because the suspect lay toward the opposite end of that continuum.

In the area of screening potential foil voices, then, my own practice has been informed by the voice quality framework, even if it has fallen well short of any full voice quality profiling. Nonetheless, the outcome of this survey shows that formal componential description of voice quality has not played a major role in forensic speaker identification. We now turn to reasons why that is so.

REASONS FOR THE LACK OF VOICE QUALITY ANALYSIS

Lack of Awareness

One possible reason is a lack of awareness among those involved in forensic phonetic casework that a systematic framework for voice quality analysis is available. Looking at the small number of standard reference works in the field, this seems unlikely. Admittedly, Laver's framework is not referenced in Tosi (1979), which was written before the framework was widely publicized and which in any case focuses on the use of spectrographic analysis in speaker identification, or in Künzel (1987). However, it is mentioned in Hollien (1990, p. 262), albeit in connection with the effects of psychological stress in the voice; in Baldwin and French (1990, p. 57); and in Rose (2002, p. 280). The existence of Laver's framework is therefore signalled in the forensic phonetic literature. Furthermore, part of my own research (Nolan, 1983, Chap.4) explicitly sought acoustic correlates of the terms in the framework, so at the very least my own non-application of the framework needs to be explained elsewise.

Lack of Training

A more plausible reason is the fact that traditional phonetic training generally does not include the systematic analysis of voice quality. Rose (2002) notes the following: 'Since [the componential analysis of voice quality] is not considered part of traditional auditory-phonetic training, the number of phoneticians proficient in this approach is much smaller than those proficient in describing phonetic quality' (p. 280).

This focus is understandable because most phonetic training (aside from that targeted at speech pathology) takes place in the context of language analysis. The framework of traditional phonetics, embodied most prominently in the International Phonetic Alphabet and the theory behind it (see International Phonetic Association, 1999), provides a method for recording the audible details of vowels, consonants, and prosodic characteristics such as intonation—all the dimensions which have the potential to play a role in linguistic contrasts of one sort or another. With appropriate training, which consists in intensive practice in discriminating and producing sounds within and beyond his or her native language, the phonetician can describe in quite some detail fine differences in pronunciation. As a result, the phonetician has a considerable advantage in bringing to consciousness, and being to able to organize, evaluate, and communicate, delicate distinctions of pronunciation, but in a context where differences between speakers have to be set aside. Such a linguistic-phonetic training puts little or no emphasis on vocal effects which pervade the whole of a person's speaking, whether or not they are of organic or learned origin. Indeed, the organically-based differences between speakers have to be factored out if, for instance, a class of students is to learn a particular reference vowel, because they all have different vocal tracts.

In my case, I was fully conversant with Laver's framework, because, as noted earlier, my own research used it, and I have attended a training course in Vocal Profile Analysis based on the framework, and yet my forensic analyses draw very little on the framework. There are clearly other factors at work.

Practical Considerations of Time

One such factor is that carrying out a complete voice quality profile of two samples would be a time consuming task. The samples would have to be evaluated for around 40 different settings, most of which require careful and repeated listening. This is in the context of a task for which consideration must be given to other aspects of the speech, notably the fine detail of the pronunciation. The magnitude of the task, which would form only a subpart of the total evaluation of the samples, may contribute to the lack of analyses in forensic phonetics (where analysis is often carried out under severe, externally imposed time scales), and explain why any analytic comments which are to be found in reports concern only one or a small number of settings, specifically ones which are particularly salient in a sample.

Quality of Samples

I suspect a more fundamental barrier to the application of componential voice quality analysis lies, however, in the nature of the samples available for analysis. In the standard situation, a recording made of a criminal in the commissioning of a crime has to be compared with a reference recording of a suspect. In the United Kingdom, the reference recording is commonly of a police interview with the suspect. There is no legal barrier in the legal jurisdictions of England and Wales, Northern Ireland, or Scotland, to the interview of the crime under investigation serving as the reference sample of the suspect's speech, or, indeed, a recording of an earlier interview connected with an unrelated crime and taken from the police archive if the suspect declines to speak during the relevant interview. Apparently, this strategy is not available to the authorities in all legal systems, but, in my view, it is a reasonable procedure because the suspect is made aware in general terms that what he or she says under questioning may be used in the prosecution's case. I suppose the suspect might understand this to mean 'what I say' not 'how I said it,' but I think such an objection would be an exercise in sophistry. So, the reference sample is very often a recording made in the police interview room. The quality of the recording is typically fair, as long as the suspect is near enough to the microphone, and the interviewing officers refrain from talking over the suspect.

The limiting factor on phonetic analysis will be the incriminating recording. With a few exceptions, this will be either telephone speech or a covert recording from a hidden microphone. Commonly, the telephone calls are hoax calls to the emergency services, attempts to defraud banks, threatening or obscene telephone calls, kidnap or other ransom negotiations, or wire-taps of crime-related telephone calls. Covert recordings are made by undercover police officers or other volunteers wearing hidden microphones in encounters with suspected criminals. The telephone carries the speech signal only in a very band-limited form. Any sound energy below about 300 Hz, and any above about 3500 Hz, is lost, and there may be distortions of the spectral shape particularly in the vicinity of these cutoffs. For comparison, the first harmonic of a male voice may be as low as 75 Hz, and significant fricative energy may be present up to 10000 Hz. Covert recordings may be subject to similar restrictions if the signal is transmitted to a recorder elsewhere, and both telephone and covert recordings are prey to contamination from noises such as traffic or other speech in the background. Calls which are routinely recorded, such as those to the emergency services or to banks, are recorded on bulk recorders which may further degrade the signal, as may answering machines or hand-held recorders used by people trying to record telephone messages. All in all, the sample of speech from the 'unknown' is like to be of very poor quality compared to anything a phonetician or linguist would normally encounter in research.

What are the consequences of this? One is that the phonetician is actually quite limited in his or her stock-in-trade activity, the analysis of sounds. I have had to challenge in court an assertion to the effect that 95% of the consonants were available for comparison between the defendant's sample and the incriminating sample. It may be that the words used exemplify virtually all of the consonants of English, but in the acoustic signal, none of the fricatives or affricates, comprising nearly half the consonant inventory, will be present in a way which would allow them to be heard as such (without the ear filling in from the context of the utterance), let alone subjected to a detailed comparison for between-speaker differences.

As far as voice quality is concerned, we need to consider separately the laryngeal and supralaryngeal contributions. The way the vocal cords vibrate leaves its mark on the voicing source spectrum. For instance, the breathier the phonation, the sharper the fall-off in energy in successively higher harmonics, and (up to a point) the tenser the phonation the shallower the fall-off. Nolan (1983, p. 142–155) shows the effect on the long-term average spectrum of adopting various of the laryngeal components in Laver's system. Another common quantification (Ní Chasaide & Gobl, 1997, p. 442–443) is the ratio of the first harmonic to the second harmonic or to other higher harmonics; the breathier the voice, the greater the dominance of the first harmonic. Perception of the full range of laryngeal components, especially breathy and whispery settings, will depend on the presence of noise in parallel with the voice source.

All of these acoustic manifestations of laryngeal voice quality will be distorted by the bandwidth limitation inherent in telephone and telephone-like transmission. The long-term spectrum will be truncated at low and high frequencies, the first two or three harmonics (of a male voice) will be missing, and laryngeal noise may be masked by transmission noise. If judgments are to be made about the laryngeal voice quality of such a sample, they can only be made via a rather elaborate process of perceptually reconstructing what the sample would have sounded like had it not been passed through the telephone. Undoubtedly, we have quite a bit of skill in doing this, because we are generally able to associate the voice of a familiar person over the telephone with that person, and indeed recognize callers with varying degrees of accuracy; but it remains to be demonstrated that the componential and independent judgments involved in the auditory analysis of laryngeal voice quality could be accurately carried out in a way which normalizes for the effects of bandwidth limitation.

Given these problems with judging laryngeal voice quality components, is there a sense in which the expert who glossed voice quality as 'the overall impression created by the combination of resonances "overlaid" upon the stream of speech' is nearer the mark? In practical terms, are supralaryngeal settings, whose effects are found mainly in the relative frequencies of formants (Nolan 1983, Ch.4), a more reliably perceivable element of voice quality in the forensic situation? The answer is probably 'yes,' but even here we must expect some problems. Formants which stray outside the 300 to 3500 telephone bandwidth will be lost, and may be attenuated near the edges of the pass band. Künzel (2001) discusses the potentially distorting effect of the telephone on measurements of the first formant frequency, particularly in vowels where it is low; and this effect could in principle result in changes in the perception of supralaryngeal settings. The perception of nasality may be particularly problematic as it characteristically adds a resonance near or below the first formant, in the low frequency region filtered out by the telephone. Once again, whether the telephone signal retains enough information for the true voice quality setting of the speech to be reconstructed is an empirical matter.

The message from this section, then, is that there are severe doubts over the possibility of doing accurate componential voice quality analysis on band-limited speech. Perhaps it is not a coincidence that in reviewing my case materials, I found I had come nearest to applying voice quality analysis in the preparation of voice parades, where the recordings were all free of the limitations of the telephone.

However, if voice quality analysis is compromised by the telephone, this raises an interesting problem. If the information is not there to do componential analysis, how is it there for a global judgment such as 'a good match in voice quality between the telephone call and the suspect's sample?' The answer is that it is not, and the attempt to make such a judgment may often involve a dangerous leap of faith. The situation is not much better than in the case of consonant comparison. My concern over the issue of 'voice quality' in noncompatible recordings is reflected in a comment from a recent report of mine:

> A comparison of the voices is made more difficult because the interview recording is rather 'boomy' with apparently some room resonance, whereas the covert recording is more like a telephone recording with relative de-emphasis of the 'bass' component .... Voice quality is very hard to judge given the difference in the characteristics of the recordings.

There has been very little discussion in the forensic context of the effect of bandwidth limitation and other distortions, and they are rarely alluded to in statements when 'voice quality' is found to match or be very similar. I take the view that pronouncements about the similarity or dissimilarity of 'voice quality' between forensic samples, if one of them is telephone speech, are of rather limited probative value. Filtering the reference sample to make it resemble telephone speech may be of some value for a direct comparison, but it runs the risk of making the two samples sound more similar than the speakers actually were. A significant amount of potentially discriminating information is neutralized whether one or both samples are band limited.

How, then, should the forensic phonetician carry out speaker identification if not by assessing 'voice quality?' Does voice quality analysis have any role? I give brief answers to these questions later after considering four further reasons which I believe militate against the adoption of systematic voice quality analysis.

The Comparison of Samples: a 'Gestalt' Process?

Technical speaker identification is often seen as primarily a matter of comparing two samples, and noting the similarities and differences. It may well be that in matters of direct comparison, human perception operates rather well on a 'gestalt' basis. That is, there may be an overall character to a voice which is not evident, or rather not straightforwardly evident, from a separate consideration of the component parts. If, for instance, we had to assess whether two very similar faces are the same person or a different person, a feature by feature analysis might leave us uncertain, whereas we might instantly know the answer from seeing them side by side. When it is a matter of describing or categorising a voice, componential voice quality analysis is essential; whereas for a simple 'same–different' discrimination, direct global comparison may be best.

Unfortunately, there is a fatal flaw with this approach to technical speaker identification, or indeed any forensic evidence. The similarity of two samples is not by itself enough to make an identification. Those two samples not only have to be similar, but they have to be similar in ways which set them apart from the rest of the relevant population. We have to ask not only 'how likely is it that we would find this blood group at the scene of the crime if the suspect is the person who bled there?' The answer, if the blood is the same type, is 100% likely; that's the only blood type he could leave. But we also have to ask, 'how likely is it that we would find this blood group if someone else was the perpetrator?' The answer to that depends on population statistics. If the blood group is very common in the relevant population, and every second person has it, then lots of people could have left it and the blood evidence only slightly increases the probability of the suspect being at the scene of the crime. If the blood group is very rare, it greatly increases the probability. This rather obvious but often dangerously neglected point is expressed formally as the 'likelihood ratio' of the Bayesian approach to forensic evidence which is gaining ground in some subfields of forensics (for a general introduction see Robertson & Vignaux, 1995, and for a detailed application in speaker identification, see Rose, 2002).

In the case of judgments on vowels and consonants, it is clearly not enough to find one similarity after another if these similarities are common to most or many speakers in the dialect. In relation to a 'gestalt' judgment of voice quality, the danger is more that the listener's frame of reference may be wrong. Unless the expert is a speaker of the dialect in question, the 'gestalt' judgment may be overwhelmed by a similarity which is characteristic of the dialect rather than the two individuals. This is a bit like comparing two different photographs (naturally not identical) and deciding that the faces shown are the same person, whereas in fact they are different people—of a racial type with which the viewer is relatively unfamiliar, for instance.

This is why, even in the matter of judging voice quality as a 'gestalt,' it is not enough merely to compare the two samples. The comparison must also be, implicitly at least, with the relevant population as a whole. Once the risk of being overwhelmed by similarity and wrongly attributing it to personal voice quality rather than dialectally determined voice quality is acknowledged, it suggests that perhaps the assessment of voice quality should proceed by a framework-referenced approach rather than a pairwise comparison. This, however, brings us back to the problem that a componential analysis of the voice quality of telephone speech is likely to be very incomplete (or else unreliable). Remember, however, that 'gestalt' judgments of voice quality in this circumstance will be at least as unreliable.

Stylistic Variation

Another possible reason for the reluctance of forensic phoneticians to engage in voice quality profiling is that it would often result in different profiles for two samples where the speaker was in fact the same. This is because the style of speaking in the reference recording and the unknown recording can be quite different. The reference recording may be a relatively low-key and rather formal discussion in the interview room, whereas the incriminating recording may be a quick-fire colloquial exchange between fellow criminals, an argument with threats, or a breathy-voiced obscene telephone call. Voice quality varies with speaking style and pragmatic function, and so the forensic phonetician has to decide whether an obvious difference of voice quality between the reference and unknown samples could be accounted for by stylistic variation. I wrote the following in a recent report: '[The defendant] is "softly spoken" in the interview tapes, while the caller [the perpetrator] is quite strident, and the two can be equated in terms of voice quality only by mentally reconstructing what each might sound like speaking in the other way.' Ideally, samples would be long enough to exhibit a range of speaking styles from which a rounded picture of the speakers' voice quality could be inferred; but in practice, this is scarcely ever the case.

Any 'mental reconstruction' of voice quality is a leap of faith on the part of the analyst, but it is one that is nevertheless frequently made. Componential analysis of voice quality would force the analyst either to treat each difference as weighing against identity, or to explain it with respect to some known model of variation. This would be the same as in the analysis of pronunciation, where it is perfectly reasonable to say, for instance, that the perpetrator's sample consistently realises /t/ as glottal stop in medial and final position, and the defendant's sample shows alternation between [t] and glottal stop, but that this is consistent with what is known about how speakers of this dialect vary between less formal and more formal circumstances, and therefore that this pattern is not inconsistent with the defendant being the speaker of the incriminating sample. An equivalent example for a componential analysis of voice quality would be if an incriminating sample of the perpetrator, talking with his fellow criminals, manifested harsh whispery voice and a degree of raised larynx, which were both absent from the defendant's sample. If these were known to be sociolinguistic variables in the dialect in question, they could be discounted by appeal to different speaking styles (cf. Esling, 1978, who found whisperiness and harshness to be associated with lower status Edinburgh speakers and creakiness to be associated with higher status speakers).

All such interpretation is, of course, a kind of speculation, and would have to be signalled as such. Cynically, one might suspect that a blanket, impressionistic statement of 'similarity of voice quality' would be preferred by prosecutors because it is more convincing (although less justified) than a carefully argued interpretation of matching and nonmatching voice quality components—as well as being more feasible in terms of time. But such blanket statements should be read with great caution when there are stylistic differences between samples.

The Importance of Instrumental Acoustic Analysis

It is now generally accepted that the best approach to technical speaker identification involves the combination of auditory and acoustic analysis. It is perhaps tempting to see acoustic analysis as beneficial because it is quantitative and therefore more 'scientific' than impressionistic auditory analysis, but the real argument for it is rather different. I have argued (Nolan, 1991, 1997) that auditory analysis can best establish the linguistic sameness of two samples, that is, that they match in terms of accent, that which is common to all speakers in a community regardless of their vocal tracts. The main tool of the auditory analyst, the IPA, is a linguistic phonetic framework. Beyond linguistic phonetics, to enter the domain of what depends on speakers' vocal apparatuses, we need to make acoustic measurements. Indeed, our ear is inherently insensitive to some of the between-speaker acoustic differences which arise from different vocal tracts (Nolan, 1994). Measurements of formants will give us a direct reflection of the size, shape, and dynamic changes of the vocal cavities, and measurements of fundamental frequency will give us a rather less direct reflection of the dimensions and dynamics of the vocal cords.

If it were possible to apply the full apparatus of componential voice quality analysis to forensic speaker identification, there would be an argument for saying that, in fact, auditory analysis can go well beyond the linguistic domain. To describe two samples as denasalized, (lip-) protruded, and palatalized with whispery voice alternating with whispery falsetto takes us well into the realm of the individual (assuming these settings are not characteristic of the dialect in question) and would increase the likelihood that the same speaker was involved. However, I have argued earlier that the commonest circumstance of technical speaker identification, where one of the samples is of telephone speech, severely limits the feasibility of voice quality analysis, particularly of laryngeal settings.

If acoustic analysis is now accepted as an essential part of technical speaker identification, there are two consequences. First, acoustic analysis is the best way to reveal what is missing from the signal in degraded recordings. It shows that, in telephone speech, much of the high frequency energy of fricatives is missing, and likewise the noise which might betray whispery voice. It therefore, perhaps, curbs our enthusiasm for making bold statements about a match of voice quality. Second, an expectation of acoustic quantification is not easy to satisfy in the case of voice quality. Voice quality components, as long-term trends or biases in speaking, require by their nature rather extensive stretches of speech for measurement. Long-term average spectra require around 15 sec of continuous speech to settle down, perhaps longer if the content of different samples is not the same (Nolan, 1983, p. 143). The quantification of supralaryngeal settings is not straightforward; the method used by Nolan (1983) requires the measurement of formant frequencies at over a dozen linguistically equivalent events, and these are unlikely to present themselves straightforwardly in forensic samples.

The move toward acoustic analysis, then, highlights the limitations of forensic samples for serious voice quality analysis. It is also the case, as I argue later, that voice quality information is captured in other ways by acoustic analysis. The conclusion, then, is that the increasing importance of acoustic analysis in technical speaker identification is another factor which has militated against the development of componential voice quality analysis in this field.

The Dynamic Nature of the Speaker's 'Signature'

Voice quality analysis within Laver's framework involves static abstractions from the flow of speech. A supralaryngeal or laryngeal setting constitutes a bias or average deviation away from a hypothesized neutral reference. On the other hand, on the basis of my practical experience and of theoretical considerations, I suspect that the nearest we will come to finding a speaker's unique 'signature' will be in the detailed dynamics of speech, for instance in the movements of formants. This is because the dynamics of the acoustic signal receive the imprint of both the speaker's vocal anatomy and his or her learned patterns of articulation. Anatomy will determine the range within which formants can vary, dependent on the size and proportions of the vocal tract, and also the regions where particular articulations need to be made to produce the necessary acoustic effect. The articulatory pattern will have to satisfy the need to achieve the linguistic target within the constraints of the individual's vocal tract; however, we may also assume that there will be some latitude for variant adequate articulations, from which the speaker selects one for habitual use. Furthermore, although there may be linguistically determined 'targets' in the speech stream which demand rather accurate acoustic achievement, transitions between those targets may allow more individual variation.

Take, as an example, the English sequence /aik/ in a word such as 'like.' Here, in linguistic phonetic terms, there is scope for fine 'idiolectal' variation between speakers of the same dialect in the quality and the dynamics of the diphthong. In physical terms, each vocal tract will determine a specific configuration of formant frequencies. Velars are notable for exploiting an area of the vocal tract where constriction anywhere within an extensive area will cause the acoustically defining proximity of second and third formant, in a way in keeping with Stevens's Quantal Theory of speech (e.g., Stevens, 1989); however, each speaker's choice of location, combined with individual anatomy, potentially causes detailed difference in the dynamics of those formants. Preliminary investigation of this sequence by McDougall (2002) has duly shown that dynamic characterizations result in effective discrimination of speakers.

The detail of formant dynamics in segmental sequences results crucially from the interplay of linguistic targets, individual vocal anatomy, and speaker-specific articulatory strategies for realising those targets and integrating them in the flow of speech (see Nolan, 1983, chap. 3, for a study of idiosyncrasy in coarticulation). The result of this interplay is a pattern which is likely to manifest considerable variation between speakers. Although voice quality, both organically determined and chosen, will influence the formant pattern, the focus of voice quality analysis, in abstracting away from the dynamic details of speech production, may be inherently less suited to determining identity than would at first sight appear.

A STRATEGY FOR SPEAKER IDENTIFICATION

Let me first summarize what I think is the core of the most effective strategy for technical speaker identification in the typical forensic case where the unknown sample is a telephone recording. There should be a (primarily) auditory analysis of accent and an acoustic analysis of linguistically equivalent events; ideally, words spoken in the same prosodic context. These two analyses should proceed interactively. The ear of a trained phonetician with knowledge of the dialect (firsthand or from reliable sources) is by far the most accurate and efficient tool for deciding whether two samples are linguistically the same. If there are pronunciation differences, these must be taken as showing that two speakers are involved unless the differences can be explained by reference to established models of variation, such as a sociolinguistic model. If the two samples are linguistically the same, it remains possible that the speakers are the same.

Acoustic analysis, particularly of formant frequencies and trajectories, can then show whether there is overlap or separation of the samples at the physical level. For instance, Fig. 15.1 shows formant data from a known (K) and unknown (U) sample, both of which unusually were of telephone speech. The graph plots the second formant value at the start of the /ou/ diphthong (as in 'know') against its value at the end. It can be seen that the samples, despite one or two outliers in the U sample, cluster separately. The difference is clearly audible, incidentally, as a fronter quality in K's diphthong. Fig. 15.2 shows an equivalent plot of the /au/ diphthong (as in 'mouth'); again, although there is no such clear auditory difference, and the number of tokens available is quite small, separate clusters are beginning to emerge. Analysis of several further vowels or diphthongs revealed separation rather than overlap, and so I was able to conclude that despite a broad match in accent (phoneticians may like to guess what it was), it was most unlikely the speakers were the same. If there had been consistent overlap, the conclusion would have been that it remained fully possible that one speaker made both calls.

I noted the following in the report: 'In almost all [vowels examined], [K]'s formant frequencies are higher than those of [U], even where linguistic phonetic quality is similar. This is most easily explained on the assumption that [K] has a shorter vocal tract than

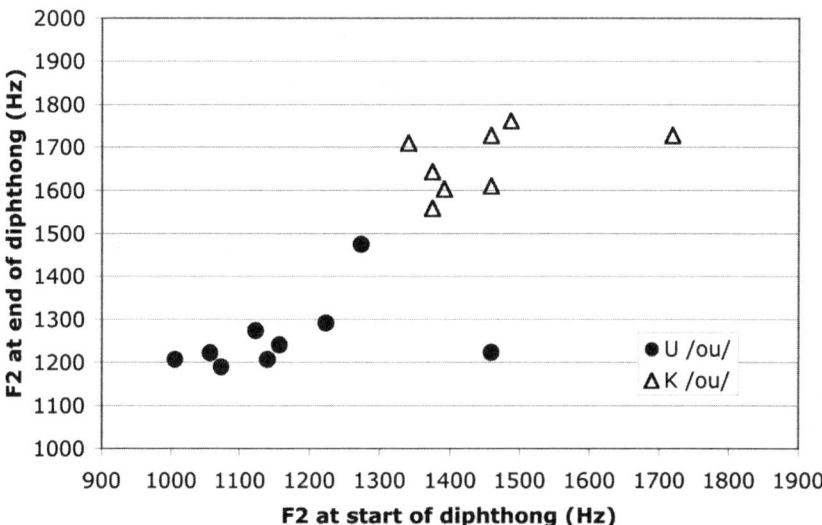

FIG. 15.1. Frequency of the initial against final second formant value in the /ou/ diphthong (as in 'know') for tokens from a known (K) and unknown (U) speaker.

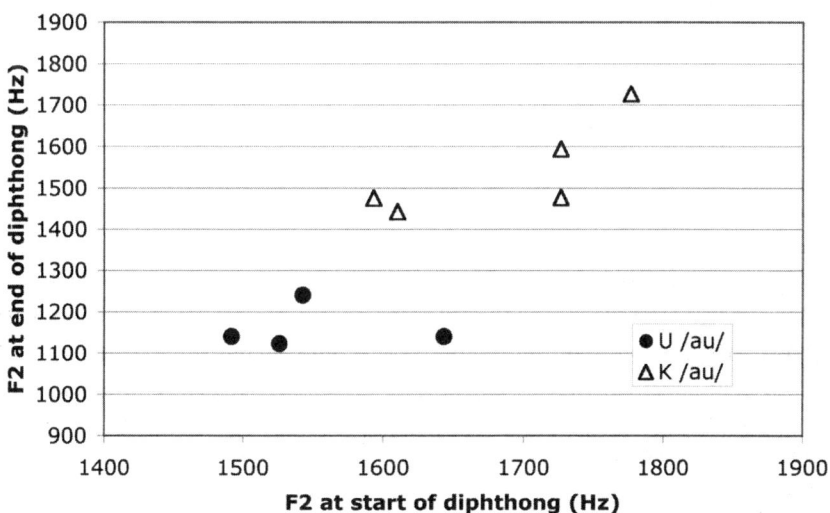

FIG. 15.2. Frequency of the initial against final second formant value in the /au/ diphthong (as in 'mouth') for tokens from a known (K) and unknown (U) speaker.

[U].' This, in effect, is a comment on anatomically determined voice quality. It may also be that K's higher second formant values in Figures 15.1 and 15.2 result from a slight tendency to palatalize, absent from [U], which would be voice quality of the habitual kind; however, for forensic purposes, there is no need to agonize over whether this is the case (unless there were a model of variation to suggest that palatalization would be stylistically appropriate in one of these phone calls and not the other, which is highly unlikely). The simple observation is enough, namely that the acoustic output of the speakers in the two samples is consistently and repeatedly different. In this way, the voice quality of the samples is not a matter for global impressionistic judgment, or componential analysis, but emerges from detailed local analysis of the acoustic facts.

THE ROLE OF VOICE QUALITY ANALYSIS

Does the fact that the most direct and effective demonstration of the origin of two speech samples depends on direct acoustic observation mean that the componential analysis of voice quality has no role in the realm of forensic phonetics? I think this would be too narrow and pessimistic a view.

For one thing, forensic speaker identification is such a difficult task that all possible tools should be brought to bear on it. It would, therefore, be very desirable if those engaging in such work had been trained in the use of Laver's componential framework for voice quality analysis. In the same way that standard phonetic training sensitizes the phonetician to detailed segmental differences which might escape the untrained listener, so voice quality training will undoubtedly make the phonetician more receptive to subtle differences in voice quality components. For instance, if the phonetician had the sense that one sample sounded as if it had a lowered larynx setting, he or she might be prompted to look at first formant frequencies, and specifically those of open vowels, because Nolan (1983) showed that larynx lowering had a dramatic lowering effect on the first formant very specifically of such vowels. Finding such a pattern would not disambiguate whether the speaker of that sample simply had a long pharynx, or was larynx lowering; however, in the absence of a model to explain larynx lowering in that sample and not the other, the finding would point against the same person being the speaker in both. More generally, there is no doubt that having an analytic framework for phonetic phenomena makes one more aware of them, and a phonetician trained in voice quality analysis will have an advantage over one without specific training in such a framework.

For another thing, although I have emphasized the problems which telephone speech creates for voice quality analysis, there are tasks where the forensic phonetician has available full-bandwidth recordings of potentially quite good quality. Of these, I briefly alluded earlier to the creation of voice parades, where the initial task is to select foil samples appropriate to the suspect. Here the value of acoustic analysis is rather limited, because the goal is a parade which must be fair auditorily. If an interview tape is available for the suspect, recent practice (which is well founded) uses other interview tapes as foils, 'sound bites' being extracted in every case to disguise the nature of the interview. Extensive full-bandwidth samples of all speakers are therefore available, and it is feasible to evaluate them with respect to the voice quality framework. Whether a full profiling is profitable, or, as I have done, it is adequate and more cost-effective merely to note salient voice quality components, is an open question. Whichever is done, voice quality analysis may help to screen out samples which a witness will discard from consideration as irrelevant to the voice heard at the time of the crime because of some salient and inappropriate voice quality component, thereby reducing the effective size of the lineup.

Perhaps above all the relevance of Laver's voice quality framework is in providing part of the conceptual infrastructure for thinking about how speakers differ. It reminds us that how a speaker sounds depends on more than his or her dialect and vocal anatomy, including also idiosyncratic choices made about the global posture and dynamics of the vocal organs. It warns us, too, that although many of these choices may be permanent, there is also great potential for flexibility in the sound of the voice. Voices will never be as reliable indicators of their 'owner' as fingerprints. Anyone who is tempted to think otherwise should listen to the tape accompanying Laver (1980), on which the author demonstrates the components of his framework.

REFERENCES

Baldwin, J. (1979). Phonetics and speaker identification. *Medicine, Science and the Law, 19,* 231–232.

Baldwin, J., & French, J. P. (1990). *Forensic phonetics.* London: Pinter.

Beck, J. M. (1988). Organic variation and voice quality. Unpublished doctoral dissertation, University of Edinburgh, Scotland.

Beck, J. M. (1997). Organic variation of the vocal apparatus. In W. J. Hardcastle & J. Laver (Eds.), *A handbook of phonetic sciences* (pp. 256–297). Oxford, England: Blackwell.

Esling, J. H. (1978). Voice quality in Edinburgh: A sociolinguistic and phonetic study. Unpublished doctoral dissertation, University of Edinburgh, Scotland.

Hollien, H. (1990). *The acoustics of crime: The new science of forensic phonetics.* Plenum: New York.

Honikman, B. (1964). Articulatory settings. In D. Abercrombie, D. B. Fry, P. A. D. MacCarthy, N. C. Scott, & J. L. M. Trim (Eds.), *In honour of Daniel Jones.* London: Longman.

International Phonetic Association. (1999). *Handbook of the International Phonetic Association.* Cambridge, England: Cambridge University Press.

Künzel, H. J. (1987). *Sprechererkennung: Grundzüge forensischer Sprachverarbeitung* [Principles of forensic speech processing]. Heidelberg, Germany: Kriminalistik Verlag.

Künzel, H. J. (2001). Beware the 'telephone effect': the influence of telephone transmission on the measurement of formant frequencies. *Forensic Linguistics, 8,* 80–99.

Laver, J. (1976). The semiotic nature of phonetic data. *York Papers in Linguistics, 6,* 55–62.

Laver, J. (1980). *The phonetic description of voice quality.* Cambridge, England: Cambridge University Press.

McDougall, K. (2002, December). Speaker-characterising properties of formant dynamics: A case study. *Proceedings of the 9th Australian International Conference on Speech and Science Technology, Melbourne,* 403–408.

Ní Chasaide, A., & Gobl, C. (1997). Voice source variation. In W. J. Hardcastle & J. Laver (Eds.), *A handbook of phonetic sciences* (pp. 427–461). Oxford, England: Blackwell.

Nolan, F. (1982). Review of The Phonetic Description of Voice Quality by J. Laver. *Journal of Linguistics, 18,* 442–454.

Nolan, F. (1983). *The phonetic bases of speaker recognition.* Cambridge, England: Cambridge University Press.

Nolan, F. (1991). Forensic phonetics. *Journal of Linguistics, 27,* 483–493.

Nolan, F. (1994). Auditory and acoustic analysis in speaker recognition. In J. Gibbons (Ed.), *Language and the law* (pp. 326–345). London: Longman.

Nolan, F. (1997). Speaker recognition and forensic phonetics. In W. J. Hardcastle & J. Laver (Eds.), *A handbook of phonetic sciences* (pp. 744–767). Oxford: Blackwell.

Nolan, F. & Grabe, E. (1996). Preparing a voice line-up. *Forensic Linguistics, 3,* 74–94.

Robertson, B., & Vignaux, G. A. (1995). *Interpreting evidence.* London: Wiley.

Rose, P. (2002). *Forensic speaker identification.* London: Taylor & Francis.

Stevens, K. N. (1989). On the quantal nature of speech. *Journal of Phonetics, 17,* 3–45.

Tosi, O. (1979). *Voice identification: Theory and legal applications.* Baltimore: University Park Press.

Author Index

Note: *f* indicates figure

A

Abberton, E. R. M., 291, *319*
Abbs, J. H., 137, *141*
Abercrombie, D., 39, 57, 286, 295, 309, *319*, 348, 350, 354, 368, 369, 373, *379*
Abramson, A. S., 355, *382*
Abry, C., 137, 138, *141*, 204, 207, 212, *226*
Ahmad, K., 362, *379*
Akahane-Yamada, R., 75, *89*
Alajouanine, T., 136*t5*, *141*
Al-Ani, S. H., 361, *379*
Alphen, P. M., van, 67, *87*
Alpher, B. J., 203, 204, *223*
Amman, J. C., 23, *36*
Anderson, A., 193*n5*, *196*
Anderson, J., xiv, *xvi*
Anderson, S., 94, 96, 97, 109, *124*
Andrésen, B. S., 177, *194*
Annamalai, E., 148, 161, *170*
Anthony, J. K. F., 361, *383*
Archibald, J., 120, *124*
Arnfield, S., 236, *260*
Arnold, G. E., 254, *260, 364, *382*
Arnott, J. L., 326, *346*
Arokianathan, S., 165, *171*
Arseni, C., 136*t*, *141*
Asher, R. E., xiv, *xvi*, 148, 150, 161, *170*
Assmann, P. F., 238, *260*

Atkinson, J. M., 264, 279*n*1, *290*
Auer, P., 271, *280*
Ayers-Elam, G., 217, *223*

B

Baer, T., *382*
Baken, R. J., 290, 291, *319*
Bakker, J., 76, 83, *87*
Balasubramanian, T., 150, 158, *170*
Baldwin, J., 389, 395, *409, 410*
Ball, M. J., 27, *36*, 290, 295, *319, 320*
Barney, H. L., 7, *21*
Barrière, M., 305, *321*
Barry, W., 43, *59*
Bauer, L., 68, *87*, 110, *124*, 230, 257, *258*
Båvegård, M., 327, *344*
Bayerl, S., 65, *88*
Beck, J. M., 390, *410*
Beckman, M., 8, *21*, 206, 217, *223, 224, 225, 256, *259*
Beddor, P. S., 74, *88*
Bell, A., 131, *141*, 349, 356, 367, *379*
Bennett, E., 324, 339, *345*
Berke, G. S., 292, 293, *320*
Bernard, J. R. L., 235, *258*
Bertoncini, J., 305, *321*

Subject Index

Note: *f* indicates figure, *n* indicates endnote, *t* indicates table

A

Acoustic
    analysis, xiii, 169*n*2, 179, 181–184,
            251–252, 290, 307, 403–404
    characteristics, 12, 25, 176–177, 295,
            363, 365
    constraints, 26
    cues, 110
    distance, 167
    measurement, 295
    pattern, 43*f*
    phonetics, 95
    profiling methodology, 174, 179, 191
    signal, 41, 289, 398
    vowel space, 9, 205, 207, 211, 213
    waveforms, 208, 237, 372
Acoustics, 27, 33, 355–356
    of speech, 117
    of voice production, 290
Aerodynamic
    aspects of phonation, 291
    constraints on voicing, 24–27
    factors, 4–8, 28, 352–354, 355
Aerodynamics, 27, 33
Affrication, 27, 28*t*, 29
African languages, 4, 73
Air
    cavity, 33

    pressure, 176, 375
    spaces, 32*f*, 33
Airflow
    channeling of, 365, 373
    escaping pulmonic, 363
    measurement, 290–291
    turbulence of, 351, 364, 367
Airstream, 371–372
    obstruction to, 176
    management, 51
    pulmonic egressive, 352
Airway, 369
Allophones, 72, 117, 181–182, 192
Alveolar
    approximant, 76
    closure, 41
    contact, 45
    gesture, 45, 53*f*
    release, 52
    stop, 4, 43–44, 47, 53–54
    voiceless stops, 72
Alveolars, 43–45, 47, 52, 53*f*, 53–54, 72, 76,
        153, 175, 387
Alveolar-velar sequence, 46*f*
American
    English, 166–168, 181, 190, 215, 267
    languages, 27
Amplitude of voicing (AV), 332
Aphasia, 53, 54*f*, 137